FIELDS OF FIRE

FIELDS OF FIRE
A LIFE OF SIR WILLIAM HAMILTON

DAVID CONSTANTINE

Weidenfeld & Nicolson
LONDON

First published in Great Britain in 2001
by Weidenfeld & Nicolson

© 2001 David Constantine

A CIP catalogue record for this book
is available from the British Library.

ISBN 0 297 81888 0

Typeset by Selwood Systems, Midsomer Norton

Set in Monotype Garamond

Printed in Great Britain by
Butler & Tanner Ltd, Frome and London

Weidenfeld & Nicolson
The Orion Publishing Group Ltd
Orion House
5 Upper Saint Martin's Lane
London WC2H 9EA

CONTENTS

ILLUSTRATIONS

Mrs Cadogan, a miniature by Norsti (Royal Naval Museum, Portsmouth)

Portrait of Sir William Hamilton, c. 1789–1790, by Hugh Douglas Hamilton (Hamilton Collection, Lennoxlove, Haddington, East Lothian)

The English Garden at Caserta by Jacob Philipp Hackert, 1792 (Palazzo Reale Caserta)

View of the Villa Emma at Posillipo by Xavier della Gatta, 1795 (Private Collection)

Plan of Milford Haven (by permission of the British Library, Add. MS 38361, ff.54v–55)

Frontispiece, by Christoph Heinrich Kniep from *Engravings from Ancient Vases*, 1791 (Ashmolean Museum, Oxford)

Plate 14, by William Tischbein, of Volume 1 of *Engravings from Ancient Vases* (Ashmolean Museum, Oxford)

Map of Vesuvius (Library of Queen's College, Oxford)

Emma, Lady Hamilton dancing the Tarantella by Mariano Bovi, 1796 (© the British Museum)

The Muse of Dance, possibly by James Gillray, 1807 (Paul Mellon Collection, New Haven)

Nelson, by Friederich Heinrich Füger, 1800 (by courtesy of the National Portrait Gallery, London)

Dido, in Despair! by James Gillray, 1801 (© the British Museum)

A Cognocenti contemplating ye Beauties of ye Antique, by James Gillray, c. 1801 (© the British Museum)

ACKNOWLEDGEMENTS

To the librarians, curators and staff of many institutions in Britain, France, Germany and Italy, also to many individuals in all those countries, I owe sincere thanks. Hamilton was a very English Scotsman and of a very particular social class but his interests and contacts were European and socially various. Assembling his life in so many places in Europe – from Aberystwyth to Weimar, from Oldenburg to Naples – seemed emblematic of his range; and the kindness and practical help I had in all those places from so many different people reflected the best spirit of his own wide and humane dealings.

To work on this book I was given periods of leave from the University of Oxford and from Queen's College; the College also gave me generous financial assistance. I am deeply grateful for both. In Queen's Library, I had access not only to Hamilton's own publications but also to much else of his eighteenth-century context; an enormous privilege, which I value and am grateful for. Altogether my debt to Queen's College, to the cheerful and expert people in the Library and to many colleagues, is large, and with renewed thanks I acknowledge it here.

My brother, Stephen Constantine, read the whole typescript, as did also June Cross. They encouraged me in my belief in the subject and in numerous ways helped me to do better in the final stages. I thank them both.

My closest friends and my family have lived with Sir William Hamilton for as long, if not quite so obsessively, as I have. A biographer with nobody to talk to would soon go mad. They were always there, listening, asking and answering. The thanks I owe them cannot be said; at least, not here.

Chronology

CONTEMPORARY EVENTS

Pope's *Essay on Man*, Voltaire's *Lettres philosophiques*

Charles III crowned King of the independent Kingdom of the Two Sicilies

---

Birth of Hamilton's 'foster-brother', the future George III, excavations beginning at Herculaneum

---

War of the Austrian Succession

Handel's *Messiah*

British warships threaten Naples

Death of Pope

Jacobite invasion, death of Swift

Battle of Culloden

Battle of Laffeldt

Peace of Aix-la-Chapelle, Montesquieu's *Esprit des lois*, excavations beginning at Pompeii

---

First volumes of Buffon's *Histoire Naturelle* (including *Théorie de la terre*), birth of Goethe

---

George III becomes Prince of Wales

WILLIAM HAMILTON'S LIFE

1751–6 Hamilton equerry to George, Prince of Wales

1752 Hamilton in Paris, his mother dies there; Henry Seymour Conway buys Park Place

1753 Hamilton promoted to Lieutenant; his sister Jane marries Lord Cathcart

1754 Death of Hamilton's father

1755

1756–63

1756

1757 Hamilton courting Lady Diana Spencer; sits to Joshua Reynolds; as aide-de-camp of Conway takes part in the expedition against Rochefort

1758 Joins Society of Arts; marries Catherine Barlow; leaves the army

1758–64 Spends his time between London and Pembroke

1759

1760 Moves from Charles Street to King's Mews as the new King's equerry

1761 Sale of his first collection of pictures; elected to Parliament as Member for Midhurst

1762

1763 Applies to replace Sir James Gray as Envoy in Naples

CONTEMPORARY EVENTS

Accademia del Disegno founded in Naples

Lisbon earthquake, Royal Herculaneum Academy founded in Naples, Society of Arts in London

---

Seven Years War

Birth of Mozart

Benjamin Franklin's electrical experiments in London

Birth of Nelson

Voltaire's *Candide*, death of Handel, Ferdinand (aged 8) becomes King of Naples under a regency

---

Accession of George III, birth of Beckford

Rousseau's *Nouvelle Héloise*

Rousseau's *Du contrat social*, accession of Catherine the Great

---

Treaty of Paris, Wilkes affair, Winckelmann's *Geschichte der Kunst des Altertums*

1764 Secures job as Envoy in Naples, his credentials dated 31 August, he and Catherine travel out through France, crossing from Marseilles they are blown into Livorno, see Horace Mann in Florence, arrive in Naples 17 November

1765 Sale of his second collection of pictures in London, immediate interest in the antiquities and natural history of Naples, by summer already has a good collection of vases; birth of Emma

1766 Writes to Royal Society about an eruption of Vesuvius, elected Fellow

1767 Hamilton promoted to Plenipotentiary; d'Hancarville and Winckelmann working on his vases; violent eruption of Vesuvius

1768 First volume of the *Vases* published; February to April in Rome with Catherine and Stormont; elected to Etruscan Academy

1768–70 Hamilton tries to find a post elsewhere

1769 Greville visits; death of Catherine's mother; tour of Sicily with Catherine and Fortrose; second volume of *Vases* published; d'Hancarville expelled from Naples

1770 Mozart at the Palazzo Sessa, Charles Burney visits, Hamilton repeatedly applies for leave

1771 August, back in England, offers his vases to the British Museum, death of his sister Jane, awarded Copley Medal

1772 Invested as Knight of the Bath, elected Fellow of Society of Antiquaries, Museum buys his vases for £8400, September leaves for Naples going via Ferney (Voltaire) and Vienna

1773 January, back in Naples, resumes his interests, applies for Paris

1774 January, considers standing for Parliament; still occupied with antiquities and natural history

CONTEMPORARY EVENTS

Mozart and father in London

Death of the Old Pretender

Winckelmann murdered in Trieste, marriage of Ferdinand and Maria Carolina, Cook's first voyage, Royal Academy founded

Emperor Joseph of Austria visits Naples, Wedgwood opens his factory at Etruria

Birth of Beethoven, Wordsworth, Hölderlin, Hegel

Dispute with Spain over Falkland Islands

Cook's second voyage

Goethe's *Werther*, accession of Louis XVI of France

WILLIAM HAMILTON'S LIFE

1775	Applies for Madrid; death of Cecile (a foster child?); Hamilton applies for leave and thinks he may not come back to Naples
1776	Again applies for Madrid; returns to England on leave via Geneva and Paris; *Campi Phlegraei* published and Volumes III and IV of the *Vases*
1777	Elected to the Society of Dilettanti, Catherine unwilling to return to Naples, slowly back through Germany arriving November, beginning of correspondence with Joseph Banks
1778	
1778–9	Letters to Banks (now President of Royal Society), in August 1779 a vast eruption of Vesuvius
1779	War between England and Spain; Buffon's *Epoques de la nature*
1780	
1780–1	In June 1780 talks of standing for Parliament again, in September hears of the continuing cult of Priapus in Isernia; Beckford in Naples (November), his relations and correspondence with Catherine
1781	
1782	Emma moves in with Greville, her child (not by him) born end of February; Anne Damer in Naples, Catherine's last letters to Hamilton, he buys Portland Vase, Beckford in Naples again, death of Catherine 25 August
1783	Hamilton's grief over Catherine, she is buried at Slebech, he diverts himself, applies for leave, visits the zone of the earthquakes in Calabria, back in London by August, meets Emma, commissions her portrait, attends meetings of the British Museum as a Trustee

American War of Independence, Cook's third voyage

American Declaration of Independence, Adam Smith's *Wealth of Nations*

Tanucci replaced as First Minister in Naples

War between England and France, Acton arrives in Naples, deaths of
Voltaire and Rousseau

War between England and Spain, Gordon Riots in London

Kant's *Kritik der reinen Vernunft*

Britain concedes American Independence, Herschel made Astronomer
Royal

Earthquake in Calabria, Treaty of Versailles, Pitt's Ministry (until 1801)

WILLIAM HAMILTON'S LIFE

1784 Often with Mary Hamilton, dealings with Duchess of Portland to sell her the Vase, in June with Greville to Pembroke and Scotland, in London society, in September leaves for Naples through France, meets Lady Clarges in Turin and Rome, November back in Naples; December Beckford disgraced

1785 Lady Clarges in Naples, the Queen wants an English Garden at Caserta, Greville tries to interest him in Emma; in May tour in the Abruzzi, in August to Ponza and Ventotene; Greville becomes more pressing

1786 March, Mrs Damer staying; on 26 April Emma arrives with her mother, Hamilton at once infatuated, Emma resists, by December they have reached some accommodation, *Priapus* published

1787 Emma ensconced, her 'Attitudes', Goethe's visits, Graefer's work on the English Garden, association with Tischbein

1788 Rumours that Hamilton and Emma are married, Tischbein frequenting their household, Greville urging more investment in Milford

1789 Dowager Duchess of Weimar and party visiting, Hamilton tours Puglia with Emma, begins collecting vases again, Emma wants marriage

1790 Milford: Greville eager, Hamilton cautious, Act of Parliament for development there; in England widely believed he and Emma are already married, publication of the Second Collection proceeding

1791 Heneage Legge warns Greville that Emma is likely to get her way, in March she and Hamilton set off home via Venice, in London by the middle of May, many visits, made Privy Counsellor, marries Emma 6 September in Marylebone Church, back to Naples via Paris and Geneva, Prince Augustus in Naples, Hamilton keeps an eye on him

CONTEMPORARY EVENTS

Handel celebrations in London

Death of Frederick the Great, Mozart's *Nozze di Figaro*, Goethe in Italy (until April 1788)

Mozart's *Don Giovanni*, Farnese antiquities moved from Rome to Naples

---

Flaxman in Naples, George III suffers a bout of madness, birth of Byron

---

Thanksgiving in St Paul's for George III's recovery, convocation of the Estates General, Fall of the Bastille, Declaration of the Rights of Man, Blake's *Songs of Innocence*, French émigrés in Naples

Burke's *Reflections on the Revolution in France*

Grenville at the Foreign Office (until 1801), Paine's *Rights of Man*, death of Mozart, Flight to Varennes, Church and King riots in Birmingham, Declaration of Pillnitz

---

WILLIAM HAMILTON'S LIFE

1792 Borrowing for work at Milford, Greville supervises, Hamilton frequently expresses contentment with Emma, in November he is ill

1793 Fear of revolutionary politics in Naples, Volume I of Second Collection published, lavish entertaining at the Palazzo Sessa, Neapolitan troops to Toulon, in September Nelson visits

1794 February, trip to Rome, Hamilton bothered by the expense of Pembroke and by more diplomatic business than ever, Jacobin conspiracy in Naples, colossal eruption of Vesuvius in June, Hamilton makes himself ill observing it. Emma: 'Everybody that sees us are edified by our example of conjugal and domestic felicity.'

1795 Hamilton: 'I am well and comfortable in my family,' Emma intimate with the Queen, Hamilton ill again, too much business and entertaining, more plots

1796 Fatigue and illness, anxiety about holding his job, money worries, trying to sell his Second Collection, Volume II published. Emma: 'Our house ... is like a fair.' Death of Antonio Piaggi

1797 Asks £7000 for his collection, wants to come home and sort out his affairs without resigning his post, bids for a pension 'beyond the usual', French get closer

1798 French in Rome, Hamilton told he will not get the pension he has asked for and does an inventory of his pictures, fears general ruin, Nelson in Naples after the Battle of the Nile, French disperse Neapolitan army and advance on Naples, evacuation to Palermo, *Colossus* sinks in Scilly with a third of Hamilton's vases

CONTEMPORARY EVENTS

Unrest in England, death of Emperor Leopold II, assassination of King of Sweden, Brunswick Manifesto, storming of the Tuileries, Battle of Valmy, September Massacres, France declared a republic, beginning of the Revolutionary Wars, French fleet threatens Naples, Wollstonecraft's *Vindication of the Rights of Woman*, birth of Shelley

Execution of Louis XVI, France declares war on Britain, occupation of Toulon, execution of Marie Antoinette, the Terror, evacuation of Toulon, Blake's *America* and *Albion*

Execution of Robespierre, Blake's *Songs of Experience*

Hardship and unrest in England, violent hostility to the King, birth of Keats

Napoleon's campaign in Italy begins, Spain declares war on Britain, Jenner performs first smallpox vaccination

Death of Horace Walpole, Treaty of Campo Formio, French set up North Italian republics

French enter Rome and take Malta, invade Egypt, Battle of the Nile, Ferdinand marches unsuccessfully against French, Wordsworth and Coleridge *Lyrical Ballads*

WILLIAM HAMILTON'S LIFE

1799 Court in Palermo, Hamilton ill, French in Naples, counter-revolution begins in Calabria, Hamilton wants to come home, feels he has to stay for Nelson and the Court; Naples recaptured, reprisals, Hamilton in debt and, with Emma and Nelson, becoming ridiculous

1800 In London Greville petitions for Hamilton with no success, Paget arrives to take over his job, trip to Malta with Nelson and Emma, their child conceived, they leave Palermo in June, from Livorno to Trieste, then via Vienna and Dresden home, Hamilton ill and distressed on the way, London in November, snubbed at Court, Christmas at Fonthill, Volume III of Second Collection published

1801 Leases 23 Piccadilly, debts in Naples and Palermo, Horatia born, Hamilton petitions for his due from Government, sells pictures and Second Collection of vases at Christie's, gives Piaggi's Vesuvius diary to Royal Society, in July visits Pembroke, Emma gets Merton Place for Nelson, Hamilton lives between there and Piccadilly

1802 Much unpleasantness in Hamilton's domestic life, money worries, in the summer he tours Pembroke and the Midlands with Emma and Nelson, pleads for some peace and quiet

1803 Gives Piaggi's Herculaneum papers to Dilettanti, last changes to his will, last conversation with Greville, dies peacefully 6 April, buried at Slebech 19 April

CONTEMPORARY EVENTS

French occupy Naples, set up the Parthenopean Republic, Ruffo's army recaptures Naples, Napoleon becomes First Consul

---

Fox censures Nelson in Parliament, Austrians defeated at Marengo

---

New ministry in England, George III ill again and tormented by his doctors, Battle of Copenhagen

---

Treaty of Amiens, Napoleon Consul for life

Resumption of hostilities

PREFACE

By the principles of the French Revolution, largely betrayed in its practice and in the ensuing wars, any human life would be worth a biography. You might study anybody and be instructed, entertained and moved. But the famous are the easiest and in some periods the only possible subjects, because they leave traces; obscure lives are, precisely, obscure.

Any human life would be interesting, both in itself and in what it represents; thus in the particular and in the typical. But again, this twofold interest is more easily revealed in famous and public lives and especially in lives taken up in a shift or acceleration of human history. People may know at the time that irreversible changes are under way and that as large or small agents they are involved in them; or such change and their involvement may only become apparent to hindsight. Living their own lives as best they can, taking decisions, making mistakes, people will at the same time be more or less conscious of their lives as in some sense representative. Goethe, dispassionate observer at the Battle of Valmy, 20 September 1792, indicated the historical significance of the moment to the Prussian soldiers around him. When the smoke of their cannonade had cleared, they saw the army of the new French Republic still standing firm. Goethe commented: 'From here and from this day forth the history of the world is changed, and you can say that you were there.' Goethe noted particularities – later at the siege of Mainz, for example, how small and ragged the French dead were, how big and well-dressed the Germans – but he had sensed as well a seismic tremor in Europe's history.[1]

On 14 July 1798 Louis XVI, at Versailles, came back from doing what he did most days – hunting – and wrote in his journal the one word: 'Nothing.' In Naples Sir William Hamilton's life was sweet. He was fifty-eight, but vigorous and contented. He was collecting vases again, still climbing Vesuvius, and had Emma Hart, not half his age, as his mistress. His summer duties were not onerous. He had to show the Dowager Duchess of Saxe-Weimar and her party around the sites. He invited them to his villa at Posillipo. There were *parties de plaisir* on the water, they heard Emma sing, they admired her. It was the beginning of August before news 'of the late Extraordinary Revolution in France'² reached them. By October the first *émigrés* had arrived. Later came the threat, after that the armies. 1789, though he could not know it then, made a caesura in Hamilton's life. After Bastille Day the life he lived and the world he represented were heading towards their common end.

Looked at a little differently, from a more personal point of view, his life might be said to have had its caesura seven years earlier, in August 1782, when his first wife Catherine died. She and Emma, very different women, are, so to speak, the signs of his life in its two unequal halves. By the summer of 1789 Emma Hart had been his mistress for perhaps three years; two years later she achieved her aim, and he married her; but he was buried at Catherine's side, leaving Emma to Nelson who in turn, two years later, left her to the Nation.

Hamilton's life, at least after 1764 when he became a public figure, is pretty well documented. He kept open house in Naples for more than thirty years, and has a regular part, not always flattering, in the memoirs and correspondence of his numerous guests. His life ended in scandal, because of Emma and Nelson. He was much written about, and his own surviving correspondence is voluminous. There are his almost weekly letters to a succession of Secretaries of State; to fellow diplomats and other political figures; and to the men who shared his passions for volcanoes and the arts. His biographer has two main difficulties. The first is a usual one: seeing the wood for the trees, the shape in all the material. The second – connected – is how to get through or around the public personae (by which word I do not mean anything false) to anything more personal and perhaps essential. In his letters to his nephew Charles Greville, his niece Mary, and his friend Sir Joseph Banks, he relaxes, and speaks in a tone that, as you get to know him, sounds most characteristic; but that style or character is itself never sentimental or effusive. Nobody will deny him an inner life, but, though he lived into the Romantic age, he remained a man of the previous generation. He was very unlike his young kinsman William Beckford, for example, who, as to sensibility, had far more in common with Catherine Hamilton.

Hamilton had only a conventional interest in literature, but his own writing, at its best, is lively and effective. Many of his letters and most of his writings in the natural sciences show him off as a good practitioner in the best pre-Romantic eighteenth-century style. One of the new emphases in this biography will be on Hamilton the writer. It is a pity he is not better known and more available in that capacity.

I have been preoccupied with Hamilton, in one fashion or another, for many years. Finally I felt that I must close my account with him. Brian Fothergill wrote his biography in 1969 and Flora Fraser wrote Emma's in 1986, and I gratefully acknowledge that I owe them a good deal. In addition, there was an excellent exhibition dedicated to Hamilton's life and works in the British Museum in 1996, and the accompanying catalogue, by Ian Jenkins and Kim Sloan, is a great and beautiful treasure house of knowledge. Still I thought I could shape something after my own understanding of the man. I have materials that Fothergill either did not have or did not use – for example, papers in the Krafft Bequest in Paris, the Hamilton and Greville papers in Aberystwyth, and a collection of Hamilton's notebooks in the Bodleian Library; also perhaps a stronger sense of Hamilton's European, particularly German, connections and importance; and a greater interest in him as a writer. For further justification I might say that biography resembles translation: there are no definitive versions, they will always need doing again. Thirty years after the last attempt I was intrigued to see what I might make of the same fellow human being.

David Constantine
December 2000

Chapter 1

LIFE BEFORE NAPLES,
1730−64

William Hamilton was born on 13 December 1730. Father and mother, both of that same great Scottish family, are remembered rather unfavourably in contemporary accounts. He was Lord Archibald Hamilton, seventh son of the third Duke of Hamilton; she was Lady Jane Hamilton, daughter of the sixth Earl of Abercorn; he had been married and left a childless widower twice already; she compensated him then with six girls and four boys. He had served in the navy and held various public offices; but he is remembered chiefly for being eclipsed by his wife, the energetic Lady Jane, a favourite and perhaps also a mistress of Frederick, Prince of Wales. At Poor Fred's court she is said to have governed absolutely. She became Lady of the Bedchamber and Mistress of the Robes there in 1736, and advanced so many of her clan at Carlton House that whenever the Prince met a newcomer he addressed him as 'Mr Hamilton', assuming he would be one. She was ousted in 1745, on a pension of £1200 a year. Never very pretty, she looked the worse for 'having lain many years by a man old enough to be her father and being the mother of ten children'. That man himself, so says the same witness, the spiteful Lord John Hervey, 'was of so quiet, so secure, and contented a temper, that he seemed cut out to play the passive character his wife and the Prince had graciously allotted him'.[1]

Hamilton rarely mentions his parents. Neither with his father, fifty-eight when he was born, nor with his mother, busy advancing and intriguing, can the relationship have been very close. Hamilton said of his father that he gave up 'twenty years before he died, calling himself a dying man'.[2] His mother's death, at least, is said to have distressed him. She affected his life most by bringing him into the

I

court of the Prince of Wales, a fraught and unedifying ambience, and into a relationship like that of foster-brother with Frederick's son, the future George III. And that relationship did matter: Hamilton would look to it for protection.

Hamilton was the youngest of Lord Archibald's sons. As such he had to shift for himself. The family name gave him status, but not the wherewithal to live as he liked. Being the youngest son, and having to make his own way in the world, was a constant ingredient in Hamilton's self-image and a determining factor in his affection for his nephew Charles Greville, similarly disadvantaged. In letters the two men allude to their common predicament more than once. It inclined Hamilton to be helpful in the matter of Emma Hart, and in the end to make Greville, not Emma, his heir.

Hamilton was born at Park Place, just east of Henley. It was, according to Horace Walpole writing in about 1787, 'by far the finest place upon the Thames'. He meant the four hundred acres of park and ornamented grounds. The house itself he described as 'indifferent'.[3] (It was demolished in 1870 and something no better erected.) Lord Archibald and Lady Jane sold the property to the Prince of Wales around 1738, but retained a dwelling for themselves on the estate. George, the future king, was born in June that year. By then her liaison with the Prince was long established and either at his houses in London or at Park Place his son and hers must, by her arrangement, often have been together. On his deathbed, aggrieved, Hamilton remembered that privileged infancy: 'My Mother reared us & the same Nurse suckled us.'[4]

The Prince of Wales died in 1751. In May 1752 Park Place was bought by Henry Seymour Conway, and it is his work on the gardens that Walpole, his cousin, so approved of and that can, largely, still be seen today. Hamilton became Conway's aide-de-camp for a while and later, as envoy in Naples, had him as one of a series of Secretaries of State. He stayed at Park Place with Catherine shortly after their marriage and visited whenever he came home on leave. These local and personal connections are typical of the period. They make up the small circle within which the relatively powerful looked to one another to get on.

At the age of nine Hamilton was sent to Westminster School which, by all accounts, with Dr John Nicoll as head, was a better public school than many in that day. The boys were flogged rather less. Two of Hamilton's fellow pupils became his lifelong friends. One was David Murray Stormont, later the seventh viscount, who, like Hamilton, had a career as a diplomat abroad and whose second wife was Hamilton's niece. The other was the son of the Lord Hervey whose memoirs, fortunately not published till 1830, were so caustic on the subject of Hamilton's parents. The younger Hervey, Frederick, as Bishop of Derry and Earl of Bristol, lived a life of exemplary futility on the public stage. Stormont and Hervey went on to university, but in 1745, at the age of fifteen, Hamilton's schooling was over.

Since Hamilton never speaks about his childhood we are left with these few facts, and they are of a very external kind. But childhood shapes the adult whether he broods on it or not; and Hamilton's taught him what he himself would call his 'philosophy', or at least the need for philosophy; which is to say, taught him self-reliance, stoicism, and not to expect too much of people. His own parents must have inured him to many things, and besides them he saw the royals at close quarters in their familial dealings, and that will have lowered his expectations further. Hamilton spent almost all the years of his life in close proximity to royalty, and often writes very scathingly about the vulgarity, corruption, cowardice and brutality of the Neapolitan version; but the spectacle at home, from his infancy till his death, was itself not always uplifting. There was, for one thing, the perennial Hanoverian hatred between father and eldest son. George III was born at Norfolk House, St James's Square, because his grandfather, George II, would not have the Prince of Wales in the palace. His older sister Augusta was lucky to have been born indoors at all. In her case the Prince himself, to spite his own father and mother, fearing their baleful influence, harried his wife in labour from Hampton Court:

> Her pains came on so fast and strong, that her water broke before they could get her out of the house. However, in this condition, M. Dunoyer, the dancing-master, lugging her down stairs and along the passages by one arm, and Mr Bloodworth, one of the Prince's equerries, by the other, and the Prince in the rear, they, with much ado, got her into the coach; Lady Archibald Hamilton and Mr

Townshend remonstrating strongly against this imprudent step, and
the Princess begging, for God's sake, the Prince would let her stay
in quiet where she was, for that her pains were so great she could
not set one foot before the other, and was upon the rack when they
moved her. But the Prince, with an obstinacy equal to his folly, and
a folly equal to his barbarity, insisted on her going, crying 'Courage!
courage! ah, quelle sottise!' and telling her, with the encouragement
of a toothdrawer, or the consolatory tenderness of an executioner,
that it would be over in a minute ... There were in the coach,
besides him and her, Lady Archibald Hamilton, and Mrs Clavering
and Mrs Paine, two of the Princess's dressers; Vreid, his *valet de
chambre*, who was a surgeon and man-midwife, was upon the coach-
box; Mr Bloodworth, and two or three more, behind the coach; and
thus loaded he ordered the coachman to drive full gallop to London.
About ten this cargo arrived in town. Notwithstanding all the
handkerchiefs that had been thrust up Her Royal Highness's petti-
coats in the coach, her clothes were in such a condition with the
filthy inundations which attend these circumstances that when the
coach stopped at St James's the Prince ordered all the lights put
out that people might not have the nasty ocular evidence which
would otherwise have been exhibited to them of his folly and her
distress.[5]

No sheets being available, the Princess of Wales was put to bed
between two table-cloths, and at a quarter to eleven, Sunday 31 July
1737, 'was delivered of a little rat of a girl, about the bigness of a
good large toothpick case'.

Relations between George III and his own heir apparent became
over the years, and especially during George's madness, very squalid
indeed. These things were well known, gossips and cartoonists of
the day had no compunction. Hamilton, born into it and a professional
observer all his life, knew better than most what life at Court was
like.

On 27 January 1747, aged sixteen, Hamilton joined the Third
Regiment of Foot Guards, at the lowest rank of commissioned
officer, that of ensign. A week later he disembarked at Willemstad
in the Netherlands, for the tail end of the War of the Austrian
Succession. He was not especially young by the standards of the day,

and to join up and go to war was quite a normal course for a son with a name and no fortune.

England was at war, more or less seriously, for most of Hamilton's life, usually against France, or against Spain and France, in a variety of alliances. England's continual hostilities against one or both of those countries extended almost world-wide, over colonies in South and North America, in the West Indies, in India. Wars were always either in progress, or threatening at one flashpoint or another. But wherever they were fighting, the essential issue was power in Europe, and the arch-enemy was France. In the Netherlands, when Hamilton arrived there, British troops, alongside Dutch, Hanoverian and Hessian, were fighting for the Austrian cause against the French and the Prussians. Hamilton served in the last two years of this war, and in the first two of the Seven Years War, which was the next. Thereafter, from Naples, he followed his country's involvements as a diplomat. They came closer and closer, finally overwhelming him.

Two of Hamilton's order books have survived, for the periods 4 February–31 May 1747 and 1 December 1747–23 April 1748. They are bound stiffly in vellum, and are of a size to fit in the pocket like bulky chequebooks. In them, day by day, Hamilton took down the orders and instructions that concerned the regiments and, occasionally, himself in particular. They document the running of the eighteenth-century British Army, and make a dense context of external details in which to site the young ensign. Much of the daily business is discipline, and especially the behaviour of the soldiers towards the local people, 'the Boors'. There must be no insulting or thieving from them, no hunting or unlicensed foraging on their land. Drunkenness and swearing must be dealt with. And lechery controlled: 'A Return of the Poxed Weomen in the Several Brittish Regiments to be given in Immediately that they may be Sent to the Hospital.'[6] There are instructions concerning dress – of the living: 'No man to presume to take off the Lace from his old hatt till he receives his new one';[7] and of the dead: 'the Nurse of the Ward wherein any Man Dies take care that he be Buryed in his Worst Shirt'.[8] Along with the orders come the punishments. There were regular courts martial. On 27 January 1748, for example: 'Joseph Rydon Soldier in Col. Lee's Regiment & James Ferguson Drummer in the Same Tryed for Sheep Stealing [were] Sentenced ... to receive 1500 Lashes with the Cat of Nine Tails at Six Different times & in Equal Proportion'.[9] Five hundred lashes here, a thousand there, for stealing shirts, for 'having an Intention to Steal a horse from a Boor of the Country'.[10] An officer gets cashiered for going AWOL, a private gets hanged for the same. One man, sentenced to death, was pardoned and discharged 'for being an Idiot and not fitt for Service'.[11] Or a death sentence might be commuted if the soldier agreed to go and serve (and die more slowly) in the West Indies. Hamilton was ordered to be present at many of these trials. And having witnessed the sentencing he must also, often, have witnessed its carrying out.

Hamilton's commander-in-chief in the Netherlands was the Duke of Cumberland, who was just back from Culloden where his efficient slaughtering of the Jacobite Highlanders had earned him the sobriquet 'Butcher'. What action Hamilton saw is difficult to establish. The first of the order books tracks him from the coast to Tilburg and via Alphen down to Schild and Bowell; the second from winter camp at Breda through Tilburg, Boxtell, Uden and Mill to the Maas, and from there down to Hellenzait near Venlo. From Bowell, where that order book closes on 31 May 1747, the armies advanced to Laffeldt, just west of Maastricht, where on 21 June the British and their allies were heavily defeated by the French under Marshal Saxe. On the British side nearly six thousand were killed or wounded. On 14 January 1748, still in camp at Breda, the regiments had orders to submit 'a return of the Cloathing & Accoutrements lost at the Battle of Leveldt'.[12] Nathaniel Wraxall, who got to know Hamilton in 1779, says of his army days: '[He] was at the battle of Fontenoy, as well as, I think, at that of La Feldt.' Fontenoy can't be right. It was fought on 11 May 1745, before Hamilton joined up. So the following anecdote (which Wraxall wished 'it were possible to relate with delicacy') must derive from Laffeldt:

'We were exposed,' said [Hamilton], 'on that occasion, as is well known, to a very severe and murderous fire of artillery, for a long time, without the power of moving: so peremptory were the orders issued, that we should remain on the ground where we were stationed. The cannon balls, from time to time, swept away whole Files, produced sensations by no means agreeable, even among the firmest persons present. I had then an opportunity of seeing

6

exemplified, the physical effects of fear on the human body. Many of the British Grenadiers, though capable of actively facing death in any shape, and ardently desirous to march against the enemy, yet experienced, internally and involuntarily, the most violent pains. Unable to support them, pressed by an irresistible necessity, and compelled to remain fixed in the same place, several of them *se detroussoient, presentoient le derriere aux canons de l'ennemi, & firent feu;* thus endeavouring to exhibit a proof of their contempt for the very danger, of which they felt within themselves the strongest sensations.'[13]

After Laffeldt the French won further victories in the United Provinces, but when the war ended, with the Peace of Aix-la-Chapelle on 18 October 1748, neither they nor any other of the participants, except perhaps the Prussians, had much satisfaction. 'Stupid as the Peace' became a saying in Paris at the time. 'Stupid as the War' would have been more apt.

Hamilton's next and final involvement in warfare as a combatant came in September 1757, at an engagement against the French port of Rochefort, one of several undertaken in that year and the next as an English contribution to the Seven Years War. The expedition, like most of the others along the French coast, was notably unsuccessful. They idled at Newport on the Isle of Wight for nearly a month, waiting for the fleet to assemble and the winds to turn favourable; sailed then on 8 September, Hamilton as aide-de-camp to General Conway on board the *Neptune*. On the 23rd the little island of Aix, just off Rochefort, surrendered after bombardment by the *Magnanime* under Captain Howe. Conway stood by, with three battalions, but in the event had nothing to do. Thereafter the commanders dithered. Having finally ordered an attack on the town, they lost their nerve and aborted it. On the 30th the fleet headed home.

Even without any enemy action Hamilton seems to have come quite close to getting killed, through the idiocy of his commanding officer. On the Île d'Aix Conway was amusing himself. Horace Walpole tells the story (as he had heard it from Hamilton himself) to Horace Mann: 'Mr Conway was so careless and so fearless as to be trying a burning-glass on a bomb — yes, a bomb, the match of which had been cut short to prevent its being fired by any accidental sparks of tobacco – Hamilton snatched the glass out of Mr Conway's hand.'[14]

Parliament, the public and the King were furious over Rochefort. There was an inquiry, the commanders were vilified, nearly court-martialled. At Court Conway was snubbed and humiliated. So closely associated with him, perhaps Hamilton too was touched by the opprobrium and inclined to quit.

England's chief interest in the Seven Years War, which she entered on the Prussian side against a coalition of Austria, France, Russia, Sweden and Saxony, was, as usual, to reduce French power; and in this aim, by 1763, she was successful, especially in Canada, where James Wolfe took Quebec, and in India. But by then Hamilton had ceased to be involved.

In the interim between the two wars Hamilton, though still in the service, seems to have been free to do much as he liked. Though not well off, he cannot have been desperately straitened, and he began to develop, outside the army, talents and interests which later, outside the world of diplomacy and etiquette, would constitute his best and most enjoyable life. In 1750 he had violin lessons with Felice de Giardini. This great violinist and prolific composer, having played in orchestras in Rome and Naples, had just arrived on tour in London, and would stay for thirty years. Hamilton became an accomplished performer; there was always music in his house in Naples. Quartets by Giardini were played on one of the evenings when Goethe visited, for example.

Besides music, Hamilton loved pictures, and met other men who did. Through Seymour Conway he had an early entrée into the circle of connoisseurs and virtuosi around Horace Walpole. Altogether the 1750s were a lively time for the arts. In London there were many auctions and exhibitions. The Society of Arts was founded in 1755, the British Museum opened to the public in 1759. Hamilton was elected to the former in January 1758 (proposed by James Stuart, who had surveyed and recorded the ruins of Athens), and from Naples he became a regular contributor to the collections of the second. In 1757 he first sat for his portrait for Sir Joshua Reynolds.

When Prince Frederick died, Hamilton's 'foster-brother' George, not yet thirteen, became Prince of Wales, and Hamilton was appointed one of his equerries. This gave him some small additional income and ensured his position at Court. His mother, who had done so much to place him there, died the following year, 1752, in December. She was in Paris at the time with her husband, her daughter Jane and Hamilton himself. She was buried in the cemetery of Montmartre. On 25 November James Wolfe wrote to his mother: 'I have been introduced to Lady Archibald Hamilton. She is so well known that I need say no more.' In his next letter, 4 December, to his father, he reports her death the night before 'of a fever, after an illness of a few days'. The family, he says, are 'in the utmost grief and distress'. He adds: 'Lord Archibald is extremely old and infirm; his son and daughter are both very young.' Wolfe, himself only three years older than Hamilton, calls him his 'friend and companion' and promises to look after him.[15] He had been with him in the Netherlands (but in the Twelfth Regiment) and would be again at Rochefort. Two years after that he was killed at Quebec.

Hamilton's own army career advanced as far as it ever would in June 1753, when he was promoted lieutenant, with permission to style himself 'Captain', which he duly did. In 1754 his father died. The close deaths of both parents, as well as the marriage of his sister Jane (to Lord Cathcart) which came in the year between them, will have impressed upon him that he needed to fend for himself. If he left the army he must have some other livelihood: another career, or an heiress, or both.

Younger sons were especially at risk. Having no funds they tended to live as though they had. But there is no evidence that Hamilton, though he was certainly acquiring expensive tastes, ever came near to ruin and disgrace. As a young officer, particularly in the period of idleness between the two wars, he doubtless amused himself in the usual ways. Long after his marriage there are one or two reminders of wilder days in letters from his friends. In one from Lord Fortrose, for example, 16 April 1771: 'It takes some time, to be sure that a Rake is reformed, tho I will appeal to Mrs Hamilton if according to the proverb, they do not make the best Husbands.'[16] I doubt if he was ever much of a rake, but he did have a weakness for women. Lord Pembroke, writing on 6 March 1766, professed astonishment at his becoming virtuous: 'Your Chastity merits to be recorded to future Ages. Tell me honestly – how long do you think it will last? Resist temptation too! That's too much.'[17] Fortrose was with Hamilton and Catherine on a tour of Sicily in 1769; Pembroke got to know him in 1756, and was intimate with him by 1762. So perhaps he had a reputation and reformed more slowly than he should have. But Hamilton was nothing like Pembroke, who told Casanova in London in the summer of 1760 that he moved from woman to woman daily, so great was his disgust.[18]

In 1757, just prior to his participation in the desultory business at Rochefort, Hamilton was courting Lady Diana Spencer. She married the day he sailed, but it seems that by then she had already jilted him for someone else – not her husband-to-be – and he was philosophical. Then in January 1758 he married Catherine Barlow and in May left the army.

When Hamilton resigned his commission his commander-in-chief, Lord Roshes, wrote that it was a pity he should quit a profession he liked and for which he was (in Lord Roshes' view) 'perfectly well qualified';[19] but this was a politeness. After eleven years in the service he had risen only to the rank of lieutenant, and his own comments on his career, few and far between, are all somewhat self-deprecating and regretful. He told the painter Wilhelm Tischbein that he had realized soldiering might not be quite his metier when an enemy bullet carried away the point of his spontoon;[20] and in 1794 he confessed to William Beckford that 'from my early Entering into the Army my Classical knowledge is very scanty indeed'.[21] At that time he was engaged with Tischbein in the publication of his Second Collection of vases, and his detractors liked to claim, precisely, that he was himself no expert and that he exploited the scholarship of others.

Catherine Barlow, the woman Hamilton married on 26 January 1758, was the daughter of John Barlow of Slebech,[22] near Haverfordwest, and Ann Barlow, née Skrine, whose family were from Somerset. Ann was John Barlow's second wife. She married him in 1735, he died in 1739, leaving her the estates and the numerous farms in Pembrokeshire that would eventually pass to Hamilton and then to Charles Greville. Ann did not marry again. Catherine, born in 1738, was her only child; the bond between them, without a father, was close, and critical in the making and shaping of Catherine's character. For one thing, she inherited and developed her mother's rather anxious piety. Their address at the time of the marriage was given as Clarges Street; Hamilton's as Curzon Street; very close together at the Green Park end of Piccadilly. The match suited all parties. It gave Hamilton land and an income. On her side, Ann Barlow will have been content to see the rather introverted and not very robust Catherine placed with a good-natured young man. And doubtless mother and daughter valued the association with his ancient and important family. In 1780, when his nephew Greville was in the same position (needing to marry), Hamilton wrote to him frankly about his own marriage:

> A disagreeable rich Devil the Devil himself cou'd not have tempted me to marry, but I have realy found a lasting comfort in having married (something against my inclination) a virtuous, good-temper'd woman with a little independent fortune to which we cou'd fly shou'd all other dependencies fail, & live decently without being obliged to any one. I can not tell you ... how often such a thought has comforted me, when I have had reason to be out of humor with the great world.[23]

Though 'something against [his] inclination' (would he have preferred Lady Diana Spencer?) the marriage was by the standards of his class and perhaps by any standards a successful and happy one. In that letter to Greville, characteristically, he understates its value, as though it were mainly material. But two years later, when Catherine was dead, he knew full well and readily admitted what he had lost. She was gifted and serious; they had things in common, notably the love of music.

It was understandable that Hamilton should leave the army after marrying Catherine. Her fortune relieved him of the need to soldier for a living; also there was a war on, in which he might get killed. But it was by no means clear when he gave up that career what he should do instead. Catherine's estates in Pembrokeshire certainly wanted seeing to, but though Hamilton was often there he had no wish to become an established country gentleman. Throughout his life he would speak of retiring into Wales only as a last resort, but when he married he had no particular calling in London either. Having been equerry to the Prince of Wales from 1751 to 1756 he resumed that office, but to the King, when the Prince became King

George III in October 1760. This increased his income slightly and enabled him and Catherine to move from Charles Street, their first married home, to lodgings in the King's Mews, rent free; but more than that what was it? Nobody ever made a life out of being an equerry. Then in 1761, in the elections following the accession, Hamilton 'entered parliament', as one of the two MPs for Midhurst in Sussex. He was elected – 'appointed' would be more exact – to serve the Court party, under the new King's favourite, Lord Bute, against the old order of Pitt and Newcastle; and perhaps he did so, from time to time. But it is not recorded that he ever spoke in the House or concerned himself with any important issue. In fact he seems to have attended infrequently and reluctantly. He wrote from Pembroke in October 1763 (to Charles Jenkinson) asking for assurance that the House would actually sit in November as announced; he was anxious not to come to London unnecessarily as he had done, he complained, the year before.[24]

The family house in Pembroke was at Colby Moor, about six miles east of Haverfordwest. It was built by John Barlow around 1710, and had a view north towards the Preseli Hills over the Moor in which the dead were buried after a skirmish there between Royalist and Commonwealth forces in 1645. Bits of armour were dug up in Hamilton's day. The house itself, let out when Catherine and Hamilton went to Naples, was not in the best condition; extensive roof repairs were done in 1768; not much of it is left in the present building. The Hamilton and Greville papers in the Library of the University of Wales largely have to do with the estates in Pembroke, and they give a good idea of the kind of business Hamilton would have been closely involved in had he remained in Britain and lived at Colby for a part of each year. His tenants there, the Philipps family, write to him about his shrubberies and a thriving plantation of beech, pines, larch, plane, sweet willow and chestnuts. His agents keep him informed about the progress (never very great) in extracting coal and anthracite from collieries at Cresswell, Swanshill and Newton. There are notes of sales of oxen, sheep, colts and horses at Wiston Fair; bills from the blacksmith, or for lime; an enquiry after a lease on the kelp at Pembroke Ferry; prospects for hake fishing off Milford, and for the opening of a packet boat route and postal link between Milford and Waterford. That last scheme was taken up much later and furthered by Greville; but everything else is very local, modest and perennial. The sums of money involved – the rents, a contribution to the upkeep of the roads – are small; and the struggles and squabbles, viewed on any but the most parochial scale, are trivial. From afar his tenants wait to be told by him how they should vote in Parliamentary elections. It is all a long way from Naples, from the glamour of Vesuvius, from the gross and the brilliant company at Court and at the Palazzo Sessa, and half a guinea here (for the education of poor children at Wiston) and £6 16s there ('for 24 wethers') sit oddly next to the vast sums he would spend later on vases and other virtu.

When they were in London, the Hamiltons lived sociably enough. They held musical evenings at home, as they would later on a grander scale in Naples. A note from Catherine, for example, invites Charles Hamilton and his wife (also called Catherine) to their lodgings in the King's Mews, for dinner and to hear 'Miss Blossett's Singing'.[25] In 1764 Mozart came to London. He was eight years old, being shown off by his father. He performed at Court on 27 April and again on 19 May. Perhaps Hamilton and Catherine were there. Certainly before the end of June (when Leopold fell sick and retired to Chelsea) Wolfgang was at the Hamiltons' home at one of their evenings. He would be their guest and performer again six years later.

As to the other arts, now with more funds at his disposal, Hamilton, like many in his circle, attended auctions and bought pictures. Long before he got to Italy he was already set in the repeating pattern of assembling collections and being obliged to sell them. He always spent beyond his means, and when those were increased by marriage he still overspent. He sold one collection, mostly of pictures, in February 1761 and a second sale, which he must have put in train before he left England, took place in January 1765. His young nephew Charles Greville, himself already a collector and later Hamilton's partner and accomplice, wrote after the first: 'I did not much relish your Pictures being turned out of Doors, before I read that you took the good ones into favour again.'[26] That was often the way: he bought back what, when it came to it, he could not bear to be parted from. If eighteenth-century collectors learned anything from their passion it must surely have been that possession is precarious and temporary. They lived in a constant systole and diastole of gathering and dispersal, ending in the auction of everything when they died.

Turned thirty, Hamilton could not be said to have done much with his life. He had taken part but not, as they would have said in those days, 'gloriously', in the petering out of one war and the desultory starting up of the next; he had married in the usual way, cultivated his wife's estates, bought and sold pictures and curiosities. He was an equerry and a Member of Parliament, nothing much in either office. In the early 1760s, more and more discontented in his situation, he was looking out for ways of changing it.

He was unhappy on his own account, and also on Catherine's, whose health, never robust, every British winter made worse. Her complaints were various, in part nervous, but mostly she was described as asthmatic. Her prescriptions – still there among Hamilton's papers – are, from July 1758 onwards, often for expectorants.[27] The winter of 1762–3 was exceptionally severe; the Thames froze so hard at Twickenham that carriages could drive across it. That spring Catherine was said to be 'plagued with the asthma', and even in May not well enough to travel.[28] But by then, having heard something of interest on the grapevine, Hamilton had begun the enquiries and dealings that would secure her survival. Early in 1763 he pulled gently at one string, Lord Bute; on 11 April at another, his under-secretary, Charles Jenkinson:

> The last time I took the liberty of troubling Lord Bute about an affair that I have much at heart, both on account of Mrs Hamilton's ill state of Health, and my own situation, his Lordship was so good as to say, that he wou'd turn it in his mind and do the best for me that he cou'd. I was, and am still thoroughly satisfied as to Lord Butes kind intentions towards me and therefore did, and do rely solely upon his Lordships goodness. Will you then be so kind as to let Lord Bute know from me that as I understand Sr. James Grey will be at home very soon, and have reason to beleive that he does not mean to return to Naples, I shall esteem myself for ever under the greatest obligation to his Lordship, if he wou'd procure me the promise of succeeding Sr. James in case he shou'd not return.[29]

Gray was at sea even as Hamilton wrote, heading for Marseilles and home, ostensibly for a period of leave but in fact, after ten years in

Naples, pleading ill health, he was intending to resign. Hamilton's wish to get abroad, and presumably by this means, must have been talked about in his family at least. His niece Charlotte wrote in May: 'I suppose I shall lose you … pray are you to go?' and her husband added this postscript: 'Does the former scheme of your going abroad, &c, take place?'[30] In the event the scheme was a long time realizing. In October 1763 Hamilton wrote again to Jenkinson, from Pembroke, saying he would be obliged to retire there altogether 'unless I have more luck than has hitherto attended me'.[31] And Catherine wrote to her namesake sister-in-law: 'I wish we were all setting out for Naples together – but Alas! I fear that Scheme is a little in the Castle-Building System.'[32] It was the following April before Hamilton got what he wanted. Sir James Gray, conveniently recovering his health, moved to the senior post in Madrid, and Naples fell to Hamilton. His obituarist in the *Annual Register* stated for certain that he owed it to the King's 'immediate protection', but his closer benefactor was the new Prime Minister, George Grenville. This was generally known at the time, and Hamilton gratefully acknowledged it.

It cannot be said that Hamilton was *driven* to get to Naples, certainly not in the way that the passionate classicist Johann Joachim Winckelmann (an extreme example, admittedly) was driven to get to Rome. Neither for his career – he had none – nor by the inner logic of his life so far was he bound to move to Italy. An opening appeared, he tried for it and was lucky. It got him out of circumstances in which he was not content; it would be good for his wife's poor health; and as an amateur of the arts he would be sure to enjoy himself in the land that, had he been wealthier, he would have toured at an age when he was marching through the Netherlands under the Butcher of Culloden.

The rightness of the move would only become fully apparent later. It was salvation, quite late in the day, into a life he could really call his own.

Word soon got round that Hamilton was going to Naples; also that he thought of applying for promotion from Equerry to Groom of the Bedchamber, because to foreigners *Chambellan* would sound better than *Ecuyer*. It interested a Mr Minchin of Caversham. He wrote asking might he get Hamilton's old position, and do it for no pay? And what about his parliamentary seat in Midhurst? He invited Hamilton to call, he was only six miles from Park Place, he could offer him excellent fishing.[33] Hamilton kept that letter, and thereafter many of the same genre. Place-seekers spied a vacancy as vultures do the likelihood of a carcass. The practice was known as 'jobbing'. Hamilton professed to despise it, but did his share of it when necessary.

Hamilton and Catherine were preparing to leave for Naples. They went to Pembroke, to settle things there and say goodbye – a final goodbye, as it turned out – to Catherine's mother.

Hamilton had an audience with the King, and kissed hands for his appointment on 13 July 1764; on 31 August he received his credentials and his instructions as Envoy Extraordinary to the Kingdom of the Two Sicilies. His only predecessor in the post was Sir James Gray, appointed in 1753. Prior to that British interests in Naples had been looked after by a consul, and Gray's appointment as ambassador was a mark of their growing importance. Hamilton prepared himself by reading through Gray's correspondence, ten years of it, with a succession of Secretaries of State. He learned what kind of reports he would be expected to write, and in ten handy notebooks made extracts and notes to take with him to Naples.[34] The chief matter occupying Gray, and in a tiresome manner it would take up a good deal of Hamilton's time also, was the regulation of trade between Britain and Naples. In the British view a treaty signed with Madrid in 1667 (before Naples had any independence from Spain) sufficed and was still binding; but the Neapolitans continually ignored or modified it, and wanted a new one. For the whole of Gray's term of office wranglings over this went on and on. Hamilton must have been heartily sick of it, from reading Gray's letters, even before he arrived in Naples and had to face its endless continuation. So he read his way into the job, noting also, whenever Gray had noted it, an earth tremor or an eruption of Vesuvius.

The Hamiltons travelled out through France. In Paris they met the abbé Ferdinando Galiani, a learned and witty man only four and a half feet high. He was Secretary at the Neapolitan embassy. He wrote to Minister Tanucci in Naples, preparing the way for Hamilton: 'I was enamoured of him. Either I am grossly deceived or Your Excellency will love him greatly, even more than Gray. He has more

16

innocence and candour, and no less ability.'[35] Galiani gave Hamilton a copy of the French translation (just published) of Winckelmann's account of the excavations at Herculaneum; and, carrying this with him to Naples, Hamilton became the agent of its dissemination in a language the Neapolitan scholarly world could read. They were incensed by what they read, for the pamphlet was scathingly critical.

In Lyons on 19 October the Hamiltons bought a hundred bottles of Burgundy, and spent three hundred pounds on clothes.[36] Much of the best in clothing available in Naples came from Lyons. They seem to have kitted themselves out at source, perhaps a little more cheaply. This expenditure on necessary costume was the first of many such.

They sailed from Marseilles for Naples, but hit bad weather. Hamilton wrote: 'We had indeed a very rough passage and for Mrs Hamilton, to whom the sea was quite a new object, it was dreadful. I found it very unpleasant, though I have been more used to it.'[37] They were driven ashore at Leghorn and rather than sit out the weather in that port they went to Florence, where they were hospitably accommodated by the British ambassador, Sir Horace Mann. Mann knew of Hamilton's appointment from Horace Walpole who had announced it to him on 8 June. 'You have a new neighbour coming to you,' he wrote, 'Mr William Hamilton ... He is picture-mad, and will ruin himself in virtu-land. His wife is as musical, as he is connoisseur, but she is dying of an asthma.'[38] Indeed, Catherine was poorly when Mann received her. He reported to Walpole: 'She, poor, good, sickly creature, was seized with a fit of the asthma as soon as she got out of her coach at my door, and could with difficulty get to her apartment.'[39] She recovered, and a few days later they rejoined their ship at Leghorn. They arrived in Naples on 17 November 1764.

Chapter 2

NAPLES

The Kingdom of the Two Sicilies, consisting of Sicily itself and the whole lower half of the Italian peninsula (as far north as the Papal States), became an independent kingdom only in 1734 when the Infant Charles of Spain wrested it back from Austria, and his father, Philip V, ceded all Spanish rights in it. Charles was crowned Charles III in Palermo the following year, but made Naples his capital and in the course of a largely peaceful reign did much for its grandeur and for the arts and sciences. Under him the great San Carlo opera house and palaces at Portici, Capodimonte and Caserta were built or begun; academies were opened, the excavations at Herculaneum and Pompeii were advanced and the finds displayed and published. His reign ended in 1759 when, on the death of his insane half-brother, Ferdinand VI, he was obliged to give up the throne of Naples and succeed to the throne of Spain, it having been agreed by international treaty that Naples and Spain could not share a monarch. Charles made his second son heir in Spain and his third son, Ferdinand, only eight years old, King of Naples. His eldest was disqualified, being an imbecile. Ferdinand had a regency council over him. Its two principal members were the Marquis Bernardo Tanucci, who had been Charles's First Minister since 1734, and Prince San Nicandro, who, as Ferdinand's tutor, did much harm.

England's political interest in Naples when Hamilton went there was slight. In 1742, during the War of the Austrian Succession, British warships had appeared in the bay to persuade Charles – by threatening bombardment – to withdraw his support for the Spanish side and to remain neutral. This confirmed Charles in his dislike of the English. Though independent, Naples' ties with Spain were naturally strong, and they remained so even after Charles's abdication, through the First Minister Tanucci. Over many years Hamilton countered that inclination, and steadily improved the Court's relations with England. Much of an envoy's job consisted in competing with the envoys of other nations, for his own nation's advantage. Generally the competition had to do with trade. Naples traded with England, the balance being greatly in England's favour; but traded even more with France, and that rivalry was always the most belligerent.

Until 1793, when England entered the Revolutionary Wars, Naples, as Hamilton frequently observed, was rather a backwater and his office of minor importance. The great embassies were those in Madrid, Paris, St Petersburg, Vienna and Constantinople, and Hamilton knew very well that for a career in diplomacy he must move, as Gray had done, to one of them. For several years he did think of moving, and tried to; but without success. He stayed put, on the periphery. Only at the end of his time, and by then he was an old man, did his backwater become a political epicentre. Neither in the army nor in parliament had he been very effective; then serving abroad he was in a place that for most of his time there was of little consequence.

But this biography is concerned much less with the art of diplomacy than with what Hamilton himself called 'the whole art of going thru' life tollerably', which was, in his view, 'to keep oneself eager about any thing'.[1] And for that he could not have been better placed.

Naples was the largest city in continental Europe after Paris; its population was about four hundred thousand, not counting the soldiery and the numerous foreigners. Much of its life, then as now, was on the streets and along the waterfront, on show. Travellers from the north felt hit on arrival by life lived more extravagantly, with more show, noise, gaiety and violence, than anywhere else on their itinerary. The city assaulted the senses, all of them, but perhaps especially the eyes. All classes in Naples loved spectacle and displayed themselves: the nobility in their carriages along the Mole, the Corso or the Via Toledo; the mob, the *lazzaroni*, in rags and half-naked or completely naked, everywhere. The buildings, secular and ecclesiastical, were grand and crass in their showing off. And in that ambience huge public spectacles were staged – a *cuccagna* at the least excuse, most lavishly during carnival and the carnival every year louder and louder so that by the 1780s it was pulling in the tourists even more than Rome. There was an indolence about Naples – *otiosa* was her classical epithet – and an anarchic energy and ebullience that would have drawn the travellers south, even without the rest.

And the rest was extraordinary. Many thought the site – the sea in a bay, the amphitheatre of hills, the volcano – the most beautiful in the world. From one vantage point or another the setting was a pleasure for the eyes, and ordinary life in it seemed marvellously enhanced. When the boats went out at night to fish under their lanterns, they were the stuff of pictures, fit to be looked at, and doubtless the fishermen knew it. At night, from the water or from lodgings on the western headland or suddenly at the end of a long slit of a street, the fires of Vesuvius were visible and the smoke, more or less reddened by fire, and often also a red trickle of lava. In daylight the mountain might be grey with ash, now and then it was white with snow, through which the red lava ran. Such phenomena were almost continuous, they fascinated, they drew observers to them closer and closer, really into danger. Vesuvius was more active in Hamilton's day than at any time since Pliny's. There were half a dozen major eruptions during his residence, they wasted the surrounding country, threw the city into darkness at noon, clogged it with ash, the lava reached almost into the streets. In 1767 and again in 1794 he was the eager and intelligent observer of Nature's violence at its most spectacular and gigantic. Few lovers of the earth's phenomena have been so gratified.

All the vicinity of Naples – the Campi Phlegraei, the ancients called it, the flaming fields – is deeply unstable. The land can't stay still. It has sunk mosaics and the Roman road under the sea at Baia, raised up the columns of a Roman market hall from under the sea at Pozzuoli. Close by, it gave birth to a mountain overnight. The instability when Hamilton was there – in those Fields themselves and also further south, in Sicily and Calabria – was extraordinarily evident; and it excited him. The land is 'curious', it attracts the 'curious', so many of them, mostly English, trekking from the Solfatara to the Grotta del Carne, to Lake Avernus and the Monte Nuovo, and writing so many memoirs, journals and letters, they almost dull the places with their repetition. Yet even now, even trashed by modernity, the Campi Phlegraei are weird, deeply intriguing and disturbing; and from Hamilton, in his accounts, that fundamental risky strangeness of the locality gets its proper due.

Stranger still perhaps – yet more 'curious' – were (are) the buried cities, whose goods and treasures in Hamilton's day were being fetched forth out of an inexhaustible mine. The first shaft into Herculaneum was accidental – they were sinking a well and drove through the crust into the buried theatre. Thereafter they mined the site, sending out horizontal feelers till they hit a house: which they entered and ransacked, in-filled and moved on. Over much of Pompeii there was only a shallow covering, which appears in the prints and paintings of the time like a shaggy pelt. It was fertile earth. And the peasants, tending their vines, had for generations, until the official digging began, dug down into the mine below and sold off whatever they found to anyone interested. Then after 1748 the city's streets and skeletons, temples and guardrooms, began to be opened up, and the finds, together with those from Herculaneum, accumulated in the new royal palace at Portici. Excavations continued in spasmodic and haphazard fashion for most of Hamilton's term of office. Continually things of interest and beauty were being fetched into view. More even than in Rome (where digging in vineyards and in the gardens of villas brought bronzes and marbles to light) in Naples the curiosity was perpetually teased and nourished.

Walpole had said of Hamilton that he was 'picture-mad', and he was; but for ancient vases he was soon madder still. These, like the finds in the buried cities, came out of the ground, out of tombs mostly north and east of Naples, in places colonized or traded with by the Ancient Greeks. Collecting and publishing these vases Hamilton made a real and lasting contribution to knowledge, and significantly affected contemporary opinion and taste. Vases and the volcano (and more generally vulcanology) became his two chief passions in the arts and sciences, and for that combination Naples in the late eighteenth century was the best place in the world.

Hamilton's first year in Naples was the seed of all the rest. By the end of it his passions were established and the factors that would shape almost the whole duration of his professional life were already in play.

He arrived on 17 November 1764; he wrote his first dispatch to his Secretary of State, Lord Halifax, on the 20th; met Prime Minister Tanucci two days later; and on the 25th, a Sunday, he presented his credentials to King Ferdinand IV, still only thirteen years of age, at

Portici. Neither with Tanucci, 'much troubled with the Gout',[2] nor with the King can the conversation have been very full: the former had poor French, the latter none, and Hamilton could not 'as yet pretend to converse in Italian'.[3] The Court was at Portici, four or five miles east of Naples, for fear of infection in the city itself, and remained away for another month.

Catherine Hamilton was ill, it had been thought she must get to Naples or die, Walpole implied she would soon die anyway. And Naples when they got there was full of sickness. Hamilton wrote to Lord Halifax: 'I never go out without being greatly Struck with the numberless emaciated objects that present themselves in every Street.'[4] When Sir James Gray had begged to be excused from returning to Naples 'for reasons of health', it was not that he was ill but that he feared he soon would be. In 1764 there were bad food shortages, in some areas amounting to famine, throughout the kingdom, and the starving came into Naples for relief. They fought – with knives – for bread. They overwhelmed the hospitals. Hamilton wrote:

> From the enquiry I have made I am not surpris'd that there should be Sickness in the Hospitals when I am told there are near two thousand in one Hospital crowded together with no other covering than a Shirt which they have worn four months & that they have actually been within these few days four & twenty hours without bread owing to the failure of the Charitable subscriptions that have hitherto supported them.[5]

But he never seems apprehensive, either for his ailing wife or for himself. Instead, the tone of voice is at once what henceforth it most characteristically will be: that of a man looking about him with the liveliest curiosity. By 19 December, still a week before the Court thought it safe to return to Naples, he was writing of Catherine that she was 'amazingly recovered' and that he was sure the mild climate would 're-establish her entirely'.[6]

Hamilton's lodgings were in the Palazzo Sessa which is reached from the present-day Piazza dei Martiri down the Vico S. Maria a Capella Vecchia. Here he had his chief residence throughout his time in Naples. Before him, for seven hundred years, the place had housed a religious community, but they were suppressed by Tanucci shortly before Hamilton's arrival, and a large part of their property passed to the Marchese di Sessa, who rented out all the southern side and some of the west, more than a dozen rooms, on two spacious floors, to Hamilton for 800 ducats (about £150) a year. There, just to the west of the Palazzo Reale and the San Carlo Opera House, he had a view – wonderfully enhanced by alterations in 1785 – over the bay to Vesuvius. And the house itself actually backs into a hill of the volcanic rock out of which the *pozzolana* cement for the building of most of Naples is derived. From the courtyard of the Palazzo Sessa there is access to caverns in the yellow rock which in Hamilton's day housed a factory of spinners and weavers, and also, from time to time, colonies of robbers and murderers. It was a perennial issue whether the Neapolitan authorities had the right to trespass through British Embassy property, to root them out. With or without permission there were occasional pitched battles under his windows, the earliest soon after he got there, the bloodiest in the spring of 1791, lasting three hours, two murderers killed before the others could be arrested.[7]

Arriving as Envoy Extraordinary, Hamilton took over from a *chargé d'affaires*, Philip Changuion, formerly secretary to Sir James Gray and left behind by him. He stayed on, serving Hamilton, until the following June, then went home, via Florence. Hamilton wrote of him to Mann: 'We have parted good Friends, & I verily beleive him to be an honest Man but it was impossible for us to go on together, especialy as he soon disgusted Mrs. Hamilton by his ill bred manner & to be sure they hated one another most cordially.'[8] Still Hamilton did his best for him, and was probably instrumental – perhaps via Conway – in his being placed for a year with the Duke of Richmond in Paris. And the King of Naples gave him a diamond ring.

Another person in post when Hamilton arrived was the English Consul Isaac Jamineau. He had been there since 1753, would remain till 1779, and on him Hamilton and Catherine (and many others, it must be said) were of one mind. They found him insufferable; he presumed too much, far beyond his station. Jamineau recurs in Hamilton's correspondence, as leitmotif and *bête noire*.

It was the Envoy's job to report to his Secretary of State, and this Hamilton did, except when on leave, every ten days or so and in some periods more often than that, for thirty-five years. He wrote his letters in draft, then in fair copy. Often there was not much to report, and he would apologize, to one lord or another, for bothering him with trivia. As he wrote his reports it was borne in upon him how far he was from the centre of things.

The post was slow and unsafe. Letters between Naples and London took three or four weeks, but longer in bad weather and during civil and international strife. Interested parties and the idly curious would open them along the way; and small wonder, they were so blatantly addressed. Whenever he could, Hamilton entrusted his dispatches to English travellers heading home: thus in February 1765 he used Henry Ellis, a retired explorer wintering in Naples, to carry the old cyphers safely back. He had brought new cyphers with him from London, and was instructed to return those Gray and Changuion had been using.

In drafting a letter Hamilton marked any part of it that in fair copy should go into code; or he might write the code in there and then between the lines, for transcription later into his fair copy. The codes were numerical, and he was advised not to use them too often for fear they would be broken. He seems to have suspected his letters would be opened before they left the Kingdom of Naples since the things he puts in cypher are often of a kind that might interest or offend the Neapolitans. On their army for example, the following sentence: 'The Troops in general exceedingly ill clothed and accoutred; and worse disciplined.'[9] A comment on Tanucci's inclination towards the English and dislike of the French and an enquiry as to how francophile the Neapolitan envoy in London is, are also sent in cypher.

Hamilton gathered information on the State of Naples and supplied the English government with it in his dispatches and in long enclosures: on the population, parish by parish; on the army and the marine; on the ports, castles, defences; on public order, or the lack of it (two or three murders a day, five 'on Sunday last ... the Police is so bad here & justice so Slack').[10] Beyond that he said what he could about international affairs, all the while supposing that his Secretary of State would know already and better from elsewhere. In August he wrote a longish review of relations between Spain and Naples and in November, in cypher, warned that Austria, Spain and France were colluding in a bid to have Corsica annexed to the

Kingdom of Tuscany. He noted the death of Emperor Francis I in September 1765 and the appointment, soon after, of a new ambassador from Vienna to Naples, Count Ernst Kaunitz.

But the Envoy's chief responsibility was relations between England and Naples, and they were largely commercial. He was there to defend English interests and privileges, and by English captains arriving and by English merchants resident in Naples he would be continually pestered with complaints and claims. First appeal was normally to the consuls, but if they could not settle things the Envoy must. In January 1765 Hamilton took up the case, outstanding from the previous April, of a Captain Nottingham whose ship had been forcibly brought into the port of Messina; in March he received, via Isaac Jamineau, a petition of the English merchants protesting against restrictions imposed on them in breach, so they said, of the treaty of 1676. The status of that treaty remained an issue throughout Hamilton's term of office. But whether the Neapolitans respected it or not, whether English privileges were upheld or infringed, the balance of trade was massively in England's favour: £416,298 in the year October 1763–October 1764, according to the statement drawn up and returned by Hamilton.

It was the Envoy's job to keep things that way and, more generally, in all areas of national interest, to press for the home advantage. Preparing himself, the first note Hamilton had made out of Gray's correspondence was this: 'Take care that the same respect is shown to you as to the M[inisters] of Fr— and Sp. and other Crowned heads residing at the Court of N in the same character.'[11] Being almost literally a born courtier, he soon saw how to assert himself, and thus also his country, in the intriguing world of Neapolitan politics. Prime Minister Tanucci gave audiences on a Wednesday and ambassadors wishing to see him were obliged to wait in an antechamber 'with the very lowest people'.[12] Early in the new year Hamilton could boast that he avoided this: he announced his arrival to the Minister *in advance*, and was seen without waiting. His tactics (and progress) thereafter are pretty well characterized by that first step.

English politics reached Naples not just in letters from home but also in the persons of certain travellers. John Wilkes arrived in Naples on 26 February 1765. He had left England in December 1763 to avoid prosecution for seditious libel. Having persistently insulted Lord Bute he had turned, in issue No. 45 of *The North Briton*, to insulting his successor, George Grenville. En route through Rome, Wilkes became friends with Winckelmann; James Boswell followed him to Naples for his friendship. He arrived with his mistress Gertrude Maria Corradini and her mother and set up home in Naples for five months. Hamilton reported on him, his erstwhile colleague in parliament. He had met him at Lady Orford's, a usual assembly point for the English in Naples, but declined to visit or receive him. Bute was the man Hamilton had first applied to for the Naples job; Grenville was the man from whom he got it; Bute's son, John Stuart Mountstuart, arrived in Naples soon after Wilkes and was often Hamilton's guest.

Wilkes lived quietly enough. He set up a press – so Hamilton informed Lord Halifax (and Horace Mann) – and was printing an edition of the works of the Reverend Charles Churchill, his friend and collaborator, just deceased. Reporting on troublemakers was part of the Envoy's brief: Gray had on the Old Pretender ending his days in Rome; Hamilton would on the Young, also in Rome.

To respectable visitors coming with letters of recommendation Hamilton's house was from the first and for thirty-five years always open. This also was his job, but, being naturally sociable, he wearied of it less soon than others would have done. During the winter months numerous travellers called, most but not all English, and he and Catherine presented them at Court and invited them to their weekly Assemblies, or to their musical evenings or to their box at the Opera. Samuel Sharp, visiting in November 1765, gives a good account of this hospitality:

> Mr. *Hamilton*, the Envoy, a very polite Gentleman, receives company every evening, which conduces much to the pleasure of the *English* residing here. It is the custom, when neither at the Opera, nor any particular engagements prevent, to meet at his house, where we amuse ourselves as we are disposed, either at cards, the billiard-table, or his little concert; some form themselves into small parties of conversation and as the members of this society are often Ambassadors, Nuncios, Monsignoris, Envoys, Residents, and the first quality of *Naples* you will conceive it to be instructive as well as honourable.[13]

Edward Gibbon came in February 1765; Boswell in April, but associating with Wilkes, he did not call. And many others, high and not so high. What Hamilton wrote to Horace Mann in February 1765 about Mr and Mrs John Dick is worth quoting, because it characterizes him:

> Mr. & Mrs. Dick seem to like the Country & Climate here better than the inhabitants, & I dont wonder at them, but as I am likely to pass some time here I continue to suit my self to them & pass over the faults that the total want of Education must necessarily produce & then I find they have some valuable quality's, in short it is the best way to be resolved to be pleased.[14]

He was less fastidious than Catherine who could not stomach the 'ill-bred' Changuion. True, he was rude about the Neapolitans (all the English were). Thus to Mann in April:

> The more I see of this Country the more I like it & the more I see of the people the less I like them, such a mean pittiful way of thinking mixt with low interested cunning I never met with, & makes me determine to have no further connection with them than is absolutely necessary. I was unwilling to beleive all I heard against them, but now I protest I fear it is but too true. I dont mean only the lower sort, for I rather think the higher you go the worse they are.[15]

But after ten years in post the King took to calling him 'Paesano Nostro'[16] which must have pleased him since he passes on the appellation to more than one of his correspondents. If people were not to his taste he could bear it better than Catherine. He got along with the world, wryly, not expecting much. Never in a lifetime would the King have called Catherine his compatriot. The necessary attendances in society fatigued her. Hamilton wrote in February that she had 'suffer'd a little by the Carnaval Balls';[17] and three or four years later, inviting her sister-in-law to visit them, she wrote of their life in Naples thus:

> We live in so English a Stile that you need not fear any of the Italian ceremonies and nonsense with us. We enter as little as we can into their stupid Assemblys, – in the Winter are almost entirely

with the English, in the Summer live much to ourselves.[18]

The Envoy looked after the English in Naples and was not always rid of them when they left. They – and others who never came as far as Naples – used him as agent; they asked him to get them things: tortoiseshell, lavas, marbles, minerals, the fiery aphrodisiacs known as *diavoloni*, snuffboxes, books. For the richest of his clients he purchased and committed to the seas (not always luckily) the expensive volumes of the *Antiquities of Herculaneum*, as the Neapolitan Academy published them. Charles III would at first not part with them for money, but would give them away from time to time as a mark of favour; then policy changed, and the English bought them. Gray, ordering two for friends, warned Hamilton that the volumes would be 'a constant source of trouble',[19] and they were, from the first year onwards. In September 1765 a Mr Howard, of Worksop, wrote to have them, presuming on the slight acquaintance he and Hamilton had made in Paris. Scores of these tomes, at seven guineas apiece, passed from Naples to the British Isles through Hamilton, the Envoy. He took orders the other way too: from the Spanish envoy Clementi, for an English coach, in October 1765. Later it would be race horses, Irish wolfhounds, optical instruments, gardening tools, gardeners, to please all kinds of people.

There to be helpful, especially towards compatriots, the Envoy and his wife had among many duties and functions that of consoling and diverting the newly bereaved. See Naples and die. It was often literally so. They came south for their health, out of the fogs and the cold, but were already too far gone; or arriving healthy, they contracted something local and died of that. Catherine, herself a survivor, looked after motherless English children or wrote to a mother in England whose son she had watched dying.[20]

By November 1765 Hamilton was perfectly master of his job; he knew what manner of things he would henceforth have to deal with; for him as Envoy all years after the first would be much the same, until the wars intruded. On Christmas Eve he wrote to Mann that Catherine, though not 'quite well of late', had had 'no return of her old asthmaticky complaint'; so there too the worry was slight. In a place where there was 'as little news as any place in the World', where there was 'nothing new ... but that wickedness rather encreases',[21] Hamilton was at liberty to enjoy himself. In June, answering a letter from Lord Palmerston, he had apologized for having nothing entertaining to relate: 'You know that Politicks in this Country is at a very low Ebb indeed, & Cicisbé nonsense is not worth writing about.' On that last business – love-affairs, a 'cicisbeo' was a married woman's lover – he added: 'As to any experience of my own in the Cicisbé way I soon saw that it was liable to produce many more disagreable circumstances than agreable ones, besides that it wou'd not have been very agreable to Mrs H.' Accordingly, he turned all his leisure hours 'either to the study of the natural History of this Country or to Antiquity'.[22]

Hamilton was soon at Pozzuoli and Solfatara and began his obsessive climbing of Vesuvius. In September 1765 Joseph-Jérôme Lalande came to Naples, writing a guide-book, and Hamilton, already a local expert, climbed the volcano with him. For Vesuvius, as for the buried cities, there was soon no better *cicerone* than Hamilton. He lived with the volcano. He could see it from home and from the Palazzo Reale; driving out to Caserta (where the Court withdrew for much of the winter, hunting) he observed it for miles in the east along the way; at Portici he was on the hem of its southern slopes. Today, with its broken crown and dead appearance, it has been fetched almost into the suburbs, among two million people, like a sinister relic. At night the lights of traffic and villas speckle it quite high. It last erupted in 1944, and the question – so the experts say – is not whether it will again but when.

There is no evidence that Hamilton was *much* interested in volcanoes before he came to Naples, but having one – and such a one – on his doorstep, for his interest and knowledge he was soon famous in Europe. In the learned world he became 'le Pline moderne'; even Emma, for a time at least, called him 'Uncle Pliny'.

By 19 December 1764, having finished 'all ceremonials', Hamilton had already seen the bronzes from Herculaneum in the museum at Portici, and admired them 'most exceedingly'. Thereafter he kept abreast of the new discoveries. In June 1764 he wrote to Palmerston:

The Works of Herculaneoum have been discontinued till lately & those of Pompea go on slowly, at the last they have also found a Theatre tho' I can not say it appears to me to be certainly so. In a

room just by this building was found a Venus of marble coming
out of a Bath & wringing out her wet hair what I thought most
remarkable was that all her *tit bits* such as *bubbies mons Veneris* &c
are double gilt & the gold very well preserved, the rest of the marble
is in its natural State.[23]

In November Tanucci ordered a new procedure at Pompeii. Henceforth, so Hamilton reported,

the workmen ... should not remove any inscription or paintings
from the Walls, or fill up after they have search'd so that travellers
will soon have an opportunity of walking the Streets & seeing the
houses of this Ancient City ... as commodiously as Naples itself ...
The principal Gate of the Town, a curious Temple dedicated to
Isis, & part of the theatre are already clear'd, they are in wonderfull
preservation.[24]

Hamilton was often at the sites, not only with important visitors,
but also for his own curiosity, as amateur and collector. Discoveries
were as constant a feature of Hamilton's time in Naples as were the
threats of the volcano to bury them again.

But another factor manifested itself during that first year in
Naples and would operate in all the years to come: Hamilton's
impecuniousness. If there was no high status in being Envoy Extraordinary at the Court of Naples there was no money in it either.
Hamilton's pay on appointment was £5 a day, but it and the
reimbursements of his numerous and large out-of-pocket expenses
were very often late in arriving from a notably tight-fisted Treasury.
Hamilton was always short of cash and died in debt. In September
1765 he had a candid letter from his London banker, George Ross
(to whom he owed £1600), urging him to appeal to his friend General
Conway (then conveniently his Secretary of State) for a rise in status
to that of Plenipotentiary and a corresponding rise in pay to £8 a
day. He suggested he might engage Earl Spencer, who had been in
Naples in the previous year, to testify to Conway how expensive
things had become. But if the approaches failed, as Ross feared they
might, then: 'you must even have patience ... depriving yourself of
the favourite passion of buying pictures.'[25] Walpole had forecast that

Hamilton would 'ruin himself in virtu-land'. Having in January 1765 sold his pictures in London, he was collecting again in Naples, but principally vases.

Chapter 3

VASES AND THE VOLCANO

The two passions started together, and by early 1768, after scarcely three years pursuing them, Hamilton had made a name for himself in both.

He must have begun collecting vases almost at once, even as his paintings were being sold in London. Sir William Farington, visiting Naples at the end of April 1765, saw his collection of 'Etruscan Vases' and described it as 'very Fine',[1] and Hamilton himself told Lord Palmerston on 18 June that he already had 'a great number of Etruscan Vases'.[2] He was not the only collector and the objects were not, at that time, in short supply. In late 1763, publishing the first edition of his *History of Ancient Art*, Winckelmann claimed to have seen 'many hundreds' of them; in the second edition (which he was working on until his death in 1768) he wrote that 'several thousand' had been preserved.[3] They came from tombs in the vicinity of Naples, ancient Campania, especially at Nola, Capua and Trebbia. Hamilton got them from dealers, or from other collectors – from Prince Porcinari, for example, in 1766; but also, with what authority who knows, he opened tombs himself. There is an account of his doing so, near Capua, with an illustration showing the skeleton among its pots, in his first publication (in Volumes II, p. 57, and IV, pp. 42–3); and the frontispiece of his second (dated 1791) shows him present with Emma Hart, soon to be the second Lady Hamilton, at such an opening. How many vases he actually had in his collections is surprisingly hard to determine. An abstract of the first, printed in 1772, says there were 730, but higher (747) and much lower (347) figures have also been given; in the second collection, according to Tischbein, there were 1591.[4]

Hamilton, like everybody else, called his vases 'Etruscan'. They were so called, sometimes from a nationalistic or dynastic bias, by early collectors and commentators who believed or wanted to believe them to be the work of the Etruscan people whose empire extended over most of Italy before Rome's did. The correction of this view proceeded through the latter half of the eighteenth century. Hamilton, as collector and publisher, together with Winckelmann and d'Hancarville, his associates in the venture, contributed greatly to the process. The correct view is that most such vases are Greek; the best were made in Corinth and Athens in the fifth century BC and traded in southern Italy, probably for gold and bronze work; others, many of them also very fine, were made in Southern Italy itself, in Magna Graecia, by Greek colonists. Winckelmann was moving towards that verdict before he saw Hamilton's collection, and what he saw there increased his conviction; and Hamilton himself, before he had any dealings with Winckelmann, already doubted the usefulness of the term 'Etruscan'. He wrote to Palmerston: 'My opinion is that but few are realy Etruscan but made by Greek & Roman Artists in that taste which was introduced when the Etruscans were brought into this Country to shew their different Games.'' Soon he would be more definite and accurate, following Winckelmann.

His letter to Palmerston continues:

> I think one day or other of publishing my collection as I am sure it wou'd be a very valuable present to antiquarians. There is a taste & Ellegance in their shapes & tho' the figures are not always correct yet their is a choise in the attitudes, & a je ne sçais quoi of Ellegance that the Moderns do not arrive at.

That was in June 1765. By the autumn he had decided to publish, and was advertising for subscribers. There was some altruism in the scheme, which he developed as it proceeded. He would make his vases available and useful to others. But also, if the publication was successful, he might recoup not only what it cost (a good deal) but also at least something of what the vases themselves had cost. And it is possible that from the first he intended to sell and meant the publication to advertise his wares.

Hamilton did not have the scholarship to write a commentary on his own vases, nor the technical expertise to engrave them and see them through the press. He was the collector and the sponsor but for publication had to employ other men. Chief among these was the dubious d'Hancarville who, having been put in charge, regularly spoke of the whole work as his. He was an adventurer and went under various names. Pierre François Hugues seems to have been his real one, Baron du Han or d'Hancarville were the ones he preferred. He had been on the move, not to say on the run, among the cities of Italy for years, coming to Naples, with a bad reputation, in October 1763. Hamilton was in dealings with him by May 1765 at the latest; liked him and trusted him and was notably slow to believe the worst of him. If by June Hamilton was thinking of publication it is probable he already had d'Hancarville in mind; indeed, publication of the growing collection of vases may well have been d'Hancarville's idea. So the Ambassador, before he had been in post more than half a year, was engaged in a project both sumptuous and risky.

The volcano was risky too. By June 1765 Hamilton had begun his fascinated daily study of its signs and wonders. These were increasing, after a quiet five years. Hamilton wrote to Palmerston: 'The Mountain has been noisy of late & throws out a great deal of thick smoak so that I am told by the learned that an Eruption is not very distant in all probability.'[6] The learned were right. In November snow fell, in December there were rumblings, volleys of ash, more show of flame at nights. 'Enshort,' Hamilton wrote to Horace Mann, 'she is in labour & will in all probability soon bring forth something more than a *ridiculus Mus*.'[7] The labour continued, under more snow in January. Hamilton went to the crater and was nearly brained: a stone three times the size of his head fell within a yard of him. In March the smoke, ever thicker and darker, assumed the pine-tree shape observed by the younger Pliny in August AD 79. Hamilton returned, this time with Lord Hillsborough whose wife, despite trying the cure at Solfatara, had died a month before. Hamilton thought the mountain might distract him from his grief. It did, it pulled him closer than was safe. Hamilton wrote: 'His Lordship was displeased that I wou'd not let him go nearer than 30 yards of the Mouth.'[8] Next day another English party – Mr Hervey, Mr Fuller and Mr Trent – were not so cautious. They went to the edge and peered down. Hervey, Hamilton's old schoolfellow, soon to be Lord Bristol and Bishop of Derry, saw 'two large mouths from whence the mountain frequently threw up two or three hundred red hot stones'.[9] One hit his arm, tore his clothing, wounded him two inches deep, caused him to bleed profusely, sent him to bed with fever for five weeks. 'Another lamed Mr Fuller & a third knock'd the stick out of Mr Trents hand.'

Pulling people to it, the mountain then excited a madness in them, rather like canon-fever. At nights now the phenomenon was glorious and the explosion of the stones being flung up 'like that of a Mortar Battery, so loud as to make the Windows shake at Portici' and audible even in Naples. An outbreak of lava was expected, 'a curiosity', Hamilton wrote, 'I own I long for much'.[10] It came on Good Friday, 28 March, towards Portici. Hamilton spent the night on the mountain. 'The lava had the appearance of a river of red hot and liquid metal, such as we see in the glass-houses.' It ran for several weeks. On 12 April he was by it all day and night, climbing to its source. He wrote: 'It ran with amazing velocity; I am sure, the first mile with a rapidity equal to that of the river Severn, at the passage near Bristol.' The adjacent ground quivered 'like the timbers of a water-mill'. On the lava rode a scum 'which in the day-time had the appearance of the river Thames ... after a hard frost and a great fall of snow, when beginning to thaw, carrying down vast masses of snow and ice'. For his similes, to describe something beyond all his previous experience, he reached back to England, to familiar industries, to his journeys into Pembrokeshire and to the hard winter of 1763–4.

During May that eruption abated. Hamilton took a final view on 3 June and a week later sent an account of the whole event to the Royal Society. It was his first such report. He prefaced it modestly: 'I shall confine myself merely to the many extraordinary appearances that have come under my own inspection, and leave their explanation to the more learned in Natural Philosophy.'[11] That would always be his forte: autopsy, saying what he really saw without prejudice or exaggeration; but before long he did have explanations and in that particular branch of natural philosophy he was the most learned. He might have got himself elected to the Royal Society, through one or other of his aristocratic friends, just as a gentleman; but his Fellowship, coming in September 1767, was on the better grounds of the paper he had sent them in June. And doubtless the Society wished to secure him as their own correspondent in such a curious locality. His paper was read over two of their meetings, on 5 March and 2 April 1767. By then, during the winter while the mountain dozed, he had busied himself collecting salts and sulphurs at the crack the lava had issued from and in the crater itself. He enclosed them in another letter to the Society on 3 February.

The vases meanwhile were not neglected. The project had been advertised, subscribers sought and found. D'Hancarville wrote a Preface, dating it 30 April 1766, in which he stated his patron's desire, through publication of the vases, to influence taste and effect an improvement in the contemporary arts. Being, he says, 'less flattered with the advantage of possessing [the vases], than with that of rendering them useful', Hamilton will make them available, in engravings and exact drawings, so that artists, and especially the manufacturers of earthenware and china, may have in them the models and deduce out of them the principles for further production. D'Hancarville concludes: 'We hope that Artists, thus enlightened in the true principles of their Art, will soon annihilate those Gothick forms which habit alone renders supportable.'

In late October Prince George August von Mecklenburg-Strelitz, younger brother of the English Queen Charlotte, arrived in Naples from Rome, where he had been tutored by Winckelmann. Because of the royal connection, Hamilton looked after him in Naples, and through him entered into dealings with Winckelmann who, then overseeing the printing of the first two volumes of his *Monumenti Antici Inediti*, was looking for people to promote it outside Italy. Through Mecklenburg, Hamilton promised him some help in England. It is likely that in doing so he was hoping to enlist him alongside d'Hancarville in the further publication of his vases. Certainly, by the end of January 1767 he must have made him some such proposal, either directly in a letter or through Prince Mecklenburg who returned to Rome on the 25th. Thereafter, in letters to friends, Winckelmann spoke of his involvement in the project as definite and by 2 April he was receiving the first engravings as they left the printer's. The vases, already engraved, wanted explanations; and these Winckelmann was to supply, no doubt in the manner of a *catalogue raisonné*, as he had done, in 1760, for Baron Stosch's collection of gems and, in a different format, for the works (mostly from Cardinal Albani's collection) he had just published in the *Monumenti Inediti*. He was the best and recruiting him was a coup. Throughout the spring and summer he and Hamilton corresponded (though only one of their letters – Winckelmann to Hamilton, 7 April 1767 – has come to light);[12] and in the autumn they met.

It was Winckelmann's fourth visit to Naples and, because of his critical account of the excavations at Herculaneum, brought in by Hamilton in 1764, he came rather apprehensively, fearing a beating or even assassination. In the event no such ill befell him – Hamilton's protection must have helped – and he enjoyed himself among the vases and under and on the now stupendously active volcano. He arrived at the end of September, lodged with d'Hancarville (overcoming a worry that the man's bad name might harm him), and had the vases around him in his room. He saw a good deal of Hamilton; they went on excursions together.

Again that April snow had covered the mountain, a curious harbinger of the fire to come. All summer the warning signs increased. On 6 October Hamilton wrote to the secretary of the Royal Society, foretelling an eruption. It came on Monday the 19th, the most violent for more than a century. Hamilton was at his villa between Pompeii and Herculaneum, making observations. When the first lava flow opened he climbed with his guide to see it from as close as possible. They were almost caught out:

I was making my observations upon the lava … when on a sudden, about noon, I heard a violent noise within the mountain, and at about a quarter of a mile off the place where I stood, the mountain split and with much noise, from this new mouth a fountain of liquid fire shot up many feet high, and then like a torrent, rolled on directly towards us. The earth shook at the same time that a volley of pumice stones fell thick upon us; in an instant clouds of black smoak and ashes caused almost a total darkness; the explosions from the top of the mountain were much louder than any thunder I ever heard, and the smell of the sulphur was very offensive. My guide alarmed took to his heels; and I must confess that I was not at my ease. I followed close, and we ran near three miles without stopping; as the earth continued to shake under our feet, I was apprehensive of the opening of a fresh mouth, which might have cut off our retreat. I also feared that the violent explosions would detach [some] of the rocks of the mountain of Somma, under which we were obliged to pass; besides, the pumice-stones, falling upon us like hail, were of such a size as to cause a disagreable sensation upon the part where they fell. After having taken breath, as the earth still trembled greatly, I thought it most prudent to leave the mountain, and return to my Villa, where I found my family in a great alarm, at the continual and violent explosions of the Volcano, which shook our house to its very foundation, the doors and windows swinging upon their hinges.[13]

He returned with his household to Naples, calling at Portici on the way to warn the Royal Family they should flee. The lava advanced, from three vents; the air thickened to an impenetrable fog; ash, pumice and cinders rained steadily on Naples and on ships twenty leagues away. On Wednesday the mountain quietened, 'though the lavas ran briskly'; towards nightfall they slackened. Early that morning Winckelmann, d'Hancarville and a close friend of Winckelmann's, the traveller Riedesel, together with three servants and a guide, went against the tide of evacuation and flight, to Portici, and from there climbed over the old lavas to the new. They wanted to get to the source, it was a two-hour climb, finally over lavas that were burning hot. Their guide was unwilling to go on, but they forced him, with a stick. At the mouth they undressed and picnicked among the fires, naked, roasting skewered pigeons on the lava streams and circulating the wine. Baron Riedesel will not have looked good in the nude. He was small, hunchbacked and ugly. But Winckelmann's letters to him, though censored by their first editor and even allowing for the effusiveness commoner in that day, are fond, even passionate. And d'Hancarville fascinated Winckelmann. He had the sort of panache and effrontery that Winckelmann himself, of even lower social origins and troubled with a sexuality he hardly ever dared express, never quite managed.

Riedesel, after his travels, settled into a career in European diplomacy; d'Hancarville lived the life of a scholar and a scoundrel into a brilliant old age; but Winckelmann met Arcangeli, his murderer, on the waterfront in Trieste. There on the mountain, at a naked barbecue over the lava flows, he seems at an extreme, too near the edge; as he always was, in fact.

Riedesel, just back from a tour of Magna Graecia and Sicily and planning a journey to Greece, frequented Hamilton in the meantime. I mention him in the trio on the mountain to indicate how closely respectability (Riedesel's, Hamilton's) consorted with its opposite.

In Naples the sun was dimmed and through the smoke and ash appeared only faintly from time to time like a moon. There was panic, rioting and religious ecstasy. The women loosened their hair and went in a throng barefoot; troops were sent to contain the prisoners in their gaol; the mob demanded the relics of Saint Januarius and set fire to the Archbishop's gate when he refused them; then the King, fearing worse and worse, obliged him to, and a procession of twenty thousand streamed to the Porta Maddalena and opposed the head of the Saint against the fury of the mountain. The mountain quietened, the mob first abused their Saint for having allowed it to cause them such alarm, then fell on their faces in worship and afterwards returned to the Cathedral, singing his praises for the miracle he had done.

Having already given his Secretary of State, Lord Shelburne, a long account, Hamilton wrote up the whole eruption, once he was sure it was over, for the Royal Society on 29 December, enclosing a map, drawings of the changing shape of the crater between 8 July and 29 October, and a painting of the lava in transparent colours which would give the best idea 'when lighted up with lamps behind it'. This letter, read at the Society on 11 February 1768, is substantial, vivid and precisely informative. It is writing done by a man who knows his subject, a man in his element who has something new and important to say. It was published, like his first, in the Society's annual journal, the *Philosophical Transactions* (with extracts in the *Annual Register*). Year by year, having begun late, Hamilton increased his authority and his reputation.

The first volume of his *Vases* came out that winter, at the very end of 1767 or the very beginning of 1768. The work's full title in English was: *Collection of Etruscan, Greek, and Roman Antiquities from the Cabinet of the Honble. Wm. Hamilton His Britannick Majesty's Envoy Extraordinary at the Court of Naples*. The text was in English and French, and the name the work usually went by was *Etruscan Vases* or *Vases Etrusques*. The volume contains a long essay by d'Hancarville on the arts, history and manners of the Etruscans, then the beginning of what (in Volume II) would become a *very* long essay, also by him, on sculpture and painting. There are explanations of two vases and of the twenty-three vignettes that decorate d'Hancarville's text. The rest of the volume, its chief attraction, consists of one hundred engravings of vases, sometimes as many as half a dozen per vase: line drawings with exact measurements, and full colour reproductions of the paintings on the vases; but these all without a word of identification or explanation.

Leaving out the explanations was doubtless a shrewd move, in that whoever wanted them would be induced to buy the second volume, in the hope of finding them there. It seems certain that Winckelmann was intending to supply them. Even without being identified or explained, the vases thus published would have the effect that Hamilton desired. The prints were obtainable loose, and might be studied or displayed simply for the vases' shapes and for the interest and beauty of the paintings. In March 1768 Josiah Wedgwood met Hamilton's brother-in-law, Lord Cathcart, in London. Wedgwood, expanding his business, was building a new factory, to be called Etruria, in what would become the Potteries. Cathcart lent him prints from Hamilton's first volume, and when the factory opened, in June 1769, the first six pots fired were decorated, red on black, with figures taken from Hamilton's vases. Wedgwood acquired all four volumes – some at least through the generosity of Sir Watkin Williams Wynn, a good friend of Hamilton – and used them like a pattern book. His 'Etruscan' line was especially successful, but prints from Hamilton's collection had their effect on other products too.

Lovers of Classical Antiquity in the eighteenth century saw very little of the best Greek work. The great bronzes in the museums of Delphi and Athens came out of the sea only quite recently. Amateurs in Rome in Hamilton's day saw mostly only Roman marble copies of long-lost bronze Greek originals. At Portici there were the startlingly lively bronzes of athletes and dancers brought out from under the ash; but taste in that time was largely formed by the Laocoön, the Apollo Belvedere, the Medici Venus, so that people did not have eyes to see what little there was to see. With the vases they could get nearer, and Winckelmann and Hamilton together sharpened their sight to something better than all the hundreds of marble copies of statues in the galleries of Rome. Very little Greek painting has survived, none by the named masters such as Zeuxis and Apelles; and the discovered wall-paintings in the buried cities, though often beautiful and in the simple fact of their survival always poignant, were still only poor after-images of a fabulous beauty lost for ever. But there on the finest vases, those from fifth-century Corinth and Athens, the art of painting came out of the ground in miniature and at its best. Winckelmann saw this ever more clearly as his life hastened to its violent end. Having lived with Hamilton's collection he called it 'a treasury of Greek draughtsmanship and the clear proof of the perfection of their art'; these vases, he said, showed you at once, and better than any other surviving works, all the enormous ability and confidence of the ancient artists.[14] And the importance of the collection was stated very definitely and correctly by the manufacturer Josiah Wedgwood in his catalogue of 1779:

And as it is evident the finer sort of *Etruscan Vases*, found in *Magna Graecia*, are truly Greek Workmanship, and ornamented chiefly with Grecian Subjects, drawn from the purest Fountain of the Arts; it is probable many of the Figures and Groupes upon them, preserve to us Sketches or Copies of the most celebrated Greek Paintings; so that few Monuments of Antiquity better deserve the Attention of the Antiquary, of the Connoisseur, and the Artist, than the *painted* Etruscan Vases.[15]

Hamilton appears on the title-page of the first volume of his *Vases* as 'Envoy Extraordinary', but long before publication that denomination was incorrect. In December 1766 he had pleaded, again, for 'the additional Character of Plenipotentiary' and for the extra £3 a day that would bring. His salary, he claimed, even supplemented by the whole of his private fortune, was not sufficient to meet 'the numberless Expenses' an ambassador in Naples faced.[16] This time his application was successful. He heard early in February 1767, by which time the title-page was already printed. On that of the second volume, out in October 1769, he was 'Envoy Extraordinary and Plenipotentiary'. The 'additional Character' is one more marker, like the publication itself and his election to the Royal Society and his contributions to their journal, of the success he was achieving in the first years of his embassy.

On 20 October 1767, having treated his Secretary of State to a long description of the violence of the volcano, he asked him for leave; and not to return to England but to visit Rome. This was granted two months later. At the end of January 1768 he made his preparations – settled bills, changed a thousand Neapolitan ducats into Roman sequins, and installed a Mr John Osborn in his house as *chargé d'affaires*. He was in Rome by the 2nd or 3rd of February, with Catherine.

He had asked for six weeks' leave, but took nine and certainly enjoyed himself. He wrote to Lord Shelburne: 'Rome greatly surpasses my expectations. It is here alone that a true idea can be formed of the magnificence of the Ancients, of their perfection in the Arts, and of the excellent Raphaels Pencil.'[17] He was described as 'indefatigable' in the 'pursuit of virtú';[18] that is, he went among the dealers and spent large sums of money. Beyond that, he did the sights in a serious and methodical way. He had the best guides: James Byres, who had been in Rome for ten years and offered his clients a course costing twenty sequins and lasting as much as six weeks; and Winckelmann, Papal Antiquary. On the whole Winckelmann disliked the English in Rome almost as much as he did the French. He found they had more money than manners or good taste. But even before he had met Hamilton, on the basis of the letters they were exchanging, Winckelmann described him as a man with whom one could talk rationally about Antiquity, who would not, as he put it, muddle any such discussion with questions of conscience or religion. The worst he ever said of Hamilton, still in advance of his visit to Rome, was that doubtless he would look around with a dealer's eye. But in Rome he gave him two days a week and concluded – Winckelmann's opinions often ran to extremes – that he was the greatest living connoisseur of pictures.[19]

Around the middle of the month Hamilton and Catherine were joined by Lord Stormont. He was ambassador in Vienna, recently bereaved and feeling his loss very badly. He had come to Naples at the end of November, in poor spirits. Hamilton wrote to Mann about him: 'His disorder is certainly nervous and brought on by grief for the Loss of his Wife.' And he added, in cynical mode, *'an uncommon case*.[20] Having diverted Lord Hillsborough from *his* grief by showing him the volcano Hamilton tried to do the same for Lord Stormont with the sights of Rome. Years later, in London after Catherine's death, Hamilton talked about Stormont to his niece Mary: how he would have lost his mind in grief but for his (Hamilton's) 'attention & care'. Mary noted: 'My Uncle made him go with him to *Rome* & study the fine Arts, & constant attention to other objects work'd ye desired effect, & his Mind by slow degrees regain'd composure.'[21]

Winckelmann approved of Stormont as much as he did of Hamilton, calling him 'one of the most learned men I know ... the most learned man of his class'. In their company, he wrote, he could be entirely candid,[22] a remark which says something about the perceived open-mindedness of the two English gentlemen and perhaps more still about Winckelmann's anxieties.

Hamilton visited the studios of some British painters – certainly David Allan and James Barry – but he and Catherine sat for a double portrait to a pupil of Raphael Mengs named Anton von Maron. They left a cameo and a dress with him that they wished her to be depicted wearing. These were returned in September. The portrait hung in the Palazzo Sessa and was packed for the hurried departure in 1798; but its whereabouts now are unknown.[23] Another of Maron's clients in the spring of 1768 was Winckelmann. Hamilton saw that portrait in the making and declared the head to be the finest he had ever seen.[24] In the finished painting the shape (and threat) of Hermes Conductor of Souls is visible behind the sitter's back.

In Naples meanwhile d'Hancarville and his wife were packing and dispatching copies of the first volume to London booksellers and working 'day and night' on the second. He wrote congratulating Hamilton on having Winckelmann as guide – 'you gain a lot seeing the statues with him' – and urging his further involvement in the project.[25] Hamilton seems to have hawked the first volume in Rome a little; Earl Fitzwilliam, at least, complained of being pestered to buy it. In March then, doubtless in recognition of that publication, he was elected to the Tuscan Academy.

Expected back on 8 April Hamilton was certainly there by the 12th. Osborn left at once. 'I am sorry to lose him,' Hamilton wrote, 'he is certainly a valuable young man.'[26] He was called back to

London and from there, for several years, he took the liveliest interest – a candid *self*-interest – in Hamilton's career.

Winckelmann left Rome a month after Hamilton, for Germany. He had been in Rome for thirteen years, during which time he had become a European celebrity. His visit home would have been his triumph. The previous autumn in Naples and all that winter his friend Riedesel had been urging him to accompany him to Greece. He had had several such opportunities to fulfil what he frequently called his heart's most passionate desire, but this was the best, the most tempting and the most realistic. He turned it down, and went north. He travelled with the sculptor Cavaceppi and no sooner were they over the border than he began to groan 'torniamo a Roma, torniamo a Roma'; but desperately unhappily pushed on as far as Regensburg, where his courage for the enterprise failed him and he turned and fled, leaving the hapless Cavaceppi, with no German, to fend for himself. In Vienna he spent some time prostrated in a hospital, but had an audience with the Empress Maria Theresa and, bearing gifts from her, headed for Italy. In Trieste, on the waterfront, looking for a ship, he took up with Francesco Arcangeli. For three days the two men were often together, on the waterfront or in Winckelmann's hotel room. Arcangeli bought a knife and a garotte and on the morning of 8 June used them to kill him. He was soon apprehended and readily confessed. He was broken on the wheel, 'downwards', thought to be the more humane way, death coming quicker.

Volume II of Hamilton's *Vases*, dated 1767, actually came out in October 1769 and its frontispiece is an ornate memorial to Winckelmann. In the preface to Volume I of his Second Collection (1793) Hamilton mentions 'the learned abbé'; but nowhere else among the thousands of his papers is there any word on the subject of Winckelmann's life and violent death. There may be no mystery in this. Hamilton, in his long public career, met many hundreds of people, several of them important and interesting; and given the numerous accidents of transmission and preservation it is hard to use the absence of reference as evidence of anything. Still, the gap is intriguing. Hamilton was one of the very last connoisseurs to have the benefit of Winckelmann's learning and enthusiasm. Is not mentioning him an ingratitude? Or a deliberate keeping clear of a life both more *louche* and more passionately focused than his own?

Chapter 4

THE KING

Naples, when Hamilton and Catherine returned from Rome, was in the throes of preparation for a royal wedding. King Ferdinand was to marry Maria Carolina, a daughter of the Empress Maria Theresa, to improve relations between the Bourbons and the Habsburgs. By proxy he had married her already, on 7 April; now she set off from Vienna, for Naples, to celebrate the real thing and to begin her long married life with the king they called 'The Nose'. She was sixteen, eighteen months his junior.

Ferdinand had come of age on 12 January 1767 but was not much more in charge of affairs of state after that date than before it. His education had eradicated what little interest in them or aptitude for them he might ever have possessed. All he could do and had any interest in doing was hunt. His tutor, Prince San Nicandro, was of the opinion that that was all a nobleman, and how much more so a king, needed to do. Another factor in this pedagogy was the fear that the young King might become an imbecile like his grandfather Philip V or his uncle Ferdinand VI of Spain, or his poor elder brother whom he had by-passed to the Neapolitan throne. His tutor and even his father thought the outdoor life might keep him sane. The imbecile brother was kept in the palace, but discreetly displayed from time to time, so that the populace might be all the gladder of the robust specimen ruling them instead.

Since Ferdinand scarcely changed throughout the thirty-six years of Hamilton's dealings with him it will be as well to characterize him now, at the time of his majority and his marriage, when he was the subject of much observation and commentary, most of it appalled. Some characterization of Ferdinand is necessary in order to understand what Hamilton's job entailed; what he, in the service of his own king, thought it necessary to do. Settled in his own passions, which were the arts and natural history, Hamilton was tolerant of other people's; and though in some respects fastidious he had also roughed it enough in the army and on the volcano and had seen enough of the Court in England not to feel in his dealings with Ferdinand an incapacitating degree of disgust. Later, taking up with Emma, he told his friend Banks that he had long made a study of 'the animal called Woman';[1] but he had equally of the 'animal called Man', and seems not to have expected very much from either. So he viewed Ferdinand 'philosophically' and reported on him in tones of varying degrees of amusement, anger, sorrow, pity, revulsion and contempt.

As a youngster Ferdinand was covered in herpes, thought by the doctors then to be a sign of health. His brother-in-law, the Emperor Joseph II of Austria, visiting in March 1769, described him thus:

> He must be five feet seven inches ... very thin, gaunt and raw-boned ... his knees always bent and his back very supple, since at every step he bends and sways his whole body. The part below his waist is so limp and feeble that it does not seem to belong to the upper part, which is much stronger. He has muscular arms and wrists, and his coarse brown hands are very dirty since he never wears gloves when he rides or hunts. His head is relatively small, surmounted by a forest of coffee-coloured hair, which he never powders, a nose which begins in his forehead and gradually swells in a straight line as far as his mouth, which is very large with a jutting lower lip, filled with fairly good but irregular teeth. The rest of his features, his low brow, pig's eyes, flat cheeks and a long neck, are not remarkable.
>
> Although an ugly Prince, he is not absolutely repulsive: his skin is fairly smooth and firm, of a yellowish pallor: he is clean except for his hands; and at least he does not stink.[2]

His young wife described him as 'ein recht guter Narr',[3] and that was perhaps the best that could be said of him: that he was a fool, without much malice in him. Many women liked him; and his subjects – the *lazzaroni* at least – adored him and were loyal to him long after he had ceased to deserve loyalty from anyone. He was 'il re nasone', and also 'il re lazzarone'. Brought up rubbing shoulders with 'the lowest sorts of people' theirs was the only language he spoke, broad Neapolitan. Theirs was the company he liked best, his beaters, fishermen, Liparote soldiers and sailors.

I said, following Maria Carolina, that he was – 'without much malice'. Perhaps so, by the standards of the day. He had first been engaged to her elder sister Maria Josepha, but she had died before she could become his wife. Obliged by etiquette to mourn her, he was prohibited from hunting. The boredom nearly drove him mad. Hamilton, arriving to offer his condolences, found Ferdinand acting out the young woman's funeral, to pass the time:

> Having selected one of the Chamberlains, as proper, from his youth and feminine appearance, to represent the Princess, they habited him in a manner suitable to the mournful occasion; laid him out on an open Bier, according to the Neapolitan custom at interments; and in order to render the ceremony more appropriate, as well as more accurately correct, they marked his face and hands with Chocolate drops, which were designed to imitate the pustules of the small-pox. All the Apparatus being ready, the funeral procession began, and proceeded through the principal Apartments of the palace at Portici, Ferdinand officiating as Chief Mourner.[4]

True, he was only sixteen and it was somebody else's (a courtier's) idea. But fun, for him, often meant some indecency; also, often, the discomfiture of other people. He liked tripping courtiers up, or whirling them round in a dance until they tottered, or tickling them, or kicking their backsides, or putting marmalade in their hats; he chased after ladies, with mice. Worse, Hamilton observed in him 'a disposition to Tyrannical cruelty both towards His Servants and the Animals which unfortunately fell into his hands'.[5] He combined the two, according to Winckelmann, by forcing his coachmen to swallow frogs alive. He did operations on living pregnant deer, to discover their young.[6]

Chiefly Ferdinand hunted. Nothing, if he could possibly help it, ever got in the way of that. On the morning after his wedding night he rose early as usual, left his young wife sleeping ('poleaxed', as he put it, adding: 'And she sweats like a pig'),[7] and went hunting. This was his outfit:

A large hat let down on every side, a shaggy grey coat with pockets
hanging half-way down his legs, an old leather waistcoat, breeches
of the same, a large pouch containing his bags of small shot and a
hunting-knife like a bayonet, heavy grey stockings of beaver and
wool, which not being suspended fall in thick folds over his shoes,
a long and heavy Spanish gun on his shoulder, a powder-horn
dangling beside it with a knitted green game-bag, and various whistles
attached to his button-holes.[8]

He returned in his filth, with his pockets full of birds. His dogs had
the run of the palace. He slaughtered tirelessly, year in year out. He
had commandeered the craters of extinct volcanoes, to be reserves
for him. Into one such enclosure, five miles in circumference, he
drove 'about 500 wild boars, 1500 stags & fallow deer, foxes and
hares innumerable'.[9] Then killed them. He loved killing, he loved it
in quantity, he loved the bloody heaps when there was nothing left
to kill, and would roll up his sleeves and gleefully climb into them
and begin the flaying, the disembowelling and the jointing. That was
his one real forte, butchery. He counted every cadaver. For want of
anything more interesting, Hamilton would often pass on a statement
of the year's total to his Secretary of State. It was neatly set out, in
two columns. In the first was the King's own personal tally; in the
second that of his attendant company. In 1789, for example, his was
5487 pieces, theirs 42,672.[10]

That was all the arithmetic Ferdinand needed, just as all the writing
he ever did was lists of his favourite beaters. Coming back from
hunting, stinking of it, bloody with it, he fell asleep in the carriage
and on waking confessed he had been dreaming of it. On innumerable
occasions, over thirty-six years, Hamilton accompanied him. It was
a mark of favour to be asked. The way to the King's heart, and to
influence over him, was through hunting. So for weeks at a time, in
the coldest seasons, in snow and freezing rain, Hamilton abandoned
Catherine and his social obligations in town and went off with the
King into the mountains behind Caserta, to Persano, Venafro, Monte
Dragone. Together they slaughtered deer, birds, boar, hares, foxes,
wolves and the occasional bear. Hamilton boasted of these occasions.
It showed he was doing his job: he got invited and the French
ambassador did not; but he could never feel quite so full-bloodedly

enthusiastic as the King. (Who could?) He wrote: 'I am almost ashamed of the slaughter we committed in the forest in 13 days, no less than 1346 *pièces de gibier*, among which were 170 wild boars, above 1000 deer, 7 wolves – I myself killed one day 3 boars & 8 deer.'[11] Rather shamefacedly he admitted to having 'something of the Nimrod'[12] in him, and nephew Charles and his circle of virtuosi in London did sometimes worry that he was going to the bad and begged him to say less about cadavers in his letters and more about pictures, vases and volcanoes. Typically, Hamilton might regret the waste of time, and he thought that hunting as the King practised it was 'Carnage rather than Sport';[13] but he went along, to serve his own King, he said, and because it was in his nature to accommodate himself and to feel at even the worst things only a moderate disgust. And perhaps he hated the futilities of etiquette even more and enjoyed the licence the King allowed his entourage in the open air. And loving volcanoes he was glad to be in among them, even extinct, even given over to carnage.

Ferdinand, like the Emperor Claudius, farted whenever he pleased, in whatever company; best to, so he told his brother-in-law, for health reasons. And this same unlucky relative by marriage, the Emperor Joseph, an enlightened and cultured man, while his sister was singing at the harpsichord after dinner, was summoned to 'the close-stool' by Ferdinand, who hated being alone. The Emperor relates the whole event:

> I found him on this throne with lowered breeches, surrounded by five or six valets, chamberlains and others. We made conversation for more than half an hour, and I believe he would be there still if a terrible stench had not convinced us that all was over. He did not fail to describe the details and even wished to show them to us; and without more ado, his breeches down, he ran with the smelly pot in one hand after two of his gentlemen, who took to their heels.[14]

Did Ferdinand have no saving graces? For many years at least he loved his wife; indeed, he was uxorious. She could always command him by slowly peeling off one of her gloves. There is no evidence that her estimation of him improved over the years.

But by the common people, whose company he much preferred, Ferdinand was loved rather like Januarius, their saint, in a way at once reverential and coarsely intimate. He was mythic and ordinary. He was their King, who came in from fishing and sold his catch on the waterside for the highest possible prices and doled the money back into the crowd. Like any good bad emperor, he gave them circuses, he gave them the carnival, and the elaborate and violent *cuccagna*. For this particular entertainment the Land of Cockaigne itself was constructed:

> A hill appears exactly opposite the palace, from the centre of which bursts forth a fountain, and falls into a bason at its foot; the base represents incrustations of rocks and shells like grotto-work; such is the appearance from the windows of the palace; but this grotto-work is composed of nothing else than dried fish varnished and gilt, and intermixed with loaves of bread so well placed as to deceive the eye. On the sides of the hill (which is covered with green boughs), appear living lambs ornamented with ribands and artificial flowers; in another part are calves and some oxen: amongst the boughs geese and pigeons are nailed fast by the wings. On the top stands the figure of Apollo playing on the lyre.[15]

Like the Christmas cribs, on which an equal amount of time and trouble were expended and which also might involve living figures, Cockaigne was a spectacle in itself, ornate, vulgar, childish, crowded, a lavish delight. But, unlike the cribs, it was not there to be looked at. It was there to be assaulted, ransacked and consumed. At a given signal the mob stampeded, the edifice was sacked, everything edible was eaten or carried off (the birds ripped from their fastenings left their wings behind). The fountains flowed with blood as well as wine. The *lazzaroni* fought and stabbed and fell from the heights, royalty and the gentry watched from their balconies. When she first witnessed it, for her nuptials, the young Queen Maria Carolina was moved to pity by the sight of oxen, cattle, sheep and lambs being torn to shreds; and Ferdinand on future occasions allowed at least the larger beasts to be butchered decently before his people charged. The English, like Lady Anne Miller quoted from above, having nothing worse than Tyburn and bear-baiting back home, watched this barbarity in fascinated horror. 'I was so sick in the stomach,' says Lady Anne, 'that all eatables went exceedingly against me; and it was with difficulty that I could sit down to table at my return.'[16]

Chapter 5

AMUSEMENTS AND SUCCESSES,
1768–73

The nuptial celebrations were very fatiguing. The ambassadors and the great Neapolitan families all competed. The dancing and feasting moved from house to house. Before it had well begun Hamilton was wishing it was over; but he will have suffered less 'by the Fêtes' than Catherine who, he reported early in June, had already been 'confined two days' by them. Often his letters mention her health; it was always an issue and sometimes a worry. On their return from Rome he commented, to Horace Mann, that he thought her much better than before the trip; she seems to have told her mother the same; but Hamilton himself then contradicted that bulletin, causing the mother to write back in great disappointment that Catherine had 'so much of her old disorders remaining still about her' and was still 'a poor nervous creature'.[1] But those weeks in Rome, seeing the sights, must have been strenuous; so if she was never very robust she was no weakling either. She proved this the following year, 1769, on a tour of Sicily.

On 10 January Hamilton applied for leave, 'for about 3 weeks or a Month'.[2] He could claim it to be in the line of duty that he should get to know the other of the 'Two Sicilies'; but chiefly he wanted to see Etna. His application was granted at the end of February; but he postponed the excursion so as to be on hand to help entertain the Emperor Joseph, arriving to inspect his new brother-in-law, the lamentable Ferdinand. Hamilton, having shown the Archduke Leopold around the curiosities of the place a year before, was now in demand to do the same for Joseph, his brother. As *cicerone* he was the best. It was in his nature to be obliging, but he also had an eye to the advantage, his country's and his own, that might ensue from pleasing the Habsburg Emperor. He wrote in modestly boastful tones to his Secretary of State that his house was 'the only one, positively the only one, that the Emperor [had] honor'd ... with his presence'.[3] But on Vesuvius the enlightened despot did not behave well. 'I accompanied him to the summit,' Hamilton wrote, 'and with concern saw him break his cane over the shoulders of the Guide, Bartolomeo, for some slight offence which he had given his Imperial Majesty.'[4] Bartolomeo had one eye, he was known as the Cyclops, he and Hamilton were often on the mountain together.

That winter and spring the English flocked into Naples. Among them were Sir Watkin Wynn, who in Florence had donated £100 to the fund got up by Boswell for Paoli's rebels in Corsica; then the Earl of Pembroke, an old friend who, rather embarrassingly for the diplomat Hamilton (having to deal with the French ambassador), was intending to go to Corsica and seek out Paoli in person; and in March, for a couple of weeks, his nephew Charles Greville. Hamilton knew him well and loved him already. His mother's marriage with Lord Brooke (after 1759 Earl of Warwick) had not been happy and she had found support for herself and her children in her own powerful family. Hamilton, having no son, developed a particular relationship with his nephew. By now, going on twenty, Greville was a confirmed and busy amateur of virtu. After a hectic time seeing the collections in Rome, he came to Naples increased in the passion for collecting that he and Hamilton shared.

Another visitor at this time was Kenneth Mackenzie, Lord Fortrose. He was twenty-five and likeable enough for Hamilton and Catherine to want him as companion on their tour of Sicily.

Having attended to the Emperor Joseph, Hamilton was free to leave. An unhappy prompting came on 18 April. He wrote to Greville:

Mrs. H. has just received the unfortunate account of her mother's death, & is in a situation you can imagine, as you know the tenderness of her nature. I shall hasten my departure to Sicily in order to divert her.[5]

Remarkable how often Hamilton sought by an expedition to divert a person from grief. They sailed next day.

Catherine's relationship with her mother, until her marriage perhaps exclusively close, had continued after August 1764, when she and

Hamilton left for Naples, in fond and frequent letters. Only the mother's, and only some of them, have survived; but the daughter's are reflected in these and the nature of the correspondence is evident. They wrote often. Ann Barlow thanks Catherine: 'You are vastly good to let me hear so constantly from you,' though a vivid account of Vesuvius's activity made her rather fearful: 'I shall ... be glad to hear that all your fine & horrible sights are over, & that the Mountain is all quiet again'; and she hoped that Hamilton, having made himself sick (not for the last time) on the fumes, would learn 'to be more carefull for the future'. She wrote affectionately to him too, about the estates, about his financial situation, about the likelihood of his returning on a visit; ending with abrupt love: 'Look to my dear child.' It is only from her that we know that Catherine's pet name was Kitty: 'I do heartily rejoice to hear of the continuance of my Dear Kitty's health'; in Hamilton's letters she only ever gets mentioned as Mrs. H., or Lady H., never even as Catherine. In her last years Ann Barlow was often ill, and her letters then, in tone and sentiment, anticipate those her daughter would write, to William Beckford and to Hamilton himself, as she approached her own death. For example:

> I am exceedingly well satisfied & contented with all my weakness, & recieve it as the vehicle that is to convey me to a better country hereafter. I would not have my dear Kitty infer from hence that I am in any present danger, for it is most probable that I shall live to see her & you once more, wch. indeed is the only thing for which I wish to Live everything else is exceedingly indifferent to me.[6]

That was in March 1767, she died two years later, not having seen them 'once more'; and to divert Catherine, Hamilton brought forward the trip to Sicily.

Since he was not leaving the Kingdom there was no need to appoint a *chargé d'affaires*; the Danish ambassador promised to keep an eye on things. In the event they were away not one month but three. Much of this time was spent at sea, or waiting for a better wind in places they had not intended visiting. Crossing to Palermo should have taken three or four days, but they were blown down the coast of the mainland, to Baia, and it was 5 May before they arrived. From Palermo they tried the sea again, to reach Catania, but were driven to Malta, where they spent ten days. Finally, returning from Messina, they were becalmed for three days among the Lipari Islands. Hamilton reported to Lord Weymouth, his Secretary of State, on the inhabitants of Palermo – 'as indolent and inactive as at Naples, but the nobility ... better educated and much more conversable'[7] – and on the armed forces of Malta; but mostly he and his party pursued their own interests. They toured the south and the west. They visited Syracuse and the great temples at Agrigento, Segesta and also, very probably, Selinunte (from Castelvetrano).

Closer still to his principal passions, Hamilton saw a large collection of vases – probably Prince Biscari's in Catania – and had them copied, thinking to use them in the remaining volumes of his own *Etruscan Vases*; he looked at pictures, and was tempted by a Guido Reni in Palermo; he made the acquaintance of local antiquaries and naturalists, some of whom, notably Gasparo Recupero, he corresponded with and protected thereafter. Recupero, 'an ingenious priest of Catania', was writing a natural history of Etna which Hamilton feared he would never finish 'for want of proper encouragement'.[8]

Hamilton and Fortrose had Recupero with them as guide and expert when they set off from Catania on 24 June to climb the volcano. They were two days ascending. The first night they spent in the convent of the Benedictines. Next day they explored the mountain thrown up by the eruption of 1669 and the caves and tunnels under it. That night they camped, high up, with a blazing fire against the bitter cold; and set off at one in the morning, across the snowfields, to be at the summit by sunrise. Their view then was a circle of nine hundred miles, land and sea laid out as on a contemporary map. And what Hamilton chiefly saw mapped there was volcanoes, active and extinct, all 'evidently raised by explosion ... some ... so far mouldered down by time, as to have no other appearance of a crater than a sort of dimple or hollow on their rounded tops'. He saw the craters as 'suspended funnels, under which are vast caverns and abysses'.[9] Back in Naples he wrote to Horace Mann: 'Mount Etna ... is realy a most magnificent Volcano, Vesuvius appears to me now a meer Mole hill in comparison. Mount Etna has thrown up above fifty such upon its flanks.'[10]

Hamilton's tour of Sicily was a part of his thorough exploration of the Kingdom, not as ambassador but as vulcanologist. Annually during this period the Royal Society published his vivid letters. In their *Transactions* of 1770 he contributed to an increasing literature on Etna. Baron Riedesel, Winckelmann's close friend, had climbed the volcano in May 1767, and must have discussed it with Hamilton during his long stay in Naples (before leaving for Greece) in 1767–8. Hamilton's account, translated into French, was appended to the French edition of Riedesel's tour in 1773. Patrick Brydone, who toured Sicily and climbed Etna, also with Recupero, in the early summer of 1770, acknowledged Hamilton as his inspiration and in his *Tour through Sicily and Malta* (1773) often cites him. In Palermo, in the library of Prince Torremuzza, Hamilton discovered a description of the colossal eruption of 1669, written by John Heneage Finch, the third earl of Winchelsea who, returning home from Constantinople, where he had been ambassador, happened to be in Catania when the volcano blew up. Hamilton brought this very rare publication back into scientific ken by including it in his own letter to the Royal Society. Thus the tradition was reinforced and extended.

Catherine did not climb Etna, but the trip was adventurous enough even without that excursion. Hamilton wrote to Mann: 'Few Strangers visit those parts & Ladies seldom indeed, so that Mrs Hamilton was made much of as you may well imagine.'[11] How happy she was, how much the journey diverted her, is not recorded; but for a woman thought five years previously to be on the point of death, three months of such travelling were surely a considerable achievement. Perhaps her ups and downs and indispositions in Naples were more a matter of temperament than of health. She was happiest living quietly, or at least away from the Court and the 'stupid Assemblys' of the local upper classes.

Catherine held an assembly of her own at the Palazzo Sessa, on Mondays. These were very cultured occasions. Lady Anne Miller attended one in January 1771. 'Before the Italians came in,' she wrote, 'I could have fancied myself at an assembly in London.'[12] Their chief glory and Catherine's passion, that in which she could more than answer Hamilton in his, was music. Arriving in Naples the Hamiltons continued the musical entertainments they had given, since their marriage, at the King's Mews in London. They kept good performers among their servants and paid professional musicians such as Emanuele Barbella to play regularly at their 'academy'. The Mozarts, father and son, having visited them in London in the summer of 1764, renewed their acquaintance at the Palazzo Sessa on 18 May 1770. They had come from Rome and that evening put on their summer outfits for the first time. They looked, so Mozart wrote to his sister, 'lovely as angels'. He wore a coat of fiery red moiré silk with silver lace borders and pale sky blue lining.

Catherine played for them, on a Tschudi harpsichord from London that Leopold, much impressed by it, described in some detail. He was impressed by Catherine too. He called her 'a very agreeable person'; reported that she trembled at having to play 'in front of Wolfgang', but that her playing was 'uncommonly moving'.[13] She busied herself on the Mozarts' behalf – they were touring to make some money – and arranged a concert at the house of Count Kaunitz, the Austrian ambassador, ten days later. Perhaps they played at Lord Fortrose's too. There is a picture by Pietro Fabris which, some believe, proves it.[14] They were in Naples until 25 June, and the Hamiltons must have seen them, and heard Mozart play, several times during those weeks. Hamilton never mentions him.

Much of Hamilton's life has to be fitted together from his visitors' accounts of it. One such visitor, later that year, on tour through Europe, collecting materials for his *General History of Music*, was Dr Charles Burney. He attended two of the Hamiltons' Assemblies (29 October and 5 November 1770) and was also their guest at the Villa Angelica under Vesuvius and in their box at the opera. Hamilton was at his most obliging. He got Burney access to the collections at Portici, introduced him to others who might help with the *History*, and generally brought him into congenial musical company. Burney, though anxious that war with Spain might hinder his return to England, greatly enjoyed his weeks in Naples and wrote them up in the liveliest way. He was travelling with Captain John Forbes, brother of the Scottish painter, Anne. They arrived at Hamilton's villa on Friday 26 October, in time for dinner. 'After dinner,' Burney wrote,

we had music and chat till supper. Mr. H. has 2 pages who play very well one on the fiddle and the other on the violoncello. Tho' my companion was not invited to lye there nor did intend it, yet he was easily prevailed on to pig in the same room with me who was, and a field bed was put up on the occasion. As soon as it was dark our musical entertainment was mixed with the sight and observations of Mount Vesuvius, then very busy.

Hamilton had 'glasses of all sorts and every convenience of situation', to observe from his windows the stones flung up red hot a thousand feet or more from the crater. He showed Burney a copy of the letter he had written to the Royal Society ten days before on 'The Soil of Naples and its Neighbourhood'. 'After supper,' Burney writes, 'we had a long dish of musical talk relative to my history.' The Hamiltons were rather tired of Neapolitan music, and were 'glad to return to that of Corelli, Geminiani, Handel, Vivaldi etc for the sake of harmony and variety'. As to his hosts' abilities: 'Mrs H. has a very neat finger and plays the harpsichord with great delicacy, expression and taste. Mr. H. is likewise a pretty good performer on the violin.'[15]

Next morning, in foul weather, Hamilton took his guests exploring the lower slopes of the mountain. To go higher would have been dangerous, he thought. Back in Naples two days later they were guests for a musical evening (till two in the morning) at the Palazzo Sessa. They heard Barbella on the violin, and Orgitano, Lord Fortrose's music master and one of the best harpsichord players in Naples. Burney noted:

> But Mrs. H. herself is a much better performer on that instrument than either him or any Italian I have heard since I crossed the water. She has great neatness and more expression and meaning in her playing than any lady I ever heard, for ladies, it must be owned, tho' often neat in execution, seldom aim at expression.[16]

Like Leopold Mozart a few months earlier and William Beckford ten years later, Burney emphasizes the emotional expressiveness of Catherine's playing. It was through music that she came into her own. The only known portrait of her, painted by David Allan in 1770, shows her playing her piano (a *Tafelklavier*) in the villa at Posillipo, Vesuvius visible through the open door across the bay. So she certainly had an instrument at each of three of their dwellings, and perhaps at Caserta also.

Burney called again next day (Tuesday 30 October) and was received by Catherine who talked to him about their tour of Sicily and got her Sicilian maid to sing and play the tambourine for him. The evening before, Hamilton had lent him his account of the tour, sent to the Royal Society on 17 October 1769. Brydone and his young charge, William Fullarton, just back from Sicily, and Fortrose, who had been there with the Hamiltons, were often in the company that Burney frequented during his stay.

There were two more evenings at Palazzo Sessa, both till the small hours, and between them a visit to the opera in the Hamiltons' box. Though music was the main entertainment and the main subject of conversation, Burney also saw Hamilton's vases, his paintings, his books, and many curiosities, 'both natural and artificial'.[17] He was lent things in manuscript to read. Arriving for dinner in the mid-afternoon, staying for tea and supper, each sociable occasion might last ten or twelve hours. The company would enlarge and diminish (only a select few being invited to stay on for supper) and disperse for different amusements around the house. It was a spacious, leisurely, generous hospitality, within its own conventions easy and informal. People came together who were keenly interested in things other than show: in music, painting, antiquities, travel and natural history. Through Burney, an eagerly receptive guest, we get a good sense of the sweetness and richness of life in Naples as the Hamiltons lived it; and because Burney's chief interest was music we see Catherine at her happiest and best. 1770 in the Palazzo Sessa and in the villas by the sea and under the volcano was as good a year as any that would follow when Catherine was dead and in a louder manner Emma entertained.

Vesuvius for much of that year was 'very busy' or 'very turbulent'.[18] There was an eruption in March, the slight shock of an earthquake in October, a strong flow of lava in November and December, fireworks all the time, but no great damage. In fact it was just as visitors and local enthusiasts would wish it to be: a continual excitement, a constant changing spectacle, and quite without equal as a backdrop or accompaniment. Having viewed Hamilton for a while alongside Catherine as hospitable host, here he is on the volcano in December, betraying her with the lava and another man's wife:

I was upon the Mountain & walked upon the banks of rivers of liquid fire ... donnant le bras a Madme. Hampden, and as perfectly secure as if we had been walking on the banks of the Arno. it is hard labour to get up to the Streams but as there are no explosions of Stones from the mouth there is no danger, & the rivers being narrow you can approach them with safety – Nothing can express the glorious scene of Saturday – There were numberless Cascades of fire, the Scoria of the Lava formed arch'd bridges from Space to Space and the Lava ran rapidly under these arches whilst we stood upon them with great security. Mrs. Hampdens beautifull face lighted up by the reflection of the fiery Streams was not a circumstance to be forgot – I was half in love with her before we went to Vesuvius but her courage & the passion she has taken for my favourite object here, has quite undone me.[19]

She was twenty-one. He would see her again, as a widower, in October 1784, but courted her companion, the widowed Lady Clarges.

During 1769 and 1770, unusually, Naples was not quite on the periphery of European politics. In Corsica Pasquale Paoli, hero-worshipped by Western liberals, fought bravely against the Genoese and then, when the island was sold to them, against the French. He was defeated in 1770 and retired to London. England's quarrel with Spain (and her ally France) over the Falkland Islands escalated towards a war, which would have been hard for the Neapolitan court – Bourbon and increasingly anglophile – to manage. By December things looked bad; then France pulled out and Spain had to compromise. In March the war between Russia and Turkey moved into the Archipelago and the Peloponnese. Empress Catherine incited the Greeks to revolt. Philhellenes in Europe watched with interest. Hamilton regularly sent on bulletins to London.

Such politics would not have held an ambitious diplomat in Naples, it is true; but add their passing interest to the numerous other more powerful attractions of the place – the antiquities, the natural history, leisure (summers on Ischia), intelligent and lively company, the conditions for physical well-being – and it might seem no sane man would ever want to leave. But by the autumn of 1768 (perhaps even earlier) Hamilton was trying seriously to do just that.

Though promoted to Plenipotentiary early in 1767 he still had money worries. In fact, they increased as he strove 'to make a figure adequate to the Character' he had been honoured with. Thus the royal wedding, so he told his Secretary of State, asking for an extraordinary allowance, had cost him 'upwards of one Thousand pounds Sterling', four hundred going on 'an addition of Jewels which were necessary for Mrs Hamilton's appearance at Court'.[20] But worry over money would not in itself make him want a move. After less than four years in the job, perhaps unsettled by two months in Rome, he began angling to improve his state.

His agent was the young man who had been his *chargé d'affaires* while he was away, John Osborn, now back in London in the Foreign Office. To him, on 6 September 1768, Hamilton confided that he was minded to come home for a few years, for fear he would be forgotten if he didn't; but also asking about the embassy in Vienna. The man in post there was Lord Stormont, who had been with the Hamiltons in Rome. Hamilton's aim, it seems, was to set himself up as his successor, with time in London first as the necessary staging post. Vienna was a senior embassy, more pay, more status, more at the centre of things. Osborn's reply on 2 December candidly admitted his own self-interest: he wanted the Naples job and would be willing to do it at the Envoy's (not the Plenipotentiary's) rate. Though much Hamilton's junior, he set out for him with typical eighteenth-century directness how he, Hamilton, might manage in England on £3 a day plus his equerry's pay plus the revenue from his estates which would surely increase if he were on the spot to manage them himself. Hamilton, docketing this letter, added the note: 'NB an Eye on Naples'.[21] He wrote back on 9 January, that 'no present Plan of operations can be carried on to our mutual Satisfaction & Advantage';[22] but revived the discussion on 29 August, again having been away (to Sicily) and after having had from the Emperor Leopold himself the strongest encouragement to seek to succeed Stormont. Osborn's response (22 September) was that Stormont had no wish to vacate Vienna. Might Hamilton like Madrid instead, or Constantinople? Both were open. Hamilton wanted neither. For his part, Osborn still wanted Naples.

In November 1769 Hamilton wrote twice more, and between January and March 1770 another five times to Osborn, always on the same subject: Vienna.[23] Finally then, on 13 March, he wrote to his Secretary of State, Lord Weymouth, asking for Vienna even if the post were downgraded from Ambassador to Plenipotentiary or Envoy Extraordinary, and mentioning the Emperor's stated desire to have him succeed Stormont. 'I should be very happy,' he wrote, 'if my poor abilities could be employ'd for His Majesties Service in a more active scene than this Court affords.'[24] It all came to nothing – Stormont stayed put for another two years (when he moved to Paris); and on 17 April Osborn wrote suggesting that he, Hamilton, might like to come home on a pension, of perhaps £1000 a year, and let him, Osborn, have the job in Naples. Hamilton scrawled on this letter: 'Pension – no – no – no', and again the business lapsed.[25] These abortive negotiations are perhaps worth dwelling on, if only to indicate that at a time of great enjoyment and success Hamilton was ambitious or restless enough to want a change.

Thwarted over Vienna, almost at once (by 11 May 1770) he applied for leave instead. But even in this he was baulked and put off. He applied again formally on 14 August, for 'three or four Months' in the following spring, adding that Osborn would be a suitable stand-in during his absence. He wrote again, having heard nothing, on 23 October; again on 18 December – and was finally refused, because of the Falklands Crisis. When that had passed he applied again, on 26 March 1771, again for 'three or four Months'; and got it at last on 21 May. In the meantime (January–February), in a renewed correspondence Osborn alerted Hamilton to a vacancy in the Order of the Bath (which he duly applied to fill, his second such application) and reported his own posting as Envoy Extraordinary to Dresden. After that, as their interests separated, dealings between the two men lapsed for some years.[26]

In December 1769, with two volumes of *Etruscan Vases* still to publish, d'Hancarville was expelled from Naples and took up residence in Florence. Hamilton, still trusting, asked Horace Mann to look after him:

> He has been sent out of Naples in a very rough manner indeed, so much so that I thought he must have been guilty of some state crime – but his papers are untouched & no reason given for this violence but that it is the will of H. Sicilian Majesty ... His knowledge of the Antiquities of this country & the perfection of his Etruscan

work ... is I believe the real cause of his disgrace.[27]

Envy perhaps came into it but his ostensible offence was trying to get out of debt by publishing pornography. In Florence he found new protectors, but before long had begun to queer his pitch there too. Gradually Hamilton was obliged to think worse of him. A correspondent in Florence, Thomas Crofts, sent him this sketch early in 1771: 'There is a seducing Plausibility in all his Schemes which would take in the most prudent & wary, were there not striking Features in his Character which must waken the Suspicions of the most cullible & incautious.'[28] By now Hamilton must have numbered himself among the latter. Still, ever the gentleman, he arranged for the man's wife, left behind in Naples, to be conducted safely to Florence. The man himself meanwhile had pawned the plates of the *Vases* and was hiding from his creditors in a convent.

Applying for leave Hamilton had pleaded that he had 'some private affairs to settle'[29] in England. One of these was to raise money by selling his vases. Though d'Hancarville's own 'private affairs' had halted the publication, and sales of the first two volumes had by no means recouped either their costs or the outlay on the vases themselves, still those volumes were at least a good advertisement and, through Wedgwood's factory at Etruria, they were beginning to have some tangible good effect. Hamilton packed up his collection and shipped it to England. He also had a picture to sell, *Venus disarming Cupid*, then believed to be by Correggio. In early June 1771, after seven years away, Hamilton and Catherine set off for home.

In December 1770 Hamilton had pressed his application for leave (of 'about three Months') in these terms:

Surely such a request after so long a Residence cannot be thought unreasonable or the quantity of it add to the clamours that have been raised at home upon the Subject of the non-residence of the Ministers at their Posts.[30]

Ministers, like bishops, often preferred not to be where their duties were. Disappointed in his bids for Vienna Hamilton seems to have been in no hurry to return to Naples. He stayed away nearly nineteen months, more than a year in England, the rest travelling out and back.

The Hamiltons were in London by 10 August. A fortnight later Lady Mary Coke saw them at Lady Hertford's. The company divided, some playing cards, some listening to music. The Hamiltons 'belonged to the musical party'. Lady Mary noted: 'Mrs Hamilton never look'd so well in her life, but is much discontented with our climate, & seems to say she will be glad to return to Italy.' It rained and rained. Hamilton seemed to Lady Coke to have aged more than the seven years he had been away.[31] It was perhaps that he was sunburned. Walpole, seeing them in October, said of Hamilton: 'Vesuvius has burnt him to a cinder'; and of Catherine: 'She looks better, but the climate affects her strangely.'[32] Like Lady Mary, he doubtless meant the English climate.

Altogether the Hamiltons' first return to England was something of a triumph. Against all expectation Catherine had survived, and had developed her musical talent and enlarged her reputation, as Burney, returning ahead of them, must surely have confirmed. And Hamilton, having done nothing to make a name for himself before leaving England, had done a good deal by the time he returned. From Naples he had established himself in the British (and European) world of the arts and the natural sciences. During the year in England that position was acknowledged and consolidated.

His collections arrived in November. Astutely – since he wished to sell them – he let Horace Walpole, consummate gossip, have a private view. The Hamiltons stayed at Park Place, Henley, with Seymour Conway, but also in the King's Mews, their old lodgings. Still an equerry, Hamilton doubtless had rights there. The vases and the other items, including the supposed Correggio, were put on display at Lord Cowper's. Lord Cowper himself lived in Florence. Perhaps Hamilton made the arrangement passing through. Walpole, having on 13 December been shown the collection, 'though ... not yet in order fit for the vulgar eye',[33] fulfilled his function and put the word around:

Mr Hamilton has brought over a charming Correggio, and a collection of Tuscan vases, idols, amulets, javelins and casques of bronze, necklaces and earrings of gold from Herculaneum, Pompeii, and Sicily; sacrificing instruments, dice of amber, agate, etc. ... The picture may as yet be had for £3,000 and the antiquities for £8,000.

They are a little dear, but the first is delightful and the latter most entertaining.[34]

The 'Correggio' remained unsold – Hamilton left it in London with his nephew Greville – but the antiquities interested the British Museum and Parliament voted the necessary money, £8400, in February 1772. This was a large sum, but still less than Hamilton had spent acquiring and publishing the vases. Wedgwood and his partner Bentley, on the other hand, in a variety of products, turned the resource to very good account. By his own estimation he soon brought to the nation, that is, to his firm, three times what the nation had voted for the purchase. No wonder he referred to 'Sir William Hambleton' as 'our very good Friend'. They did an 'Etruscan bas-relief portrait' of him in April 1772 and seven years later included him, in jasperware, in their series 'Eminent Moderns'. He was in their stock catalogue till 1788. The tributes and the firm's success gratified Hamilton, no doubt. The Etruscan portrait carried a dedication praising his generosity as a means 'not only of improving and refining the public taste, but of keeping alive that sacred fire, which his collection of inestimable models has happily kindled in Great Britain'.[35] Though he might speak disparagingly of 'the old dons'[36] running the Museum he was proud to see 'the Hamiltonian Collection' housed there and pleased when people wrote to tell him how well it looked. Still, he had debts; he needed what he had hoped to raise on his 'Correggio'.

Even as his virtu arrived in England Hamilton was being honoured by the Royal Society for his work on volcanoes. At its meeting on 30 November 1771 the Society presented him with their Copley Medal, an award deriving from a bequest of Sir Godfrey Copley and made annually for some outstanding contribution. The citation refers particularly to Hamilton's account of Mount Etna (published in the Society's *Transactions* of 1770), but it was his whole scientific oeuvre to date that they were acknowledging. And before he returned to Naples, Thomas Cadell, a bookseller on the Strand, had undertaken to publish all of these writings in one volume, as *Observations on Mount Vesuvius, Mount Etna and other volcanoes*. With two volumes of the *Vases* out (and being sold by Cadell) Hamilton was in two important areas of learning an established authority. In February he was elected

Fellow of the Society of Antiquaries, to whom he would later send an account of the discoveries at Pompeii.

Elsewhere too Hamilton sought and got recognition. He wanted the red ribbon of the Order of the Bath. This Order, founded in 1725 by George I, had thirty-six members, as well as the Sovereign and a Grand Master, and vacancies occurred only when a member died. In February 1771 John Osborn had alerted Hamilton to the death of Sir Andrew Mitchell in Berlin, 'that you might immediately write to yr. friends in England'.[37] Doubtless Hamilton did, and not for the first time, but again unsuccessfully. Then almost on the day of his arrival back in London, on 7 August 1771, he had another chance, by the death of Sir Francis Delaval. On 30 August Lady Mary Coke noted: 'Mr Hamilton has got the red ribbon'; but two days later, listing those present at a private party, she added after Hamilton's name 'who has not got the red ribbon'.[38] It had gone to Sir Charles Hotham-Thompson. Hamilton was at that party with his nephew Greville and with Lord Fortrose, just arrived from Italy. The reversal must have been rather embarrassing. Fortunately there was soon another death, Lord Chandos this time; and by 15 December Walpole was spreading the word that Hamilton, finally, had been successful. It is worth noting – in anticipation of later and unhappier days – that being foster-brother to the King did not mean he could count on immediate favours.

Hamilton (with Sir Charles) was invested on 15 January 1772. Fees for the privilege came to £343 16s 4d. But that was nothing to what his installation cost him six months later in Westminster Abbey. Just before leaving England he had a bill from his jeweller George Robertson, £66 of it for ornamenting Catherine, and the rest, £968, for his own diamond star and other insignia.[39] The bill for his robes has not survived, but it won't have been negligible. Status, in England as in Naples, was expensive. In 1773 David Allan added the star to his portrait, painted three years before, of Hamilton seated by Catherine at her pianoforte. It carries the motto of the Order: 'Tria juncta in Uno' – 'Three joined in One' – which would acquire such a scurrilous sense after 1798 when Hamilton, Emma and Nelson were a public spectacle.

By one society or another the Hamiltons were much taken up during their stay in England. In the latter half of September 1771 they made a sort of progress through Warwickshire and North-amptonshire, staying at Warwick Castle, home of the Earl of Warwick (elder brother of Charles Greville), and at Drayton (the Germains) and Burghley (the Cecils). And later, perhaps in the spring or summer of 1772, they must have made time to visit the Barlow estates in Pembroke, more of which had come to Catherine after the death of her mother in 1770.

The family concerned them on Hamilton's side too. In November 1771 his sister Jane died suddenly in St Petersburg. She was married to Lord Cathcart, the British ambassador there. It is likely that Catherine, who had been her fond correspondent, was at least as affected as Hamilton by the bad news when it came. At the end of August 1772 they began making preparations to return to Naples. Twenty boxes of their furniture and apparel were loaded on to the *Lemmon*, sailing from London; but they postponed their own depart-ure, waiting for Cathcart, who had resigned his post and was coming home. He arrived on 10 or 11 September. After Stormont, here was another bereaved ambassador, and one whose bereavement they shared. They spent a week with him, before setting out on the long overland way back.

Like many people, indeed like most people of a certain class and education, they called on Voltaire at Ferney just north of Geneva. He was seventy-eight, and well used to being viewed by tourists, particularly the English. After Boswell and Lord Hervey the Ham-iltons will have seemed quite modest and civilized guests.

From Ferney they headed east to Vienna. Altogether their route back to Naples was astonishingly indirect and arduous. They were in Vienna for three weeks in October–November, staying with Lord Stormont, the ambassador and their good friend. They found him still, in his own words, 'condemned to deep and remedieless sorrow'.[40] Hamilton had wanted to succeed him as ambassador; and though that had come to nothing he did have the satisfaction of being told, by Prince Kaunitz, that he would have been their preferred choice. By the Imperial Family too both the Hamiltons were shown particular favour. When Catherine played for them at a dinner in the Palace of Laxenburg the Empress gave her a kiss and a gold enamelled snuff-box with the royal cypher set in brilliants. And breaking all precedent – he never visited foreign ministers – the Emperor called at Stormont's residence and spent their last evening with them.[41] Thus the contact, established in Naples in the spring of 1769, was resumed and fortified; and no doubt Hamilton thought it might serve him one day.

Catherine wrote to Lady Mary Coke about her success; 'in raptures', according to Lady Mary, who had herself been well received by the Empress a few months before. Of the snuff-box she said: 'I fancy it is the same that she had once design'd for me.' Naturally she hated Catherine thereafter and observed a year later, when Catherine refused to receive the Duchess of Beaufort at the Palazzo Sessa, that 'the favours she received at Vienna has had a bad effect on her understanding'.[42]

Winter was well begun when they left Vienna and Catherine, leaving with a cold, became feverish en route. They had got beyond Klagenfurt as far as Spital and there she was laid up. In typically flippant tone Hamilton reported to his nephew Greville that with the aid of a medical handbook (Tissot's *The Family Physician*), over five days, he had undertaken her cure himself. He concluded: 'Luckily there was a lake close by, & I amused myself with catching pike.'

He was writing to Greville from Venice, on 23 November. Their route thither (and Venice itself was out of the way) lay through the Tyrol to Bolzano, Trento, Verona and Vicenza. Between the latter two places, he wrote, 'the rains overtook us ... and we had liked to have been drowned, as there was $3\frac{1}{2}$ ft. of water in the road for three miles'. Catherine, convalescent, did well to survive. Between Trento and Verona, near Rovereto, Hamilton pursued his volcanic obsession:

> I saw most noble havock, certainly made by volcanick explosion, tho' no one could give me any account of it. The earth has opened in many parts for the space of 4 miles, & thrown up the rocky soil in huge masses in a most wonderfull manner. Had I been alone I shou'd have stopped, &, I am sure, have had matter for a letter to the R. Society.[43]

They had a week or so in Venice, seeing the sights; thence to Florence, where they arrived on 11 December, for a further week. Their host was Sir Horace Mann. He wrote to Walpole that Catherine 'had suffered much in the journey from Vienna'.[44] Hamilton had business in Florence, with d'Hancarville, whose creditors had just seized the plates for the last two volumes of the *Vases*, pawned though they already were. Mann recounted the whole *histoire* to Walpole, concluding:

> Nobody can as yet foresee how the work can be completed. But after all, though it may be important to Sir William on account of his private engagements, is it so to the public from the nature and merit of the work? It is not thought so here.[45]

After Florence they halted awhile in Rome. Here Hamilton did one or two things more in the line of ambassadorial business. He met the Pope, Clement XIV, and took stock of the Young Pretender, Charles Edward Stuart. Dealings with either were a delicate matter, and Hamilton, once back in Naples, was careful to report on them at some length to his Secretary of State, to shield himself against any spiteful gossip. Hearing that Hamilton was in Rome, the Pope wanted to meet him, as a connoisseur, not as a diplomat. Britain had no ambassador to the Papal States, and Hamilton, to avoid suggesting any such relations, arranged to meet the Pope privately, through the painter and antiquary Thomas Jenkins; and after thanking him for favours shown to British residents in Rome, their further conversation, so he reported to Lord Rochford, was all on antiquities about which, according to Hamilton, Clement knew very little.

Bonnie Prince Charlie and his wife, living in Rome as the Count and Countess of Albany, could be observed at church. Hamilton had last taken a look at him in 1768, and reported now, with loyal satisfaction, that he appeared 'much thinner and more declining'. His understanding, Hamilton learned, 'was almost ruin'd'; indeed, he was 'universally looked upon as in a great degree out of his Senses'.[46] Hamilton got most of his information from the Abbé Peter Grant, a Scot and a Jacobite so long resident in Rome and so well connected that for British travellers he had almost an ambassadorial function there. Hamilton knew him already, from a visit to Naples, liked him – they had a love of antiquities in common – and moreover appreciated his courtesies to British travellers. So he consorted with him freely. In Naples then the rather poisonous consul, Isaac Jamineau, spread tales that he, Hamilton, was a closet Papist and Jacobite. Hamilton appealed to Rochford to put the man in his place; which Rochford, after a further complaint, nearly a year later finally did: 'The Difference between your Station and That of Sir Wm. Hamilton is too obvious to make it necessary for me to point out a Line for your Conduct...'[47]

Hamilton was back at his post, after an absence of more than eighteen months, on 6 January 1773. Copies of his book, *Observations on Mount Vesuvius, Mount Etna and other volcanoes*, published in London as he was leaving England, had been sent by sea and were there in Naples for him when he arrived. In his absence Britain's interests had been looked after by the Reverend William Preston; 'a sensible prudent & learned Man',[48] Hamilton called him. At the end of March Preston set off for England, accompanying Lord Findlater and carrying with him a copy of Hamilton's book, to present to Voltaire as they passed through Switzerland. He wrote from Lausanne: 'Mons. de Voltaire ... expressed himself much obliged to you on the Occasion, and said that he had expected your work with much Impatience.'[49] Doubtless Hamilton had promised him the gift, when he and Catherine called. A fortnight later (17 June 1773) Voltaire wrote himself: thanking him, agreeing with his central thesis that volcanoes throw up mountains (though he added, rather deflatingly, that ants do the same), and developing a lengthy contrast between the Alps in their frozen stability and the Campi Phlegraei in their torrid instability. Hamilton must have been well pleased with his letter. He sent a copy to Horace Walpole, who, less agile mentally than the Sage of Ferney, found it incoherent.

Chapter 6

'GOING THRU' LIFE
TOLLERABLY', 1773–80

On 15 June 1774 Hamilton wrote to his colleague Lord Grantham, ambassador in Madrid, who had spent some weeks in Naples as a young man:

> This Court removes at stated Seasons to Caserta, Persano Ischia, Naples &c. His Sicilian Majesty hunts, shoots, fishes, sails and exercises his two Regiments as usual. St January performs his miracle in the usual manner, and at the usual Seasons ... The Fair, the Cucagna's, Processions, &c present themselves also in their Seasons, and in short everything goes on at Naples exactly as Your Lordship remembers...[1]

Back in post Hamilton performed his duties and amused himself as usual. By November 1774 he had been doing so for ten years. He was, in his own expression, 'Le Doyen du Corps diplomatique'. From elsewhere during those ten years ambassadors had come and gone, three from Spain, three from France, three from Vienna, Turin, Copenhagen, but he stayed put, favoured above all others. He was the King's 'compagno', 'Paesano Nostro',[2] already a fixture and an institution, and still only a third of the way through his total term.

Hamilton's most serious pastimes were, as before, the arts and the natural sciences. From home he had gratifying reports of the fine appearance his collection made in the British Museum, and of its good effects. His friend Dr John Elliott wrote:

> Your collection forms one of the greatest and most admired ornaments of the Metropolis, even Foreigners come to see it. I have with much satisfaction seen the advantageous manner, in which the inestimable remains of antiquity are arranged. I really think, that the

national taste has received a rapid improvement from them; in place of the ponderous dull ornaments, we formerly had, we have now the pleasure of seeing new embellishments daily rising up, where every thing is formed in the elegant manner of the Ancients. The Furniture of even the houses is already changed. These improvements are totally owing to that choice collection, which you have set before the publick. In the most ordinary houses, in place of the unnatural, the distorted chinese figures, we see the chimney peices and cabinets decorated with vases, equal to the Etruscan.[3]

This sounds like flattery and exaggeration, but there is some corroborating evidence in Hamilton's own direct dealings with British manufacturers. I have already mentioned his contribution to the success and the profits of Wedgwood and Bentley. He wrote to them in March 1773, ordering a dinner service for the Maltese ambassador and encouraging them in the productions that owed most to his vases:

Your Etruscan ware is universally admired. I hope you continue to meet with the encouragement you deserve. I will surely send you some drawings of the fine shaped vases soon; continue to be very attentive to the simplicity and elegance of the forms, which is the chief article, & you cannot consult the originals in the museum too often.[4]

Soon after, he wrote to their competitor Matthew Boulton in Birmingham, urging him to develop a line in glassware of an antique kind. He sent specimens of ancient glass to Charles Greville, believing them to be what the Greeks and Romans called *Murrhine*, with instructions that he should forward them at once to Boulton. He was very pressing:

Vases of good forms of this kind of composition, imitating onyx, verd-antique, serpentine, &c., with or moulu, wou'd be charming. I have wrote [Boulton] a letter with my remarks & hints, but I hope you will go this summer & see that he works at the Murrhine new manufacture, for so he may call it if he succeeds.[5]

And two years later he was in dealings with another Birmingham man, Henry Clay. Greville had sent him some of Clay's work.

Hamilton replied: 'The dressing boxes à l'Etrusque are delightfull, I am sure they must meet with great success, for they are in as pure a taste as can be.'[6] He wrote to Clay, congratulating and encouraging him. Clay's reply was fulsome, and also shrewd. He thanked Hamilton for the particular encouragement, and went on:

At the same time that I acknowledge myself obliged to Your Excellency on this account I must confess that I think myself, Mssrs. Wedgwood & Bentley and every Englishman (but particularly us) under still greater obligations to you for the usefull patterns which we have had so abundantly in your Etruscan publication, to which alone we are indebted for the gradual progress we have made in this kind of Painting so well & so deservedly received by the Publick. – I am waiting very anxiously for the Publication of the third & fourth volumes.

Those volumes finally came out in 1776. D'Hancarville's creditors, holding the plates against his debts, would only let him consult them, to write his accompanying essays, one at a time.

Hamilton must have shown Clay an opening. Clay's letter continues:

I am much obliged to Your Excellency for the hint of Snuff Boxes of this taste [Etruscan]. I have now put some in hand which will be exceedingly elegant and if it will not be obtruding too much I will beg the favour of you to point out to me a good Shop in Naples where they will be well received, and that your Excellency will be so kind as use your interest in procuring me permission to send an assortment of them, with Tea Trays, Tea Cadie's, Tea Chests, Quadrile Dishes, &c of Papier.[7]

It was usual for British ambassadors to be asked to serve home industry in this way. Cathcart and his wife in St Petersburg had been helpful to Wedgwood and to Boulton. But Hamilton was especially effective, as collector and publisher of inspiring vases, then as the agent for products deriving from them.

Clay made use of Hamilton at home as well as abroad. At the end of November 1775 he called on Greville in London with the news that he had just been appointed japanner to the King. He wanted permission to print the encouraging letter Hamilton had written him in July, by way of self-advertisement. He had written an introduction to it, which Greville thought 'very awkward', and improved. Forwarding this to Hamilton he added: 'I told him that it could not be displeasing to you to appear from a distance superintending the Arts in this country.'[8] That was of course exactly the capacity in which Hamilton wished to appear.

Hamilton was proud of his collection in the British Museum, and from Naples sought to increase its glory by getting the Trustees to buy another of his acquisitions, the so-called Warwick Vase, dug up, the surviving pieces of it at least, by Gavin Hamilton near Hadrian's villa at Tivoli in 1769–70, sold to Hamilton and restored for him, at considerable expense, after engravings done by Piranesi. Hamilton presented a set of these to the Museum in 1775, and Greville in London did his best to persuade the Trustees to buy the thing itself. Hamilton wrote: 'I shoud realy be unhappy if that superb piece of antiquity was not to be at the head of my collection.' He presented himself as both disinterested – prepared to be out of pocket for the Public Good – and interested in his own good name:

> I do assure you I have the collection at the Museum so much at heart that tho' I can ill afford to lose such a sum as £350, which is (I believe) abt the cost of my vase, I should rather give it to that collection than let it go elsewhere for twice the sum.[9]

It was, he said, 'the honour of the Hamiltonian collection' that spurred him on. In fact he was asking £500, which the 'the old dons' of the Museum were unwilling to give, and the Vase went to Warwick Castle, the home of Greville's elder brother, the Earl of Warwick.

In the summer of 1774 Hamilton made what he called 'a little Picina' in the rocks below his villa at Posillipo. It was a natural basin which the sea could flow in and out of. This gave him, 'the means of examining the manners of many curious sea-productions'. In arts and sciences, he was a collector. He wrote to Greville: 'I have all sorts of insects & will have all the polype kind, besides I have a longer reservoir for the great fish. I am at work upon the torpedo of which I have many living.' He was curious. When his captive cuttle fish laid eggs, he opened one, and 'having taken off the black outward skin, found the embryo in a transparent bladder in which it swam, & being disturbed it squirted its ink even into the egg'.[10] The embryo now imprisoned in its own gloom was exactly what he would call 'curious'. The fishermen knew his interests and fetched him creatures they netted that were sufficiently strange, and he kept them alive or pickled among his other curiosities.

Something very curious occurred at Lord Tylney's on 15 March 1773. Tylney, long established in Florence, had five hundred guests that night at the house he took in Naples for the winter months. Hamilton was among them, sitting on a card table, 'conversing with Monsieur de Saussure, Professor of Natural History at Geneva', when there were cries of '*un fulmine, un fulmine!*' and lightning passed through nine of the rooms, leaving in all of them 'evident marks of its passage'. A servant asleep on the stairs and leaning his head against the wall 'had the hair entirely singed from it on that side'. Hamilton observed: 'It is very certain that the profusion of gildings, which is remarkable in this house, and the bell-wires, prevented the lightning from making more use of the company to conduct it in its course.' He and Saussure went back next day and, starting on the flat roof, traced the passage of the lightning down the clues of blackened gilding. He wrote the whole thing up, with diagrams, for the Royal Society.[11] Electricity was a craze among the learned then. Hamilton had brought a machine back with him from London, for performing electrical experiments, and it was, he said, the wonder of Naples. He used to boast that the Palazzo Sessa was one of only two houses in the whole of Naples fitted with a lightning conductor.

The natural world interested Hamilton in all its manifestations, but especially the volcanic. His travels, and his letters published in the *Transactions* of the Royal Society, brought him into correspondence with natural scientists and fellow enthusiasts in Italy, France, Switzerland and Germany. Canon Recupero, his guide on Etna in 1769, sent him regular accounts of his own explorations and discoveries on that volcano; and John Strange, an eminent geologist appointed British resident in Venice in 1775, discussed with him such matters as the presence of sea shells in the deposits of Vesuvius. Hamilton wrote:

I have a stone found in a hollow way on Mount Vesuvius full of Sea Shells which no doubt was thrown out of the crater ... at some very ancient period, perhaps at the time when this Volcano first rose out of the Sea which it undoubtedly did.

Recupero had noticed strata of clay lying between distinct strata of volcanic matter. This observation corroborated Hamilton's own. Eruptions and the time between them could be dated. His mind was turning on the great age of the earth:

> I have discovered that in all the Mountains of Tuffa, & which ... I clearly prove to owe their existence to Volcanick explosion, there are scattered marine Shells, & exactly of the sort that inhabit these Seas at present. They may be call'd recent for they are almost as fresh as if they had been shut up yesterday, & as this is thought to be an ancient Country we may conjecture what others must be where the shells have undergone various chimical operations of nature, & such changes as can only be produced by a long series of Ages.[12]

According to the theologians, the earth, God's creation, was 4004 years old when Mary gave birth to Christ. The Flood took place in 2349 BC. Anyone studying the stratification even of such recent deposits as those of volcanoes soon necessarily began to wonder whether in that time-scale there was time enough. Francis Rawdon, writing from Ischia in August 1774, said Hamilton had calculated that it took a thousand years to produce two to three inches of soil. And he added: 'Sir William does not mention [it] in public on account of [its] contradicting the chronology of Moses so palpably.' Canon Recupero, Rawdon said, 'who was writing the natural history of Aetna, was warned by the Jesuits not to disagree in opinion with Moses, upon which he stopped his work, declaring he could not in conscience allow the mountain to be only 6000 years old'.[13] In that light, Hamilton's donation of his *Campi Phlegraei* to Catania Library in 1778 is almost a subversive act.

Horace Bénédict de Saussure, Hamilton's companion at Lord Tylney's on the night of the lightning, was first a botanist then an outstanding geologist and mountaineer. He was to the glaciers and snowy peaks of the Alps what Hamilton was to the lavas and cinder cones of the Two Sicilies, their energetic explorer and chronicler. They geologized together in the vicinity of Naples in 1774, and from

Geneva on his return Saussure sent Hamilton a lengthy essay on the geography of Italy, as he had observed it on his way home.[14] Quite an archive of such accounts, sent to him or diligently sought out by him, might be reassembled from among Hamilton's papers, now scattered far and wide.

Saussure was a Neptunist: he believed all rocks and minerals were deposited from aqueous solution or suspension. Hamilton was rather of the other camp, the Vulcanists, who thought that fire, through its agent the volcanoes, was the chief maker. Though land often rises out of the sea in Hamilton's cosmogony, the first mover, below the sea bed, is volcanic. All his letters on volcanoes, collected together, were published in two volumes, as *Campi Phlegraei*, in 1776. Introducing the letters he declares himself to be against any system, Vulcanist or Neptunist: 'Aware of the danger of systems, I have kept clear of them, and have confined myself to the simple narrative of what I have remarked myself.' He offers, he says, 'accurate and faithfull observations on the operations of nature, related with simplicity and truth'.[15] Nevertheless, having 'anatomized' (his word) quite a tract of a particularly interesting area of the earth, he had formed, if not a system, at least decided views. His premise is that we have to enlarge our thinking. I found this scribbled admonishment in one of his notebooks: 'The dangerous Error of limiting the Order of Nature to our Confined Ideas.'[16] Escaping from that confinement, viewing events with an almost inhuman detachment, he managed to think of volcanic activity, even including the earthquakes of 1783 and the eruption of AD 79, as ultimately productive and creative. Thus he can say of the latter catastrophe:

> But to consider such partial misfortunes, on the great scale of nature, it was no more than the chance or ill fate of these cities to have stood in the line of one of it's operations; intended perhaps for some wise purpose, and the benefit of future generations.[17]

Which, to anticipate a little, sounds like Goethe's ironic observation at Pompeii: 'There have been many disasters in the world but none which has afforded so much pleasure to posterity.'[18] In fact 'the wise purpose' that Hamilton discerned in volcanic operations consisted chiefly in the dramatic production of islands, sudden mountains and an earth that in time became abundantly fertile. Ploughs and moles are his two best images for such violent workings. He writes:

I imagine the subterraneous fires to have worked in this country, under the bottom of the sea as Moles in a field, throwing up here and there a hillock, and that the matter thrown out of some of these hillocks, formed into settled Volcanoes, filling up the space between one and the other, has composed this part of the continent, and many of the Islands adjoining.

And again:

May not subterraneous fire be considered as the great plough ... which Nature makes use of to turn up the bowels of the earth, and afford us fresh fields to work upon, whilst we are exhausting those we are actually in possession of, by the frequent crops we draw from them?[19]

In that spirit, in half a dozen letters, Hamilton had by 1776 comprehensively described the operations of Vesuvius and Etna. *Campi Phlegraei* collected these letters and added to them fifty-four dramatic and beautiful coloured drawings – or rather, as Hamilton said, 'prints imitating drawings' – by his painter Pietro Fabris. These prints, etchings, all hand-coloured, are a glorious work in their own right; Hamilton appends a text to each, modestly explaining what it depicts. Their colours – the black, the red, the gold, the blue – are so intense, and the human figures in them so demonstrative of relative smallness and amazement in the face of the wondrous phenomena, that Hamilton's passion for the fiery territory seems perfectly expressed and understandable. Cascades of lava, zig-zags of lightning on coal-black emissions a mile high. When Hamilton was made Knight of the Bath Horace Walpole tried to persuade him that his natural element, and a safer one, was watery: but without any doubt it was fire he loved.

Campi Phlegraei was the interim balance of his vulcanology, not its final total. There was always more to do. In the summer of 1774, whilst that volume was in preparation, he wrote to Greville, asking him for Joseph Banks's account of Iceland's volcano, Hekla, 'as I am going on with the subject of Volcanoes'; and in the following summer to Strange asking could he get him, from the Bishop of Derry, a print of the Giant's Causeway 'as soon as possible, as it will be of service to me in the work I have in hand'.[20] He meant to settle the current dispute between Neptunists and Vulcanists about the origin of basaltic columns in favour of the latter. And returning from leave in England, in the autumn of 1777, he took a leisurely route through Germany, five days of it by boat up the Rhine from Bonn to Mainz, and studied the evidence of ancient volcanic activity along the way. He saw men paving the courtyard of the Elector's palace at Düsseldorf 'with a lava exactly like that of Etna and Vesuvius'. In Cologne he saw 'numberless basaltic columns inserted in the walls of the town ... posts in the streets, and every door ... very like the basaltes of the Giant's Causeway, but without their regular articulation'. They came from the Elector's quarry at Unkel. 'Walls of most of the ancient buildings in the town of Cologne were of a tufa exactly resembling that of Naples and its environs.'

His boat trip then was full of interest. He stopped off to visit the quarry and pottered in the dead craters of three of the Siebengebirge. A man with a harmless obsession, in territory feeding it, is an engaging phenomenon. He wrote to the Royal Society as soon as he was through, 'from on board a Yacht on the Rhine, near Mayence, Sept. 29, 1777'.[21]

In the summer of 1779 Vesuvius obliged Hamilton with so vast an explosion that he brought out a supplement to *Campi Phlegraei* in tribute. By then, with his guide Bartolomeo, the Cyclops of Vesuvius, he had been to the crater fifty-eight times and at least four times as often on other parts of the mountain. 'And after all,' he wrote, 'I am not ashamed to own, that I comprehend very little of the wonders I have seen on this great laboratory of nature.'[22] But Bartolomeo had taught him a trick or two, at least: how to walk over rivers of lava, for example, on the cooling crust of scoriae that they carry.

Ottaiano, to the north of the volcano and directly in its line on this occasion, was in great danger. Hamilton wrote:

Had the eruption lasted an hour longer, Ottaiano must have remain'd exactly in the state of Pompeii which was buried under the ashes of Vesuvius just 1700 years ago with most of it's inhabitants, whose bones are to this day frequently found under arches, and in the cellars of the houses of that ancient city.

At the palace of the Prince of Ottaiano, 'The white marble statues on the balustrade made a singular appearance peeping from under the black ashes, which had entirely cover'd, both the balustrade, and their pedestals.'[23]

One of the strangest and yet most likely things throughout Hamilton's time in Naples was the continual dialectic of excavation and reburial. As the finds were taken out of the ground at Pompeii and Herculaneum, villages nearby and indeed the Palace of Portici itself, in which the finds were housed, risked being buried. In 1794 Hamilton climbed a church tower in Torre del Greco and looked down on a town overwhelmed by forty feet of lava. For thirty years he had been following the slow clearance of more and more of Pompeii. He reported on it to the Society of Antiquaries at the end of 1774. His report, as printed in *Archaeologia* in 1777, is a series of engravings with explanations, in many of which there are details of a peculiarly striking kind. In the armoury, for example: helmets 'not unlike the hats used by the firemen in London'. In a room adjoining a baths there was the skeleton of a washer-woman:

> She seems to have been shut up in this vault, the stair case having been filled with rubbish, and to have waited for death with calm resignation, and true Roman fortitude, as the attitude of the skeleton really seems to indicate.

She prefigures the female dead found in the rubble of Calabria in the spring of 1783. Hamilton was several times present when skeletons were exhumed at Pompeii, most notably at 'a sort of Villa Rustica' outside the city. There the paintings discovered were 'as fresh as the day they were executed'. But just near the gate, he writes:

> I saw lately a skeleton dug out; and, by desiring the labourers to remove the scull and bones gently, I perceived distinctly the perfect mould of every feature of the face, and that the eyes had been shut. I also saw distinctly the impression of the large folds of the drapery of the toga, and some of the cloth itself still sticking to the earth.

The city was first covered by a shower of hot pumice-stones and ashes, and then by a shower of small ashes mixed with water. It was in the latter stratum that the skeleton above described was found. In the Museum at Portici a piece of this sort of hardened mud is preserved; it is stamped with the impression of the breast of a woman, with a thin drapery over it.[24]

Hamilton remembered these excavations during the colossal eruption of 1794, when, as it seemed, the cities were close to being buried again. He describes the impression of the face as being like 'a mould just taken off in plaster of Paris'; and added, after recalling the young woman's breast, the memory of a find in the volcanic tufa in the theatre at Herculaneum: 'the exact mould or impression of the face of a marble bust ... the bust or statue having been long since removed'.[25] These accidental preservations anticipate those done by Giuseppe Fiorelli in the 1860s. He brought forth the citizens of Pompeii from under the crust, in all their agony, by filling their hollow moulds with plaster of Paris.

Pompeii was (and is) inexhaustibly interesting and poignant. Skulls of prisoners in the barracks were placed on shelves in there 'for the inspection of the curious'. Of the washer-woman Hamilton says: 'It was at my instigation, that the bones were left untouched on the spot where they were found.'[26] Lady Anne Miller, visiting in 1771, was much affected by the skeleton of a poor slave, 'who probably had been employed in heating a bath'. She took away one of his vertebrae, for a pious souvenir.[27]

Plate XI in Hamilton's report to the Society of Antiquaries is an 'Interior View' of the Temple of Isis. And there is a picture of the first excavations of this important site in *Campi Phlegraei*. In a niche at the temple 'was found a marble statue of a female, with her fore-finger on her lips'.[28] By that gesture she can be recognized as Polyhymnia, Muse of the silent art of Mime, which would be Emma's art. Altogether, this fetching of the statues and the remains of the once living out of the ground is an eerie anticipation of Hamilton's tutoring Emma in the art of reanimating the classical past, its paintings and its statuary, in her *poses plastiques*.

I began this chapter with Hamilton's remarks to Lord Grantham on the sameness and repetitiveness of life in Naples. The serious amusements described above were themselves nothing new, but they mattered to Hamilton and do perhaps also in a more general sense exceed and survive the often trivial, ridiculous or brutal context in which year after year he served King George III.

Naples continued in its usual round of violent life and death. After the carnival of 1775 came an epidemic of a putrid fever, 'principally among the lower class of people',[29] for a while as bad as in 1764. Hamilton saved a couple of lives with Dr James's Powder. After that the Queen, so far only the mother of two daughters, gave birth to an heir presumptive, and the city went into celebrations. The usual dramas of the Neapolitan Christian year, the liquefactions of the Blood of Saint Januarius in the cathedral, the great procession to Santa Maria di Piedigrotta, for example, were augmented to the point of frenzy when, in August 1779, Vesuvius threatened to put an end to them and everything else. Then:

> All publick diversions ceased ... and the Theatres being shut, the doors of the churches were thrown open. Numerous processions were formed in the streets, and women and children with deshivel'd heads, filled the air with their cries, insisting loudly upon the reliks of St Januarius being immediately opposed to the fury of the Mountain; in short the populace of this great city began to display it's usual extravagant mixture of riot, and bigotry, and if some speedy, and well timed precautions had not been taken, Naples wou'd perhaps have been in more danger of suffering from the irregularities of it's lower class of inhabitants, than from the angry Volcano.[30]

In the spring of 1779 there were processions of penitents, and the head of the patron saint was lifted up to induce the sky to rain. In April 1773 Hamilton, just back in post, reported a greater than usual number of robberies and murders. The prison island of Ventotene, unable to cope, had been allowed to empty its five hundred convicts on to the capital's streets, a decision thought by many, so Hamilton reported, to be 'very impolitick'.[31] The King of Spain's eldest son, Philip, whom Ferdinand had overleaped to rule, was shown from time to time in his further degeneration. Hamilton viewed him in December 1775. He was incontinent, melancholic and unable to feed himself, but violently lascivious, with a morbid love of gloves.[32] He died the following year, of smallpox. Ferdinand himself meanwhile did what he always did: slaughtered and flayed and never wearied of it. At Persano in March and April 1776 3000 men and 835 dogs were employed in the sport – or 'continual dissipation & Carnage rather than Sport', as Hamilton, in a moment of disgust was moved to call it. Reporting that on one day 2309 deer were killed, 200 of them by the King, 69 by the Queen, he added:

> I must own that so much bloodshed deserves a more serious name than that of Sport, & I should fear that the heart of a person accustom'd to the Sight of so much blood might be in danger of becoming callous to all tender feelings...

Still he went along, as part of the job, because it was an honour, because it distinguished him above the French ambassador, and because, for a while at least, in moderation, he enjoyed it. Did the Queen enjoy it too? It was expected of her. In December 1778, nine months pregnant, she was nevertheless 'often of the BoarShooting parties' and shot, according to Hamilton, 'remarkably well with ball'.[33] A week later the heir presumptive, Prince Carlo Tito, died, but she had in 1777 given birth to another son, Prince Francis, and was about to give birth to a third. Maria Carolina was almost always pregnant. Occasionally Hamilton reported it to his Secretary of State, as a matter of some slight interest, if she happened not to be.

When heads of state arrived and wished to see the sights, it was Hamilton who obliged. Thus he conducted Archduke Maximilian around 'the Antiquities and Natural curiosities' of the region in June 1775, had him as guest at the Palazzo Sessa, laying on 'a Concert of Musick'; and dined with him at Portici. The following April it was the Archduchess and Duke Albert of Saxony. They showed him and Catherine particular favours in return. He commented to Viscount Weymouth:

> The very long stay I have made in this Country & my love for Antiquities & natural history have acquired me the Character of the best Cicerone of Naples & its environs which has procured me a great deal of honor to be sure, but attended with some fatigue.

He could also say of himself (having just entertained the Duke of

Ansbach Bayreuth): 'my House is so well known over Europe that of late years most Travellers of distinction have been immediately address'd to me'. Travellers, and especially the English, arrived in great number. For the Carnival of 1778, a particularly grand affair whose highlight was a masque of the Entry of the Grand Signior at Mecca, they drew on their bankers to the tune of at least £50,000, a sum which reduced by one sixth Britain's favourable balance of trade with Naples.[34] Hamilton wrote scathingly to his nephew Greville about their fellow-countrymen: 'Last year the Arts and gaming were the prevailing passions with the English, this year it is drinking & gaming.'[35] That was in March 1775. There were always at least sixty of them in town. In the autumn Charles came out himself, on his second visit, and was doubtless more congenial company. Then the following spring came the Duke of Hamilton, barely twenty, with his tutor John Moore and in Naples, to Moore's consternation, became the inseparable companion of Sir Harry Fetherstonhaugh, who five years later had Emma as his mistress at Up Park, before losing her or disposing of her to Greville. In Naples Sir William dealt kindly with both young men, ten years before he inherited their cast-off.

Naples throughout the years I am surveying here remained, in Hamilton's words, a 'remote & indolent quarter of the World'.[36] There were some local troubles: bandits in Calabria became so bold that troops had to be sent against them in the spring of 1779. In the autumn and winter of 1773 there was serious unrest – Hamilton called it revolution – in Sicily; and violent disturbances continued sporadically for several years. In November 1775, in Naples itself, complaints were posted up 'that the Sovereign thought of nothing but his amusement whilst the Prince Minister & the Chief Magistrate ... suffer'd the people to be abus'd & oppress'd'. Underweight loaves were hung near the notices as an instance of what was meant.[37] But no coherent protest would ever develop. The common people of Naples, perhaps the most anarchic and violent in Europe, were immunized against revolutionary ideas, if not against smallpox and putrid fevers, by their fanatical adoration of royalty.

When Hamilton returned from leave in November 1777 Prime Minister Tanucci, after forty-two years in power, had been replaced by the Marchese delle Sambuca. But a more significant novelty, a sort of precursor of the more critical times to come, was the arrival, in August 1778, of General Sir John Francis Acton. This extremely competent man, English by birth (though actually born in Besançon and never quite master of the English language), had served first in the French navy then, very prominently, in the Tuscan. He came to Naples on loan from the Grand Duke of Tuscany, 'to give his advice & assistance towards the putting His Sicn Majestys Marine (hitherto neglected) upon a more respectable footing'.³⁸ But the Queen fell in love with him and advanced him until he became indispensable. She herself had begun to be assertive. Constant pregnancy notwithstanding – she viewed it as Ferdinand's effort to keep her in her subordinate place – she insisted, once she had given birth to a son and heir, on her right, inscribed in the marriage contract, to be a member of the Council; and there she began to be powerful. Instrumental in getting rid of Tanucci, she soon reduced Sambuca in favour of the newcomer Acton and, in collaboration with him, sidelined her husband into his largely futile pastimes. The Queen, and Acton, were subjects on which Hamilton reported at length to his Secretaries of State; by July 1779 they were, he said, governing the country; but their greatest importance was still some years away.

With hindsight, of course, it is obvious that the age of revolution and irreversible change had already begun. Consciousness is usually a long time catching up. At Lexington and Concord on 19 April 1775 the fighting started between Britain and the rebellious American colonies; on 4 July in the following year Congress adopted the Declaration of Independence, in the preamble to which were set out truths which now seemed to them self-evident: that every citizen has the right to life, liberty and the pursuit of happiness. These truths, once put about, could not be revoked or contained. The idea of a better order was released on the world; the Ancien Régime began its long rearguard struggle. The idea itself, needless to say, at once became embroiled and disfigured in world politics. France sided with America, not for the sake of a better order but to make up the losses she had sustained in the Seven Years War. In February 1778 she signed a treaty of commerce and alliance with the Americans, which, without any formal declaration, effectively put her at war with Britain. Lord Stormont, the ambassador, was recalled from Paris.

These critically important events touched Naples only somewhat, but enough to be a first indication, which nobody then could read, of how things would develop. Britain asked Naples not to export gunpowder 'or other Warlike Stores' to the American colonies.[39] Naples complied. Relations between the French and the British ambassadors cooled still further. There was an anxious wait to see what Spain would do. Hamilton thought she would keep out, and was, according to Walpole, thunderstruck, when she declared for the French side and entered the war against Britain in June 1779. Naples' official position was strict neutrality, but, through Acton and the Queen, Hamilton had them leaning towards England, and could report with some satisfaction that the French looking for favours – timber to build more ships, for example – were refused. Even when Spain entered the conflict Naples was still anxious to stay in Britain's good books. Hamilton's position at the Neapolitan court during this period of war was curious. It struck him so particularly in February 1780 when, hunting with the King, the company passed the night together 'in a straw Cottage'. He wrote to Lord Hillsborough:

> I cou'd not help reflecting then upon the singularity of my situation; that in the midst of a hot war between Great Britain and the united powers of Spain and France one of the King's Ministers shou'd be sleeping quietly in the same room with the King of Naples, Son to the King of Spain, and Brother in Law to the french King.[40]

If the pleasures and pastimes of Naples continued much the same, so too did the annoyances and the worries. Apart from Neapolitan etiquette – which he claimed not to understand even after ten years at the Court – and the eternal arguments over the Treaty of 1667, Hamilton was more plagued than ever by his consul Isaac Jamineau. In 1767, calling him a 'little absurd Animal', he had written to Sir James Gray: 'I could forgive his Absurdity but he is so bad at bottom & I fear sooner or later he will force me to endeavour at getting rid of him';[41] but ten and twelve years later he was still in post and still a nuisance. He got above himself; he had a seal cut 'of his own portrait with the Consular fasces as the distinctive mark of *his* office', and generally gave himself the air 'of a sort of minister'.[42] When the Secretary of State, Lord Rochford, had rebuked him Catherine became fearful that he might really do them some harm.

She appealed to Greville to find out what Jamineau – perhaps back in England briefly – had been engineering against Hamilton there. Hamilton seems to have been rather indolent in his own self-defence. Jamineau stopped being a bother only when he was replaced in Naples, in 1779.

Money was another perennial worry. Hamilton was, as ever, short of it. He wrote to Greville in December 1774 that he had 'worse than nothing' with his banker, 'owing to the great arrear of the Civil List'. He urged Greville, in parliament, to hurry along the payments if he possibly could.[43] Being Ambassador cost more than the British Treasury was prepared to pay. Things got worse the following year, when the heir presumptive was born and Ministers were honour-bound to celebrate. Hamilton appealed in vain to his Secretary of State for an extra allowance to do so. Most of his colleagues in the *corps diplomatique* had already had 'a supply from their respective Courts on this account'. The Danish minister, for example, had been paid £300. Hamilton got nothing. He wrote back politely and phlegmatically: 'I have no family & can upon extraordinary occasions, or when the Civil list is in Arrear, supply that immediate want by anticipating a portion of my private income as I have done hitherto.'[44]

The late or non-payment of salary and allowances was only one among several small and sometimes not so small humiliations from London that came with Hamilton's job. Concerned for his standing, perhaps he felt that being in Naples, on the periphery, in a backwater, made him more liable to demeaning treatment. That would explain, as self-assertive reaction, his frequent reminders to his Secretaries of State that he was successful, influential and important at the Court of Naples, beyond any other foreign minister. Still he must have felt that success in Naples did not amount to much, since Naples itself did not. The advantages of his post, its pleasures and satisfactions, were many and obvious, and in the areas of his life which mattered most to him he had made a name for himself and had won the respect of intelligent and energetic contemporaries, in large measure by virtue of having been so long in Naples. On balance ought he not then to have been content? In fact, in the years after his return from England, exactly as in the years prior to that first leave, Hamilton repeatedly tried to change his situation.

In November 1773 he wrote privately to Lord Rochford, bidding for the embassy in Paris. His approach was somewhat oblique. He had, he said, made the acquaintance of a M. Laborde, a lover of music and natural history and moreover the 'Premier Valet de Chambre' of Louis XVI. Laborde was eager for him to succeed Lord Stormont in Paris. Hence the letter to Lord Rochford.[45] Nothing came of it. In January he tried something else. He approached Lady Orford who, though she lived in Italy for the last thirty-six of her three score years and twelve, still had some English parliamentary boroughs in her gift. She was wintering in Naples, 1773–4, and when Hamilton asked her, she offered him Callington in the West Country. Horace Walpole, her relative though not her friend, wrote to dissuade him from standing. It would be costly, he would have to lay out two or three thousand pounds on the necessary bribes and expenses, and still might not be elected. And even if he was he could not be sure of any further advancement, which he would need, to live comfortably. Walpole concluded: 'You may judge therefore whether this is a proper moment for quitting a certainty for a great improbability.'[46] Hamilton let the idea drop; but it became common knowledge that he was looking for a move.

A year later there was another opportunity. On 2 January 1775, having told Lord Rochford of his pre-eminence among the foreign ministers in Naples, he went on: 'Yet I cannot help regretting that it is not in my power to exert my poor endeavours in His Majestys Service to better purpose than my present situation will admit of.'[47] He said much the same on 25 February and 7 March, first to Lord North then to Lord Rochford, but now with the specific request that he might be promoted to the embassy at Madrid if, as was being forecast, Lord Grantham vacated it. He made the bid sound altruistic. His situation 'in point of self comfort' could never be more agreeable than it was in Naples; but he wanted to be where he could serve the King of England better. And he argued that it would be an easy transition to Madrid from the Kingdom of the Two Sicilies, 'a country so dear, & in a manner belonging to the King of Spain'. His further ground for the request, candidly admitted, was ambition: 'I have always held it right to have an ambition of getting at the head of ones Profession'; he said exactly the same to Greville a week later, telling him he had made the bid. If we take the statement seriously, then we have to suppose that in some part of himself at least

Hamilton felt he had failed, since he never did get 'at the head', despite many efforts to do so. Another consideration, admitted to Greville, and North and Rochford will not have needed telling, was that if he got 'an Embassy', that is one of the first-rank ambassadorial posts, he would have 'better pretensions for something comfortable at home' in the latter days of his life. So the one failure comprehended another. He cited the example of his predecessor Sir James Gray, who had abandoned Naples and wangled Madrid; but did not manage to follow in his footsteps.[48]

At this point Hamilton must have renewed his dealings with John Osborn, who was coming to the end of his time in Dresden. Osborn wrote to Hamilton on 28 March: 'What you mentioned to me relative to Ld Gr—m will not I beleive take Place at present.' There was, for a while longer, to be no vacancy in Madrid. Grantham wasn't moving because Lord Holderness in Berlin, who had seemed to be dying and whom Grantham wished to replace, recovered. It seems that Osborn had a part in Hamilton's grand design. He wrote: 'In Answer to the Proposal you communicated to me, I can in Confidence acquaint you, that should any Plan for you at any Time succeed, I have reason to think that I should be destined to releive you at Naples.'[49] In the event, no plan at any time did succeed.

As he had done in 1770, when he failed to get Vienna, Hamilton in 1775, having failed to get Madrid, applied for leave instead. In June he wrote to Greville: 'We shall probably set out on our way home about April next.' At that point he had not made his application. Perhaps it was not strictly leave he meant then, but homecoming proper. He went on: 'I think with you it is probable some event may prevent our return hither,' then stated his hesitation, and the pros and cons behind it, pretty clearly:

> I am very determined not to quit this hold unless I have a good temptation, for, after all, what is desirable in life but passing one's time honourably and agreeably, both of which I do here? I only regret the want of a friend or two; but where is happiness compleat?[50]

In September he had such a friend, for a while at least, when Greville came visiting. Then in November he applied formally for leave – 'as my private Affairs in Wales have much need of my presence'. He asked for a few months, in the following spring.[51]

In London, as word got round, the usual jockeying for advantage began. Hamilton's brother had a letter from one Ralph Woodford, 'with Regard to Sir William Hamilton's Intentions of coming Home this insuing Spring, and to it's being said his Meaning is not to return'. Woodford had been ambassador in Denmark. Now he was home on a pension of £800 a year. Would Hamilton swap him Naples for his pension? He wondered

> whether the sooner We put Our irons into the Fire will not be the better, I mean before Sir William Hamilton actually leaves Naples, before his Design becomes known here, or that Government being embarrassed by Applications can distress him by Offers inadequate to his Ideas.[52]

And Stephen Sullivan, having breakfasted with Charles Greville, wrote to Hamilton on 4 January 1776, reporting Greville's disclosures:

> you might have had Spain long ago, but was then too immers'd in Volcanos to bear the idea of quitting Naples – that you propos'd visiting London this Summer, when you would endeavor to procure something at home – but still should a Vacancy happen for Spain, he believ'd you would apply for it.[53]

There is no evidence that Hamilton 'might have had Spain long ago'. All his recorded attempts to move anywhere were unsuccessful. Sullivan was writing to him because he wanted a job in the embassy in Madrid. By January Hamilton had heard he had leave. On 12 March, perhaps rather alarmed at the rumours spreading about his intentions, he wrote to Greville:

> I am not anxious to change my situation which is now made so pleasant to me. I have you know applied for Spain & if I am thought of on a vacancy well, if not *je me consolerai aisément*; nothing but the superiour character cou'd tempt me. Pray always say that my intention is to return here.[54]

It was again reported, again falsely, that Grantham would soon quit Madrid; and on 9 April Hamilton made his usual bid, in the usual terms, again vainly.[55]

During their first years in Naples Hamilton frequently remarked on Catherine's improved health. On leave in England, in 1771–2, it was noticed, and she said herself then that she would be glad to get back to Italy, where the climate did her good. Thereafter, however, for the remaining years of her life she seems to have felt less well. The trouble, to judge by the few scattered comments on her state, was an aggravation of her characteristic nervousness and anxiety.

Dr John Elliott's advice, offered soon after their return to Naples in January 1774, addressed her physical condition:

> I hope every year will add to the strength of her constitution, I see no alteration that can be made in the plan of management, which her Ladyship follows. The more she is in the water in fine weather, so much the better, but of all things, let her be careful not to expose herself to that peircing wind, which is so dangerous at Naples.[56]

She was always under the need to take care of herself, and of her spirits as much as of her 'constitution'. Hamilton spoke about her nervous disposition as a well-known and unalterable fact. That was how she was, very unlike himself. In June 1774 they were both involved in trying to prevent what they thought would be a disastrous marriage. Hamilton commented to Greville: 'It is a great distress to Ly H., but as I am like yourself, a philosopher, I take the good & the bad as they come, patiently.' His fuller account, again to Greville, of his own part in the affair is worth quoting since it proves not so much his 'philosophy' as his susceptibility to young women (the one in question here was twenty-two):

> I think I told you in my last about poor Wittick. Her parents will not consent to her marrying Guido & have order'd her home, she will not obey; we have turned away Guido & as I realy think she will not be happy in this country I endeavour to persuade her to forget him, but that will not do. The struggles between love and duty make her very interesting. I take her hand, the poor thing squeezes it when she thinks of Guido, & cries, & in the midst of all this distress the devil will have it that —— & I grow confoundedly confused in all my councils.[57]

What distressed Lady H. interested and excited Sir William.

In the following year something truly distressing occurred, or is said to have occurred. Fothergill asserts, as a fact, that 'a child, dear to both of them, died after a serious illness'. And he adds: 'She has been described as their daughter.' But he does not say by whom. He supposes her to be the girl Greville asked after in March 1769, having just then visited the Hamilton household in Naples.[58] Greville wrote: 'I hope little Checille is quite recovered.'[59] Since there is no record of Catherine having had any children – her delicate health makes it unlikely – nor of Hamilton himself having fathered any illegitimately (and in those days he would doubtless have owned up), Fothergill concludes that the child must have been adopted. Greville's spelling of her name strongly suggests that she was Italian. Still she remains very mysterious. There is no other mention of her in Hamilton's surviving correspondence, nor, apparently, in that of the notably inquisitive Queen of Naples; and without knowing Fothergill's authorities for her illness, death and status in the Hamilton household, I can do no more than repeat his story, as others have done. Did she die in the epidemic in the spring and early summer of that year? Hamilton reports the high mortality, but says nothing of any death that touched him closely. A letter he wrote to John Strange in July 1775 has a black seal, a marker of recent death closely touching the sender or the recipient; but the letter itself makes no allusion.[60] Greville's second visit fell in the autumn. Odd that he never mentions the little girl whose health had interested him after the first visit.

If Cecile was the Hamiltons' adopted child and if she did die in 1775 then we can agree with Fothergill that Catherine must have suffered greatly. But nowhere – to my knowledge – does she express any such sorrow; nor does Hamilton, in her name or his own. Yet they both speak of her other distresses precisely in these years.

There were two such occasions in January 1776. Hamilton, applying for leave, had recommended a Mr Christopher Hervey to be *chargé d'affaires* in his absence; but when his leave was granted he was told not to appoint any replacement but to use the Portuguese ambassador instead. Hamilton was puzzled, but Catherine, so he informed Greville, was made very anxious. She suspected that Jamineau had wanted the job, and that, disappointed, he was working to harm Hamilton in London. Hamilton observed to Greville that she had 'the art of ingeniously tormenting herself'; and when she then wrote to him, asking him to get to the bottom of it, she herself referred to her 'working anxious mind'.[61] Doubtless there was nothing more in the arrangement than London's meanness and usual lack of interest in Naples. I mention the matter here because, though trivial, it characterizes Catherine. Her own mother had commented in a letter of May 1766 that 'there are no disorders so horrible as those upon the mind, whether real or imaginary'; and though she was actually referring to the sufferings of some third person, she speaks with feeling, for herself and for Catherine too.[62]

What occurred later in January 1776 was more serious, and real enough. Their servant Giovannini, who had been with them for more than ten years, was shot dead in the crossfire between two rival groups of soldiers at Caserta. Hamilton described the incident to Greville, adding: 'We are both much grieved,' and concluding: 'Lady H.'s love to you. You may imagine the present state of her nerves.' On 15 May the Duke of Hamilton wrote from Rome, thanking his kinsman for the hospitality he had shown him in Naples. He sent his regards to Lady Hamilton, and in the tone easily adopted by men, even very young men, on the subject of women, even, in this case, the wife of his host, he added: 'I hear she has taken to the reading of godly books since I left Naples.'[63] Becoming, like her mother, pious, would be taken in the men's world as another symptom of her chronic nervous trouble.

The Hamiltons set off for home at the end of May. They went via Florence, calling as usual on Sir Horace Mann. Thence to Geneva, where they had some conversation with Charles Jenkinson, former under-secretary to Lord Bute. He had been in parliament with Hamilton, but stayed in politics, doing ever better for himself and finishing as the first Earl of Liverpool. He was the man Hamilton had appealed to in 1763, about the job in Naples. Wraxall said of him:

> It was not difficult, on a short Acquaintance, to discover that he
> had read Men, more than Books; and that his Education had been
> of an inferior, as well as limited kind. He neither manifested the
> elegant Information acquired by visiting foreign Countries, nor the
> classic Ideas and Images, derived from a Familiarity with the
> Productions of Antiquity.[64]

From Geneva the Hamiltons went on to Paris, to visit Lord Stormont, ambassador there and now recovering from his 'remedieless sorrow' in a second marriage, to Hamilton's niece, Louisa, daughter of the Cathcarts, now both dead. Of this new Lady Stormont, just twenty, it was reported (by Hamilton's other niece, Mary, also just twenty, who had it from Jenkinson): '[She] is rather difficult to please and manage, & does not conduct herself quite so amiably as Lord Stormont wishes.' Mary went on:

> It is a great pity Lord Cathcart required his daughter to marry a man so much older and, whom the world in *Paris say*, she evidently dislikes. Mr. Jenkinson says Lady Stormont will not comply properly with the etiquettes required, as Lady to the English Ambassador; it is to be hoped that Lady Hamilton will prevail on her to alter her conduct.[65]

Second marriage to a woman not half the widower's age was common enough. In Paris that summer Hamilton saw a mild version of his own future *ménage*.

He and Catherine were in England by 20 September. Like the first period of leave the second extended way beyond the 'few months' Hamilton had asked for. They were in England almost a year and away from Naples half a year longer. But less is recorded this time about their occupations. They were expected at Park Place and must have stayed there. They saw Walpole and the usual circle. And they must certainly have gone into Pembroke to look after the 'Welsh affairs' that were Hamilton's grounds for seeking leave at all. Apart from that, there was further recognition of Hamilton's status in the arts and sciences. Already a Fellow of the Society of Antiquaries and of the Royal Society and a member of the Society of Arts and the Tuscan Academy, on 2 February 1777 he was elected to the Society of Dilettanti and received at their meeting a month later. The Dilettanti, founded in 1734 for purposes that were largely social and convivial, had established themselves more seriously in the 1760s by sending the architects Stuart and Revett to Athens and Richard Chandler and his party through much of Greece and Asia Minor, and by publishing the excellent work that resulted from these expeditions. Hamilton qualified for membership in that tradition. Volumes III and IV of his *Vases* had just appeared. In Joshua

Reynolds's two group portraits of the Society, painted in 1777, Hamilton is there among some familiar names: Greville, Fortrose, Watkin Williams Wynn, and Joseph Banks whom he was just getting to know. He has a Greek vase (and a glass of claret) on the table before him, and is pointing to an illustration in his book. The Dilettanti gave him another gentleman's club to go to, if he liked, when he was in London.

It was only now, on his second return to England, that Hamilton saw the collection he had sold to the British Museum in 1772, fittingly displayed there under the portrait of him painted in Naples by David Allan in 1775 and dispatched at once by the artist as a gift to the Museum. Though in that portrait references are made to Hamilton's achievements in the arts and sciences – a vase on his left, a view of Vesuvius through the window on his right – principally he appears as ambassador and Knight of the Bath, in all his expensive costume and regalia. Back in London now he sat nine times during June to Reynolds for a portrait more as a dilettante and a connoisseur, still a vase on his left and Vesuvius on his right, but more comfortably dressed, seated, with Volume I of his *Vases* open on his knee.

In July the Hamiltons were preparing to leave. They had been in England during the first year of American Independence, as the war, for the British, went badly, and being often no doubt in the company of people who had a say in such things, Hamilton will have felt the remoteness of his posting in Naples. Still, he wanted to return. If he had made any efforts to secure himself something viable at home, they were unsuccessful. Catherine wrote to his niece Mary. She had no family of her own, and kept up a fond correspondence with the women on her husband's side. She wrote:

> Both Sir Wm & I are determined to see you before we go, which he says will be about Saty Se'ennight; he takes leave of his Majty on Wedy, & we both take leave of their Majesties on Thursday; this will be a melancholy ceremony for me for I am thoroughly unwilling to go, ... if Hamilton had the same way of thinking, I am inclined to believe we should give up everything & take care of our own Estate, which would be a much more comfortable Scheme than our present situation, & I believe a more lucrative one.[66]

Five years earlier she had been happy to leave, for a climate in which she felt healthier. Did she now feel strong enough to live through the British winters? More likely it was quiet she wanted and a better place of respite from her nervousness and anxieties. But they left at the beginning of August and she would never see England again.

Their route was through Germany. I have already said how much Hamilton enjoyed it. Besides traces of volcanoes, they saw one Elector's palace at Düsseldorf and another's at Mannheim. Their host at Mannheim, according to Mary, who had it from William Preston, 'spoke in the highest terms of Sir Wm. & wished it had been possible to have known more of him & enjoyed his company for a longer time'. And she added (she was writing to Catherine): 'Tell Sir Wm … that he is very insinuating and has the art of pleasing universally.'[67] They were in Augsburg, staying at the inn Zu den drei Mohren, on 7 October. Mozart was there on the 11th, but they had gone by then. More's the pity: it would have been a pleasure to Catherine as great as were the volcanoes to her husband.

Returning in 1772 Catherine had fallen ill on the way. This time there was an accident of some kind, by which she was much shaken. To his Secretary of State, on 25 November, Hamilton announced their arrival in Naples thus: 'After a tedious & rather hazardous journey owing to uncommon inundations, Earthquakes, bad roads & worse horses we arrived here on Thursday last.' Then in his first letter to Greville he added this PS: 'Lady Hamilton has not yet recovered her fright, but upon the whole is tolerably well.' Whatever it was, Mary had heard of it – 'a shocking accident' – from the King. She wrote to Catherine: 'Thank God *you* sufferd no worse than fright, tho' I feel for your poor Swiss, & hope he is perfectly recover'd.'[68] For these journeys, over the Alps at the onset of winter, travellers needed to be pretty robust, and it is doubtful if Catherine, returning unwillingly, had the heart for it.

Not long back in Naples Catherine had to deal with Lady Maynard, and Sir William with the enraged Lord. The quarrel was this. Nancy Parsons, a tailor's daughter, having been the mistress of various dukes, had now made it to be a viscount's wife, Lord Maynard's, a young man, and she wanted assurance of her status by being presented at Court. Such introductions, for women, were effected by the ambassador's wife, who in this case, for reasons of propriety, refused to do it. In fact, whenever Lady Maynard called, Lady Hamilton was not at home. Lord Maynard wanted to fight Sir William, but made do with threats to complain to George III. Hamilton wrote pre-emptively and at great length to his Secretary of State, and there the matter ended. Lady Maynard stayed a year in Naples and was certainly not ostracized, but Catherine would not see her, which Hamilton approved, and the King of Naples himself made it plain that he did not want her to be presented. The incident is worth mentioning only to show what manner of folly the Hamiltons were necessarily involved in, and also because of the irony that in his second marriage Hamilton would seek for Emma precisely the kind of recognition that Lord Maynard was seeking for the erstwhile Nancy Parsons.

In January and February Catherine was often alone. It was the hunting season, or one of the hunting seasons. The Court removed to Caserta, Catherine went too, but Hamilton was away with the King, killing animals. Catherine wrote to Mary:

> They set out at break of day, dine in the field, & he comes home just to drink tea, when he returns again to the Palace where he plays at a game called Biribis with the King & Queen, they afterwards sup, & he is home a little after 9 o'clock.[69]

A month later Hamilton himself makes it seem rather worse, in a letter to Greville:

> Ly H. wou'd not stay at Naples alone (for without me she kindly says is being alone), so that she has led the life of a hermit these two months, as I am out before daybreak, come home after dark & have just time to dress & go to Court to play at Biribis with their Sicn Majesty's.[70]

More than once Catherine said of herself: 'I am a bad Courtier.'[71] But in that same year she was described by the singer Michael Kelly as 'the finest piano-forte player in Italy',[72] and music on one keyboard instrument or another was her consolation in her hermit days.

And she enjoyed the summers, when, because of the heat, most of the English had gone and the Court itself made fewer demands. She and Hamilton spent a good deal of time at their villa at Portici, among vineyards under Vesuvius, or at the 'casino', their little house on a rock, with three rooms and a kitchen, a terrace with an awning

over it, and 'a very diminutive garden',[73] at Posillipo. The latter place
was out of the sun by two in the afternoon, and they dined there
early, perhaps with just one guest, and went into town in the evening,
for an opera at San Carlo or a musical assembly at their own Palazzo
Sessa. To convivial people they were always hospitable. The young
Lord Herbert, in Naples for a month in August and September,
dined with them, or with Hamilton alone, usually at Posillipo, almost
every day. Hamilton took him boating, and up Vesuvius, and almost
every evening he called on them in town.

The correspondence between Hamilton and Joseph Banks began
in November 1777. Banks was well travelled by then. He had been
with Cook in the South Seas, and before that in the far north, around
Newfoundland and Labrador. His third great voyage was to Iceland,
in 1772. Hamilton had been reading his published works, at least
insofar as they concerned volcanoes, since shortly before he set off
for England in the summer of 1775; and the two men became friends
during that period of leave. The letters they exchanged are among
the best in all of Hamilton's correspondence. They had lively interests
in common. Banks was made President of the Royal Society on 30
November 1778, which ensured Hamilton's continued involvement
in their meetings. Having been by far the more adventurous of the
two, Banks felt himself now too sedentary. He wrote to Hamilton,
who was always out and about after volcanoes: 'I read your Letters
with that kind of Fidgetty anziety which continualy upbraids me for
not being in a similar situation.'[74] He sent Hamilton accounts of
travels to the Azores and in the South Seas, and a list of rare
botanical books to look out for in Naples. Hamilton sent him corals,
serpents, madrapores, notes on freaks (a spaniel with a tuft of hair
in its pupil), accounts of volcanic rain over Sicily, and the relics of
the Worship of Priapus, of which more later.

Banks suggested to Hamilton that his motto should be 'Labor ipse
Voluptas'.[75] He meant his work on volcanoes, which was manifestly
a keen pleasure. In September 1778 Vesuvius 'began to fire away' in
a sort of prelude to the vast explosion a year later. Hamilton wrote
to Banks:

I coud not resist & when the violence of the Explosions abated
which was towards Midnight I went up to the Lava & tho' I have

seen this Phenomenon so often I cou'd scarcely leave that Curious Spot before day break I long'd for you Solander & Charles Greville, for tho' I have some company with me on these expeditions sometimes yet they have in general so much fear & so little curiosity that I had rather be alone.[76]

Daniel Solander was a Swedish naturalist, assistant librarian at the British Museum, and, like Banks and Hamilton, already honoured by Wedgwood in the series 'Eminent Moderns'. He had been with Banks on the *Endeavour*. Hamilton certainly missed such company in Naples. After his return in 1777, lack of friends – rather than his distance from the political centre – was his chief complaint.

Hamilton acquired a companion of sorts, one both he and Catherine became fond of. It was a monkey called Jack, from Chandongo on the Malabar Coast. Banks, but not only Banks, was treated to full accounts of this creature's appearance, character and deeds. Hamilton got him in the autumn of 1777, sustained him through the winter by keeping a good fire in the house, and introduced him to Banks in February 1778: 'He is black with a light brown beard, his hands remarkably well made he bites his nails & keeps them in charming order and every motion genteel.' He had a curiosity to match any in the Royal Society: 'My Wife retired into a closet lately & I caught him with is eye at the Key hole which he constantly repeats when any Ladys go into that retreat.'[77] And, 'by way of laughing at antiquarians', Hamilton taught him to use a magnifying glass, to look at cameos and intaglios, which he did 'very gravely'.[78]

Jack was well established in the household and in his master's daily round of pleasures by the summer of 1779, when Lord Pembroke's son, George Herbert, came visiting. The young lord's diary for 29 August begins: 'Sir William called on me at eight to carry me on the water to see him, his monkey and one of his boatman's boys bathe, the said company bathe together every morning. The monkey is a very remarkable clever fellow.' Hamilton wrote his young guest a detailed account the following summer, which deserves quoting at length, since it characterizes Hamilton (his sense of humour) as much as it does the monkey:

Jack is greatly improved, but bites now & then as Yr Lp may

remember he could when you was here. The battles between him & my Boy Gaetano (whom you may remember to have a St Januarius, a I.C., & a Pulinchinello tattooed on his arm) when he is naked & going into the Sea with me in the morning are really curious. He never bites him but plays him all sorts of tricks, his favourite one is to pull him by his —— & then he always smells his fingers; the other day he pull'd rather hard & the boy clapped his two hands upon it whenever the monkey approached. Jack made use of a most excellent expedient to put the Boy off his guard. He passed by him & kept his hind parts close to the Boy who was setting at the head of the boat, & who no longer fearing him removed his hands; Jack who was squinting back immediately siezed his prey with one of his feet, which you know are equally handy, & held him fast to the great entertainment of the Watermen & myself.[79]

Jack had been ill, and his improvement, alas, was only temporary. His death came at the beginning of a mixed and highly characteristic passage in Hamilton's life.

Chapter 7

MIXED EVENTS,
1780–AUGUST 1783

Ferdinand had a palace in Naples, close by the Opera House, but spent more time elsewhere, for the hunting. Caserta, begun in 1752, was still only in the process of becoming the grossest palace in Europe, but in July 1780, finally, one suite of rooms was made habitable for the royal family when they visited; but long before then Ferdinand and his favourites, chief among them Hamilton, had been there in autumn and winter, housing frugally, for the hunting in the mountains behind the building site. Further north, further into the Apennines, there were other domains, notably at Persano, a vast extinct crater, and at Venafro, which had important classical remains, in which Ferdinand was not interested. Throughout 1780 the Court, and Hamilton with it, shifted in perpetual restlessness from Naples, to Portici, to Caserta, with forays beyond. But this constant progress, camping at one place and another, was entirely usual, and had its reason in the hunting. Carnival that year was a repeat of the very successful and costly spectacle of 1778, the entry of the Grand Signior to Mecca.

At home, in early June, in the so-called Gordon Riots, London was given over to violence and anarchy for some days. Among the many properties attacked by the anti-Catholic mob were some lived in by the ambassadors from continental Europe, which was embarrassing to civilized British ministers at those courts. Hamilton again toyed with the idea of standing for Parliament, this time on his own patch in Pembroke; mused that on the whole he would be content to stay in Naples for the rest of his life; but still thought something might supervene to cause a change. By 1780 however he was less and less actively seeking one. He thought Catherine not only well but also, more surprisingly (given her reluctance to leave England in the summer of 1777), even fonder of Naples now than he was himself.

In September 1780, discussing the fate of younger sons with his nephew Greville, Hamilton reflected that his marriage, though not entered into very willingly, had on the whole been a happy one. In these last two years of Catherine's life we see the couple most distinctly in their fundamental differences, and yet in an affectionate and companionable estate that Hamilton would miss very sorely when it ended. For the present, however, he reported that she was well: 'Lady H. is better than I have known her to be some years, but the E. India Monkey is dying, which grieves us both . . .' He supposed the servants had poisoned him.[1]

As the monkey declined a new interest came Hamilton's way. He had word from a correspondent in Isernia, a remote town in the Abruzzi then just being opened up by road-building, that the ancient fertility god Priapus was alive and well and still being worshipped by the women of the region every September in the church of Saints Cosmo and Damien. His account was so entertaining, and to an antiquarian so interesting, that Hamilton determined to get to the place itself and collect evidence, just as soon as possible. Autopsy was always his way. Priapus and the phallic ex-votos of Isernia turned amusingly in his mind that winter, as another subject for the delectation of his learned friends at home.

Hamilton insisted that Catherine was well, but when he moved with the court to Caserta a cold, soon becoming a cough, prevented her from joining him. She wrote that she longed to be with him, 'the air and quiet of Caserta', but above all being with him would speedily cure her. That year in fact the air of Caserta was malarial. 'The yellow-green & ghostly countenances of the poor inhabitants of the low ground,' Hamilton wrote, 'is really terrible. Many have died.'[2] Catherine, he reported, was 'a little indisposed', and the Queen visited her. He cites this as an instance of particular favour (and thus of the importance of his own position at court); the Queen visited Catherine in her own house and stayed more than two hours without ceremony. Since Catherine disliked the Queen the favour was, for her at least, a mixed blessing.

Jack died. His death was very affecting. Hamilton reported it to the young Lord Herbert:

Our poor Jack, your Friend, Alas! is dead. Nothing could be more moving than his illness & death; it half kill'd Lady H, for he never would leave her a moment. He grew quite gentle & and for the last month was without a chain, and never attempted to bite. He shewed us that his disorder was in his breast. He would do any thing for us, & and finding that glisters [clysters] did him good he would turn up his tail & ask for one every morning. He really was the most extraordinary animal, if it was one, (for I am sure I have several servants in my house that deserve that apellation more than him) that ever I saw. He was ten times wiser than when you saw him, and was improving daily. His lungs were decay'd. I have preserved him in Spirits & intend him for the British Museum.[3]

Hamilton diverted himself with hunting and with thoughts of Priapus. (Vesuvius was quiet '& little virtu stirring'.[4]) Catherine, much alone, was herself diverted by the arrival in Naples of her husband's second cousin, William Beckford, aged twenty, and travelling in the grip of unspeakable passions, which by the time he reached her he had further indulged, in Venice. His relationship with the first Lady Hamilton (he lived to know the second also) was certainly important, though perhaps more to her than to him. He had just read *Werther*, and was himself an extreme example of the type. She made him the object of feelings that otherwise went without an object in her life. In their correspondence, largely preserved, the pathos and poignancy are almost wholly on her side.

Beckford reached Naples on 3 November, and there and at Caserta stayed a month, much of it in Catherine's company while Hamilton was '*nimroding* it away upon the Mountains'.[5] Between Beckford and Catherine music was a powerful bond; or, better, the medium of their dealings with one another. Hamilton loved music too, and it affected him; but not as it did Catherine. He never used it as Catherine and Beckford did, to excite feelings, express them and in so doing excite them further. Both could compose and improvise and used the instruments to think or dream aloud. Beckford reported: 'Sir Wm hunts all day long with the King upon the Mountains whilst we indulge our imaginations at home and play strange dreams upon the piano forte and talk in a melancholy visionary style.'[6] Music went over into talk and talk into music. They indulged in hours and hours of a pastime that enervated them both. Through music they entered other enthusiasms. Like Werther, they had a passion for Ossian, Homer and Nature. Twice Beckford's age, Catherine was quite coeval with him in the Gothick and the Pre-Romantic. Their relationship was then further intensified by her religious desire to save him from 'the Gulph'[7] she saw him pulled towards. So even whilst through music she and he were raising their feelings beyond the expressible into the unbearable she was mindful, in her conscience, of her duty to pull him back, and she warned him against music as against something sweetly sinful on which he would drift into perdition. Beckford must soon have confessed to her his liking for young, even very young, boys; perhaps his infatuation at home for the eleven-year-old William Courtenay, certainly his affair in what she called 'the *pestilential* air'[8] of Venice with the youth Connaro; and she fought with him, as she understood it, for his very soul. And clearly the whole thing, the confessions and the admonitions and the mutual excitement through music, was compellingly enjoyable.

In her letters to him after his departure, she insists that her concern for him, her admitted affection and tenderness, were all maternal. '*My Child* ... My dear Child', she calls him, again and again; signs herself 'yr truly affect Motherly friend'; sides with his own mother (with whom she was in correspondence) in the struggle for his soul. Indeed, she says it outright: 'I look upon you as my Child,'[9] and doubtless it was so, for this childless woman, but with a troubling admixture of another strain of feeling that she was duty-bound to repress and which continually, in their music together, and in her music alone when he was gone, she allowed and increased.

Catherine's husband was neither philistine nor unfeeling; but his sensibility was quite unlike hers and his second cousin's (of whom he was nonetheless genuinely fond); really, it was an age away. They were both, the boy and the woman old enough to be his mother, of the epoch of 1774, the year of *Werther*. Though in her letters to Beckford she speaks loyally and affectionately of Hamilton, she knew their differences. One ragged sentence says a good deal: 'My companion (tho' not bless'd or rather curs'd with our kind of feels [=feelings] [but?] as worthy Man as breathes) he loves you sincerely, admires you, & will help me to take care of you.'[10] But Catherine herself had Beckford's 'secret', the confession of his vice; she cherished it as the mark of their intimacy. Each bound the other to show their letters to no one. Hers are unsigned, or only with the compressed little cypher 'CH'.

Beckford left, he was in Rome on the evening of 5 December, and wrote to Catherine the following day, as did she to him. She added a postscript on the 11th, having received his letter. One quotation will suffice to show the state she could work herself up into by dwelling on the peril he was in:

> I cannot express the anxiety of my mind about you, I have travelled with you all the way there, & am still going on with you; my fears augment as you approach the *pestilential* air – my imagination paints you so strongly to me, that I see every tear you shed, & hear every sigh, I stretch out my arm & would feign pluck you out of the danger which stares you in the face (& which Alas! you do not (or will not) see, & grasp nothing but air, & the sensation betrays me into trembling & tears, I then fly to my Piano forte & there your Voice pursues me, its sound is still in my ears...[11]

She felt better when he got beyond Venice, and worse again when he lingered in Paris. She wanted him back in Naples with her, under her supervision; but she feared the 'fatal corruption' of Italy's 'tainted' air,[12] and selflessly wished him safely home, under the supervision of his real mother.

Hamilton meanwhile was writing to thank Lord Herbert (Lord Pembroke's son, the same age as Beckford) for two gifts, just received: more Giardini concertos, published in London, and 'a charming print' of work done by the woman whom years before he had wanted to marry, Lady Di Beauclerk (née Spencer):

> I always thought Lady Di, had more true taste than any creature living and I defy any artist in Europe to compose two figures with more grace and simplicity than these two delightfull little girls. Do kiss the hand that produced them, (as my proxy) the first opportunity and tell her Ladyship that I can never cease being her admirer, as I was long before you was born, and when your graceless Papa used to laugh at my tender feelings, for with him you know -Sh-cum-Sh is the beginning of love & kiss my A—e is the end of it.[13]

Then he went on to describe the death of Jack.

Catherine was ill for much of 1781. On 5 March, she apologizes to Beckford for not having written: '[I] was so ill before I left Caserta that I was unable to do so from the State of my nerves.' Writing on the 19th she concluded: 'I would say much more, but have a terrible cold & am obliged to go to my bed.' More seriously on 8 May, again apologizing for not writing:

> A Severe illness put it out of my power, & I had occasion to think myself hastening fast to the end of my Earthly journey – I cannot tell you what was the matter with me, but I never was so weak in my life, so much so both in body & mind that had a pistol been presented to my head I should not have withdrawn it.[14]

It must be this illness, or particular recurrence of her chronic condition, that Catherine's doctor, Alexander Drummond, is addressing when, on 19 April, in response to her complaint that he was not taking her troubles seriously enough, he wrote her the following candid analysis:

> You are subject to complaints, which being constitutional, must be difficult to remove, and which have therefore troubled you already, and perhaps may in future continue to trouble you, in a variety of different forms. These complaints however, I consider as much more troublesome than dangerous, and by no means inconsistent with your outliving those who seem to be stronger, and enjoy an uninterrupted course of good health. But while I thus acknowledge you to be seriously and unavoidably ill, I must not forget to say that you would be better if your temper were better suited to your situation, and your mind so interested in other things as not to brood so much over your bodily distresses. You are too much of a great, and too little of a fine lady, to be as well as you might be. Had you been poorer you would have found a constant occupation in your household affairs, which would at last have become an amusement to you. Had you had a turn for a gay life, that would have overbalanced your fondness for vegetating at home, and made you find health in dissipation, while you sought only to gratify your vanity. As it is, you are but too much a prey to ennui. And it is this which is the parent of your lowspirits, mingles with all your

constitutional ailments, is mistaken for them sometimes; and always aggravates them.[15]

He prescribed '15 grains of Squills a day, twice that weight of Colomba-root' and tar-water, a pint or a pint and a half a day. Ennui for Catherine, however, was not 'vegetating at home', where she could write to Beckford and play the pianoforte; it was the world of the Court. In June, still lingering, with the excuse of illness, at Portici, where she liked to be, after the Court had returned to Naples, she wrote, as her respite neared its end: 'I grieve to think that in a Week I must launch into the World of ennui, for which I am less fit every day.' In November she wrote to Beckford that she had been 'for some months' more ill and nervous than she could express.[16] So the sum total of illness that year, the year before her death, was great.

Doubtless Hamilton read Homer, but he never speaks of him, unless in connection with the paintings on vases. Catherine and Beckford read him, in Pope's translation, and enthused together over their favourite characters and scenes. Catherine had a passion for Hector. She writes: 'My hero is Hector ... I love Hector, & have a confidence in him; there is a mixture of tenderness that draws ones affections. The Scenes between him & Andromache are touching to the last degree.' Beckford's hero was Achilles, and not Achilles the great killer but rather Achilles the lover of Patroclus. The Homeric texts not only served Catherine to express her own ideals; they were also a battleground on which she fought Beckford for the good of his soul. When he turned her more towards the *Odyssey*, reminding her that in Naples and its environs she was in the supposed zone of Circe and indulging himself with thoughts of lolling among the lotus-eaters for ever more, she answered sternly with the *Iliad*, its martial virtues, and her hero Hector, in his love for his wife and child and for his homeland, which he went out to defend, and died. She had composed a dead march, to accompany the bringing of his body into Troy. 'It began with the Morning dawn, & Cassandra's spying the procession from the Walls, & as it goes on is intermix'd with the screams & laments of the people.'

Obsessively in the last two years of her life she reverts to this march, exciting herself unbearably not just with the music and the imagined cries of Cassandra and the people but also with visions of the scene itself, of how it would look if she were a painter and could depict it. She found other companions or accomplices in this worship, when Beckford left. One was the gothically impassioned Abbé Sterkel, who had twice been at the point of death through the power of music and who, like Beckford, conversed with her on an accompanying pianoforte. Another was the young German painter Friedrich Heinrich Füger, who under her inspiration hurried off to paint a picture of Hector upbraiding the effeminate Paris with a frown.[17] Füger is better known for his portrait of a modern hero, whom Catherine would not live to meet: Nelson.

Hamilton meanwhile was himself reanimating the Ancient World, or seeking out traces of its continued vitality. In February 1781, doubtless from Venafro where he was killing boar with the King, he made an expedition to Isernia, to find out for himself about the surviving cult of the god Priapus. He consulted the Governor of Isernia, who corroborated the account he had already received from his correspondent in the autumn of the previous year. He wrote to Greville, who put the word around. In May Lord Pembroke asked to be informed. He had a reverence for Priapus: 'So superb a deity ought allways to have been treated with every possible mark of religion and respect; but, from the natural perverseness & exclusive monopoly of the Christian faith, he has been neglected too long a series of ages.'[18] Alas, the Christians were about to repress him again. Hamilton intended witnessing the ceremony himself, that September, but Isernia becoming better known, once the new road brought the outside world in, the Bishops banned the holy goings-on, for their indecency; so that when, having in July promised Banks a full account, Hamilton delivered it in a letter on 30 December 1781, he was writing about a festival already lost.

But this is how it was. Every year on 27 September the women of the villages, all in their local costumes, came into town and purchased wax ex-votos 'representing the male parts of generation, of various dimensions, some even of the length of a palm', and offered them in the church, saying: '*Santo Cosimo benedetto, cosi lo voglio.*' Any man afflicted or unhappy in that part presented it itself at the altar and the priest anointed it with Saint Cosmo's oil, saying: '*Per intercessionem beati Cosmi, liberet te ab omni malo.*'[19] Hamilton collected a good number of the wax ex-votos, known as the saint's 'Great Toe', intending them for the nation. Pembroke commented: 'I shall like to see our matrons handling the great toe of Santo Cosmo in the British Museum. I wish you would send me one for mine'; and Hamilton concluded his July letter to Banks thus: 'That your *Great Toe* & your purse may never fail you is the wish of Dr. Sir yr most faithfull humble Wm. Hamilton.'[20]

Distinct in and perhaps even separated by their interests and their characters, Hamilton and Catherine do also appear in these last months of their life together at their most companionable. It is Catherine who supplies the testimony, in letters to Beckford and to Hamilton's niece Mary. She particularly enjoyed the summer retreat under the volcano at Portici. She wrote to Mary: 'We live as English a life as we can make it. In the Morning we go out in an open Chaise, I work, & draw, in the Evening we have musick, afterwards I work & Sir Wm reads to me.'[21] The letter is undated, but may well refer to their stay at the Villa Angelica in the early summer of 1781, after her severe illness; certainly it characterizes the life there, that she liked best. She added these details to Beckford, on 8 May:

> My companion is very busy cutting Walks & making a kind of labyrinth in a Shrubbery on the foot of Vesuvius behind our house – it is chiefly composed of Myrtle, Chinese Cyprus, & Spanish broom, the two former high enough to give a thick shade.

The 'companion', before her letter was finished, could be heard 'practising away with his Violette'.[22] They had the King's vast private bosquet to walk in (a fence and a guard at the gate kept the world out) and in June, when the Court had left and Catherine was still convalescent before another illness, they discovered a wood:

> Such a wood! – Wild Walks – a mixture of beach, Oak, Arbutis, Cypress, &c &c mix'd with the flowering Myrtle & other beautifull Shrubs – the Shade too thick for the hottest sun to penetrate except here & there little plots of grass so surrounded as to give them such an air of Solemnity that you might fancy them to be the haunt of some Nightly beings – to add to the pleasure the Wood was full of nightingales, & passeri Solitarias – to which we listen'd till the Sun was near Setting.

True, here and in the long description of the sunset which follows, she is writing in Beckford's style – no worse, in fact rather better – and the scene was so of his kind that she and Hamilton cried out almost simultaneously: 'How Beckford would enjoy this!'[23] Nevertheless it is a pleasure shared by man and wife, for all their great differences, and one very characteristic of their best life together.

Hamilton ended the year writing about the survival of Priapus. As the new year, 1782, began, Catherine was dying and her replacement, Emma, moved into the wings of Hamilton's life. At Up Park in Sussex Sir Harry Fetherstonhaugh, her protector, had tired of her. In January she appealed to Greville to replace him, which he did, pregnant though she was, on terms of the strictest chastity and obedience. He established her, with her mother, in a little house on the Edgware Road, not far from Tyburn, near the modern Marble Arch, and there she kept house for him, whenever he chose to be home. Catherine was in a new apartment too, in bitter cold Caserta, in rooms hung with tapestries from the Palazzo Pitti that had once belonged to the Medicis. She sat there wondering what scenes the figures on these tapestries had witnessed. She wrote to Beckford, 'Sir Wm. is half angry with my fondness for this frightfull furniture, but it serves for food to the imagination, & that is no bad thing when he is out hunting wild boars, & I am sitting shivering alone under a snowy Mountain.'

She felt 'as stupid & chilly as a swallow in Winter'.[24] In that month and the next the cold was very severe. There was snow on Vesuvius; in Naples the fountains froze, indoors the temperature was minus seven. Hamilton was much taken up entertaining the Grand Duke Paul. This young man, Catherine the Great's son and heir to the Russian Empire, was a disappointment to his host, King Ferdinand. For their common amusement, at a cost of 14,000 ducats, Ferdinand had confined 'about 500 wild boars, 1500 stags & fallow deer, foxes & hares innumerable' in the reserve at Persano, but Paul had no interest in hunting and declined the invitation.[25] Ferdinand rode off and killed it all himself. Hamilton was left to show Paul and his Duchess the sights, which he duly did. The Duke's behaviour in the carriage was odd. He flung himself repeatedly on his wife, kissing and embracing her 'with as much warmth as he could have shewn if they had been alone, and newly married'. Hamilton averted his eyes, but the Grand

Duke called for his attention: *'Monsieur Le Chevalier, J'aime beaucoup ma femme.'* Hamilton observed (to Wraxall): 'It was impossible not to credit the assertion, after the proofs which he had just exhibited.' The proofs resumed, as did the Grand Duke's commentary: *'Vous voyez que J'aime beaucoup ma femme.'* Hamilton: 'I could only express my satisfaction at his felicity.'[26] On Vesuvius, the couple suffered considerably, the Duke's lungs being 'very weak, & his body ill formed & not strong', and the Duchess 'rather corpulent'. Her feet came through her shoes. Grand Duke and Duchess were in the end, so Hamilton reported, 'quite knocked up'; but rewarded him nonetheless with 'a fine gold snuff-box all over diamonds'.[27] Anne Damer, General Conway's daughter, came visiting. She was an artist whose work, and person, Hamilton admired as much as he did Lady Di Beauclerk's. She did some sculptures in Naples, one of Ceres in particular, about which he wrote enthusiastically to Walpole. Anne Damer was one of several women on whom his thoughts lingered when Catherine was dead, and before Emma moved in. Emma herself meanwhile had given birth to her first child, a girl whom she called 'little Emma' and whom she deposited at once with her grandmother in Hawarden. Thus liberated, she sat to Romney, at Greville's expense, as Nature and as Circe. In the latter role she was wonderfully effective and later in Naples also, in the very home of Circe as Beckford had pointed out, she sustained it convincingly, for a little while.

On 24 April Hamilton applied for permission to convert the top floor of his residence, the Palazzo Sessa, into a new apartment. His reason: to give Catherine more air and light. It was already too late. Hamilton wrote to Greville on 14 May: 'My utmost ambition is now to be left where I am ... for I find I grow old apace, and such a climate as this in old age is no inconsiderable object, & to Lady H's tatter'd constitution is become essential.'[28] In fact he had years ahead of him, and a passage of rejuvenation too; but Catherine was resigned to dying. That spring she wrote three long letters to Hamilton, for him to find after her death; they are her last testament to him, and her plea, from beyond the grave, that he mend his ways and look more to the after life. A year before, so ill then that she thought herself already 'launching into the World of Spirits', and already finding 'every occupation & Object of worldly eagerness' despicable, her only regret, one that broke her heart, so she wrote to Beckford, was leaving her companion, and the thought 'that he probably would never have anyone so tenderly & strongly attach'd to him' as she had been.[29] Her letters in the spring and sumer of 1782 are mixed the same. Thus on 7 April:

> How shall I express my love & tenderness to you, dearest of earthly blessings! My only attachment to this world has been my love to you, & you are my only regret in leaving it. My heart has followed your footsteps where ever you went, & you have been the source of all my joys. I would have preferr'd beggary with you to kingdoms without you. But all this must have an end – forget & forgive my faults, & remember me with kindness.

Hamilton at his fondest never spoke *of* her like that, and I doubt if that was ever his private tone *with* her either. The other two documents – one is a soliloquy rather than a letter – are undated, and are if anything more helplessly effusive. He is absent, hunting no doubt, but her feelings seem to exceed any such real occasion:

> How tedious are the hours I pass in the absence of the beloved of my heart, & how tiresome is every scene to me. There is the chair in which he used to sit. I find him not there, & my heart feels a pang & my foolish eyes overflow with tears. The number of years we have been married, instead of diminishing my love have increased it to that degree & wound it up with my existence in such a manner that it cannot alter. How strong are the efforts I have made to conquer my feelings, but in vain. How I have reasoned with myself, but to no purpose. No one but those who have felt it can know the miserable anxiety of an undivided love. When he is present every object has a different appearance, when he is absent how lonely, how isolated I feel. I seek peace in company, & there I am still more uneasy. I return home, & there the very dog stares me in the face & seems to ask for its beloved master. Alas! I have but one pleasure, but one satisfaction, & that is all centred on him.

She makes her feelings sound not only heartfelt, but illicit, as though for a lover. But she concludes: 'Oh, Lord, bless & convert to thy faith my dear, dear husband & grant that we may live to praise &

bless Thee together.' And that anxiety for his soul reaches out to him also from the third document:

I feel my weak, tottering frame sinking & my spirits fail me; my only regret in leaving this world is leaving you; was it not for that I should wish the struggle over. But my heart is so wrapp'd up in you that you are like the soul that animates my body. You never have known half the tender affection I have borne you because it has never been in my power to prove it to you – forgive this effusion of my heart. I feel myself every day declining. You are absent from me, & God grant I may ever see you again. The dissipated life you lead, my dr. Hamilton, prevents your attending to those great truths in comparison of which all is folly – for God's sake do not reject those truths, nor despise the plain simplicity of a religion upon which our salvation depends...'³⁰

Hamilton, not yet in receipt of these writings, went on as usual with his interests: in June – almost certainly then – buying the Barberini Vase from Byres, who called on him from Rome; and in July – after months of putting the man off – he finally visited the Radnorshire artist Thomas Jones in his studio and commissioned a large picture of the Campi Phlegraei from him.

Beckford meanwhile, now of age but no wiser, was back on the continent, and in grand style, in a train of three coaches, he was heading south. He reached Naples early in July, and was accommodated in the Hamiltons' villa at Portici. On the 8th he accompanied Catherine on what was perhaps her last outing, in a carriage through the King's *boschetto*. But there is no record this time of musical and confessional intimacy between them. Since seeing her last he had 'consummated' his relationship with the by now thirteen-year-old William. He had gone beyond being saved by Catherine; not that he had ever seriously wanted it. Moreover he and his party were ill, of malaria, and lay confined at Portici in considerable misery and distress. Catherine's doctor, Alexander Drummond, rode out to treat Beckford, on a horse he could not manage, and was thrown, and died of his injuries the following day, 13 August. Drummond was much loved among the British in Naples. He gave his services free and had stayed on, when he might have advanced more elsewhere, because he liked the place, making do with very little. It is probable that his death, since she was fond of him and dependent on his professional care, hastened Catherine's own. It came two weeks later. She was, in Hamilton's words, 'carried off by a putrid fever',[31] on 25 August 1782, aged forty-four.

Among Catherine's favourite lines in the *Iliad* were these:

> May I lie cold before that dreadfull day
> Press'd with a load of Monumental clay
> Thy Hector wrap'd in everlasting Sleep
> Shall neither hear thee sigh nor see thee weep.[32]

She had tried to set them to music, without success. The second of them must have thrilled her in a peculiarly unhappy way, since among her many mental torments was a morbid horror of being buried alive. In her letter to Hamilton of 7 April, that he would find in her workbox after her death, she wrote: 'I entreat you not to suffer me be shut up after I am dead till it is absolutely necessary.' Then she goes on, as though to counter the horror by force of conjugal love: 'Remember the promise you have made me that your bones should lie by mine when God shall please to call you, & give directions in your will about it.' That promise mattered to her, she reverted to it: 'Remember your promise of being lay'd by me, when God calls you away';[33] and he kept it.

The place where they would lie together was not anywhere in Naples. It was the Barlow vault in Slebech Church in Pembroke. She had a long journey, going ahead of him. The procedure was established: embalming, then the wait, perhaps a long wait, for a ship whose captain would be willing to carry the unlucky cargo of a corpse. The expatriate dead were sometimes shipped home falsely ticketed as statues, to circumvent the sailors' superstition. But Hamilton found a Swedish captain who would take the first Lady Hamilton home without that subterfuge, and on 20 September he wrote to the Neapolitan authorities for the necessary permission.

Beckford had left Naples by then, his party diminished by the death of his harpsichordist, John Burton, of malaria on 3 September. He died in delirium, cursing Beckford for bringing him to Naples. Word of Catherine's death reached England about the time she was setting off for burial. Greville wrote, with somewhat cold condolences and a word of praise to his uncle for always having shown 'that kindness and attention to her which she deserved'. And he added, perhaps not just in flattery: 'I have often quoted you for that conduct.'[34] Walpole wrote to Mann: 'Our papers say Lady Hamilton is dead at Naples. I am very sorry for her; but I hope, as she was a good fortune in land, that Sir William loses nothing by her death.'[35] In fact he lost a good deal; he seems really to have surprised himself by the degree of his grief. He admitted it frankly, to his sister the Countess of Warwick: 'In spite of all my Philosophy I am quite unhinged by the cruel separation from an amiable and true friend'; and to his niece Mary:

> In spite of all my philosophy & that I know that all regrets are vain, I cannot help indulging myself in them every moment. A chair, a table, a pianoforte, alas every little circumstance calls to my mind those happy moments that are gone for ever ... I must for ever feel the loss of the most amiable the most gentle & virtuous companion that ever man was blessed with.[36]

His philosophy was stoical; and against real life, in the shape of Catherine's death, it proved less effective than he had thought it would.

Hamilton protected himself by continuing precisely in the sort of distractions that Catherine had begged him to abjure. He wrote: 'I have nothing for it but to drive away thought as much as I can'; and in this he was aided and abetted by the King and Queen. He admitted: 'My home is no longer comfortable to me';[37] so they invited him out of it as often as possible, to spend the evenings with them, and the days in the field, hunting. In letters to Beckford he described his regime of hyperactivity as the only cure. Health of the body seemed to him vital, if he was not to lose his mind. He has almost a materialist, certainly an unorthodox view of how the two combine: 'If my body should fail me I am not quite clear that the mind, Soul, or whatever you please to call it, will fish about alone; I am determined to keep the clay walls that confines *him, her, it* – in as good repair as I can.'

Accordingly, instead of brooding on absence at home, he was

'posting about from Boar to Duck, from Duck to Woodcock Hare Snipe, lark, bald Coot – & the King says please god it shall be so every day till the Month of March'. Hamilton was quite clear-sighted about the nature of such a life: 'One would imagine by the extravagant waste of time of our present way of living that the natural term of the life of Man was at least a thousand years ...' He had watched the King living thus for two decades and joined him in it often enough; and now with the added reason of self-preservation. Apart from hunting there was music. Beckford's painter Cozens, whose manners many found repellent, had stayed on in Naples and Hamilton made use of his company: 'Cozens pass'd a day with me here lately – the vermin plays a good stick upon the violoncello which was a fine discovery we play'd 4 hours – he is very firm as to time & is a lover of Handel which suited me.'

Beckford wrote from Geneva, a month after Catherine's death, a letter quite devoid of grief, concerned only with himself, asking Hamilton to find his letters to her and let him have them back. Hamilton, writing on the same day, reported that he had already found them, tied up together, as he had expected. He sealed them and promised their safe return. He mentioned also that he was keeping 'a short journal', presumably on his efforts to combat grief, which he hoped to show Beckford when he next came to England.[38] It is lost, unfortunately Documents of Hamilton's private life are very few.

Catherine's death seems to have decided the question more or less urgently posed throughout their time in Naples: whether he should move elsewhere. Writing of his loss, he continued (to his sister):

> I by no means think of exchanging the office I at present enjoy, not even for one that might be more brilliant & lucrative in appearance – I have weigh'd well every circumstance & am sure that in the ballance of my future happiness the Naples Scale preponderates.[39]

And in January he said the same to his niece Mary. Calculating (pretty exactly) that in all probability, 'barring accidents', a man of his age could 'count upon 17 more years of life', he thought he would do best to live them out quietly in Naples, in the sun.[40] But he did have in mind to return home on leave, to see to the Pembroke estates that were now, by Catherine's will, wholly his; and was only waiting for peace in the war with America, Spain and France, to apply. On 5 December 1782 George III granted the American colonies what by force of arms they had won already: independence. The war petered out, and a treaty was signed in Paris early in the new year. It was thought by many in England, because Tobago and Senegal were lost to France and Minorca and the Floridas to Spain, to be a bad peace; but Hamilton, remembering an earlier Peace of Paris that had dispensed him from further fighting, commented: 'a bad Piece I have myself experienced to be better than no Piece'[41]; and at once he applied for his leave. That was in February 1783. He had come through the winter not, I think, as through a long dark night of the soul, but through some sadness nevertheless, by dint of tirelessly hunting with the indefatigable King. He wrote now (11 February) in a good humour to Beckford, and in a real concern for that young man's well-being. It seemed to Hamilton, replacing Catherine in a sort of loco parentis, that Beckford might be saved not by moral willpower but by the outdoor life:

> Live in the air force yourself to be a Sportsman, banish books pen ink & paper & do not even suffer yourself to have a rational thought – I realy prescribe this nauseous draught to you as a good Phisician woud prescribe a dose of Jalop or Buckthorn & bleeding to such a man as the late Ld. Plimouth who was ready to burst (nay I beleive did burst) with having stuffed himself with venison &c & whose mind certainly never prey'd upon his body.[42]

In fact by then, as the hunting season ended, Hamilton's appetite for life had been whetted by the foretaste of something grander, a thing more in keeping with his most serious and passionate interest. On 5 February Calabria suffered the first shock of an earthquake; others followed, there and around Messina. By 18 February, when Hamilton first wrote to Banks about it, a disaster was under way that would devastate much of that country and cost some forty thousand people their lives. Reports came slowly to Naples, and Hamilton collected them. 'The great plow of Nature' was working with especial violence.

On 22 February Catherine, so long on her journey, was finally buried in the family vault under the floor of the chancel in Slebech Church.

Hamilton waited for his leave. On 15 April, not having heard, he wrote again to Lord Grantham; and also to Beckford: that he expected to be in London by early August at the latest, and that he would like to stay with him at Fonthill over the winter. One or two remarks indicate Hamilton's sense of the distinction, in terms of wealth at least, between himself and the much younger man. Beckford was fabulously rich. For a purchase on Beckford's behalf Hamilton asked payment as soon as possible, because 'W.B. can afford to pay interest should he out run a little, better than W.H.'; and later, sending him a parcel: 'You great folks I suppose don't mind how much you pay for Postage' – clearly, Hamilton did. And it was in that letter (29 April), referring to changes in government at home, that he added this too true to be comfortable ironic comment on himself: 'I am too insignificant an Animal to have been thought of during the great operation of the formation of the new Ministry so the letter in which I asked leave to return home for a short time & which arrived at that period remains unanswered & I am kept here.'[43] By then he was packed and ready to go and had made his usual provision: sold his horses and let his country houses for a year; still without Grantham's word. Till that came, he would visit Calabria and Messina, the earthquake zone, and satisfy the curiosity of his countrymen with a clear account. His own curiosity was keener still. 'Such great operations of the chimistry of Nature do not occur often,' he wrote to Greville; and to Beckford: that the phenomena, according to reports, were 'wonderful'.[44] He set off three days later, down the coast in a Maltese *speronara*. The artist Thomas Jones begged to be allowed to accompany him, but Hamilton refused. On such an expedition he preferred his own company. He let Jones, who was in need of a studio, have the use of the billiard room in the Palazzo Sessa, but took with him only his own manservant Abraham Cottier, to whose particular care Catherine in her testament had commended him. He was away three weeks and in that time saw his fill of wonders and horrors, which he wrote up at once on his return, for the Royal Society. His 'Account of the Earthquake which happened in Italy, from February to May 1783' is his best and most characteristic piece of writing.

Though the shocks of 5 February and 28 March had been felt in Naples their source was a long way south. Hamilton, coasting along, saw the first effects at Cedrao and St Lucido – fearful inhabitants had left their homes and were living in barracks. These were, he says, at their best, 'just such sort of buildings as the booths of our country fairs'; but many were 'more like our pig-styes'. A little further and he was at the frontier of devastation. Take a line across from Amantea on the west coast to Punta dell' Alice on the east, and everywhere south of it, the whole of the foot of Italy, in that zone every town and village had been hit, and many of them wholly ruined. 'Having little time, and much to see', Hamilton pushed on to Pizzo and landed there on the evening of 6 May. At Pizzo not many had died in the earthquakes, but their temporary housing was poor and unhealthily situated, and they were dying now, in the first of the epidemics. Hamilton slept on his boat, and was woken by the smart shock of another tremor through the still unstable shore.

Next day he sent his sailors on ahead, to wait for him at Reggio, and with Cottier went inland on horseback. He wanted to test with his own eyes the numerous barely credible stories that had reached him in Naples from 'the center of the mischief'. The way to that centre lay through an earthly paradise, 'a perfect garden of olive-trees, mulberry-trees, fruit-trees, and vines; and under these trees the richest crops of corn or lupins, beans or other vegetables'. He had come to survey the violence of Nature and the resultant human misery, but was continually diverted by scenes of surpassing beauty and fertility. This side-by-side of horror and paradise is a leitmotiv of his account. Doubtless the reality was so; but such contiguities appealed to him, he had an eye for them. 'The town of Monteleone, anciently Vibo Valentia, is beautifully situated on a hill, overlooking the sea and the rich plains above mentioned, bounded by the Apennines, and crowned by Aspramonte, the highest of them all, interspersed with towns and villages, which, alas! are no more than heaps of ruins.' He and Cottier had four days then, visiting 'every curious spot' between Monteleone and Reggio. He collected facts, many of them wonderful, from eye-witnesses, corroborating what he could with observations of his own:

> All agreed here that every shock of the earthquake seemed to come with a rumbling noise from the westward, beginning usually with the horizontal motion, and ending with the vorticose, which is the motion that has ruined most of the buildings ... I found it a general observation also, that before a shock ... the clouds seemed to be fixed and motionless; and that immediately after a heavy shower of rain, a shock quickly followed. I spoke with many ... who were thrown down by the violence of some of the shocks; and several peasants in the country told me, that the motion of the earth was so violent, that the heads of the largest trees almost touched the ground from side to side; that during a shock, oxen and horses extended their legs wide asunder not to be thrown down.

Altogether animals and birds do better than humans in earthquakes. They feel the approach of the shocks long before we do. 'Geese, above all, seem to be the soonest and most alarmed ... if in the water, they quit it immediately.' Buried alive, they can wait longer to be rescued. 'A hen, belonging to the British vice-consul at Messina, that had been closely shut up under the ruins of his house, was taken out the twenty-second day, and is now recovered.' Elsewhere mules and dogs did just as well. And 'at Soriano two fattened hogs, that had remained buried under a heap of ruins, were taken out alive the forty-second day; they were lean and weak, but soon recovered'.

There were forty thousand human dead, but it is natural, under such a mortal weight, to be particularly interested in the miraculous survivors. A man at Palmi, buried by one shock, after a second, which followed immediately, found himself sitting astride a beam high in the air. A girl was buried at Oppido with a baby in her arms. The baby died on the fourth day, but the girl came out, still clutching it, having counted daybreak, through a small opening, eleven times. The nuns died in their cells at Polistrene – all but one, and she was as old as the century. A woman four months pregnant went out to sea on the tidal wave at Scilla. She floated for nine hours, but had despaired and was trying to drown herself when a boat came by. She lived, and the child in her. The Prince of Scilla, and more than two thousand of his subjects, were drowned or battered to death by that same tidal wave.

Half the town of Terra Nuova rode away. Two hundred houses and their inhabitants rode for half a mile on the shifting land, that ditched in a ravine. There were some survivors. Hamilton wrote:

> I spoke to one myself who had taken this extraordinary journey in his house, with his wife and a maid-servant: neither he nor his maid-servant were hurt; but he told me, his wife had been a little hurt, but was now nearly recovered.

Her hurts were these: both legs and one arm broken and her skull so fractured that the brain was visible. 'It appears to me,' Hamilton wrote, 'that the Calabresi have more firmness than the Neapolitans; and really seem to bear their excessive present misfortune with a true philosophic patience.' The shifts and journeys of cultivated land were very remarkable:

> The whole town of Mollochi di Sotto ... was ... detached into the ravine, and a vineyard of many acres near it lies in the bottom ... in a perfect order, but in an inclined situation: there is a footpath through this vineyard...

Footpaths ending nowhere, water wheels raised up many feet above their water; cracks in the earth out of which came fire or the sea, and into which men and their animals vanished. Everybody spoke of a continuous and pitiful groaning underground. New lakes; the disappearance of rivers; their reappearances elsewhere, ashen in complexion or yellowish and stinking of the subterranean regions through which they had been forced to pass. Salt fish on dry land; trees neatly upside down. A poor man on a hill outside Casal Nuovo looked for his native village on the plain. It had gone. What he saw in its place was a thick white cloud of slowly mushrooming silent dust. And a ploughman near Oppido was transported with his oxen and his field across a ravine, unhurt. Having often seen the dead in their characteristic attitudes at Pompeii, Hamilton pursued the subject in Calabria:

> It had been remarked at Rosarno, and the same remark has been constantly repeated to me in every ruined town that I have visited,

that the male dead were generally found under the ruins in the attitude of struggling against the danger; but that the female attitude was usually with hands clasped over their heads, as giving themselves up to despair, unless they had children near them; in which case they were always found clasping the children in their arms, or in some attitude which indicated their anxious care to protect them.

After four days, passing through 'such misery as cannot be described', 'through rich corn-fields and lawns, beautifully bounded with woods and scattered trees, like our finest parks', he arrived in the environs of Reggio. There he met a gentleman called Don Agamemnon, owner of a garden ('of no great extent') whose crop every year was '170,000 lemons, 200,000 oranges ... and bergamots enough to produce 220 quarts of the essence from their rinds'. Hamilton rejoined his boat and, from the water, saw the whole lovely arc of the port of Messina by moonlight half in ruins. Messina was the limit. He began his return from there on 17 May.

The object of Hamilton's journey was not, he said, 'to visit ruins, but the greater phenomena produced by the earthquakes'. There were five more shocks while he was in the zone. He studied the phenomena closely, explaining what he could. This is his overview of the reach of destruction:

If on a map of Italy, and with your compass on the scale of Italian miles, you were to measure off 22, and then fixing your central point in the city of Oppido (which appeared to me to be the spot on which the earthquake had exerted its greatest force) form a circle (the radii of which will be, as I just said, 22 miles) you will then include all the towns, villages, that have been utterly ruined, and the spots where the greatest mortality has happened, and where there have been the most visible alterations on the face of the earth. Then extend your compass on the same scale to 72 miles, preserving the same center, and form another circle, you will include the whole of the country that has any mark of having been affected by the earthquake. I plainly observed a gradation in the damage done to the buildings, as also in the degree of mortality, in proportion as the countries were more or less distant from this supposed center of the evil.

He thought the cause was a deep-seated volcano, either at the bottom of the sea between Stromboli and Calabria or actually under the plain near Oppido. Some months later he learned from local fishermen that the waters in the Lipari archipelago were shallower since the earthquakes. The seabed had been lifted, which confirmed him in his first hypothesis. Modern vulcanologists would probably agree with him. Through the undersea cracks across its surface our planet's destructive and creative energy is perpetually forcing up. 'Nature is ever active,' Hamilton wrote, 'but her actions are, in general, carried on so very slowly, as scarcely to be perceived by mortal eye, or recorded in the very short space of what we call history, let it be ever so ancient.' In his three weeks in Calabria he saw the effects of one of her accelerations.[45]

1783 was a particularly good year for anyone interested in the workings of the laboratory of Nature. Though reports in those days came in slowly, students of natural history could in the end piece them together. In March 1783 a sizeable new island rose out of the sea off the coast of Iceland, and this was 'generally believed to be an effect of the late unhappy Earthquake at Messina'.[46] There was a closer coincidence still in the summer of that same year, when Iceland's Laki fissure opened, letting out lava that covered 218 square miles. More than half the livestock and a fifth of the human population (9500 people) were lost in the eruption and the ensuing famine. A blue haze lay over Iceland and northern Europe for many months and the winter was exceptionally severe, which Benjamin Franklin suggested was caused by the ash and gases of the eruption blocking the sun's rays.[47]

Hamilton was back in Naples on 23 May. Perhaps he wrote up his account there and then. That at least is the date he gives to it. Grantham had written in the meantime, and he was free to leave. He did so on the 27th. He must have sent his letter on the earthquakes ahead of him by the postal service, since it was read at the Royal Society's meeting on 3 July, about a month before his own arrival in London. By ship he had sent some particular treasures: the Barberini Vase, which he needed to sell, and the wax phallic ex-votos from Isernia, which he intended donating to the British Museum. With him he had Catherine's letters, to show to his niece Mary. He travelled slowly. In Rome he visited the galleries of the Villa Borghese, the Vatican and the new Rotunda. Between Rome and Florence he was attentive to evidence of old volcanic activity along the way. He had four or five days in Florence, did the galleries there and was presented to the Grand Duke and the Grand Duchess. He left on 12 June. His further route, jotted down on the blotting sheet in the notebook he carried with him, was Modena, Mantua, Trento, Bolzano, Innsbruck.[48] Beyond that he headed for Dresden. He was in London society again by the middle of August, a widower whose particular passions were as keen in him as ever.

Chapter 8

THE WIDOWER ON LEAVE, AUGUST 1783–NOVEMBER 1784

Hamilton's third period of leave in England, his first without Catherine, is pretty well documented, largely by his niece Mary whom he often visited and accompanied. He made one long journey, in the summer of 1784, to Pembroke and Scotland, but otherwise he was in and around London, in familiar circles. He does not seem to have gone to Fonthill to see Beckford, despite having declared that he wished to spend the winter with him.

Arriving in London, Hamilton put up at Nerot's Hotel on King Street in Mayfair. He was at St James's on 13 August, to report to the King and receive his condolences on the death of Catherine. Thereafter his friends began to see him. He was at Park Place in September, looking much older, according to Walpole who saw him there on the 10th. He talked about the earthquakes whose effects he had just come from witnessing in Calabria. Altogether his appearance must have been rather exotic. He was the 'Professor of Earthquakes', 'le Pline moderne'; and having last time said of him that Vesuvius had 'burned him to a cinder', Walpole now compared his complexion to 'the patina of a bronze'.[1] So his passions marked him. And he was further marked, and made interesting, by his bereavement.

In Mary Hamilton, the daughter of his dead brother Charles, Hamilton had a sympathetic associate in his grief. She had moved to London with her mother, that other Catherine Hamilton with whom Catherine, *née* Barlow, had kept up warm relations. Uncle and aunt equally had always been fond of Mary, 'How does my little friend Miss Hamilton do? I beg my love to her.' So Catherine had ended a letter in 1768, when Mary was twelve. In the summer of 1783 then, returning alone, Hamilton sought her company, as his niece and as a living connection with his dead wife. Childless himself, he drew

125

her to him, just as he did his nephew Charles. The two, very different in themselves, stand either side of him, like surrogate daughter and son.

Mary was also, of course, an attractive young woman whom Hamilton enjoyed being with. In the new year especially they were very often together, at the Stormonts' in Portland Place, for example – the young Lady Stormont having turned out a model wife and mother after all; at the Prince of Wales's ball; and at a dinner with Mrs Garrick who showed them mementoes of Shakespeare from the collection of her late husband, the famous actor. Other occasions were musical. On 15 March 1784, at the very elderly Mrs Delaney's, there was a concert of Handel songs which Hamilton had got set in Italy for performance as trios; he himself that evening took the second violin part. He loved Handel, in Naples he promoted his work, and he will surely have attended the performance of *Messiah* in St Paul's on 5 June.[2]

During the winter of 1783–4 Hamilton went to meetings of the Royal Society, but wrote to Banks later that he looked back on them 'with horror'.[3] Perhaps it was the incongruity of himself and his dangerous fieldwork in that context? He had dealings with 'the old dons' of the British Museum too. He was now a Trustee, and in that capacity attended at least twice, in September and December. Not until June of the following year, just as he was leaving for Pembroke, did he hand over to them the phallic ex-votos from Isernia. Perhaps before that they were being inspected by the Dilettanti, whose meetings Hamilton also attended once or twice and who, on 22 May, resolved to publish his account of the worship of Priapus, with illustrations.

Wax effigies Hamilton could afford to give away, but not the Portland Vase. Returning home, this time as in 1771, he brought with him, so he hoped, a means of reducing his chronic debts. The Vase was one of the most beautiful and famous antiquities to pass through his hands. Dating from the first century AD, found in a sarcophagus a few miles outside the old city wall of Rome, it was first recorded in modern times by the Provençal scholar Peiresc in the winter of 1600–1. Thereafter its fame never lessened. For a hundred and fifty years it belonged to the powerful Barberini family (so that it was known as the Barberini Vase), and from them, around

1780, when they needed money, it went to the dealer James Byres. When he offered it to Hamilton, perhaps in the summer of 1782, Hamilton, hard up as ever, agreed at once, for the sum of £1000. He took the vase, but still owed the money, on interest of 5 per cent. About 10 inches high the vase is made of a very beautiful deep blue murrhine glass – of the sort of glass that Hamilton had encouraged the British manufacturer Matthew Boulton to try his hand at ten years before. In the event it was Wedgwood who benefited, from close study and imitation not just of pieces of such glass (which was all Hamilton had been able to send to Boulton) but from an entire vase in it, on which had been worked, in lovely white cameo, scenes from the myth of Peleus and Thetis. Hamilton needed to sell. Quite candidly he set out his position to Mary[4] – debts, including the one to Byres, of £4000 – and employed her as his agent in his dealings with the chosen purchaser, the Duchess of Portland, 'a simple woman', according to Horace Walpole, 'but perfectly sober, and interested only in *empty* vases'.[5] She was almost as old as Mrs Delaney. Hamilton tried to get her to take his 'Correggio' too, still unsold at Charles Greville's; but she would not, he wanted £3000. (After her, through Grand Duke Paul, he tried Catherine the Great, also unsuccessfully.) But the Duchess of Portland took the vase, and one or two smaller antiquities besides. The deal, thanks largely to Mary, was concluded in the new year. Mary noted on 5 February: 'My Uncle and ye Dss settled about the Vase ... *entirely*.'[6] But it remained in Hamilton's ownership for a further six months while his artist, Giovanni Battista Cipriani, copied it. On the day of the transaction John Flaxman wrote to Wedgwood, urging him to come to London to see the vase, as he, Flaxman, just had: 'It is the finest production of Art that has been brought to England and seems to be the very apex of perfection to which you are endeavouring to bring your bisque & jasper.'[7] The Duchess herself did not enjoy her purchase for very long. She died on 17 July 1785, the vase went to auction, and her own son bought it. He lent it at once to Josiah Wedgwood, who began the difficult business of reproducing it commercially. The 4th Duke of Portland deposited the vase in the British Museum, for safekeeping, in 1810. On 7 February 1845 it was smashed into pieces by a drunk and insane young man called William Lloyd. The Museum bought it a century later and twice since then it has been taken apart and reconstructed, by experts.

Disposing of an ancient piece of virtu Hamilton was at the same time, though perhaps he did not know it, beginning the acquisition of 'a modern piece'. The phrase is Greville's,[8] and says a lot about him. Very soon after his arrival in London, in August 1783, Hamilton met Greville's young mistress, Emily (later Emma) Hart, and liked her enough to commission a portrait of her by Reynolds, as a Bacchante, despite his finances. She seems to have liked him well enough also, calling him 'Uncle Pliny', sitting on his lap, and in her letters to Greville sending him love and kisses. Her heart, no doubt about it, belonged to the nephew, her protector, but the sunburned, exotic and widowed uncle brightened her life during his months on leave. He was attentive to her, told her she could rely on him should anything happen to Greville, and generally behaved in such a way that later Greville wrote: 'I know you thought me jealous of your attention to her ...' and: 'I concluded that your regard to me had been the only reason for your not making present offers.'[9] But by then Greville was trying to get rid of her and was perhaps reading or pretending to read Hamilton's behaviour in ways that might advance his own purpose. At the very least, Hamilton admitted: 'When I was in England ... her exquisite beauty had frequently its effects on me.'[10]

By December 1783, probably dissatisfied with the job Reynolds was doing, Hamilton sent Emma to Romney, already her painter and to whom he was sitting himself, and asked *him* to do her as a Bacchante, to improve on Reynolds's. In fact the two Bacchantes proceeded together. On 12 April 1784, after 'a *Bas-Bleu* party' (the Burneys, Mrs Garrick, Horace Walpole, Reynolds and others) Mary Hamilton noted in her diary:

> Miss Palmer told me that my Uncle William had been often at Sr J. Reynolds lately; that he escorted my Cousin Chs Greville's Mistress, in a *Hackney Coach*, & that her Uncle (Sir Joshua) was painting this Woman's picture for him to take to Naples. I shall make use of this intelligence to have some entertainment in *plaguing Sir William*...[11]

In June 1784 Emma and her mother were packed off first to

Hawarden, where they retrieved 'little Emma', now two years old, out of the care of her grandmother, and then to a bathing establishment, Parkgate, on the Wirral, where Emma took sea baths and drank sea water to treat the rashes she was suffering from. During that time Emma wrote lovingly to Greville, with kind remembrances to Hamilton, and became fond of her own child. She would have liked to have her at home in London, but Greville, already with Emma's mother on his hands, wanted no such thing, and towards the end of the year the two Emmas were separated and the little one given into the care of a couple in Manchester.

Hamilton was beginning his preparations to return to Naples. He sent all his heavy luggage aboard a ship waiting in London docks, that would leave at the end of June. That done, he and Greville took the road to Pembroke, to view the estates together. This visit was important in that it aroused in both of them, but chiefly in Greville, the desire to turn the land, particularly the area in and around Milford Haven, to much better financial account. After Hamilton's return to Naples, Greville became the agent and overseer of his Pembroke estates, and would be forever pushing him to invest more money in their development.

From the family house in Pembroke Hamilton rescued a few items that had belonged to Catherine's mother: a dinner service, for example, and his own portrait, done by Reynolds in 1762. Then he and Greville headed north, a long way north, into Scotland, to visit the clan up there. They seem also to have intended to visit Staffa, to see the basalt formations in Fingal's Cave that Sir Joseph Banks had discovered on his voyage to Iceland in 1772; but something prevented them and they turned back after Loch Awe.

Emma was in London again by 10 August, Hamilton and Greville soon after that. Hamilton had four weeks before his departure. In that time he saw a good deal of Mary. She was preparing to marry a Mr Dickenson, a respectable gentleman from Derbyshire, and marriage in general and her own and other people's marriages in particular were more than once a subject of conversation between her and her uncle. Indeed, even before his return she and the second Lady Stormont had discussed Catherine's devotion to Hamilton: 'Her passion for him, for it could be call'd by no other name, was as lively to the last moment of her life as when she first knew him – she had no object

in life but him & only regretted dying because she left him behind.'
Then on the way to dinner at Mrs Garrick's, which was shortly
before Hamilton left for Naples, he related to Mary how grief-
stricken Lord Stormont had been (sixteen years ago) over the loss
of his first wife: how when he came to Naples (and was diverted
there from his melancholy by Hamilton) 'he had her *Heart in a Gold
Vase* wch *accompanied* him ... *The Heart* is now deposited at Scone in
Scotland ...' And coming away together, with 'no other light than
that of ye Stars', he and Mary had this conversation, as she records
it:

> We talk'd of people's marrying merely for ye sake of a rank or
> an eligible establishment without paying any regard to principles,
> dispositions, temper, &c. &c. I ask'd my Uncle wht he would have
> thought of me had I married Mr. S: Mr. B: or Mr. H: 'Why,' says
> he, 'I should not have so good opinion of you as I have at present' &
> though many sensible & worthy people wd act well under ye above
> mentioned motives for settling in life, it was in his opinion neither
> more or less than a *legal prostitution.*

Hard to say whether this decided opinion was to be applied to or
whether it disregarded his nephew Charles, then busily seeking for
just such a settlement. Hamilton concluded with some advice to
Mary 'wth respect to *first setting* out as a Married Woman', which she
took very well, having already in her own mind 'made a resolution
to do ye very things he pointed out'.[12]

As parting gifts Hamilton gave Mary the portrait of himself by
Reynolds which had belonged to Catherine's mother, and a book she
had made of extracts from her mother's letters. He had already given
Mary an antique ring of Catherine's and a bracelet of his own hair
which Catherine had worn from the moment they were married.
Others among her papers, which he had also intended to give to
Mary, when he came to look over them, he could not find it in his
heart to part with them.

At Windsor the King and Queen, with a nosiness they must have
thought their royal prerogative, asked him outright what his intentions
were. Mary is the recorder of this encounter; she had it from Lord
Stormont.

The Queen asked Sir William whether he went *alone* to Naples & at last fairly told him that ye King had bid her *fish out* whether he was going to marry. Sir Wm said he should be careful whom he chose. The Queen replied: 'I believe you have a bad opinion of our sex.' He assured her that was by no means the case but that he had been so happy for 22 years with the late Lady Hamilton that he should be fearful not to meet again with the same fate.

Then came the King: 'Well, & who shall you make your Heir? I suppose your nephew Mr Greville.' Since Greville was standing next to Hamilton at the time, this was less than tactful. Hamilton, however, was a professional diplomat. 'He ... answered this *improper* question very *properly* by saying that he should certainly keep that secret to himself, that no one had any claim upon him as it was not a paternal inheritance but the gift of his wife.'[13] All in all Hamilton and marriage was a topic much aired during his third period of leave.

Another encounter, centring on related matters and recorded from this late summer of 1784, shows Hamilton in a different light. The recorder, it must be said, is not the most trustworthy. He is Major-General George Cockburn, who had come out to Naples and met Hamilton there shortly after the Peace in February 1783. He met him next, so he claims, outside an inn at Abergavenny, in June 1784, when Hamilton, with Greville, was heading for Pembroke; and lastly he reports a dinner party shortly before Hamilton left for Naples, so in August or early September of that same year. Though he does not claim to have been one of the 'small party of gentlemen', a friend of his was and he had the story from him. This is what Cockburn has to say:

Sir William had been too long an Inhabitant of Naples not to have imbibed some of its immorality, and it was notorious, that after his Lady's death, tho' then a middle aged man, he gave himself up to more than a little of Debauchery, but as he well knew the danger of it, he determined to obtain some Englishwoman as a Mistress, and take her out to Naples and he mentioned this at the dinner.

Greville was at the party:

And as he heard the conversation, and knew his Uncle's wishes, he called on him next evening, and candidly told him, that he knew a Lady that would suit him, and who was very beautiful, not too young for an elderly man, and he was sure he would like her ... Neapolitan climate and manners made Sir Wm perfectly easy with his Nephew and he at once expressed his thanks, and acceded to the proposal. The good natured world however went a little further as to the negociation, and it was at the time believed that Greville ... made his Uncle come down with 100 guineas as the Fee for his negociation.[14]

The latter part can't be right – Hamilton had already known Emma a year by then and it was not until the spring of 1785 that Greville made his proposal and little by little Hamilton accepted it, and without, so far as is known, having to pay a fee; but the first part of the account *might* be roughly right. I quote the whole thing because it illustrates pretty well what gossip at least was sure of; and the detail of the fee, if not literally true, is certainly in keeping with Greville's renowned meanness.

Hamilton was at the King's levée on 1 September and left feeling that he enjoyed His Majesty's '*old* accustomed confidence'.[15] He saw his Secretary of State on the 10th; Mary begged him not to call again – taking 'personal leave' of him was, she said, more than she could bear; and he set off for Naples on the 11th. He took the route through France. He is recorded in Dijon, and then, on 14 October, in Turin. There, and again in Rome, he met Lady Louisa Clarges, aged twenty-four and very recently widowed. She was a harpist. He saw her in the company of Lady Catherine Hampden, whom he had taken to view the lava flow in December 1770 and professed himself much in love with then. Their party was travelling slowly to Naples, where Hamilton himself arrived, to resume his duties, at the beginning of November, after the usual year and a half away. His third leave in England had made a caesura in his life. Perhaps he did not know it yet, or perhaps the sadness of a homecoming to a household without a wife made him realize that something must be done.

Chapter 9

THE TRANSACTION OF EMMA,
1 7 8 4 – 6

The next twelve months or so of Hamilton's life were shaped by dealings with and at times under pressure from his nephew Charles Greville. Though each man had different needs, it seemed, especially to Greville, that by following the usual eighteenth-century doctrine of self-interest they could help themselves and one another in equal measure. The two areas of interest, separate for Hamilton but both together part of a larger problem for Greville, were Emma Hart and the Pembroke estates. Greville needed, or at least wanted, much more money than he had. He spent a good deal on his hobbies – virtu and mineralogy – and never did well enough in any career to bring him the sufficiency he felt he deserved. Visiting the estates with Hamilton in the summer of 1784 he became keen to develop them in an ambitious way: for the public good, for his uncle's and, he might hope, ultimately for his own. Hamilton went along with the idea, and left Greville, always keener than he was himself, as his chief agent and overseer in the business. But those schemes, if they ever paid off, would be a long time about it; Greville would get rich quicker by marrying an heiress, and in that campaign he must make two preliminary moves. First he must be able to appear not entirely penniless to any prospective mother- and father-in-law; and second he must clear his household of Emma and her mother. Hamilton could assist him on both counts, on the first doing himself no harm and on the second, in Greville's opinion, doing himself some good.

Uncle and nephew write very candidly to one another, and Greville in particular makes a virtue of it, so that reading his letters we can hardly imagine how anyone could have loved him. And yet both Hamilton and Emma did. Fondness for his nephew, sympathy with him as a fellow younger son, was certainly one element in Hamilton's compliance with his schemes; but another, in the matter of taking on Emma, was his own disconsolate situation in Naples after his return.

He went hunting with the King, and had the entertainment of a long letter from Greville (written on Christmas Day) on the subject of William Beckford's disgrace. Beckford had been seen in the act with his beloved William Courtenay by the boy's tutor, the Reverend Moore, who, hearing 'a creeking & bustle, which raised his curiosity', had peered through the keyhole early in the morning.[1] Beckford would soon be leaving for the continent. Was Hamilton entertained? If he thought about Catherine's long struggle over Beckford's soul he must surely have had mixed feelings.

Apart from hunting (with a new rifle given him by his friend Sir Joseph Banks) he engaged in more of what Pascal (and Catherine) would have called *divertissement*. In January 1785 Queen Maria Carolina said she would like an English garden at Caserta, and asked Hamilton if he would see to it. He wrote to Banks, to get somebody suitable sent out from England, to manage the work; and by May had himself become involved. Emma, much later, would refer to the garden at Caserta as 'Sir William's favourite child'; but Hamilton himself at the outset commented on it thus to Banks: 'I promise myself great pleasure in this new occupation. As one passion begins to fail it is necessary to form another, for the whole art of going thru' life tollerably in my opinion is to keep oneself eager about any thing – the moment one is indifferent on s'ennuye.'[2] Hard to see quite which passion was failing. He had not bought vases for a while, but only because there were none (there soon would be again); young women continued to keep him 'eager'; and in that same letter, 3 May 1785, he announced his intention of taking a tour into the Abruzzi, while the King and Queen of Naples were away in Florence, and duly did so between the 18th and the 31st of the month. His notes survive, and since he only published a part of them (in the *Philosophical Transactions*) they are valuable for showing us what he was like on his own at a critical stage of his life. And what was he like? The answer is: much the same, much as he always was, in letters, in recorded conversations. In all that handy notebook, which he used on and off between January 1783 and March 1791, there is no introspection, no private trouble or grief, nothing more personal than this statement in verse of his life-long and well-known stoical philosophy:

> Enjoy the present nor with anxious care
> Of what may spring from blind Misfortune's womb
> Appal the latest hour that life has given
> Serene & Master of yourself prepare
> For all events & leave the rest to Heaven[3]

The journey itself, which he took either quite alone or more likely with his manservant Abraham Cottier, was from Naples via Monte Cassino as far as Lake Celano, where he explored the remains of the Emperor Claudius's emissarium, and to the site of Ancient Alba. Alba and Lake Celano were quite often visited from Rome, but Hamilton's route there from Naples, climbing the river Liris, was not at all a beaten track. His notes show him at his most characteristic. He was amused: by the Abruzzesi – he had one for a guide – who 'drink like animals & can piss walking fast'; he was keenly interested: by the antiquities, by paintings at Arpino and at the abbey of Monte Cassino, by 'stories of Wolves bears & robberies'; and he delighted in a scenery 'more magnificent far than the lakes of Cumberland & Westmorland' (which he had seen the year before on his way to Scotland with Greville). He was hospitably accommodated along the way, and managed to spend a good deal of time indulging another of his passions: fishing. The Liris was an excellent trout stream, and Monday the 23rd he 'passed the whole day on the Lake Celano fishing & admiring the views', the catch there being tench, barbel and dace.

Two other notes are especially interesting, though the first only confirms what we knew already: that Hamilton liked beautiful young women. Or perhaps it would be fairer to say that he liked them best, but the human face and physiognomy altogether. On Tuesday 24th he remarked:

> Don Ladislao Matheis's mother the finest old woman I ever saw 95 yrs old D. Vincenzo Milicuccios's 2 daughters Pensioners in the Convent fine girls 15 & 17 yrs. old the eldest – such a melting eye – her mouth rather wide & very little hair upon her eye brows

Two days later he visited the Trappist monastery at Casa Mari and there watched what he called 'a good Pantomime or Tableau'. This was surely one inspiration – there were others – in his training Emma Hart only a year later to stand 'in attitudes' at the Palazzo Sessa in a style and a context anything but monastic.[4]

In letters before Hamilton's tour in the Abruzzi, Greville had been advancing ever more frankly his own financial needs and the question of what to do with Emma. First in January he got Hamilton to stand surety for a loan (to clear one of his debts) and began to muse on what his difficulties would be if necessity obliged him to marry:

> If I was independent I should think so little of any other connexion that I never would marry. I have not an idea of it at present, but if any opportunity offer'd I should be much harassed, not know to manage, or how to fix Emma to her satisfaction.[5]

And he asked Hamilton's advice, perhaps hoping he would bid for Emma immediately. Hamilton did no such thing. Instead, alarmingly for Greville, he admitted that he had said something to Lady Clarges, then in Naples, that she at least had interpreted as a proposal of marriage:

> I like her much in one of my moments of admiration I sayd to her that I wished she would take possession of my empty appartment she gravely answered that she was much flattered but had resolved never to Marry again, the Devil fetch me if I meant to propose tho I own I often have thought she would suit me well – Her musical talents you may imagine weigh greatly with me & she is gentle –[6]

He told his niece Mary that though he had not meant it as a proposal and though he was 'not the least in love' he would very likely have married Lady Clarges had she agreed. 'She seemed,' he said, 'to have many domestick qualities, & her taste for Musick was so perfect, & my present Situation so desolate.'[7] Even before he received Hamilton's letter Greville was worried by news coming back from Naples (with his own brother-in-law Sir Harry Harpur) that Hamilton was behaving there like an eligible widower. He feared for his inheritance if Hamilton remarried and had a child. He wrote on 10 March, urging him to be careful: 'They say here that you are in love. I know you love variety, & are a general flirt, & of the 60 English, what with widows & young married ladies, an amateur may be caught.'

Greville did not want his uncle caught. He began trying to steer him into thinking that a mistress would be a better arrangement than a wife, and in that capacity why not Emma, since he, Greville, needed to be rid of her? 'If you did not chuse a wife, I wish the tea-maker of Edgware Row was yours.' They might, he suggested, split the upkeep of her fifty-fifty. He reverted to Hamilton's demonstrations of affection towards her during his leave in London; praised her conduct since; and concluded:

Judge then, as you know my satisfaction on looking at a modern piece of virtu if I do not think you a second self, in thinking that by placing her within your reach I render a necessity, which would otherwise be heartbreaking, tolerable & even comforting.

Hamilton's reply to this letter has not survived, but Greville's next, 5 May, gives some idea of what he said: that he would like Emma to do the honours of his house, which was rather more than Greville had expected; certainly it was more than he allowed her to do for him; and perhaps he didn't like the idea of her passing to his uncle in so prominent a way. He wrote on 5 May, with directions as to how Emma could best be managed. He, Greville, had educated her not to expect too much. Hamilton should install her in one of his villas, in a household quite distinct from his own; by anything closer and more liberal she would only be spoiled. Still, he urged very strongly that Hamilton should take her. She already regarded him as a protector and a friend. Then: 'At your age a clean & comfortable woman is not superfluous, but I should rather purchase it than acquire it, unless in every respect a proper party offer'd.' Would Lady Clarges have qualified as such a party? Greville doubted it. And 'I know the sentiments of all your friends, & my delicacy prevented my writing on that subject, but I can assure you they feel very happy at the departure of Lady C.' And he repeated, this time citing Hamilton's brother, the Archdeacon Frederick, as another moral authority, that the wisest thing Hamilton could do 'would be to buy Love ready made'. Greville concluded his long letter with the frank request to have it in writing that Hamilton did indeed intend to make him his heir. He was after a wife worth £30,000, and such a statement would assist him in his bid. Then in case it seemed as though the offer of Emma was the *quid pro quo* for this necessary certificate he assured Hamilton that it wasn't.[8] And despite all the gossip to the contrary, this was probably the truth and Greville is best understood as asking two favours of his uncle: that he relieve him of the financial burden and hindrance to marriage represented by Emma, and that he further his chances in the market place by categorically declaring him his heir.

This was the letter waiting for Hamilton when he got back from the Abruzzi on 31 May 1785. He replied next day, first, because he was so full of it, hurrying out a summary of his journey; but then settling down to deal with the serious matters Greville had put to him. He assured Greville that, according to the terms of his will, drawn up when he was last in London, it was indeed his intention to leave the Pembroke estate to him. Were he only to think of himself, he would sell it and live on the annuity it would buy him, but

> Being a younger Brother myself & having made my own fortune and being at liberty to dispose of it as I please at my death when I can no longer enjoy it, I shall have a satisfaction in its going to a younger Brother whom I love and esteem more than any man on Earth...

And he enclosed a letter to that effect, for Greville to use in his bargaining for an heiress. But about taking on Emma he was now more cautious, both on his own account and on hers:

> Was I in England & you was to bring your present plan to bear & she wou'd consent to put herself under my protection, I wou'd take her most readily for I realy love her & think better of her than of any one in her situation but my dear Charles, there is a great difference between her being with you or me for she really loves you when she coud only esteem and suffer me – I see so many difficulties in her coming here ... that I can never advise it – Tho' a great City, Naples has every defect of a Province & nothing you do is a Secret It would be fine funn for the young English Travellers to endeavour to cuckold the old Gentleman Ins. Ambasciatore, and whether they succeeded or not woud surely give me uneasiness.

He offered to make her an allowance of £50 a year if Greville married and she had to retire to the country, and concluded: 'I do assure you I shoud like better to live with you both here & see you happy than to have her all to myself for I am sensible that I am not a match for so much youth & beauty.'[9] In a PS he asks after the portrait of her, as a bacchante, done by Romney. It was on its way to him, and duly arrived in Naples in November.

Hamilton, unlike Greville, does show some concern for the feelings of the real young woman in question. Greville, replying, felt quite competent to speak for her, saying, again, that Hamilton should settle her in one of his villas 'or rather take a small retired house on the Hill at Naples, very small; she will not want to go about ... As to Englishmen, there is nothing to fear; left to herself she would conform to your ideas ...' And again he expounded on her character and how best to manage her, and moved on then, assuming all Hamilton's doubts were now settled, to the practicalities of her removal:

> If you could form a plan by which you could have a trial, & could invite her & tell her that I ought not to leave England, & that I cannot afford to go on, & state it as a kindness to me if she would accept your invitation, she would go with pleasure.[10]

No correspondence between Hamilton and Greville survives from that summer. Doubtless there was a lull in the negotiations. In the meantime Hamilton did not invite Emma as Greville had suggested. She was packed off with her mother for six weeks, sea-bathing on the Cheshire coast. Greville's bid to marry the elder daughter of Lord Middleton, for twenty not thirty thousand pounds, failed despite the statement he had elicited from Hamilton; and he went on tour in Wales and Cornwall, interested in the commercial possibilities of clay and tin. Hamilton for his part went exploring the volcanic islands of Ponza and Ventotene in the Gulf of Naples. He was away for a week, staying first a couple of days on Ischia. Writing to Banks on 30 August, he commented: 'I thought I had done with this Subject here but rather than leave a single volcanic spot in this neighbourhood undescribed I will risk another letter to you on the Subject of my last Tour ...'[11] On that tour, travelling with a painter to depict the

islands in all their strange beauty and making his own notes in the
Abruzzi notebook on things and people of interest, he seems
contented and quite self-sufficient and proof against any amount of
bullying by Greville. But in that same month, in the letter already
quoted on the subject of Lady Clarges, he admitted to his niece Mary
that his situation was 'desolate', and added: 'When the Court is here
I live with their Sn Majesties, but now they are absent, I pass my
time rather dully, for what is a home without a bosom friend &
companion? My Books, pictures, musick, prospect are certainly
something, but the Soul to all is wanting.' And praising her own
wifely qualities – she had just married Mr Dickenson – he confessed:
'I believe if I had not been your Uncle I shoud have been apt to
have proposed to you myself.'[12] So not just his susceptibility to young
women but also his loneliness made it likely that when the winter
came on and Greville resumed his campaign, Hamilton would soon
capitulate.

Over the summer, while Greville was away, Emma's mother, Mrs
Cadogan, suffered a stroke, and when he returned in the midst of
this extra trouble he postponed the announcement of what he had
in mind for them. He even seems regretful at going through with it,
but was determined to none the less. He wrote to Hamilton about
the estates, about a scheme for planting a colony of whalers at
Milford. But still the crux was this: 'I have no other alternative but
to marry or remain a pauper.' One irony in the whole business is
that he never did marry nor did he live to profit for very long from
the estates that finally came to him on his uncle's death.[13]

In this critical period when Emma's future was being decided
there is only one surviving letter from Hamilton to Greville, written
at Caserta on 8 November. It makes no mention of Emma, except
to send regards. There is talk of the estates and of the work on his
new apartment with which he is unhappy and which will have to be
done again at great expense. On the same day Hamilton wrote
cheerfully to Banks about the English garden (Graefer, Banks's
recommended man, was on his way), about Paestum roses, about a
vast killing, in nets, of quails, pigeons and fern owls. He was finishing
his account of Ponza and Ventotene and watching Vesuvius, thinking
to add a note on its increased activity. Concern about what to do
with Emma seems wholly Greville's.

Early in December Greville acted, and informed Hamilton of the *fait accompli*. He told Emma that in the following year he would have to be away in Scotland for some months, induced her to agree that she would like to be in Naples for that time, and enclosed with his letter one from her (partly composed by him) prettily asking Hamilton to offer her hospitality so that under his protection she could further improve herself. The clear proposal, as she set it down there, was that she should be accommodated in Hamilton's house, in a separate appartment, for '6 or 8 months', at the end of which time Greville would come out and stay a while and fetch her home. Her response to a suggestion by Greville that she might not want to come back was, in his tortuous version of it, as follows:

> She would certainly be grateful to you; but that neither interest nor affection should ever induce her to change, unless my interest or wish required it, & that you could comfort her, altho' she made all the distinction of age, but that she had seen enough to value a real friend whenever she could find one, and that you had shown more real friendship to her than any person in the world beside myself, & therefore you was, after me, the nearest to her heart.

There is in that account, but perhaps only by Greville's wording or insinuation, a hint that she knew what might happen and that she would, if she had to, accept it.

As though fearful that Hamilton had lapsed from the idea and needed persuading all over again, Greville went on to extol the virtues – the beauty, good nature, tractability etc. – of the girl who loved him and of whom, after his fashion, he was himself fond. Among his recommendations of her this perhaps characterizes him best: 'As I consider you as my heir-aparent I must add that she is the only woman I ever slept with without having ever had any of my senses offended, & a cleanlier, sweeter bedfellow does not exist.'

He proposed the venture as, from his uncle's point of view, 'an experiment without any risque', assured him that of course she might come home if she wished and that of course he, Greville, would always provide for her if necessary and if he could. He added a note on what might be called the philosophy of their conduct – 'You know we are not accountable to the world further than not to offend against *bienséance*' (in his view they were committing no such offence) – and finished by asking that Hamilton pay for Emma and her mother on their journey (he, Greville, had already reserved their places on the coach) and that he send his man Cottier to Geneva to meet them. Hamilton replied to Emma, welcoming her, and sent £50 for expenses.[14]

Greville replied on 20 January, again passing on her words and commentating on them in such a way as to suggest that she would be amenable in the end:

> She has always said that if ever she was to part she might be weaned by degrees; she talks of the chances of our not meeting again, & that on the least neglect she will accept your offers, & that she will by her conduct merit your kindness. She must have in mind a stronger impression of the chances than she expresses, but says she would not put herself in the reach of chances with any person but yourself, and she does not say this from compliment, but from her heart; she would not be on the *pavé* if I was to be suddenly lost to her.[15]

We can't know exactly what Emma said, of course. Her reactions later were not what Hamilton, reading this letter, might reasonably have expected them to be. Greville was playing a tricky game, managing mistress and uncle, wholly honest with neither.

Emma and her mother, now happily recovered (she would outlive uncle and nephew), were packed off to Geneva on 13 March 1786. They were accompanied by the painter Gavin Hamilton, to whom Greville had introduced his 'modern piece of virtu' the previous November and whose praises ('He says he has not seen anything like her in G.B.'[16]) he had relayed to Sir William. He added more praise of his own in a last letter just before dispatching the person herself; congratulated her new protector: 'You will have comfort with the prettiest woman confessedly in London'; and repeated his old advice on how to handle her.[17]

Hamilton meanwhile was getting on with his life. He had to entertain Ernest, Duke of Cumberland, his wife and her sister, a party even more than usually demanding and tiresome. Queen Maria Carolina, having given birth in February for the seventeenth time, was ill then for a further two months, which meant that the Court was less accommodating to the Cumberlands than it might have been, and the responsibility for diverting them elsewhere and otherwise fell on Hamilton. And there were scores of other visiting English besides, some noteworthy, like Mrs Piozzi, formerly Hester Thrale, the companion of Johnson, and Cornelia Knight, who would on her second stay in Naples stick very close to the Hamilton ménage in the period of its greatest upheaval and notoriety.

Hamilton showed the Cumberlands the gardens at Caserta. His particular interest there, the proposed English Garden, was about to begin its realization with the arrival of the nurseryman and gardener from England, John Andrew Graefer. But just before him, by happy coincidence, another man with a passion for plants arrived in Naples. A letter from the Ambassador's secretary in Venice, written on 17 March, announced the departure from there for Naples of John Sibthorp, Professor of Botany at Oxford, and asked Hamilton to look after him.[18] He arrived on 15 April, three days before Graefer. The two men met – or perhaps they had already in Venice or Rome – and got on well enough to go botanizing together on the island of Ponza. On 7 May Sibthorp continued his travels, by ship to Greece (his magnificent *Flora Graeca* was the end product) and Graefer, with wife and family, settled in and with Hamilton as his overseer and dedicated ally began the long struggle against Neapolitan ignorance and prejudice to fashion an English garden in the midst of the overbearing French classicism of Caserta.

On 8 or 9 March the widowed Anne Seymour Damer came to Naples and Hamilton put her up in the Palazzo Sessa. She had stayed before, in the last year of Catherine's life. He announced her imminent arrival to Greville in a letter, of 7 March, which (surviving incompletely, it must be said) again makes no mention of Emma. Hamilton saw no reason why Mrs Damer should not be his guest at home, though he knew people would talk, and they did.

Emma and party arrived in Geneva on 27 March. They were met there by Hamilton's servant, not Cottier but Vincenzo Sabatino, and he conducted them the rest of the way. On 25 April, having heard they had reached Geneva and expecting them in Naples 'in a day or two', Hamilton wrote to Greville, less indulgently than usual. Greville was presuming too much. In borrowing money from Hamilton's bankers, Ross and Ogilvie, he had gone further than he had authority to go, and had named Hamilton as principal in the loan and himself only as joint security. Though Hamilton signed the bond Greville sent him, he clearly felt he was being put upon. His own financial situation was never such as to be able to take on somebody else's debts. And he issued to his nephew what was, coming from so tolerant a man, a reprimand: 'You will, I dare say, turn your mind seriously to the improving your fortune, either by marriage or getting again into employment.' He was, after all, clearing the ground for the former course by taking on Emma. And thinking of her and her imminent arrival Hamilton was by no means easy. He wrote:

> The prospect of possessing so delightful an object under my roof soon certainly causes in me some pleasing sensations but they are accompanied with some anxious thoughts as to the prudent management of the business; however, I will do as well as I can, and hobble in and out of this pleasant scrape as decently as I can. You may be assured that I will comfort her for the loss of you as well as I am able.

He emphasized that her stay with him would not be permanent and that the final responsibility for her lay with Greville.[19]

She arrived next day, her twenty-first birthday, overlapping with Mrs Damer; and it seems that Hamilton's 'management of the business' was at once and thereafter by no means prudent. He seems to have behaved neither as Greville advised nor as Emma expected, but to have thrown himself immediately into doting on her. The evidence is her first letter to Greville, written on 30 April with an appalled addition on 1 May. In the four days following her arrival he had done his utmost to distract her from her evident unhappiness at the separation from Greville. They had been at the theatre, at the opera, in a promenade along the Villa Reale with Sir Thomas Rumbold, and at the summer house at Posillipo. Hamilton had begun showing her off – in a white satin dress he had bought her (costing twenty-five guineas). And among his other gifts were 'several little things of Lady Hamilton's'. He could not take his eyes off her. 'To speake the truth,' she wrote, 'he is never out of my sight. He breakfasts, dines, supes, and is constantly by me, looking in my face.

He does nothing all day but look at me and sigh. I can't stir a hand, leg or foot; but he is marking [it] as graceful and fine.' He acted at once like a man in love with her, and doubtless said it too and promoted himself to her in that capacity. He soon disclosed, perhaps to win her by evidence of his kindness, that he had made Greville his heir. By all this attention, not just from him but from the company he took her into, she was certainly flattered, but this also troubled her. In her first letter she careers naïvely hither and thither in a welter of mixed feelings, but her refrain is her love for Greville and her determination that the uncle now declaring himself in love with her should never be what she calls – wittingly or unwittingly repeating the term used by Greville – his 'heir-apearant'. She writes:

> There is not a hardship upon hearth, either of poverty, hunger, cold, death, or even to walk barefooted to Scotland to see you, but what I would undergo...

> It is you that as it in your power either to make me very happy or very miserable...

> He can never be anything nearer to me than your uncle and my sincere friend. He never can be my lover.

> I can be civil, oblidging, and I do try to make myself as agreable as I can to him. But I belong to you, Greville, and to you only will I belong, and nobody shall be your heir-apearant...

These utterances, which ring true, are extracted out of the hectic account of how much, in a dizzy fashion, she was enjoying herself in Naples. She saw herself set alongside the other women this eminent man had an interest in. Like Mrs Damer, she said, she went out in a coach of her own, not his; for if she were seen in his she would be supposed to be his mistress or his wife; neither of which, she added, could she possibly become. She said outright in naïve gratification: 'He loves me now as much as ever he could Lady Bolingbroke ...' (She meant Di Beauclerk, whose first husband was a Bolingbroke.)

Still, on 30 April Hamilton's declared love and all his flattering attentions, though troubling, had not yet come down to propositions she must answer with yes or no.

That happened next day. Hamilton revealed to Emma that Greville had no intention of coming to fetch her, and he must have put to her there and then what she herself called 'the consequence' of that revelation. She says: 'I have had a conversation this morning with Sir William that has made me mad. He speaks – no, I do not know what to make of it ...' What he was asking or proposing was doubtless clear enough; harder for her to comprehend was Greville's treachery: 'But Greville, my dear Greville, wright some comfort to me.' And her PS was: 'Pray for God's sake, wright to me and come to me, for Sir W. shall never be anything to me but your freind.'[20]

Hamilton and Emma both had reason to feel duped by Greville. Emma more obviously and grievously; but Hamilton for his part, an ignominious part, had been assured that she would accept his offers at 'the least neglect'. Since the neglect was gross and manifest, no doubt he felt deceived, by Greville if not by her, when she still refused.

Hamilton was gentleman, or philosopher, or diplomat enough not to insist. Since she herself was never party to the deal what grounds did he have for insisting anyway? None. Besides, he wanted more than Greville had counselled him to want: he wanted real love and companionship in his home, and no young woman could be forced to give him that.

Naturally, rumours had got back to England that he was perhaps seeking it in a marriage with Mrs Damer. On 30 May, a month after Emma's appalled rejection of his proposition, he wrote to his niece Mary, always his best confidante. His letter opens like the one he had written to her in August of the previous year when the woman in question was Lady Clarges: first the coming to nothing of a possibility of marriage, then his loneliness.

Mrs. Damer has been here, lodged in my house & is gone home. It is not very extraordinary if after that, there shoud be some conjectures, but the fact is I neither am, or ever was, in love with her. I do believe if I had chosen the part of a dying lover, but I never coud act a part in my life, & consented to live at home in England, I might have succeeded. If she would have consented to take me as I am, & live chiefly here, I certainly wou'd have married her, for after having lived 22 years *en famille* it is most terrible to live chiefly alone.

He goes on then to admit what by the usual channels of gossip Mary would sooner or later have found out for herself:

I have a *female visiter* from England, that occupies a part of my House, but this is *a deed* without a *Name*; I shall say no more but that it is probable the visit will not be of long duration.

By 'deed without a name' – quoting the witches' answer to Macbeth's 'What is't you do?' – he means he will not tell her who his visitor is (he goes on to say that she has 'curiosity & cleverness enough to find out'); but he might better have called his situation with Emma 'a name without a deed'. Interesting also is his statement that she probably won't stay long. Does that mean he will send her packing if she continues to resist?

Hamilton goes on then to speak of the new apartment, first intended to give Catherine somewhere lighter and airier in her illnesses and now at last completed to Hamilton's satisfaction, just in time for Emma. 'The apartment I have fitted up in my House here is quite delightfull, & will be a great comfort to me in the latter part of my life, when it is to be hoped my follies will cease.' Mentioning his follies he is back, without naming her, to Emma and to a predicament perforce as virtuous as his strict niece could wish: 'Tho' appearances are not always true – with regard to my present situation, if you knew the circumstances, Even you woud not blame me, & no one knows better than you what is realy right or wrong...'[21]

For some months then, how many is a moot point, Emma, living in Hamilton's house, refused him the relationship she knew for certain, after 1 May, that he wanted. To his credit it can at least be said of him that he did not sulk. He continued the hectic generosity of the first four days, doing everything in his power to let her enjoy and profit by being in Naples. Of course, his thoughtful largesse was not disinterested and in the end it must have contributed to making her change her mind; but he could only hope, he couldn't know that it would. The experiment his nephew had got him into was not at all 'without risque'. He feared ridicule. Before Emma arrived he had feared being cuckolded. Now he feared he would look a fool if 'so delightful an object' as Emma were under his roof and known to be resisting him. He was quite soon something of a spectacle, being watched with amused interest. James Byres, his dealer in Rome, wrote on 14 June to the Bishop of Killala: 'Our friend Sir William is well. He has lately got a piece of modernity from England, which I am afraid will fatigue and exhaust him more than all the volcanoes and antiquities in the Kingdom of Naples.'[22] She might wear him out by resisting, or by giving in. And if she gave in he would be further worn out in combating the efforts of men more her age to take her off him. Emma herself, as a strategy against him and to touch Greville, constantly announced that she was not the uncle's but the nephew's property. This, with Hamilton doting very publicly on her, must have been cause for merriment at his expense.

Emma had four rooms in the Palazzo Sessa to live apart in with her mother; she had a carriage of her own to go out in as she pleased; and Hamilton conducted her on excursions all around, especially to the little casino at Posillipo. She was constantly in society with him, being shown off, being admired. And he engaged at once also in what she had ostensibly come to Naples for: her improvement. He got her tutors in singing and in Italian. All this we know because in fourteen chaotic letters, eliciting only one reply (and that unpleasant), she told it all to Greville. Her letters are extraordinary not least because of the contiguity in them of wildly discrepant and contradictory moods, attitudes and tones of voice. In that they rather resemble the performances for which she would soon become famous. Many witnesses remark on the rapidity with which she moved from one character and emotion to another.

One thread through Emma's letters is her love for the unlovable Greville and her real distress at his treatment of her. Thus: 'I love you with the truest affection ... Oh, my heart is intirely broke ... I am poor, helpless and forlorn.' But another strain is her exuberant, sometimes comically self-important and as it were accustomed enjoyment of the life Hamilton daily presented her with. Of course, when she relates her conquests – of the King, Prince Dietrichstein, Lord John Hervey and many others – she is trying to show the ungrateful Greville what he is throwing away. But naïve gratification mostly exceeds any such calculation: 'I walk in the Villa Reale every night. I have generaly two Princes, two or 3 nobles, the English minister, and the king with a crowd beyound us...'[23]

The conviction that she was adorable must have been powerfully borne in upon her by Hamilton's continuing in Naples, and now quite compulsively, what he had begun when he first saw her in England: reproducing her in art. His own pleasure in her seems to have been to a large extent visual. He feasted his eyes on her and pointed out her beauties to other amateurs. The natural extension of this was to have her painted, modelled in wax and clay and marble and bronze, or cut on snuff boxes, in precious stones, on rings, in silhouettes; and that process, as though to preserve her in the place whether she physically stayed or not, got well under way in the summer of 1786. Hamilton possessed her as a collector long before she let him as a lover. Emma Hart's sense of herself as quite extraordinarily beautiful and desirable was founded indestructibly during the first weeks of her residence in the Palazzo Sessa when Hamilton called up the queue of artists wanting to do her likeness, a queue that would last for years.

There is a third element in Emma's letters to Greville. It can be discerned as a constant undercurrent in all her appealing to him and in all her enjoyment of Naples and her anxious management of the provider of that enjoyment, Hamilton. It is her instinct for self-preservation. She had been a prostitute very early, at best (the stories vary) one of a 'nunnery' of girls under their 'abbess', Mrs Kelly of Arlington Street in London. By the age of sixteen, she had advanced into aristocratic protection but knew, first from Sir Harry Fetherstonhaugh and now, much worse, from Greville, how unsure that was. She knew she had to look out for herself, and that if she played it wrong she risked being back on the streets again. In accumulating 'lovers' during her first weeks in Naples, gratifying in itself, she was also doing what any young woman 'in her situation' was bound to do: look for protectors should she need them, and the richer, the more powerful, the better.

It is clear from the correspondence of Greville and Hamilton that, according to their lights, they always intended to negotiate between them some sort of fair deal for Emma; but she could not know that, and her healthy instinct was mistrust and calculation for survival. This can be seen very clearly in her letter to Greville of 22 July: 'I was told I was to live, you know how, with Sir William. No, I respect him, but no never. Shall he perhaps live with me for a little wile like you, and send me to England. Then what am I to do?' It was probably her mother – who knew enough of the world to know that Cadogan sounded better than her real name Duggin or Doggins – who told her how she should live with Sir William and had Emma not been hindered by her real love for Greville she might have accommodated herself sooner to the new situation. Objectively, Hamilton was a better bet than Greville. Though not rich he had more wealth than Greville did, also more power and influence; and he was besides kind, generous, amusing, easygoing, and in love with her; none of which could be said of Greville. Mrs Cadogan will have seen this sooner than Emma could; but Emma saw it soon enough.

Greville's one reply to her reams of writing came as an enclosure in a letter to Hamilton. What he said is revealed in her response:

> As to what you write to me, to oblidge Sir William, I will not answer you. For, oh! if you knew what pain I feel in reading those lines where you advise me to W— How, with cool indifference, to advise me to go to bed to him, Sir Wm!

The letter as a whole, long as ever, is a maelstrom of all the usual elements: she kisses it, the reply he finally wrote, she submits 'to what God and Greville pleases'. But then she is outraged. She, 'a girl that a King, & c., is sighing for!', a girl Prince Draydrixton (Dietrichstein) has called 'a dymond of the first watter, and the finest creature on the hearth', to be so insulted! 'I will go to London, their go into every excess of vice till I dye, a miserable broken-hearted wretch, and leave my fate as a warning to young whomen never to be two good ...' Besides all that she describes various people, excursions and *parties de plaisir*. But she concludes with words and in a tone that must have given Greville pause for thought: 'It is not to your intrest to disoblidge me, for you dont know the power I have hear. Onely I never will be his mistress. If you affront me, I will make him marry me.'[24]

A week later Hamilton took her to Sorrento, Capri and Ischia, and there, Flora Fraser thinks, Emma decided where her best interests lay, 'obliged' Sir William and began the process of making him marry her.

In fact, there is no conclusive evidence of Emma's giving in to Hamilton until her affectionately erotic notes to him in December and January 1786–7; which is why Brian Fothergill thinks she held out till late November, early December. The interest in when exactly is not just a prurient one. Quite important questions are raised concerning the characters, motives and behaviour of the people involved, and those questions will have significantly different answers, according to whether the month was August or December.

From 1 August to 24 October no letters have survived between the three parties. Hamilton mentions Emma in two letters to Banks. First on 4 July in a PS (having spoken of Graefer who was waiting for the King's permission to begin the garden): 'A beautiful plant called *Emma* has been transplanted here from England & at least has not lost any of it's beauty.' And secondly, 26 September:

My *visiter*, for you must know I have *one*, is as handsome as ever & in tollerable spirits considering all – it is a bad job to come from the Nephew to the Uncle but one must make the best of it & I try to see poor Charles out of his difficulties.

Fraser thinks that means she was by then already his mistress. Perhaps; but not certainly. 'One must make the best of it' sounds as though it refers to both of them, as though they were both still in an uncomfortable situation; and seeing 'poor Charles out of his difficulties' is an odd way of describing, even obliquely, a sexual success.'[25]

Then in his letter of 24 October Greville says two things which imply that Hamilton has told him (in a letter now lost) of Emma's capitulation. First: 'I know that you owe your present situation to your attentions, & not to any unfair advantage, & on her part there can be no plea but free choice...' And second: 'I have often told her that I never expected from a woman a power to withstand favourable opportunity & a long siege...'[26]

But from that letter and from Greville's next (some time in November) it is clear that their agreed plan now is that Emma should come back to England in the spring, but not to Greville, and that she should live on an allowance of £100 a year paid her by Hamilton. Greville writes: 'Your proposed provision exceeds your promise.' Before she came to Naples Hamilton had offered £50 a year. They thought Romney might be her trustee and manage the allowance.

Greville further suggested that there might be some young English-man conveniently leaving Naples, not 'any boy of family' but one 'from 25 to 35, & one who is his own master', who might make her an offer and be a suitable new protector. This continued scheming, very much in the vein of what had gone on before Emma ever left for Naples, is quite hard to make sense of. If by October she had indeed done what Greville had advised her to do: 'go to bed to him, Sir Wm', why was Hamilton sending her back? It almost sounds as if her worst fears had been realized, that having lived with him 'for a little wile' as she had with Greville, she was now being packed off back to England, and not to Greville either. And thus, that her estimation of her power, in the letter of 1 August, was wildly over-optimistic and her threat that she would make Hamilton marry her entirely empty. But their continued scheming makes most obvious sense if as late as October and November she was still proving obdurate but they still felt some obligation to provide for her. Otherwise, if she did as she was told in August and Hamilton was intending to send her home in October we should have to think worse of him than his behaviour throughout that summer and indeed his dealings with Emma thereafter give us grounds to.[27]

Fothergill disregards those phrases in Greville's letter of 24 October; Fraser acknowledges that the plan to send her back docs pose a problem, and suggests, rightly I think, that whatever footing Hamilton and Emma were on by October 1786 it was still in some way unsatisfactory. In fact, relations between all three persons were rather fraught. Hamilton had very likely revcaled to Emma just how long Greville had been scheming to be rid of her (see his letter of 24 October); Greville himself, in his ineffable conceit, felt she should have informed him at once of her capitulation (if indeed she had by then capitulated); but also felt Hamilton should have made it clearer to her that he, Greville, absolutely did not want her back.

It may be best to view the whole thing as a protracted negotiation, particularly between Emma and Hamilton. Deciding to switch masters, she needed to know what the terms would be. In the summer and autumn of 1786 Hamilton would certainly not have agreed to marry her (he was still being evasive about it in the summer of 1791). Perhaps the best she could get by the autumn of 1786 was an assurance of his continued protective interest and the promise of an allowance of £100 a year. Armed with that she was not being sent back to England but was herself insisting that she would go, perhaps still in the faint hope (Hamilton not having quite disabused her) that she might prevail on Greville after all. At the end of November then, Hamilton, actually very unwilling to lose her, gave her all the promises he could – status and protection in his house, access to Neapolitan society, endless cherishing and 'improvement' – and got from her promises that she would conduct herself, under his protection, in such a way as not to expose him to ridicule. And on that basis, as the year ended, their relationship truly began. Emma switched unequivocally from Greville to Hamilton – a wise move.

Chapter 10

PRIVATE PASSIONS IN
POLITICAL TIMES, 1787–91

On 20 November 1786 Hamilton wrote his Secretary of State, the Duke of Leeds, one of his periodic reviews of the 'remote corner of the World' in which, for twenty-two years, he had been serving the British Crown. He speaks of 'the trifling antics' of the Court; then of his own particularly favoured position there; and of the King's dissipated character. Nothing new, in fact. Noteworthy was only the greater and greater power of the Queen and of her favourite, Acton. Late in the day, too late, as it must have seemed to him, for any remedy, Hamilton draws up the balance of his career: 'I should have thought myself fortunate if my Lot had placed me in the same agreable situation at a Court of more importance where I might have rendered some more essential service to My King and Country.'[1] So he wrote with a mild regret, not knowing that before much longer he, the 'Professor of Earthquakes', would find himself at one of Europe's political epicentres.

In the mean time, with a twenty-one-year-old mistress in his house, he entered the last quarter of his life with renewed zest and interest, continuing old passions and developing fresh ones.

The new apartment, long planned and long and very expensive (£3000) in the making, was itself a passion. It became his favourite room, one he thoroughly enjoyed and that visitors admired and often wrote about. Its chief attraction was a large bow window wrapped high up around the south-western angle of the house, with a view over all intervening buildings to the bay, the sea, the promontories and Vesuvius. It is still there, above the choking streets, like the bridge of a ship, a real captain's window. The 'prospect' was at first sight breathtaking and even when accustomed always a delight and a wonder. (Lusieri's painting of it, commissioned by Hamilton, is

said to have started the craze for 'panoramas'.) Hamilton had lined
the facing walls and doors of this balcony room with mirrors, so
that their curve matched the windows and the prospect was doubled
and appeared both as a reality, outside, and as an image by means
of art, inside, behind window glass, in the collector's own home.

The painter Wilhelm Tischbein was often in Hamilton's house at
this time, first to paint Emma then to work on the Second Collection
of vases. In his memoirs, written when that to him glorious epoch
was over, he gives loving descriptions of several of the rooms. Sitting
on the cushions in that new apartment was, he says, like being out
of doors, high up on a rocky pinnacle above land and sea. It was
Hamilton's favourite place to sit and read. In the following memory
of one particular occasion Tischbein very aptly characterizes the man
in his habitat:

I visited him one day and found him alone, stretched on the sofa
with a book in his hand and laughing out loud. 'No, really,' he said,
when I asked him what he was laughing at, 'it is too ridiculous, the
things people do ... See here. There's a description in this book of
them putting a witch on trial in Palermo and burning her in public.
It is all recounted in the minutest detail and amongst other things
how in the square where the execution took place the city's finest
ladies had seats set up for them and were served with ices and
sorbets. Just imagine the scene: the ladies sitting there in all their
finery with ices in their hands, guzzling sorbets and watching in
comfort while that poor creature perishes in the flames.

Hamilton's character, his philosophy, his way of being in the world,
was expressed in the house he had inhabited, when Tischbein became
a familiar there, for more than twenty years. On the stairs he had
heads of the two philosophers, Democritus and Heraclitus, the first
laughing, the second weeping at the state of the world. They were
hung either side of a painting by Luca Giordano of a guitarist
standing between an ass and a big-horned ram and having a parrot
on one shoulder, a monkey on the other; the sense of which was,
according to Hamilton, that we are all chatterers, imitators, fools and
cuckolds. Naturally, these reflections reflect back on the man who
put them so on public view. We can be certain Hamilton knew that.

He was of the world thus satirized, not above it. Around the walls of his 'cabinet' – which was something more than a study, sometimes he slept there – in letters of gold, were maxims his visitors would suppose he lived by. Tischbein remembers: 'La mia patria e dove mi trovo bene,' which gave offence to some of his countrymen and was indeed an odd or oddly public statement from the King's Ambassador.[2] Other visitors noticed: 'Chi sta bene, non si muove.'[3] Neither quite sorts with his repeated efforts, for the first twenty years at least, to leave Naples. Tischbein actually says – and Hamilton must have told him this – that he had asked the King to leave him where he was because he loved Italy and the arts so much and thought he could serve his country there; not quite the whole truth.

The room was hung with a variety of pictures. According to Tischbein: 'The whole seemed a chaos, but if you only looked at it aright you recognized in it the room's occupant, a man of sensibility and intelligence, who had arranged the different objects with good taste and discrimination. The walls expressed his character.' Still the principle seems to have been one of startling juxtaposition, a side-by-side of images as discrepant as the sorbet and the fire; or as paradise and ruin such as he had witnessed in Calabria in 1783. Such irreconcilable contiguities in some way deeply appealed to him. In his cabinet – as Tischbein remembers it in epitome – he had the quick and lively sketch done by his old flame Di Beauclerk of her children, sent to him by Lord Herbert in 1780; numerous pictures of Vesuvius and Stromboli in their violence; a little pastoral painting by Heinrich Roos; then pictures of a warrior, a great scholar, a famous beauty: all set in close juxtaposition.

Tischbein revered Hamilton, and had a sincere affection for him too; he calls him his great patron and also, fairly, without presumption, his friend. Friendliness seems to have been the quality that first came to mind when people remembered Hamilton. 'Who has more friends than you?' John Elliott asked in 1774;[4] and the number grew and grew. Tischbein again:

> In Lord Hamilton I had a great patron and friend. Very naturally this lover and connoisseur of the arts became for me the foremost man in Naples. And in every respect he was an extraordinary person. He had in the highest degree the gift of being agreeable to everyone,

and with his candour and honesty he drew people to him in such a winning fashion that each among all his numerous acquaintances believed himself his best friend. He was a man of the world, who knew how to acquire and enjoy the amenities of life. Not a moment passed him by unused. He was altogether a good, an excellent, a wholly exceptional person.⁵

Tischbein got to know Hamilton in the spring of 1787, when, largely because of Emma, he was happy and generous with his happiness.

In the middle of November 1786, whatever Hamilton's domestic situation was by then, he moved with the Court to Caserta for the hunting, to the accommodation that Catherine, when she did accompany him, had found chilly and dispiriting. Emma will hardly have taken to it either; that winter was exceptionally cold, and perhaps as part of the agreement being reached between them she seems to have visited him in Caserta but to have stayed mostly in Naples, proceeding with her improvement and receiving visitors.

Emma's first note to Hamilton, on 26 December 1786, after a long silence on her part and thus a break in the evidence, comes as a shock: 'Yesterday when you went a whey from me, I thought all my heart and soul was torn from me.' This is her sudden new appearance: wholly in love with him, wholly devoted. 'How I wish'd to give you some warm punch, and settle you in my arms all night.' He was away with the blood-drenched King, but came home when he could, to a home now a good deal more comfortable. On 8 January Emma went to have her likeness done; perhaps it was a miniature for a snuff box. She writes:

It shall not be two naked, for it would not be so interesting, and as you will have it in a box, it will be seen a great deal, and those beautys that only you can see shall not be exposed to the common eyes of all, and wile you can even more than see the originals, others may gess at them, for the are sacred to all but you, and I wish the wos better for your sake.

His notes to her have not survived, but he wrote quite often, if only a couple of lines. From one of her replies we can catch his tone, a quieter tone than hers:

Oh, how kind! Do you call me your dear freind? Ah, what a happy creature is your Emma! – me that had no freind, no protector, no body that I could trust, and now to be the freind, the Emma, of Sir William Hamilton!

She had plenty of amusement in Naples. On 18 January she reports a visit to a particularly famous and holy nun, Beatrice Aquaviva, who was, Emma says, very smitten by Emma's beauty and said: 'You are like the marble statues I saw, when I was in the world.' A nun one day, an old man the next. Poor Banker Hart after Emma's singing was, she reports, 'quite gone'. Who wasn't? She concludes that account: 'And so the all admired me.' Her singing was divine, her beauty out of this world, and her progress in Italian quite astonishing. Her perhaps unconscious strategy in these letters was to make Hamilton see what a treasure she was, how prized by everyone she met; and so to fill him with complaisance that she loved him. 'One hour's absence is a year, and I shall count the hours and moments till Saturday, when I shall find myself once more in your kind dear arms, my dear Sir William, my freind, my All, my earthly Good, every kind name in one.'[6] Doubtless that gratified him.

At the Palazzo Sessa she received almost like the lady of the place. Philip Hackert, court painter, and Angelo Gatti, inoculator of the royal children, were frequent visitors; as was also the new gardener Graefer, who needed an ally and a confidante. Significantly, during this first absence leaving her in the house, she began to be approached for favours. It was already thought the Ambassador might be influenced through her.

By February Hamilton seems to have decided that the period of trial or experiment was over and that he and Emma were now on an even keel. He wrote to Greville, first about the estates – wondering why they weren't bringing in more than the £1200 they always did, cautious about further investments but hopeful that one day Hubberston would be as great as Portsmouth or Plymouth – then coming to Emma:

Our dear Em. goes on now quite as I cou'd wish, improves daily, & is universally beloved. She is wonderfull, considering her youth & beauty, & I flatter myself that E. and her mother are happy to be with me, so that I see my every wish fulfilled.[7]

That would be the pattern thereafter, to Greville, to Banks, almost to anybody who would listen: an insistent, slightly anxious reiteration of how well Emma is doing, how much improved she is, and how blamelessly she conducts herself. Though she loved admiration and certainly encouraged it Emma was not by nature promiscuous. Her side of the bargain when Greville took her on was fidelity, which she kept to without much effort, I should say; and likewise when she moved in with Hamilton. Sex itself, for any of that odd trio, can't have been very important or compelling. In all his portraits and extant utterances Greville seems a frigid prig, and Hamilton, though a thorough hedonist, had perhaps at his relatively advanced age (relative to hers) to some extent aestheticized sex into an act of looking. As for Emma herself, she could be playfully erotic if she thought it would please, but her own sexuality, like everything else about her, was subordinated to the even more basic drive of self-preservation; and once she could afford to worry less on that count, then to a grandiose self-dramatizing ambition. Nelson was another matter. He was perhaps her only sexual passion.

When Hamilton said in February 1787 that his every wish was fulfilled he meant that he saw a real household taking shape again. He had somebody – Emma – there who cared whether he came or went and who did her utmost to please him and make his home comfortable. And besides her, Mrs Cadogan, more Hamilton's age by a long chalk than her daughter was, contributed to what we might call the ordinary domestic agreeableness of the place, which Hamilton certainly valued. As for the mother herself, who almost never spoke and when she did – in malicious report, at least – then always comically, Hamilton, never a snob, treated her with respect and affection, as she did him. They were an odd ménage: the gaunt, aquiline and philosophic lord; the garrulous and for a while wonderfully beautiful girl; and, like something mythical, some taciturn and stoical witness of the best and the worst, Mrs Cadogan in her neat bonnet and with her partiality for a drop of English gin.

Hamilton's chief concern about Emma, once he felt sure she would not make him a laughing stock with young Englishmen, was her status in his house and the tricky question of who would receive her and who, if she was there, would visit. The King, according to Emma, was wholly in thrall, and the Queen, surprisingly, not jealous.

Both looked benignly on the relationship and were glad to see Hamilton, their friend, rescued from his loneliness; but before she married him Emma could not be presented at Court. Otherwise, Neapolitan society was notably easygoing in the matter of lovers and mistresses; and most of the English in Naples – often themselves doing things they dared not do at home – were glad to follow suit. In addition, much of Hamilton's natural circle was intellectual and artistic, and from the latter particularly Emma had nothing but sympathy and admiration. At the Palazzo Sessa, every bit as much as in Catherine's day, Hamilton after the Christmas of 1786 had all the society and good company he could wish for. His continual insistence on Emma's virtues is partly still defensive – against any who might assume that in such a liaison he could not but be ridiculous – and partly also to raise her standing to that of effective mistress of his house, so that in the end she would be accepted as the proper companion not just for an aesthete, a man of science, a man of the world, but also His Britannic Majesty's Ambassador. In so doing, of course, whether he intended it or not, he was giving her grounds to bid to be his wife.

Before very long Emma was doing the honours of his house, which was what Hamilton had said he wanted at the very outset and Greville had warned him against. She spoke in an increasingly proprietorial way about the house she was now installed in and its affairs, and Hamilton let her; he was content. He doted on her, defended her loyally, but saw her foolishness and vulgarity too and let it be. He read her no homilies as Greville had done. He told Banks she 'realy contributes much to my happiness',[8] and was grateful for that. He had a companion again. Happy in that centre, he went out energetically after all the things that amused and excited him.

Snow-covered in January 1787, Vesuvius, which had been 'open' for the past three years, Hamilton says, disgorged long lavas in May and August. Hamilton wrote to Banks but set this local volcanic activity against the news that William Herschel, the Astronomer Royal, had discovered lavas on the moon: after which, he says, 'Nous autres Volcanistes must hide our diminished heads.' But he goes on:

I was imagining that perhaps when Herschel saw this very curious circumstance it might be an Eruption like that of Vesuvius in 79 when the Lava was thrown up 11 thousand feet high & actually formed a Column of bright fire of that heigth & of a diameter of more than 2 Miles. If any of the Astronomers in the Moon had been looking at us perhaps they might have seen that Eruption.[9]

The idea that volcanic fire, the great motor of change on earth, should have worked on the moon as well, excited Hamilton's mind as a confirmation of his own maxim: that it is a dangerous error to limit the order of Nature to our confined ideas. In August he and Emma were on the mountain together, at night, viewing the great cascade of lava up close. Emma writes to Greville: 'I was enraptured. I could have staid all night there, and I have never been in charity with the moon since, for it looked so pale and sickly ... the light of the moon was nothing to the lava.'[10] The lava was not pleasing to everyone. It surrounded another of Vesuvius's tourist attractions – the Hermit's house – and occupied his chapel.

Hamilton learned from Banks that the Society of Dilettanti had published his letter on the Feast of St Cosmo or Priapus at Isernia. The letter was printed with a massive addendum in the form of a learned 'discourse on the Worship of Priapus' by Richard Payne Knight, and numerous rather comical illustrations of wax, bronze, clay effigies of 'the Organ of Generation in that state of tension and rigidity which is necessary to the due performance of its functions'.[11] Hamilton had one copy of the book 'as a member' of the illustrious Society, and six more 'in Gratitude' for his original letter. All seven were given to Greville, who sent them on and they duly arrived in October. Tischbein was shown them. Payne Knight and the Dilettanti soon panicked at their publication, which gave some offence, and did their best to call in copies from the general readership.

Besides the volcano and Priapus Hamilton went on with vases. The Portland Vase, no longer his, was the subject of letters between him and Josiah Wedgwood. After very close study of it and reflection on his own resources, Wedgwood set out his proposals for the commercial reproduction of the vase and of the figures on it. This was another instance of the influence Hamilton had consciously sought to exert on the arts in his home country. He alludes to it with some satisfaction in correspondence at this time with George Cumberland, an amateur painter and critic who had just eloped to

Rome with the wife of his London landlord. Cumberland had seen Hamilton's First Collection of vases in the British Museum, and wrote complimenting him. Hamilton replied (5 June 1787): 'It has already in a great measure answered my purpose by having been greatly assistant to the advancement of the arts in Great Britain.'[12] Cumberland was proposing to do his bit for such advancement by forming a museum of casts of the best bas-reliefs. Writing on 27 December 1787 Hamilton offered support and added:

> We have no want of Lovers of the Arts in England ... but of true Connoisseurs I know but few & when I have named Townley, Mr Lock & Charles Greville I know not where to look. I mean that are capable of judging of the Sublime & are truly sensible of the great Superiority of the Ancient Greek Artists over all that have existed since. I am happy in the thought of having introduced purer forms of vases & a purer stile of Ornaments in England by my Collection, with the assistance of Mr Wedgewood, and as the Duke of Portland has trusted him to Copy the Barberini Vase, which I had the satisfaction of placing in England, that may be of some service to introduce a better stile of bas relief.[13]

Hamilton's passion for ancient vases was reanimated when, after some years of dearth, they began to be found again in great number in the spring of 1789. Tischbein reports: 'He came to me one day full of joy and said he had been unable to resist and had begun buying vases again.' Then: 'Hamilton arrived almost every day delighted to tell me that he had bought more vases and I must come along and look at them with him.' He gives a memorable glimpse of Hamilton in the very act of acquiring: 'I saw him once, he had just come from Court, and in all his regalia, wearing the star and sash of the Order of the Garter, he was carrying a basket full of vases. A ragged lazzarone had hold of one handle and the English minister the other.'[14] By March 1790 Hamilton had nearly a hundred and was already planning their publication and eventual sale.

And another large project was under way. In August 1786 Graefer had obtained the King's permission to begin the English Garden. Fifty acres of land were given over to it, adjoining the Royal Garden at Caserta which Hamilton described as 'laid out in the most detestable taste'. Next to this then was to come a garden in 'the beauty & simplicity of our English taste'. It was to include a botanic garden, a kitchen garden and a bowling green, and naturally enough met with at best incomprehension and more generally with jealousy and hostility. Eighty men were set to work on the ground, and a further five hundred, mostly slaves and convicts, on building the surrounding wall. Hamilton was full of praise for Graefer. He wrote to Banks: 'You have indeed procured a Treasure for this Country.' The treasure none the less, 'a thorough master of his business', was subjected to all kinds of inconvenience and chicanery over wages and lodgings. His foreman, also from England, Hamilton described as 'excellent but a Drunken Dog'. He feared he would kill himself by continuing with his native tipple – rum – instead of switching to something in Hamilton's view more suitable for a hot climate, namely wine.[15] With typical generosity, Hamilton took an interest in this drunkard, and did his best for him later when he had to be shipped home. By April 1787 the bowling green was finished, and bowls were sent for, from England; by May he had eaten the first melon from the place; then a hothouse was sent for, also from England, since no seasoned wood could be found in the Kingdom of Naples. And so on. When the King did finally show some interest in what had been the Queen's idea, he proposed a labyrinth, much to Graefer's horror.

In his own house meanwhile Hamilton and Emma between them had developed a minor new art form and were treating their guests to it at the Palazzo Sessa or at the apartment in Caserta. These performances – her 'Attitudes' – were what Emma in her day was chiefly famous for, until she outdid herself in her dramatic liaison with Nelson. She stood in the character and struck the poses of figures in antiquity who would be familiar to a classically educated or even half-educated audience. There has been a lot of debate about whose idea these attitudes were. Hamilton himself is usually given the credit, in his Pygmalion-like relationship with the untutored, malleable, beautiful young woman whose native tongue was so coarse that she did best to remain silent.

The idea that statues might be brought to life had perhaps suggested itself to privileged tourists allowed into the galleries of Italy at night. Statues seen by torchlight may appear to move. Contrariwise, striking a living woman into the immobility of a work of art might well occur to Hamilton, who had both at his disposal. In an early version of Emma's act he stood her in a black box or frame in attitudes and wearing dresses modelled on those of the women in the wall-paintings at Pompeii and Herculaneum. Years before that, in 1775, he had sent to the London Society of Antiquaries an account of the most recent excavations at the buried cities. He supplied them with pictures and diagrams of the Temple of Isis, then being uncovered at Pompeii. In a niche by the main altar, he reports, 'was found a marble statue of a female, with her fore-finger on her lips'.[16] She was the Muse Polyhymnia, the Muse of Mime. She holds a finger to her lips as the gesture of her silent art. Goethe, who saw Emma perform, connected her art – and the whole modish pastime of tableaux vivants – with that of the *presepii*, the cribs, set up at Christmas in Naples, in which the Nativity was presented in fastidious detail and in Baroque histrionic style; and he suggested, though on no evidence that anyone has been able to discover, that perhaps living human figures also sometimes positioned themselves and stood immobile among the usual ones of wood. The association of immobile human figures and statuary is significant; as is also the derivation of tableaux vivants from religious art. There was certainly a tradition of didactic performances on Christian subjects at different points in the Christian year in some monastic orders; witness the 'good Panto-mime or Tableau' that Hamilton saw at Casa Mari on his tour of the Abruzzi. For Trappist monks, under the rule of strict silence, speechless mime would be a peculiarly appropriate art. It may be that Hamilton, liking what he saw there, inducted Emma into his pagan version of it as soon as he had her at his disposal.

Hamilton was Emma's first impresario, no doubt about that. Very likely he was the inventor of the art itself. But the painter George Romney deserves some credit too. Emma began sitting for him in March 1782, only two months after moving in as Greville's mistress. There were more than three hundred sittings before she left for Naples in the spring of 1786. Mostly she sat in costume – as Circe, Medea, Thetis, a bacchante. Sitting immobile in costume for a painter is perhaps not so very different from standing or posing in costume before an audience. Romney aimed at strong theatrical effects and used costume and lighting to that end. He would ask his model to

Sir William and the First Lady Hamilton
by David Allan, 1770

The Palazzo Sessa

Plate 122 from Volume I of
Etruscan Vases, showing a king
and a woman performing a
sacrificial rite

Sir William Hamilton
by David Allan, 1775

Excavation of the Temple of Isis at Pompeii, Plate 41,
by Pietro Fabris, from *Campi Phlegraei*, 1776

The eruption of Vesuvius in 1779,
plate 3, by Pietro Fabris, from the
Supplement to *Campi Phlegraei*, 1779

The eruption of Vesuvius in 1779,
plate 4, by Pietro Fabris, from the
Supplement to *Campi Phlegraei*, 1779

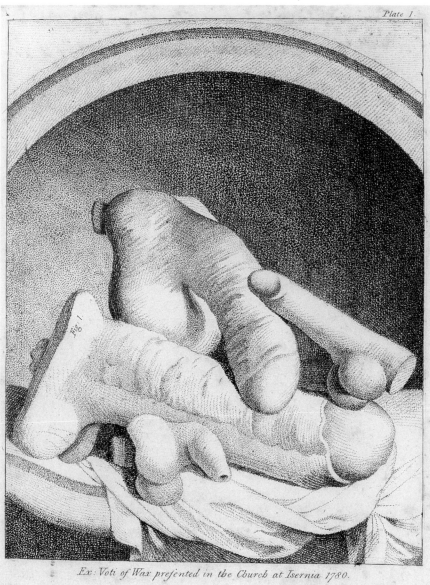

Plate 1.

Ex: Voti of Wax presented in the Church at Isernia 1780.

Phallic ex voti from Isernia, from
The Worship of Priapus, 1786

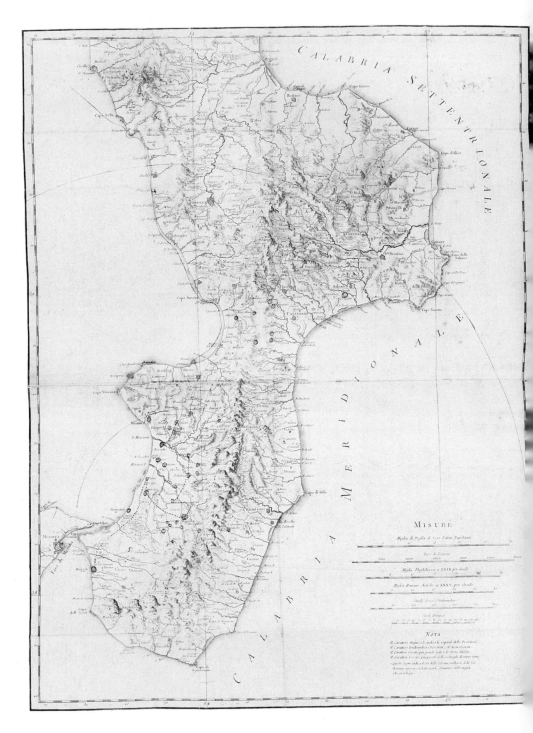

Map of Calabria, showing the areas most and less affected
by the earthquakes of 1783

Views of the Island of Ponza, 1785,
from *Philosophical Transactions*

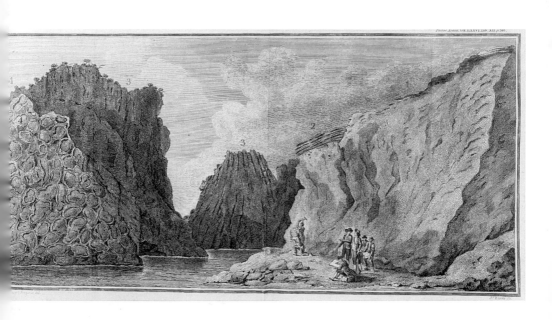

The Hon. Charles Francis Greville,
mezzotint, 1810, by Henry Meyer after
a portrait by George Romney, 1781

Emma Hamilton as Circe by George Romney c. 1782

that there can be no comfort in life
live in the air force yourself to be a
Sportsman, banish books pen ink &
paper & do not even suffer yourself
to have a rational thought — I realy
prescribe this nauseous draught to
you as a good Physician avoid prescribe
a dose of Jalop or Buckthorn & bleeding
to such a man as the late Ld Plimouth
who was ready to burst (nay I beleive
did burst) with having stuffd himself
with Venison &c & whose mind certainly
never prey'd upon his body — Follow my
advice for a year or so & then I allow
you the use of Pen & Ink books, but
in a moderate degree — if you do not do

Extract from Hamilton's letter to William Beckford,
11 February 1783, on questions of health

Mrs Cadogan,
a miniature by Norsti

Portrait of Sir William Hamilton, c. 1789–
1790, by Hugh Douglas Hamilton

The English Garden at Caserta,
by Jacob Philipp Hackert

*View of the Villa Emma
at Posillipo* by Xavier
della Gatta, 1795

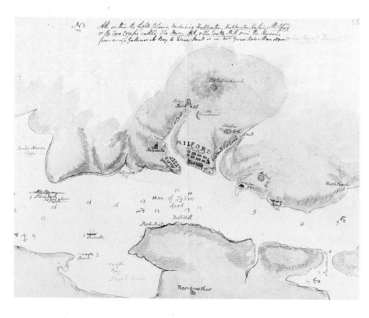

Plan of Milford Haven,
showing the area
Hamilton and Greville
began to develop

ARCHAEOPHILORVM . SODALITIO . LONDINENSI.
GVGL.HAMILTONVS.BAL . ORD.EQVES.
D.D.D.

Frontispiece, by Christoph Heinrich Kniep, of Volume I of *Engravings from Ancient Vases*, 1791, showing the opening of a tomb at Nola

Plate 14, by Wilhelm Tischbein, of Volume I of *Engravings
from Ancient Vases*, showing Telemachus, Helen and Menelaus

Map of Vesuvius, showing the extent of the lava flow in 1794,
from *Philosophical Transactions*

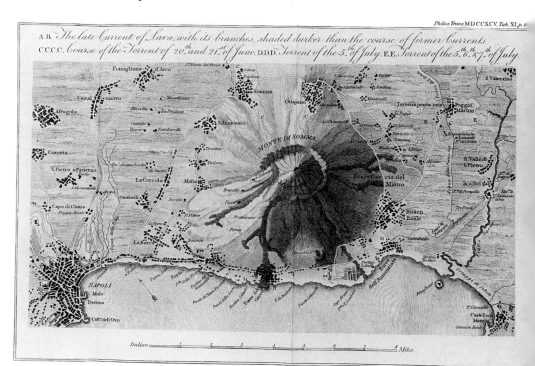

Emma, Lady Hamilton dancing the Tarantella by Mariano Bovi (after William Lock), 1796

The Muse of Dance, possibly by James Gillray, 1807

Horatio Nelson, by Friedrich
Heinrich Füger, 1800

Dido, in Despair!
by James Gillray, 1801

A COGNOCENTI contemplating ỿ Beauties of ỿ Antique

A Cognocenti contemplating ye Beauties of ye Antique,
by James Gillray, c. 1801

'imitate' or (though immobile) act certain powerful emotions, and then seek to convey them in his portraits.

No sooner had Hamilton got to know Emma, in August 1783, than he commissioned his friend Sir Joshua Reynolds to paint her portrait. He accompanied her to the sittings. Reynolds did her as a bacchante, but not very successfully. Hamilton turned to Romney with the same commission, and there too he accompanied her. So during his leave in London he had frequently seen her in costume, holding a pose, striking an attitude, requiring to be looked at. Perhaps he thought of her, posing, when he saw the Trappist monks performing their mime or standing in a tableau for Christ; and having her then in his house he made her, as Walpole put it, into his 'pantomime mistress', his 'gallery of statues'.[17]

Goethe saw Emma's act in March and May 1787, and was shown the black box or frame used in the earlier form of it. Writing to Hamilton on 18 January 1787 Emma, who in company was regularly asked to sing by then, says something which perhaps suggests she was already also performing dramatically. She writes of one admirer: 'He says Garrick would have been delighted with me.' If the attitudes began as early as that they are a first fruit of Emma's decided shift from one lover to the next. Then, in a marathon letter begun in August and finished in December 1787, she asks Greville to send her some shawls, explaining: 'for I stand in attitudes with them on me'.[18]

Goethe had been in Italy, chiefly Rome, since October 1786. He was in flight from personal and social ties at home in the tiny dukedom of Saxe-Weimar which, he felt, were killing the poet in him. He fled, telling no one what his destination was until he had actually reached it. His employer, Duke Karl August – Goethe was his Privy Counsellor – generously continued to pay him his full salary and allowed him the space and time to recover himself. Goethe, from the moment he set off, did just that. In Rome he lived among painters, and actually sought to become one of them. He was looked after there by Wilhelm Tischbein, and it was Tischbein who, on business of his own – he needed a position and was angling for one in Naples – brought Goethe first into acquaintanceship with Philip Hackert and then, through him, on 15 or 16 March 1787, into Hamilton's house at Caserta, when Emma performed. This is

Goethe's description, the earliest and one of the most ample there is:

> She is very beautiful, her figure fine and pleasing. He has had a Greek dress made for her, which suits her wonderfully well. She undoes her hair, takes a couple of shawls and goes through such a changing succession of poses, gestures, looks etc, that really in the end you think you are dreaming. You see what so many artists would have been glad to achieve, here perfectly finished in movement and change. Standing, kneeling, sitting, lying, serious, sad, teasing, extravagant, penitent, seductive, threatening, fearful etc, one flows into and out of the next. She suits the folds of her shawl to every expression and with the same two or three of them can invent a hundred different dressings for her hair. The old lord holds the lights for it and has given himself wholeheartedly to his subject. He finds in her all the statues of antiquity, all the lovely profiles on the coins of Sicily.[19]

As I said earlier, the essence of this performance is not the immobility of the stone statue or bas-relief or painted figure on a vase, but fluidity. She passes rapidly out of one character and one emotion into the next, and can do them all convincingly. Greville, who spent a great deal of time analysing Emma and expounding the results of his analyses to Hamilton, did understand (but who could have failed to?) that she was primarily an actress wanting admiration in all her roles. He offers this insight to his uncle as part of his laborious and endlessly repeated advice on how to handle her: '[She] ... is capable of aspiring to any line which would be celebrated, & it would be indifferent, when on that key, whether she was Lucretia or Sappho, or Scaevola or Regulus; anything grand, masculine or feminine, she could take up ...'[20] Typically, Hamilton developed an art form out of that ability; whilst understanding at least as well as Greville did, that in whatever she ever took up she would be acting.

James Edward Smith, the botanist who saw to the publication of Sibthorp's *Flora Graeca*, was at Caserta the same evening as Goethe. He doesn't mention Emma, but tells us there was music (by one of Hamilton's favourite composers) and he does mention Goethe. He writes:

At Sir William Hamilton's we were entertained with some charming
unpublished quartettos of Giardini's and with a greater assemblage
of literary and intelligent people than I should have expected. Here
was M. von Goethe, prime minister to the Duke of Saxe Weimar,
author of the well known Sorrows of Werter, a polite unassuming
man.[21]

Both those roles, functionary and author of *Werther*, were what
Goethe was seeking to escape by coming to Italy. In fact he began
his travels incognito, but was soon generally recognized, as here, for
who he really was. Hamilton never mentions him; but in his account
of his Italian journey, not edited and published until 1816 (shortly
after Emma's death and when Goethe was reading the scurrilous *Life
of Lady Hamilton*, just out) Goethe makes a good deal of Hamilton
and of his life in Naples with his young and beautiful mistress.
Goethe distinguished between Rome and Naples thus: 'In Rome a
man may well be happy studying, but here he forgets himself and
the world and for me it is a strange experience to move in the
company only of people enjoying themselves.' What other travellers,
viewing the common people, condemned as idleness he understood
better as a way of being in the world wholly the opposite of what
he was used to under rainy skies and the northern Protestant work
ethic: 'Northerners think any man an idler if he does not spend his
days anxiously working himself to death ... I find in this people the
liveliest and most inventive industry: not to get rich, but to live
carelessly.' And in that context Hamilton seemed to him the very
epitome of the rational hedonist, the man who – as Tischbein also
observed – knew how to enjoy the amenities of life, which were,
especially, the arts, the natural sciences, and a woman like Emma:
'Sir William Hamilton, so long an amateur of the arts and a student
of the natural sciences, has found the summit of all the pleasures of
nature and the arts – in a beautiful girl.'[22] Hamilton was, to Goethe,
at the opposite pole of the self-tormenting hero he had himself
created in his novel (so beloved by Beckford) *The Sorrows of Young
Werther*. Training himself to be a painter, Goethe was chiefly training
himself to look at things as they are in the classical daylight, without
mist and introspection. He was seeking to become what Hamilton
had been since *he* came to Italy: a lover of bare phenomena under

the sun. And one final thing: back in Weimar in June 1788, back under the rain, back in the gossip and the petty-mindedness, Goethe within a month had a young woman in to live with him, the twenty-three-year-old, socially inferior and very lively Christiane Vulpius whom he stuck by in the teeth of all the spitefulness, married at last, and sincerely mourned when she died in 1816, the year after Emma, who had perhaps, in her relationship with Hamilton, shown what could be done if you kept your nerve, and put him up to the idea in the first place. He seems to have made a trial of it when in the early summer of 1787 he returned to Rome from Naples for a further year, there for the first time in his life (he was nearly forty) enjoying a domestic uncomplicated sexual relationship, without guilt, self-torment or regret.

Enjoyment, sensuous happiness, is, in the context of traditional Christianity, a polemical act. That is how Goethe understood it, as a polemical recovery of the classical past in opposition to Christian morality, particularly in the matter of sex.

Emma was on show, there to be looked at. In that capacity she was perfectly in place in Naples of all cities then the most and the most knowingly picturesque. Goethe has often been described as an 'Augenmensch', that is, a person for whom sight is the chief of the senses, that through which most experience and perhaps also most pleasure comes; and Hamilton was one such also. Tischbein's memoirs may be said to be slanted; he was a painter and saw things that way; but again and again he draws attention to the pleasures of looking that Hamilton's life with Emma was so rich in. One instance is the swimmers below the summer house (by now christened Villa Emma) at Posillipo:

> There were often little gatherings of boys under the windows who begged us to throw coins into the sea so they could show off their skill in swimming and diving. We did, and they did. Or they wrestled on the top of a high wall, to push one another off into the sea. Often whole clusters of them hung together, falling. You saw wonderful postures and movements and the loveliest bodies.[23]

Naples was the place for such shows. When Casanova was there in the early summer of 1771 he and the Duchess of Kingston and two or three Saxon and English gentlemen (Hamilton among them) were entertained by the Prince of Francavilla at his bathing place: 'He made all his pages, lads of fifteen to seventeen, go into the water, and their various evolutions afforded us great pleasure. They were all the sweethearts of the prince, who preferred *Ganymede* to *Hebe*.'

Casanova continues: 'The Englishmen asked him if he would give us the same spectacle, only substituting nymphs for the *amorini* ...', and the Prince obliged next day, at his palace near Portici. 'We had the pleasure of seeing the marble basin filled with ten or twelve beautiful girls, who swam about in the water.' The Duchess this time, and two lady-companions, 'pronounced the spectacle tedious; they no doubt preferred that of the previous day'.[24] Hamilton's looking at Emma, and offering the spectacle of her to innumerable other eyes, belongs in that context or tradition.

Naples altogether was a spectacle, in a myriad instances constantly delighting the eye. Tischbein, for example, thought very picturesque an occasion down at the harbour when Emma pleaded for the purchase of a young Moorish girl on display among some Turkish prisoners taken in a sea battle. There it may be said that the picturesque, an aesthetic category, overrides or at least exceeds the ethical. Doubtless Emma was really moved by the young girl's plight, but in Tischbein's classicizing sketch of the encounter (which he sent to Goethe), she seems to be striking an attitude.[25] The aesthetic view of the world, like the scientific, is of itself uninterested in morality; things are more or less beautiful, more or less interesting. Hamilton, as lover of virtu and of the volcano, lived a good deal in that mode. And perhaps the aesthetic and the scientific views are actually rather akin to his characteristic stoicism, his ironic detachment, in which he at times seems heartless (laughing at the folly of sorbet and pyre) but more often humanely tolerant of all kinds of people in all their vices and foolishness in every social class.

There is no opposition of art and life in Hamilton's way of being in the world. Constantly – with Emma at his disposal – he passes to and fro between them. She brings to life the paintings, sculptures, bas-reliefs of an ancient art that he, like many in his generation, thought supreme. Like Pygmalion, he had the living statue in his bed. Polyhymnia, her finger on her lips, came out of the ash of Pompeii into his house and home. At the same time, he was busily converting the living woman into works of art, in her attitudes, and more lastingly into paintings, drawings, cameos, busts, engravings. The object herself gives the best idea of this headlong metamorphosis:

> The house is ful of painters painting me. He as now got nine pictures of me, and 2 a painting. Marchant is cutting my head in stone, that is in cameo for a ring. There is another man modeling me in wax, and another in clay. All the artists is come from Rome to study from me, that Sir William as fitted up a room, that is calld the painting-room.[26]

There were two dozen portraits of her in England before she left. By 1787 Hamilton had another dozen in his house. The walls of the Palazzo Sessa and the (improving) apartment at Caserta were hung with her, yet neither there nor anywhere else was she exhibited as herself but always as a name surviving out of antiquity: Berenice, Euphrosyne, Iphigenia; or as a type, a character: nymph, muse, seamstress, penitent, spinner, bacchante; or, if nameless, then so classicized in her hair and profile that she belongs as type among the thousands of such images. She was not, in the flesh, very beautiful for very long; in manner and physique she became rather gross; but by a frenzied industry of reproduction she was got in time into the safekeeping of the aesthetic sphere, which may or may not have been some consolation. For herself she may have needed none. It seems possible that in her self-infatuation she did not even notice that, having once outdone in her own person the ancient images of grace and beauty, she later in that changed person outdid even Gillray and Sherrard in all their skill and malice. Hamilton doted on her, but was never as blind as she was about herself. His own taste was closer to the slim spare lines of the paintings on his finest vases. Hard to say whether the versions of her by Reynolds, Romney, Tischbein, Marchant, Angelica Kauffman, Vigée Le Brun, Rehberg and numerous others, in the years to come were consoling to him.

In the first years there was no such discrepancy. Emma was beautiful, and also well behaved. She continued to improve:

> She improves daily in language & musick & loses none of her beauty ... She goes on wonderfully in Italian, French, & above all in Singing ... Emma continues to improve daily & is universally admired &

approved of ... The lovely Emma ... improves daily & is universally loved & admired ... She is clever as she is beautifull ... It is now 3 years ½ she has been with me and it is impossible that any one coud improve more than she has done in the time in every respect ...[27]

Hamilton had what he wanted. He told Greville: 'I find my house comfortable in the evening with Emma's society.' She looked after visitors during his absences, certainly to her own great satisfaction and doubtless also to his: 'The English is coming very fast, and you can't think how well I do the honours; for Sir William is out every day a-hunting, and the are all inchanted with me ...'[28] Tischbein, now in almost daily dealings with Hamilton's household, to paint Emma or to work on the vases, reports on the good life there; and in January 1789, in a sort of aristocratic re-run of Goethe's Italian journey, the Dowager Duchess of Saxe-Weimar and entourage reached Naples and stayed (with a break in Rome) for a year. They saw a great deal of Hamilton – he and the Duchess Amalia got on well – and in letters home they too report on the life he and Emma were living: musical parties on the water at Posillipo, Emma's singing, her attitudes, it all floats along in a lazy summery way as though for ever.

In August 1787 Hamilton and Emma had nine days on Ischia, visiting the Countess Mahony; in the autumn Hamilton sent to England for a bathing machine for Emma (Naples was kinder than the Cheshire coast); in April and May 1789 they did a tour of Puglia together, thirty-two days, on 'the most execrable roads', carrying tents for the nights. Had he travelled alone, Hamilton could have slept in monasteries, 'but Emma would be of the party, & she is so good there is no refusing her'.[29]

In Paris then, on 5 May, there was the first convocation of the Estates General for more than a hundred years. It was the last of the Ancien Régime. On 14 July Louis XVI noted in his diary: 'Rien'. Like Ferdinand of Naples, indeed like most kings (though not George of England), Louis was a hunter and the diary entry, quite unlike any Ferdinand might ever have made, meant he had killed nothing. That same day, unbeknownst to him out at Versailles, the Parisian crowd stormed the Bastille, demolished it, and put its governor's head on a pike. It was a while before anyone heard of this in Naples. Then (4 August) Hamilton wrote to his Secretary of State: 'The news of the late Extraordinary Revolution in France has cast a visible gloom upon the face of this Court.'[30] Queen Maria Carolina was Marie Antoinette's sister but, beyond that, perhaps the more prescient there, which would include Acton and the Queen but certainly not Ferdinand, at once feared the worst. Duchess Amalia was relaxing on Ischia. Her lady-in-waiting, a great letter-writer, Louise von Göchhausen, having described their usual days and evenings – lovely evenings with Hamilton at Posillipo – then on 11 August mentions the events in Paris: 'As you may imagine, in such a life there is very little mention of politics and the governance of the state and for an event to be talked about by the Neapolitans for a day or two it needed to be as stupendous as this revolution in France.'[31]

On 26 August, after a bonfire of the privileges, the National Assembly published its Declaration of the Rights of Man and the Citizen; like the American Declaration of 1776, only louder, nearer, less able to be ignored in its indivisible appeal. On 5 October the King and Queen of France were fetched ignominiously from Versailles into virtual custody in the Tuileries, more heads on pikes accompanying them on the dreary road. On 20 October Hamilton noted to Banks: 'the French Refugees drop in here apace';[32] the duchesse de Polignac was at Rome, the comte d'Artois at Turin. History was accelerating, a colossal and inevitable shift was getting under way. Into the aesthetic life ethical questions, in the dubious but unavoidable form of politics, were forcing themselves.

Hamilton by this time was well into his second collection of vases; Tischbein, now Director of the Academy of the Arts in Naples, was working hard for their eventual publication; and Emma was scheming to do what she had threatened Greville she would do: marry Hamilton. The new background to those characteristic activities would be revolution and approaching war.

When Hamilton told Banks on 3 April 1787 that Emma was 'tollerably reconciled to her banishment', he still spoke of her stay with him as a visit.[33] He applied for leave to come home – unsuccessfully – as early as January 1787. She would surely have come back with him had he been granted it then. Would he have left her behind on his return? By January of the following year it was being said in England that he and Emma were married. His niece Mary wrote – perhaps with not quite enough tact – to ask him was this true. Emma told Greville how he had replied:

He as given Mrs. Dickinson a choaking in a letter to-day about me. He told her I was necessary to his happiness – that I was the hansomest, loveliest, cleverest and best creature in the world, and no person should come to disturb me.[34]

Mary's account of his reply is rather different. She makes no mention of any choking or eulogy but passes on, to people wanting to know, what she says her uncle told her: 'he has no thoughts of marrying at present'; and she adds her own view, which was that he never would marry.[35] In December 1788 Tischbein mentioned in a letter to Goethe that Hamilton and Emma had secretly married; Göchhausen repeated the story, also to Goethe, a few days later.[36] Beyond any doubt, Emma was herself assiduously contributing to these fictions. She would later assert: 'I never lived with Sir William as his mistress. I was under the protection of his roof, my mother with me, and we were married in private two yeas before he married me openly in England.'[37] But on 26 May 1789 Hamilton gave Greville this account of the present state of his relations with Emma:

I endeavour to lose no time in forming her, & certainly she would be welcome to share with me, *on our present footing*, all I have during my life, but I fear her views are beyond what I can bring myself to execute; and that when her hopes on that point are over, that she will make herself & me unhappy.

He goes on to say what provision he would make if a separation did become necessary: £150 a year for Emma and £50 for her mother, 'a very worthy woman'. Clearly, she was pushing for marriage. He was anxious. He finishes:

But all this is only thinking aloud to you, & foreseeing that the difference of 57 & 22 [actually fifty-eight and twenty-four] may produce events; but, indeed, hitherto her behaviour is irreproachable, but her temper, as you must know, unequal.

He hoped to be in England in the spring of 1790. And telling Greville this, he added: 'how we shall manage about Emma is another question'.[38] That was in May 1789. Then the Revolution intervened, made it 'improper for any of his Majesty's Ministers to think of stirring from his Post',[39] and in that sense undoubtedly furthered Emma's cause. Going to England would be bound to bring the question of their status to a head. Indeed, there is evidence that Hamilton would not have taken leave in 1790 even had he been granted it. He wrote to Greville, in March: 'I wish I cou'd have come home this year, but Emma wou'd not be left.'[40] He feared that if she accompanied him she would get her way. But deferring his leave, whatever the reason, till the spring of 1791 made her stronger still, for in the meantime he grew more and more used to his house being 'comfortable' with Emma and her mother there. The English in Naples that winter (1789–90), notably the Duke and Duchess of Argyle and Lord and Lady Elcho, not only found Emma and Hamilton behaving like man and wife but also, apparently on the strength of remarks made by Hamilton himself, believed them to be just that, only Hamilton's 'public situation' preventing him from declaring it openly. Still, a year after his statement to Greville, he told first Banks, then Mary, in April and May 1790, that despite her irreproachable conduct he would not marry Emma; the reason being that because of his public position he was not free to. He told Banks such a step 'wou'd be imprudent and might be attended with disagreeable circumstances'; and to Mary he spelled these out:

As I have experienced that of all Women in the World, the English are the most difficult to deal with abroad, I fear eternal tracasseries, was she to be placed above them here, & which must the case, as a Minister's Wife, in every Country, takes place of every rank of Nobility.

'In a private station', 'in a private character', he told them both, he would marry her. To Banks then, man to man, he admitted more personal anxieties and strategies:

Besides as amidst other branches of natural History I have not neglected the study of the animal called Woman I have found them subject to great changes according to circumstances and I do not like to try experiments at my time of life. In the way we live we

174

give no Scandal, She with her Mother and I in my apartment & we have a good Society, what then is to be gained on my side? It is very natural for her to wish it & to try to make people believe the business done, which I suppose has caused the report in England. I assure you that I approve of her so much that if I had been the person that had made her first go astray, I woud glory in giving her a publick reparation, and I woud do it openly, for indeed she has infinite merit & no Princess coud do the honors of her Palace with more care & dignity than she does those of my house; in short she is worthy of any thing, & I have & will take care of her in proportion as I feel myself obliged to her.[41]

Characteristically, he acknowledges and respects her right to pursue her own interests, whilst opposing them with his.

By January 1791 Emma was sure she had got her way. Greville, expecting them back, had suggested that, for decency's sake, she and Hamilton ought to have separate lodgings. She gave him a choking:

As to our seperating houses, we can't do it, or why should we? You can't think 2 people, that has lived five years with all the domestic happiness that's possible, can seperate, & those 2 persons, that knows no other comfort but in each other's company, which is the case I assure you with ous, tho' you bachelors don't understand it.

And she added in sovereign style: 'We will let you into our plans and hearths ... Sir William will lett you know on what a footing we are here.'[42]

That footing was being observed with fascinated horror by the nicer English in Naples, among them Greville's friend Heneage Legge. He wrote on 8 March 1791, shortly before Hamilton and Emma set off, to warn Greville of what, receiving Emma's letter, he knew already. Legge writes:

The language of both parties, who always spoke in the plural number – we, us & ours – staggered me ... Her influence over him exceeds all belief; his attachment exceeds admiration, it is perfect dotage. She gives everybody to understand that he is now going to England to sollicit the K.'s consent to marry her, & that on her return she shall appear as Ly H. She says it is impossible to continue in her present dubious state, which exposes her to frequent slight & mortification; & his whole thought, happiness & comfort seems so center'd in her presence, that if she should refuse to return on other terms, I am confident she will gain her point, against which it is the duty of every friend to strengthen his mind as much as possible; & she will be satisfied with no argument but the King's absolute refusal of his approbation.

Legge took it upon himself to try to persuade Emma that she was better off as things were; naturally enough, 'she does not accede to that doctrine, & unless great care is taken to prevent it I am clear she will in some unguarded hour work upon his empassion'd mind, & effect her design of becoming your aunt'.[43]

In Paris on the first anniversary of the Storming of the Bastille it seemed to many that the Revolution was over, that things would stabilize under a constitutional monarchy, the rural proletariat contented with the abolition of feudal manorial dues, and the bourgeoisie massively empowered. Wordsworth, passing through Paris at that time, never forgot the optimism of that achieved beginning. The Revolution so far was offensive to conservatives like Burke, because it broke violently with the past; and the rest of Europe watched very warily, recognizing, as indeed Burke did, that the 'infection' was likely to spread. It was in that context of anxiety and wariness that Hamilton felt obliged to postpone his leave. The worst regimes felt most anxious. In July 1790 Hamilton reported that several French citizens in Naples – 'Tavernkeepers Shopkeepers Artists & Cooks' – had been and still were being deported for 'having had meetings at which the liberty of the Subject was discussed in terms far from being agreable to this Government'. In August the King and Queen of Naples set off for Vienna, to celebrate the marriages of two of their daughters into the House of Habsburg; but some alarm was felt at their Majesties quitting the Kingdom 'at a moment of such general fermentation'.[44] They stayed away until the following March, when Hamilton and Emma, heading for England, crossed them in Florence. Going on leave, which had seemed out of the question in the spring and summer of 1790, seemed quite all right in March 1791. The political mood was indeed less tense by then; but Hamilton's own affairs, chiefly Emma but also the development at Hubberston, were more pressing. He might well have come home in 1788 or 1789, but chose not to, because it would have forced his hand with Emma; he couldn't in 1790, because of the 'fermentation', or wouldn't because she 'wou'd not be left'; by 1791 she would be fobbed off no longer. Politics now permitted a return at a time greatly in her favour; a year later, they would again have prohibited it.

In Florence Hamilton had a letter from Beckford in Paris. He wrote: 'I look upon you as the first of connoisseurs – not only in the fine arts, but in the science of human felicity.' He encouraged him to go ahead and marry Emma. The new times seemed to him propitious to that sort (and perhaps also his own sort?) of boldness: 'The reign of grim Gothic prejudices is nearly over, & people begin to serve God & themselves in the manner they like best.'[45] Were Hamilton and Emma, the one a British ambassador, the other a virulent hater of the French, actually beneficiaries of the dawn that Wordsworth said it was bliss to be alive in? Their route after Florence was first Venice, where they consorted with various French émigrés, among them the comte d'Artois, Louis XVI's brother, the future Charles X, whom Hamilton found 'very easy, polite, & agreable';[46] then through the Tyrol. Hamilton had intended to pass through Weimar, to visit Anna Amalia, but – more's the pity, another meeting with Goethe would have been interesting – he did not make the detour, and hurried on to Brussels, even resisting the offer of Beckford's apartment in Paris.

They were in London by the middle of May, after a speedier journey than usual, and the period of leave itself was by far the shortest Hamilton ever took. Perhaps he felt it his duty not to linger. In June the French King and Queen escaped and fled, intending to return and retrieve their old position by force of émigré arms; they were recognized near the border, at Varennes, and fetched back in utter humiliation. In France things were coming to another crisis; tension rose accordingly in the old regimes. In England Tom Paine answered Burke's *Reflections on the Revolution in France* with his *Rights of Man*, and sold a quarter of a million copies (in a population of about seven million). On the other hand, in July, in Birmingham, there were 'Church and King' riots, against freethinkers. Dissenting chapels and Joseph Priestley's home and laboratory were wrecked. Perhaps Hamilton thought he should be back at his post? More likely though his urgency was personal. It is significant that he did not even find time to visit the estates in Pembroke to see what Greville had been pushing ahead with there (by an Act of Parliament, passed in the summer of 1790); he met his agents in London, and did what was necessary with them. The real pressure on him was from Emma, to go through with it and, so it seems, then to leave the country and get back to the relatively easy context of Naples as quickly as possible.

Hamilton and Emma (or Mrs Hart, as she was called in the interests of respectability) had a very crowded three and a half months in England. The awaiting company wanted to know first had they married already, and secondly, if not, did they intend to? Hamilton, visiting his sister the Dowager Countess of Warwick, gave her answers which her daughter, Lady Harpur, reported thus:

> His *Lady* is *not* his *Wife*; He told my Mother, being a Publick Character at Naples, He did not think it Right to marry Mrs. Hart; from respect to his *King*; My Mother said that was very proper, but added: 'I hope you think there is something owing to *Yourself*!' He made answer, 'O! as to that, the first object is to be Happy' — then in raptures expatiated on the Charms, Talents & Accomplishments of Mrs. H. & said she was the Happiness of his Life.

Hamilton 'looks thin', she said, '& stoops; but just in his usual Spirits, and whereever He Is, the Life of the Company'.

In London they stayed at 30 Somerset Street as Hamilton had in 1784. Early in June he was described as 'so much hurried with Business, & Visits, He has not a Moment to Himself'. His own account (to his niece Mary) is much the same, though typically he thinks of Emma:

> My old friends draw me away so much, that poor Emma passes her time but ill here, but she has the good sense to know that it cannot be otherwise & will last but a short time, when we shall get back to the very good Society which her excellent conduct has insured her at Naples.[47]

In fact, beginning on 2 June, Emma sat to Romney, thirty-six times in all, and certainly was herself not ambiguous about the chief reason for her being in England. She told Romney, according to his biographer Hayley, at once, on a preliminary visit with Hamilton at the end of May. So some had one story, others another.

On 5 June, Hamilton attended a meeting of the Society of Dilettanti, proposed his kinsman Lord Abercorn as a new member, and was presented by the Society with twenty-five more copies of *The Worship of Priapus* in the desire 'that he will distribute them among such Foreigners as he may think worthy of them & likely to do honor to the Priapeid system'.[48] (Perhaps he sent Goethe one?) Emma met the notably priapic Prince of Wales, who commissioned a portrait of her as Calypso, in a chrysanthemum tunic, stretched in front of a cave. Hamilton wrote to Mary, prior to visiting her and her husband at Taxal in Derbyshire, asking for the sort of accommodation Emma had told Greville she did not want: 'Sir W.H., & E.H. appearing to be separate must be so in your house'; and he made the distinction which had always implied that he could not marry her: 'You must comprehend that Sir W.H. is one thing, & the King's Minister at Naples, another.'[49]

Meanwhile they saw people in London, among them Sir Richard Worsley, to sell him a collection of gems, and William Beckford, who wrote to Hamilton: 'The only glorious object I have set my eyes upon since my arrival in this foggy island is the Breathing Statue you brought over.'[50] Romney dined three times with them at Somerset Street. He reported: 'Everything is going on for their speedy marriage.'[51] The visit to Taxal, late July, passed off very well; Mr Dickenson rather took to Emma. In August they did the rounds: Payne Knight in Herefordshire, arranging to sell him a collection of bronzes; Beckford at Fonthill; Walpole at Strawberry Hill; the Conways at Park Place; and a day or two in Bath. Everywhere possible, Emma performed: her attitudes, scenes from operas. Lady Harpur was still guessing. She wrote to Mary (her cousin) on 9 August: 'I believe it likely she may be our Aunt. My Mother in her last seemed to fear it; do you think it likely; I *own I think not*; for making a *Shew* of Her *Graces & Person* to *all his acquaintance* ... does not appear a *preliminary for Marriage*.'[52] She was wrong. Showing Emma off, Hamilton was showing the world that he thought her fit to be his wife. On 17 August he wrote to his old friend the Countess

Spencer, who had absented herself from Bath so as not to have to meet Emma:

> A man of 60 intending to marry a beautifull young Woman of 24 [actually twenty-six] and whose character at her first outset of life will not bear a severe scrutiny, seems to be a very imprudent step, and so it certainly would be 99 times in 100, but I flatter myself I am not deceived in Emma's present character – We have lived together five years and a half, and not a day passes without her having testified her true repentance for the past.[53]

It is clear from his dithering and from his frequent protestations of Emma's worth and suitability that Hamilton was anxious. The liaison itself had worried him, and the prospect of marriage worried him more. Neither was, to recall Greville's phrase, 'an experiment without any risque'. Hamilton felt Emma made him vulnerable, and not just to ridicule, perhaps also to disgrace. Once the deed was done he watched her apprehensively to see how she would behave. She reassured him. He joined then in a stated alliance with her against their detractors and enemies in the world. There is documentation of this in two or three of his few surviving letters to her, from Persano in January 1792, thus after their return to Naples as man and wife. She must have told him of some plot to discomfit them both, even to get him removed from his post. He replied: 'You see what devils [there are] in England! They wanted to stir up something against me; but our conduct shall be such as to be unattackable ...' And a week later: 'You see the line we have taken will put it out of the power of our enemies to hurt us.' He said: 'Your business, and mine, is to be civil to all, and not enter into any party matters'[54]; but more important than their civility and neutrality was her good conduct. How real the threats against him were is hard to gauge. I mention that instance of his anxiety here, even though it postdates the marriage, to explain *his* conduct in the summer of 1791.

In May 1789 Hamilton had written to Greville: 'I see Keith is a Privy Counsellor; if they do not make me one on my return they will have used me ill.'[55] They did make him one, which he sought speedily to make use of in a letter to the Archbishop of Canterbury, 22 August. The letter is in many ways a revealing document, worth quoting in full:

My Lord,

As Your Grace is at Scarborough and I have but a short time to stay in England I am under the necessity of solliciting a favor of your Grace in this manner instead of doing it personally as I cou'd have wished.

In short My Lord it is my intention to marry a young person with whom I have been acquainted several years & whose behaviour I think fully merits all that it is in my power to bestow. Her name is *Amy Lyons*, tho' better known by the name of Hart. Will your Grace at the request of an old Friend grant me a Special Licence as speedily as possible – as I wish my marriage to be secret untill I have left England. I flatter myself that your Grace will hear from many quarters of the merit & talents of the person that has induced me to take this Step so late in life, inshort it is my own affair and I shall be much mistaken if this Event does not insure my happiness. Excuse the confusion which I find in reading over what I have just written – it is an awkward Subject to write upon. I beleive my being a Privy Counsellor entitles my application to your Grace but I shall take it as a very particular favor shoud you grant me the request & speedily[56]

The letter does indeed read awkwardly. On the same day Emma visited Romney and was even more than usually charming to him. She knew she was close to winning.

In the event the Archbishop of Canterbury did not oblige. (Hamilton was never very successful in soliciting favours from old friends and acquaintances in high places.) Mr Dickenson, who was with Hamilton and Emma till the marriage day itself, reported to his wife Mary: 'A demur was made by the A.Bp of Canty about a special license owg to an expression in Sir Wm's application, therefore it must be solemnised in a Church.'[57] Which phrase it was is hard to guess. There are several a prickly archbishop could take exception to.

The King, who might have put a stop to the whole thing, made no objection. Hamilton went to see him at Windsor on 28 August and got most of what he wanted for nothing worse than a teasing. Dickenson again: 'The King joked him about Em. at a distance & gave a hint that he thought he was not quite so religious as when he married the late Lady H.'[58] The marriage could go ahead and duly did. 'A special licence' would have dispensed the couple from attending in any church at all; but the Archbishop had demurred. So they were married 'by licence', at least letting them off the banns, at Marylebone Parish Church on 6 September. The necessary clergyman was the Reverend Edward Barry. Emma was given away, as Amy Lyons, by Lord Abercorn, head of a powerful branch of the Hamilton clan. He approved of her, and would defend her and her marriage against detractors thereafter. He and Louis Dutens, Rector of Elsdon in Northumberland and formerly Secretary and chaplain at the Embassy in Turin, were witnesses. There is no record that anybody else was present in Marylebone Church.[59] Dutens, at Emma's request, had one of Romney's pictures of her. 'He took a deal of pains and trouble for me,' she said, 'and I could not do him a greater favor than to give him my picture.'[60] And back in Naples Hamilton commented: 'Dutens was very satisfactory.'[61] He had known him and corresponded with him for many years, but what exactly he did towards the wedding is not clear; helped it be as quick and secret as possible, perhaps. The haste and scantiness of the proceedings are due partly to Hamilton's distaste for the rituals of the Church (he wanted a bare minimum funeral too); but more, as he admitted to the Archbishop, that he wanted to get out of England before word of the deed got around.

The King agreed to the marriage, but not that Emma should be received at the English Court. The consequence of this was that she would be Hamilton's wife, Lady Hamilton, at Naples but hold no official position there; she was never the Ambassadress, though she gave herself the airs and occasionally referred to Mrs Cadogan as *la Signora Madre dell' Ambasciatrice*. And Romney provided a compensation in art. Straight after the wedding the party repaired to his studio and he did the sketches for a portrait of Emma to be called *The Ambassadress*.

Two other pieces of business were seen to during this brief and hectic stay in England. Hamilton made another will, settling on Emma a yearly income from the estates, on Mrs Doggins or Duggin ('otherwise written Cadogan') an annuity, and bequeathing the rest to his own lawful issue, if any; otherwise to Charles Greville or, after him, to his brother Robert.[62] And Mrs Cadogan, representing Emma, went north to have a look at Emma's child, now nine years old and being fostered by Mr and Mrs Blackburn in Manchester. Mrs Cadogan saw the little girl, known as Emma Carew, 'situated to her satisfaction', but the visit itself made her 'evidently more anxious'. Greville reports this in January 1792, which may mean that he had gone with Mrs Cadogan to Lancashire and does more certainly suggest – since he had to report it – that he had kept out of his uncle's and Emma's way during the last weeks of their time in England. Now that she was married and very definitely not his responsibility, he transferred the expense of looking after her child, £32.11s od for the last half-year, to Hamilton.[63]

Hamilton's old friend the Earl-Bishop of Derry wrote, rather in the style of Beckford, to congratulate him: 'upon the fortitude you have shown, & the manly part you have taken in braving the world & securing your own happiness & elegant enjoyments in defiance of them.'[64] Casanova's verdict, admittedly with hindsight, was not so favourable. 'Mr *Hamilton* was a genius,' he wrote

> and yet he ended by marrying a mere girl, who was clever enough to make him in love with her. Such a misfortune often comes to clever men in their old age. Marriage is always a folly; but when a man marries a young woman at a time of life when his physical strength is running low, he is bound to pay dearly ...[65]

Hamilton, Emma and Mrs Cadogan (now his mother-in-law) left London two days after the wedding, first for Paris. The journey usually took three to four days, so they were probably there on the 10th, but Lord Palmerston, who looked after them, does not record their arrival at his hotel till the 14th. Palmerston, an old friend of Hamilton's, had been in Paris since 9 July, perhaps on official business (carrying letters from Charles James Fox to the Constituent Asembly) and certainly observing the mood and the politics of the city. The King and Queen, he reported, after their flight to Varennes and enforced return, were 'very close prisoners in the Tuileries, no person but the National Assembly or persons with them being admitted into the gardens and soldiers encamped under their windows'.[66] Palmerston attended debates, in the Chamber and at the Jacobin Clubs, which chiefly had to do with the drawing up of a new constitution,

one drastically limiting the powers of the disgraced King. The summer
in Paris was tense. Palmerston witnessed the riot on the Champ de
Mars on 17 July, when the National Guard fired into and charged
the crowd, killing several. The new constitution was finally carried in
the Assembly and put to the King, for him to accept, on 3 September;
and he and the Queen were given their liberty, which they used to
hold court three times a week. On 14 September he came in person
to the Assembly, and accepted. Hamilton and Emma, thanks to
Palmerston and the Marquis de Noailles, were there for the occasion.
Hamilton mentions it to his niece Mary, Palmerston fills it out:

> The King's speech was short, he spoke very distinctly and audibly
> but looked distressed and unhappy. The President, who seemed to
> assume a kind of equality that to me was disgusting, made a long
> speech to him in answer ... Upon the whole, it seemed to me the
> last degree of humiliation and had more the air of a triumph over
> a degraded man than a dignified constitutional act.[67]

By a decree of the Assembly the 18th was given over to celebrations, a balloonist rose over the city, all the buildings and gardens
of the Tuileries, the Louvre, the Champs-Elysées were illuminated,
carriages were forbidden and the streets were reclaimed for music,
dancing and spectating. The King and Queen drove past along the
Champs-Elysées and were applauded; briefly, they were in the city's
good books again. Palmerston, the Hamiltons and de Noailles went
about witnessing all this. The most hopeful face to be put on it was
that now France would stabilize into a country governed rather on
the British model. Hamilton and Emma, she especially with things
to celebrate, were there in Paris in this interlude of optimism and
rejoicing. Hamilton showed her off doing what she was best at, the
attitudes, and Palmerston reported favourably on her to his wife:

> I perfectly agree with everything I have heard in commendation of
> Lady Hamilton. She is certainly very handsome and there is a plain
> good sense and simplicity of character about her which is uncommon
> and very agreeable. I have seen her perform the various characters
> and attitudes which she assumes in imitation of statues and pictures,
> and was pleased even beyond my expectation though I had heard

so much. She really presents the very thing which the artists aimed at representing.[68]

He heard her sing too, at Lady Sutherland's.

Most likely during this week, but possibly even before the momentous 14th, Emma secured her future position in Naples by getting herself presented at the French Court, to Maria Carolina's sister, Marie Antoinette. It is doubtful if Marie Antoinette knew or would have cared about Emma's failure to be received by Queen Charlotte in England. She would certainly be glad to see Hamilton, proceeding to Naples; and there is a story, which could well be true, that she liked Emma enough to entrust her with a letter, the last she wrote or managed to send, to Maria Carolina. The connection was vital to Emma; it set up her entrée into the court she was bound for, which in turn massively increased her future role there. Altogether, the Hamiltons' encounter with the Revolution was, at this early and critical time, rather detached – as foreign spectators in the Chamber and on the streets – or primarily personal, in being received by the French Queen. Certainly to Emma, and probably also to the uxorious Ambassador himself, Marie Antoinette mattered more as a means of access to the court of Naples than in her own predicament or in what that predicament represented: the brief halt in the landslide that was bearing her, her husband and the old regimes away.

The Hamiltons left Paris soon after and continued on their way through France. They noticed (so Hamilton later reported to his Secretary of State) 'a general and Enthusiastical attachment to the New Constitution'.[69] They lingered in Geneva, where Emma wrote to Mary: 'Ah Madam, how much do I owe to your dear Uncle. I feel every moment my obligations to him and am always afraid I can never do enough for him ... Am I his Wife, and I can never separate more. Am I Emma Hamilton? It seems impossible I can be so happy. Surely no person was ever so happy as I am.'[70]

They were back in Naples on 1 November. Emma was received by the Queen, and though only as the wife of Sir William Hamilton and not as the wife of the Minister the distinction made no practical difference. Hamilton was at once dragged away to Caserta, hunting; but did find time on 15 November to write a long letter from there to Anna Amalia, the Dowager Duchess of Saxe-Weimar, regretting that they had been unable to return via Weimar; and with extra-ordinary candour (writing in French) and as though soliciting the old lady's blessing, set out his reasons for marrying Emma, explained the difficulties, dwelled on her worthiness, recounted her success as his wife with Queen Maria Carolina, and concluded: 'Your Highness will forgive me if I have abused your kindness in speaking at such length about our private affairs, but after all the goodness you have shown us I thought it my duty to inform you precisely about our present lot.'[71]

Life in Naples looked set to continue much as before, with Emma happier. But the Legislative Assembly and the streets of Paris would soon decide otherwise.

Chapter 11

DOING THE STATE
SOME SERVICE, 1792–8

Leaving England in September 1791 Hamilton would be away more than nine years, the longest period throughout his career. At the end of that career, when old age and bouts of ill health (the first in his life, he says) would have inclined him to take things easy, his 'remote corner of the world' became politically important. The events begun on 14 July 1789, whose critical and hopeful continuation he had seen in Paris in September 1791, reached out in their repercussions over the Alps and down the whole length of Italy to involve him professionally and personally and to drive him from his house and home. Having frequently wished and applied to be more at the centre of things, in the end those things came to him, and took him up out of a life lived at ease in rational pleasure into the very dirty world of war, revolution, betrayal and reprisal. At the same time, and as a direct consequence of public affairs, his own private life, which since the first dealings with Greville over Emma he had been so anxious to keep from becoming ridiculous, in the eyes of many became it, with a vengeance.

Hamilton returned to Naples as a married man, and in many ways this second period of domesticity (including the years before the marriage itself) mirrored the first. In a brasher style the Palazzo Sessa became again, after a gap of perhaps five years (1782–7), a lively social place, Emma's singing and attitudes matching Catherine's harpsichord recitals. Hamilton's Second Collection of vases, begun in 1789 and beginning to be published in 1793, in some ways repeated and in some ways extended the First. And the eruption of Vesuvius in 1794 outdid even that of 1767: Hamilton wrote it up, as he had the earlier ones, and many thought it his best such account. Much then, with variation, continued or repeated the life lived with the first Lady Hamilton. Entirely new however was the context of politics.

The celebrations of 18 September 1791 had no real foundation; their occasion was soon swept away. By December some further and cataclysmic shift of history felt inevitable. Wordsworth, passing through Paris again, sensed that since his last visit in the summer of 1790 things had 'abruptly passed/ Into a theatre of which the stage/ Was busy with an action far advanced';[1] and on the 15th Beckford wrote to Hamilton in the vulcanist language that later his correspondents would often use on the subject of the Revolution: 'A thick cloud hangs over Paris at this moment, fraught with some confounded crackers. I expect an eruption any moment. The assembly know not which way to turn themselves ...'.[2] Louis, having publicly accepted the new constitution, was with Marie Antoinette in secret busily seeking to undo it. Their hopes lay not inside France but outside, with the émigrés and with the old order in Europe which had issued its first combined threat against the Revolution in the summer of 1790, when, after a conference in Pillnitz, Emperor Leopold II, brother of Marie Antoinette and Maria Carolina, had called for a league of princes 'to restore the honour of his Most Christian Majesty', Louis. And among the Revolutionaries, there were some, notably the Girondin deputy Brissot, who were calling for a war of the people against the despots.

The rulers of Russia, Prussia, Sweden, Austria, Saxony and Spain, were all in favour of active intervention. Catherine the Great declared the affairs of France to be the concern of all crowned heads. Gustavus II of Sweden was behind the Flight to Varennes; his assassination on 16 March 1792 was a marker of the way things were moving. The death of Leopold, also in March, hastened the drift. In Paris in the spring of 1792 both the court party around Louis and the radicals around Brissot, were, for very different reasons, urging France into war. Brissot wanted it in his own struggle against the Jacobins; the Court in the expectation that the revolutionary forces would at once be crushed and the old order restored by invasion. In the event both were overwhelmed by what they unleashed. On 20 April France declared war on Austria, and her ill-prepared armies crossed into the Austrian Netherlands. This was the beginning of a conflict which, with its extension into the British and French colonies, would become almost world-wide.

In July, the Declaration of Pillnitz was severely reinforced with the Brunswick Manifesto: the old order's pledge to reduce Paris to rubble and execute its citizens if the King were harmed. On 10 August what is sometimes called the Second French Revolution took place: the crowd stormed the Tuileries, massacred the Swiss Guard, tormented and incarcerated the King and Queen. In the first week of September then, in an atmosphere of paranoia, there were wholesale killings of prisoners in the Paris gaols. And at the Battle of Valmy on 20 September, the French revolutionary army stood its ground against the Prussian cannonade. France declared itself a Republic and, in titanic hubris, began the calendar again. Robespierre declared that the people of France were 2000 years ahead of the rest of Europe.

A milder self-satisfaction was being expressed meanwhile in England. Sir James Bland Burges, an under-secretary in the Foreign Department, wrote to Hamilton on 27 July 1792 (two days after the Brunswick Manifesto): 'While all the rest of Europe is more or less in a flame, we enjoy here the profoundest quiet & an increasing prosperity.'[3] That comparison, invariably in England's favour, would become a leitmotiv of much correspondence between Hamilton and home. In fact the quiet was not quite so profound as Burges thought or made out. In April Hamilton reports the efforts being made by the authorities in Naples to keep democrats and democratic propaganda out of the Kingdom. In November Greville, supervising the works in Pembroke, reported that Tom Paine's *Rights of Man* had been translated into Welsh and was being 'circulated with industry'; he thought matters 'serious everywhere', he saw 'symptoms of restlessness in G.B., and of confusion in Ireland'.[4] He had brought in six Quaker families from America, for his new settlement at Milford, thinking them, or immigrants from the colonies, safer than the Welsh. On 18 December Paine (also a Quaker) was convicted – in absentia, he had fled to France – of publishing a seditious libel in the latter half of his book. On 15 January 1793 Hamilton wrote to Banks on the threat from France: 'here where there are so few are at their ease, and Government & justice slack, we have everything to fear'; not so in England 'where there is good Government and

Justice'.[5] On 26 January Greville reported, again from Wales: 'There has been alarm universaly, & the intentions of the disaffected have extended to this country, & all sorts of sedition preached up. The gentlemen have associated to suppress disorder, & I have not been idle.'[6] Five days before that letter – Greville was expecting it but had not yet heard – the French, like the English 130 years before, had beheaded their king. The traveller Henry Swinburne, whose son had been a page with the French Royal Family and was now in Naples being rather petted by Emma, speculated (to Hamilton, 31 January 1793) on the effects that the execution of Louis might have:

> The late events must render the sovereigns still more averse to public exhibition, and I fear the fine thoughtless bonhommie days that I remember in Naples are for ever vanished, & have made way for uneasy apprehensions & forebodings.[7]

In fact, the sovereign of Naples was not at all affected thus; he and the émigrés and the usual tourists continued their holidaying in Naples much as they always had at home and abroad. But Maria Carolina, who had in her time flirted with liberal ideas and even encouraged the masonic clubs in which they were discussed, now thought more and more of vengeance against the French, and courted Emma and Hamilton, as the representatives of the country most likely to be able to deliver it. To Emma, by now her confidante, she wrote of 'l'execrable catastrophe dont se sont souillés les infames francois';[8] and to her friend the Marchese di Gallo: 'I should like this infamous nation to be cut to pieces, annihilated, dishonoured, reduced to nothing for at least fifty years.'[9]

Naples had been obliged to recognize the new Republic in December 1792. A dozen French warships appeared in the bay, and, with threats of bombardment, insisted. They were soon back again, because of damage in bad weather and, during a stay of several months, their officers added insult or further injury to injury by openly proselytizing, and fraternizing with local Jacobins. France, anticipating British reaction to their incursions in the Low Countries, declared war on Britain on 1 February 1793. At once the Mediterranean became important and as a consequence so too, for the first time, did Hamilton's post in Naples. He was given 'a Full Power under the Great Seal' to negotiate a treaty with the Kingdom of the Two Sicilies. Having been there so long he was quite clear-sighted about the kind of state Britain was allying herself with. He wrote his Secretary of State another account three days after war was declared: the dissipated but in some ways amiable Ferdinand sidelined from government, which was wholly in the hands of the Queen and Acton. And he concluded:

> The Neapolitans have certainly an utter aversion to the french, but the late Transactions in France have open'd their eyes. They are now sensible that in this Country Justice does not exist, that the Government of it is very defective & that the people have a right not to be trampled on. So that if this Government does not speedily and seriously set about a reform in all its branches, the general discontent now silently brooding, will probably, sooner or later, break out into open violence. Nature has certainly done more for the Kingdom of the Two Sicilies than for any Kingdom in Europe, and yet I have been witness myself of more misery & poverty among the inhabitants of some of its richest Provinces, than I ever saw in the whole course of my travels.[10]

Conceding the right of the people not to be trampled on Hamilton now allied his government with a government doing just that. He and Acton signed a treaty of alliance on 12 July: Britain would maintain a fleet in the Mediterranean, but Naples must contribute to it, cease all trade with France and conclude no separate peace there without British permission (and in that case must remain neutral). By then the Terror was beginning in Paris (beheading Brissot among hundreds of others), liberal enthusiasts for the Revolution were backing off everywhere, reaction in Britain against the reform groups and the Corresponding Societies got harsher, and a full European war was being fought. A British fleet under Lord Hood, blockading Toulon, was invited to take possession of that harbour by Royalists still holding out against Paris. On 28 August a force was landed to occupy the city and to make a bridgehead against revolutionary France. There was even some talk of inducing the south to secede as a separate nation under British protection.

On 11 September Lord Hood's emissary arrived in Naples, to seek the addition of Neapolitan forces to those occupying Toulon. The emissary was Horatio Nelson, captain of the *Agamemnon*. He addressed himself to the British Ambassador. Southey, going back to Harrison's *Life of Lord Viscount Nelson* (1806, supposedly written 'under the immediate dictation of Lady Hamilton'), reports the occasion thus: 'Sir William, after his first interview with him, told Lady Hamilton he was about to introduce a little man to her, who could not boast of being very handsome, but such a man, as, he believed, would one day astonish the world.' Nelson had the same opinion of himself: 'I am now only a captain: but I will, if I live, be at the top of the tree.' He wanted 6000 Neapolitan troops and Hamilton, going straight to Acton, speedily got them. 'Sir William,' said Nelson, 'you are a man after my own heart! – you do business in my own way.' Southey comments: 'Thus that acquaintance began which ended in the destruction of Nelson's domestic happiness.'[11] There was little sign then that it would. Emma seems to have preoccupied herself more with Nelson's stepson, Josiah, a midshipman who was not doing very well. Nelson and his officers, in their sole ship, were fêted, rather prematurely, as 'Saviours of Italy'. They stayed four days, Nelson dined three times with the King, always on his right hand. He left abruptly, to chase the French, and was not seen again in Naples for a full five years, during which time he and Hamilton kept up a correspondence largely on official business but in the friendliest terms. Their instant and real liking and respect for one another endured, perhaps till the very end.

On 16 October the Convention beheaded Marie Antoinette. For months Maria Carolina had been hearing of her ill treatment and wishing that France might be pulverized with all her inhabitants. The news was a fortnight reaching Naples. When it did it prostrated her, the Court went into mourning, she gave birth to another princess, and under a picture of her dead sister she inscribed: 'Je poursuivrai ma vengeance jusqu'au tombeau'; and to that end she directed Neapolitan foreign policy thenceforth.

Beckford wrote from Lisbon: 'Were there ever such times, such vertigo, such bedevilments? Society is almost totally dissolved in every part of Europe.'[12] His own relationship with society, even before the Revolution, was notably tangential. He continued wandering with his large retinue, pitching camp here and there. The Palmerstons, themselves on tour through a Europe in flames, had seen him a year before near Lausanne, and noted: 'He has a public day once a week where everybody is welcome. He has tents pitched and ... keeps half a dozen cooks and lives *en prince*, but he cannot get any good society.'[13] Now, November 1793, he was in Lisbon, as well there as anywhere.

Toulon fell to the Revolution on 19 December. Napoleon Bonaparte, then a young colonel, distinguished himself by the ruthlessness of his cannonade against the fort. Hamilton had a long account of the débâcle from Sir Sydney Smith, there with the British fleet. In the general pandemonium those foreign troops and royalists and collaborators who could, got out; the rest were massacred. The Neapolitan contingent, quite unused to war, had two hundred dead, another four hundred wounded or taken prisoner. It was early February before the survivors got home, bringing with them four hundred royalist refugees. Neapolitan Jacobins meanwhile, mostly very young men, were planning a coup, something, according to Hamilton, rather on the lines of Guy Fawkes's Gunpowder Plot. Neither they nor the secret police were very efficient; they gave themselves away in the middle of March and many were rounded up. It had been their intention to capture the castles, blow up the arsenals, murder the royal family and the ministers and rouse the populace to general revolt. The last item particularly was a nonstarter. The populace, whatever their real grounds for grievance, so loathed the French and many so loved the feckless King that they were quite immune against anything to do with the rights of man and the citizen.

Money from France was believed to have funded the plot. Hamilton wrote to Greville on 10 April: 'I hope in a few days and by a few executions all will be quiet again.'[14] The trials dragged on till October, 124 volumes of evidence accumulated against the conspirators, three of whom, finally, were sentenced to death. There was a disturbance when they were hanged, not in support of them but by accident and in nervousness. The troops fired into the loyal crowd, killing and wounding about a hundred, according to Hamilton, or forty-one according to the historian Acton.

In France the Terror ended in the execution of Robespierre on 28 July 1794. Then followed, under the Thermidorean putschists who had toppled him, a period of relative internal stability in which France was better able to prosecute the wars. In England *Habeas Corpus* was suspended, acts against Treasonable Practices and Seditious Meetings were passed and similar measures were taken in Ireland to counter the threat of French-assisted revolution there. In a word, the country was brought forcibly into unity, for a long war.

In June, as Hamilton reported it to Banks, there was 'a thumping Eruption of Vesuvius, certainly the greatest in History except those of 79 & 1631'.[15] The mountain had been quiet for seven months. Then there were signs: daily the water in the wells sank lower and lower; a thick vapour encircled the summit, just below the crater; there was a reddish cast over the sun and the moon; a small explosion, and smoke came out of the ground close to a man and two boys in a vineyard above Torre del Greco. On 12 June, about eleven at night, an earthquake passed in a wave from east to west, out of Puglia and across the Campagna Felice. All the servants' bells rang in the rooms at Caserta. The clear night went black. The eruption itself came three days later, after a second milder shock. 'A fountain of bright fire' went up from the central crater, then another from lower down, and fifteen torrents of lava made their way towards Resina and Torre del Greco. There was a thunder like heavy artillery; a roaring like the sea; and 'another blowing noise, like that of the going up of a large flight of sky-rockets' which also brought to mind 'that noise which is produced by the action of the enormous bellows on the furnace of the Carron iron foundery in Scotland'. This last comparison is very typical: it was Hamilton's way to reach for something that would bring the colossal and strange phenomena home. He had been at Carron, near Falkirk, with Greville in the summer of 1784; and since in 1794 the foundry was busier than ever making cannon (and carronades) for the war the image fits well with many others from Hamilton's soldierly past.

He and his guests moved from the Palazzo Sessa to Posillipo, to watch in more safety; but they were reached even there, by 'two small balls of fire, joined together by a small link like a chain-shot ... They separated, and one fell in the vineyard above the house, and the other in the sea.' The lava reached the sea on the 16th, overwhelming Torre del Greco on its way. Naples, night and day, was in darkness, buildings collapsed under the weight of ash and the people rose in their customary violent religious panic and ecstasy. On the 17th Hamilton went by boat to view the condition of Torre del Greco. The lava, nearly a quarter of a mile wide and thirty feet deep, had pushed out two hundred and ten yards into the sea. The sea was so hot it scalded his hand, melted the pitch on his boat and almost sank him. He landed and walked where he could in the town. Of its eighteen thousand inhabitants all but fifteen or so had escaped. Many stayed in their homes, and the lava passed around them; they emerged next day on to their roofs and fled over the red-hot hardening crust. The cathedral was buried, but for the upper part of its square brick tower, in which hung the bells, neither cracked nor melted but wholly put out of tune. Around the cathedral the lava was forty feet thick, more generally it was twelve and nearly a mile wide in places. He writes:

> I went on the top of one of the highest houses that was still standing, although surrounded by the lava; I saw from thence distinctly the whole course of the lava, that covered the best part of the town; the tops of the houses were just visible here and there in some parts, and the timbers within still burning caused a bright flame to issue out of the surface; in other parts, the sulphur and salts exhaled in a white smoke from the lava, forming a white or yellow crust on the scoriae around the spots where it issued with the most force. Often I heard little explosions, and saw that they blew up, like little mines, fragments of the scoriae and ashes into the air.

Householders, returning to salvage what they could, found looters in their homes. When on the 18th the summit became visible for a while, its shape was changed, much of the old crater had fallen in. At the end of June, with one-eyed Bartolomeo, Hamilton climbed the mountain itself, his sixty-eighth ascent in his sixty-fifth year. They saw the tracks of animals in the soft volcanic dust as fine as snow. The routes the lava had made to reach the sea were more than two hundred feet deep, and up to a mile wide. 'Ten thousand men,' he remarks, 'in as many years, could not, surely, make such an alteration on the face of Vesuvius, as has been made by nature in the short space of five hours.' He had added an extra sole to his boots, but they were still burned through before he and his guide came down.

After the lava came torrents of mud and ash, carrying away walls, trees, livestock, a team of eight oxen, and hardening over the fields and villages like cement. Early in August, when the mountain quietened, the people returned to where their homes had been, and began building again. They dug foundations in the earth that was still smouldering.

The account Hamilton wrote for the Royal Society – the letter dated 25 August 1794 and read at two of their meetings in January 1795 – was said by many to be his best.[16] He made notes as the eruption was happening, and also had the benefit of notes and drawings made for him by Father Antonio Piaggi who, for fifteen years from his little house in Resina (below which lay Herculaneum) had observed the mountain day by day, and kept a meticulous diary of its changes and activity, being paid by Hamilton £20 a year for doing so.

Piaggi, a monk from Genoa, of the Scuole Pie, had an extraordinary ability to copy texts, even those in languages like Arabic and Ancient Greek which he did not know, and so faithfully that his copies were indistinguishable from the originals. He spent forty years of his life working for the King at Portici, unrolling, on an infinitely complicated machine of his own invention, the carbonated cylinders of papyri from the House of Piso at Herculaneum. In five hours he could reveal a finger's breadth of script. Then he would transcribe it. Winckelmann, on his visits to Naples, watched, and described the process. Occasionally the King called by, and stood for hours, in a childish trance and amazement over so much patience.

Vesuvius was Piaggi's other chief employment, and the eruption of 1794 was the last he would see. In fact, it was almost the end of him there and then. He was interrupted in his observations 'by the imminent danger of his situation ... It was with difficulty that his friends carried him off alive ... in the midst of a shower of heavy cinders and sulphureous ashes.'[17] He died two years later, aged eighty-two. In his last letter to Hamilton, in November 1795, he says he has been told by his confessor that, standing now with his feet already in the grave, he should give no more thought to papyri nor to any other thing of this world but prepare himself instead 'a fare una buona morte'. He includes in his letter two little sachets, dated

31 October and 7 November 1795. One still contains its sample of the volcano's most recent ash, little black grains, like poppy seeds.[18]

Besides his scholarly letter Hamilton sent Banks a scurrilous local response to the eruption in sonnet form, together with his own translation. The title was 'The Mountain of Somma lets down his breeches and Shitting addresses his discourse to the Neapolitans'. Hamilton commented: 'It is truly Philosophical for this Eruption altho to us very serious & alarming was to Nature & Mount Vesuvius no more than having let out 3 farts a Sneeze and a Shite.'[19] He means it accords with his own philosophy: on Nature's limitless force and our smallness. And even on this occasion of truly cataclysmic violence he insisted on viewing the activity as ultimately beneficial and productive. 'A gentleman of the British factory at Naples,' he reports, 'having filled a plate with the ashes that had fallen on his balcony ... and sowed some pease in them, assured me that they came up the third day, and that they continue to grow much faster than is usual in the best common garden soil.' Indeed, Hamilton begins his letter to the Royal Society with his thesis of ultimate good by regretting that anyone could think the opposite: 'I am sorry to say, that even so late as in the accounts of the earthquakes in Calabria in 1783 ... nature is taxed with being malevolent, and bent upon destruction.' As he himself had reported, a vast terrain was laid waste and forty thousand people lost their lives. Still, Nature is not malevolent. In August 1794, after the worst eruption since 1631, he sums up his view thus: 'Let us then content ourselves with seeing, as well as we can, what we are permitted to see, and reason upon it to the best of our limited understanding, well assured that whatever is, is right.'[20]

Whilst Vesusius erupted, the Revolution in Paris was seizing up in one last paroxysm of guillotining, and the Jacobins in Naples were in gaol awaiting trial. Banks wrote that before Hamilton dealt with the volcano it would be necessary first to extinguish 'Jacobine Fire'.[21] The association of phenomena in natural science and in politics was commonplace. Goethe felt an equal hatred for any violent upheaval, in Nature or in Society; in that sense he was a coherent Neptunist, a believer in measured, very gradual evolutionary change. Hamilton as a natural philosopher loved the violent acceleration of Nature in volcanic eruption, believing it to be in the end productive; but his politics were, at their most progressive, as gradualist as Goethe's. Quoting Pope ('whatever is, is right'), he is, I should say, thinking more of purposes in Nature whose final good end we are too limited to comprehend, than suggesting that any social order, the Neapolitan, for example, is justified by the very fact of its existence.

Beckford wrote to Hamilton on 18 February 1794: 'You are very busy with your vases & yr politicks.'[22] As to politics, he was indeed busy, first with raising soldiers for Toulon, then with getting supplies to Lord Hood for further operations in the Mediterranean. He told Banks in April that he had had more business in the past year 'than in the course of 28 that preceeded it'.[23] Answering Beckford, on 11 March 1794, he puts the two occupations, politics and vases, side by side, competing: 'But I will talk no more of Politicks. Every moment I can steal from business is employed in forwarding my New Publication on the Greek Vases that form my New Collection all of which were Under Ground 6 years ago.'[24]

Hamilton employed Tischbein as editor, advancing him the money to do the job, about £600 in all; Tischbein was to pay him back in books, calculated as worth just over two guineas each. Work was under way by June 1790, after about fifteen months of collecting. Volume I was scheduled for October 1791, and that year appears on the title page. Tischbein, sending proofs of the first engravings to the Duchess Amalia in December 1790 (and asking her to show them to Goethe), announced it as almost ready for printing; in December 1792 he said it was finished; but not until 10 September 1793 were 200 copies finally dispatched to the bookseller Cadell in London. Such delays became par for the course, reasons being 'the abominable Neapolitan press' and 'various accidents & war';[25] also that Hamilton kept buying more vases. He told Beckford in March 1794 that the second volume would be 'out in two months'; Tischbein announced it as imminent ('this week') on 10 January 1795; but it was May 1796 before copies were dispatched to Cadell. Hamilton's accompanying letter to Cadell described the third volume as 'nearly finished as are the plates for the 4th & last'.[26] But then the wars, always getting closer, intervened decisively. It was late 1800 before the third volume appeared, and the fourth was after Hamilton's death. Loose prints at least were in circulation before the volumes themselves, and the first two, when they did appear, were as effective as Hamilton had hoped. The work's full title, explanatory rather than neat, is *Collection of Engravings from Ancient Vases mostly of pure Greek Workmanship discovered in Sepulchres in the Kingdom of the Two Sicilies but chiefly in the Neighbourhood of Naples during the course of the years MDCCLXXXIX and MDCCLXXXX now in the possession of Sir Wm. Hamilton His Britannic Majesty's Envoy Extry. and Plenipotentiary at the Court of Naples with Remarks on each Vase by the Collector.*

Though Hamilton wrote to Greville in September 1790: 'I shou'd hate to be looked upon as a dealer,' that is indeed how he was looked upon by some, by his guest Pryse Lockhart Gordon, for example, who said of him: 'He trafficked in the arts, and his hotel was a broker's shop. No one knew the value of a Greek vase ... better than the *cavaliere Inglese*, or where to place it.'[27] Certainly, he always intended to sell his Second Collection, and not to the British Museum – he was still cross with the trustees for not buying his Portland Vase – but to whoever would pay the most. He tried, one after the other, the Emperor of Russia, the King of Prussia and Beckford, all unsuccessfully. Tischbein reckoned he had spent 20,000 ducats on vases (about £3,800). In the end there were more than fifteen hundred in the collection. His more altruistic intention, as with the First Collection, was to improve taste and design in the fine arts and in manufacturing. He wrote: 'I wish Wedgewood had this collection two years in his possession, he wou'd profit much by them';[28] and though he did nothing to make that possible, by the publication he can still be said to have had a good effect. The vases were not engraved in full colour, as in the first publication, but in simple outline; and although this was primarily intended as an economy, it both chimed in with and furthered the sparer and, some would say, more classical style being practised by, for example, Flaxman, who, having seen Hamilton's vases and doubtless also Tischbein's drawings, was working on his own illustrations of the *Iliad* and the *Odyssey* in 1792–3. The important insight – Winckelmann's confirmed by Hamilton – that these so-called Etruscan vases were actually Greek, already fully demonstrated in the First Collection, was emphatically reinforced by the Second. Most of the vases came from tombs in Southern Italy, from Nola, Trebbia, Locri, and from sites in Puglia. A few came from Sicily, and at least two came from Greece, from Melos. It was travellers to Greece who gave Hamilton the additional proof he continued to want, that the art he was collecting and publicizing was Greek. As early as 1772, the painter William Pars, viewing the First Collection in the British Museum, had shown Hamilton pottery he had found himself in Athens in 1765–6. The paintings were very like those on some of Hamilton's vases. And in August 1792 three travellers – Graves, Tilson and Berners – who on their way out had seen Hamilton's collection in Naples, returned from Greece with fragments and whole vases very like his, which they had acquired in Athens, Megara, and on the island of Melos. Two from there they gave him for his collection. Their discoveries were final proof. He was glad to make use of the letter they sent ahead of them, from Palermo, 10 August 1792 (the day of the storming of the Tuileries) as a postscript to his Preface to Volume I.[29]

For commentaries this second time round Hamilton had neither the erudite Winckelmann nor the eccentric and brilliant d'Hancarville at his disposal, but only a man with no particular qualification for the job, his colleague in diplomacy the Russian Minister, Count Italinski. Unconfident of his own learning – it was at this time that he blamed his long years in the army – Hamilton deferred to him. Italinsky supplied his remarks in French; Hamilton translated them. But his own prefatory letters and address, plainly written, all to the point, touchingly remembering the learned abbé Winckelmann, suggest that he should have trusted himself for the explanations of the vases too. As it is, the value of the publication lies chiefly in the engravings and in Hamilton's own clear statement on the origins and beauty of the vases he had collected.

Tischbein derived a second project out of his work on Hamilton's vases. Hamilton himself had indicated how much light the paintings would throw 'upon the ancient history, fabulous history & mithology of the Greeks', since so many pieces showed particular and identifiable scenes.[30] Tischbein had the idea of using these illustrations to make up a 'Homer in Pictures'; later he also took in sculpture, cameos, coins, etc. The work was a long time under way. Driven out of Naples by the wars, he took all he could back with him to Germany, and published his Homer there in 1801, so continuing and extending his patron's good influence.

All this activity – vases, the volcano, the wars – came at a time when Hamilton, now in his sixties, began periodically to suffer from ill health. His illness in November 1792, which he describes as the first in his life, seems to have been quite serious. It lasted a fortnight. Emma, as she wrote to Greville, feared she would lose him. Nursing him, she went eight days without undressing, eating or sleeping. She called the illness 'a Liver Complaint', and 'a billious fever',[31] and the latter term became the usual one for his illnesses thereafter. He made himself ill – indeed, he says, nearly lost his life – in the summer of 1794, inhaling 'so much of the Sulphurious & Mephitic Air' of Vesuvius; but described himself in December as better in health than for some years past.[32] The following spring, however, he was low again, and again the complaint was bilious. Emma: 'The quantity of bile he as discharged these days past is incredable'; and she now says he was 'allways' subject to such attacks. There was another the following January 'which was violent, but yielded directly to a bleeding and five small doses of James's powders'. The attacks were likely whenever he was 'confined to close application'; and he tried, as a prophylactic, a regime of energetic horse-riding.[33] On 17 November 1795, he reported to Greville: 'By constant riding I have braced up my bowells & in great measure got the better of my bilious complaints that were brought upon me by constant writing & want of Exercise.'[34] Still he had recurrences, which is not surprising, as he aged and as the demands on him got worse. Altogether, professionally and domestically, he was burdened more and more as his stamina lessened.

Money worried him too. This was nothing new, but as he aged he wanted to be certain of some comfort in retirement. Greville made him anxious, pressing ahead in Pembroke with ambitious schemes. The Act of Parliament, passed in the early summer of 1790, authorized 'Sir William Hamilton K.B. his Heirs & assigns, to make & provide Quays, Docks, Piers, & other Erections: & to establish a Market, with proper Roads & Avenues thereto respectively, within the Manor or Lordship of Hubberston & Pill in the County of Pembroke';[35] but of course it was Greville who was going ahead with it. There was some serious likelihood that mail boats to and from Ireland would run six times a week if facilities were available at Milford; Greville wanted to encourage and exploit that chance. Hamilton made his own feelings pretty clear in a letter as the Act went through:

Tho' I do not understand thoroughly the nature of the act of Parliament you have passed for me, yet I see enough that it may be attended with great consequences; the whole question *to me* is whether I shall live to be benefitted by them, or whether great present disbursements must not be made in order to insure future success...

In a word (from an earlier letter – one way and another, he said the same thing to Greville many times): 'I am willing to sacrifice a little to that hereafter, but not pinch myself.'[36] He got some explanations in London in the summer of 1791, but was too taken up with marrying Emma actually to visit the works themselves; and once back in Naples, spending large sums on vases, on Emma, on improvements at Caserta, on entertaining the English, he reverts to the old worry: that disbursements for the benefit of posterity will impoverish him in the meantime and leave him 'pinched' in old age. His salary was, as always, late and inadequate, and the estates were no more productive of income than before Greville's developments there began. In January 1792 they were still only bringing in £1200 a year (though, according to Greville, their estimated value was double that). Greville, ever more confident – it was in his nature to promise himself and others more than he could deliver – raised a loan for Hamilton of £9000 (at 4 per cent, from Hoare's bank), in part to settle Hamilton's old debt (of £3400, at 5 per cent, to his lawyer in London, also called Hamilton) and the rest to go on the works at Milford. His tone towards his uncle at this stage is bossy, as though he had every right to whatever funds he thought he needed: 'I have set down without mystery everything that you can do for me at present & in future without diminution of present income.'[37]

It was precisely such diminution that Hamilton was worried about. A letter to his agent in Pembroke, John Meyrick (5 November 1793), reveals that the new loan, once the debt to the London lawyer was settled, also had to fill up the hole in his account with Ross and Ogilvie. Then, as he put it, 'having rigged out Her Ladp. to make a proper appearance as my Wife at Naples', he had about £3000 left; but feared he would still be in the red with Ross and Ogilvie, 'as it is also probable that Government may be in arrear in their payments'.

They had, he said, sometimes owed him as much as five quarters, 'upwards of 4000£'. In the two years since his return to Naples he had, so he told Meyrick, spent more than £4000 on 'Antiquities & pictures' (mostly vases), and reckoned that all he had in his house of such things had cost him in total £10,000. Having laid out his position and admitting that he was 'not very exact at accounts', he tells Meyrick he will go on with the quay and the inn at Milford, but then no more.[38]

Over the winter, to pay off Hoare, money was raised by a mortgage on the estates (the burden on them was £13,000 when Hamilton died). In March 1794 Greville assured him he should soon get £1400 a year from them clear.[39] With Britain in the wars and everything in Europe uncertain, Hamilton looked to the estates in Pembroke as his 'sheet anchor', and again and again he urges caution: 'I am determined not to risk anything that might distress me in the latter part of my life.' He quoted with approval the Irish MP 'who, when a great present expense was proposed for the benefit of futurity, desired to know what futurity had done for us'. He wrote anxiously in October to know how much had already gone on the inn and the quay, 'to which two *articles I limit all improvements* as realy my expences increase by everything growing dearer daily'. With his bankers he was always in deficit, but on that score he wrote (July 1795): 'I have valuables here that will balance that account if we escape bombardments, earthquakes, invasions, & home conspiracies'.

In October Greville informed him that despite disturbances in Pembroke the offices, the quay and the inn were almost finished;[40] but Hamilton's mind was by no means set at rest. He told his banker Ross in January that he was 'determined not to advance one farthing more on prospects'. Whatever the actual rents, they were very slow — slow as his salary — ever finding their way into his account. He wrote the same day, 12 January 1796, to Greville: 'I know no more of my affairs in Wales than the man in the moon; I have not seen a farthing return from the Welsh estates in Ross & Ogilvie's accounts.' Ross wrote to Wales himself, and managed to get £600 paid in. It is a mark of Hamilton's anxiety at these distant and as they seemed to him very risky dealings that in June he suggested selling the inn they had only just built at Milford. Greville, sanguine as ever, replied that with the Quakers now established there the rent roll should actually amount to £2279 a year. But in May 1797 Hamilton described his financial state to Banks in terms not a jot less anxious:

> My friend Charles has I know improved the future views of my Estate in Wales exceedingly and I dare say all he has done is excellent but my accounts from Ross & Ogilvie show me that not a penny of my Estate has come into their hands for 6 years passed and as I have always spent what Government allows, & the full income of my Estate & continue to do so by drawing on my Agents as usual you may judge of the sort of ballance in the Books of Ross & Ogilvie at the moment, cela fait trembler.[41]

Anxiety about money, especially the money to retire on, fretted away at Hamilton throughout his last and longest period away from home.

And the job itself was becoming tiresome, not the serious business of furthering the British war effort in the Mediterranean – that fatigued him but he accepted it as his duty and was glad to be useful at last. The English tired him, holidaying in Naples, war or no war, as they always had. As the French advanced down Italy, more and more tourists, determined not to let a European war spoil their fun, moved south to Naples in greater numbers for longer periods. All the English among them, and many of other nations also, applied to Hamilton for help in amusing themselves. His complaint to Walpole, in April 1792, may stand for many such:

> Having resided at Naples upwards of 27 years, foreigners of every denomination contrive to bring letters of recommendation and as our countrymen can without much difficulty, *paying 2 guineas at the Secretary's Office*, get a letter they now all bring me such letters and think themselves entitled to get that penny's worth out of me, and after all it is most difficult to content them. It appears to me that education in England does not improve, for of upwards of 100 British travellers that have been here this winter I can scarcely name three who can have reaped the least profit, for they have lived together and led exactly the same life they would have done in London.[42]

Three years later, despite Britain's entry into the war, the tourists were as numerous and demanding as ever:

Nothing plagues me in the business of a minister but the eternal succession of our travelling countrymen. One would have thought there were such difficulties this year, that few wou'd have arrived at Naples, yet I had 74 at dinner the Queen's birthday & Prince Augustus at their head.[43]

Prince Augustus, the sixth son of George III, was a particular charge. He spent ten years of his life in Italy, and two of them, between 1794 and 1798, in Naples. Hamilton had been instructed to keep an eye on him: having married illicitly, it also seemed possible he might turn Catholic. 'Entre nous,' Hamilton reported to Bland Burges (24 March 1795), 'he has an odd way of crossing himself when he sets down to dinner.'[44] As the French advanced it became a problem how Prince Augustus should be got safely out. All in all, Hamilton was rather weary of his compatriots as they appeared to him abroad. He even thought a restriction of Civil Liberties might be in order: 'I respect Magna Charta but wish there had been in it some little restraint upon emigrants.'[45]

Less than two years after his return to Naples Hamilton was wishing he could go home again, to see to his estates; but being for the first time necessary in his post he made no formal application for leave until April 1797, and even then, when in June of that year it was granted him, he deferred taking it up. His position in Naples was being watched with interest by people who thought they or their protégés might like to replace him. They noted his illnesses and his anxieties about his affairs in Pembroke. The first direct bid came in November 1794 from the Earl of Bristol in the interest of his son, Lord John Hervey. Hamilton had advance warning in a letter written to Emma by Joseph Denham, a merchant in Rome, whom they had met there that February. Hervey had just been sacked from his job as Minister in Florence, but had secured himself a pension of £1500 a year. Bristol's bright idea was that his old friend Sir William would take this instead and resign Naples in favour of the highly unsuitable Hervey. There was not the least chance that the British government would agree to this, and there was certainly nothing in it for Hamilton. Denham commented (4 November):

Sir William cd never be so stupid as to give up £3500 a year for less than half the money, nor agree to lose all his consequence at Naples, where I remember he told me he intended to remain even if he were to lose his place, as the air & climate agree so well with him.[46]

When Bristol arrived in Naples later that month Hamilton will at once have disillusioned him; but perhaps he was bothered by the suggestion nevertheless. The vultures were gathering.

Hamilton was telling people, Denham among them, that he would remain in Naples whether he continued as ambassador or not. When he spoke of his Pembroke estates as his 'sheet anchor' he did not mean that he thought of retiring there. He wanted them to contribute to a sufficient income for him to live or at least always winter in the south, in Naples. He had in mind to go home, but certainly not for good. He wrote to Banks in December 1794: 'Shou'd this Cursed war have an end soon I do not despair of making you one more Summer visit, but I shall never think of passing a Winter in England.'[47] That was a refrain in letters throughout 1795: he would come home for a short time, to settle his affairs, just as soon as hostilities ceased. And at the moment of his own choosing, so he told Greville on 24 March 1795, he would resign his post and stay on in Naples in retirement, on a pension. He felt the Government owed him a fair deal: 'I can say with Othello I have done the state some service ...'[48] In the end, as he saw it, the state never did pay its debt.

Early in the new year Hamilton wrote privately to Lord Grenville, his Secretary of State. The letter shows very well both his anxieties and how things were done:

As I have had within these four years past several attacks of a bilious complaint and some of which have been attended with danger I have no doubt but that your Lordship has had many applications for the Post of Naples. Some openings have been made to me by particular Persons and by way of temptation a considerable annuity offerd me in addition to whatever the King might think proper to grant me on my retreat but this kind of jobbing I have ever looked upon as highly indecent and injurious to His Majesty, and therefore paid not the least attention to such offers. I have now only to entreat of your Lordship that if any such proposals shoud be made to you Lordp. as with my consent that you will be so good as to pay not the least attention to them as I shall, as in duty bound, whenever I feel that age and infirmities begin to render me incapable of serving His Majesty at this Court as I cou'd wish, (and which thank God is by no means the case at the present moment) give the full notice thereof to your Lordship and leave the whole arrangement of my retreat to your Lordship and the King's goodness.[49]

Throughout the period of his greatest diplomatic busyness, when he truly was 'doing the State some service', Hamilton was trying to secure his future in negotiations with a system that had never been wholly accessible to him or amenable to his requests. He renewed his efforts in the spring of 1797. He told Greville that he would apply for leave

and give a look to my own affairs, and take some arrangement as to my continuing here which I certainly can not do on my present income as every expence is increased ... I am determined not to be in any way distressed in my latter days – & indeed I begin to find repose necessary & I shall seek it, but I will not give up what I have untill I see clearly what I may expect for my long Service & in which I certainly have spent more than all I have ever received from Government & my own money too.[50]

In April he applied for leave to come home 'for a short time'; was granted it, but felt obliged by his duties not to take it up. Less altruistically, he felt afraid that if he left his post he might by the wars or by a government decision be prevented from returning to it; and he did not want that to happen, at least not until he had secured himself an adequate pension. He made a bid for one at the end of the year (or very early January 1798): he asked for a net income from Government in his retirement of £2000 a year. If that were forthcoming, he said, they might dispose of his post to whomsoever they pleased. The response, in a letter from Lord Greville, on 27 January 1798, was discouraging: the state of the Civil List would not allow it, he had asked for a pension 'so much beyond the usual proportion of the retreat of Foreign Ministers to their Salary'.[51] There the matter stalled. Events overwhelmed Naples, and Hamilton's final departure, in the spring of 1800, was not at all as he would have wished.

Tischbein commented in a letter to the Duchess Amalia, on 16 December 1794: 'Hamilton looks older by the day.'[52] He was thinner, he stooped. Emma meanwhile grew ever fuller of life. She might complain of 'the fatige of a dinner of fifty, and a ball and supper of 3 hundred'; she might write to Greville: 'I am allmost sick of grandeur ... Our house – breakfast, dinner and supper – is like a fair';[53] but really she was in her element. Her vitality was vast. It became a commonplace in the mostly very spiteful accounts of the Hamilton ménage to point up their differences of age and shape to a grotesque degree. Lady Palmerston, visiting in the winter of 1792–3, was among the kindest commentators: 'Sir William looks extremely ill and it puts one a good deal in mind of January and June, for I think she is beyond May.' Four years later Sir Gilbert Elliot found her overwhelming: 'Her person is nothing short of monstrous for its enormity, and is growing every day.' Hamilton by then was, according to Lady Holland, 'old, shrivelled'; and, according to his old school friend Bristol, 'a piece of walking *verd-antique*'.[54] She and Hamilton, soon to be joined by the one-armed, one-eyed and diminutive Nelson, were a hard act for the cartoonists to follow. She performed her attitudes, and for some years at least was so striking in these that even her worst ill-wishers forgot who she was, and marvelled. And some months after Elliot had called her monstrous Tischbein reported: 'Hamilton is still collecting vases and Mylady is still being painted and sculpted, every artist has to try his skill on her.' The association there is very apt. The frontispiece of Volume I of the Second Collection is an engraving by Kniep (the artist Goethe had with him in Sicily) of Hamilton opening a tomb at Nola and Emma standing by him, surveying the vases and the skeletons. For a long time, as she performed, she continued to incarnate for him the figures of antique art. He told the traveller John Morritt in December 1795 that he had married her because 'she only of her sex exhibited the beautiful lines he found on his Etruscan vases'; which lines he continued to love on new vases and in the paintings and sculptures still being done of her. Moreover, he said to Elliot, 'she makes my apple-pies'.[55]

That reported comment is quite as significant as Tischbein's. On all the surviving evidence – his letters about her, his letters to her, the accounts of the innumerable visitors to their house – Hamilton, at least until the liaison with Nelson became scandalous, was happy with Emma and felt she had more than kept her side of the bargain. He wrote continually about her good conduct. Thus to Walpole, in April 1792: 'She is really an extraordinary being and most grateful to me for having saved her from the precipice into which she had good sense enough to see she must without me have inevitably fallen ...' And to Banks, year after year: 'She knows the value of a good reputation ... She knows that beauty fades & therefore applies daily to the improvement of her mind ... Her beauty now [December 1794] is in it's glory & with a conduct irreproachable she has gained universal Esteem ...' 'Her mind has gained & her body lost nothing of its beauty ...' But as well as beauty and good behaviour he valued company and domesticity itself. 'Without a Woman you can have no Society at home & I am sure you will hear from every quarter of the comforts of my house.'⁵⁶ Hamilton wrote to Emma from Persano (in January 1792), in response to an 'effusion of tenderness' on her part: 'We are now one flesh, and it must be our study to keep that flesh as warm and comfortable as we can.' Looking forward to Saturday (the day of his return) he wrote: 'What say you to a feet washing that night? *O che Gusto!* when your *prima ora* is over, and gone.'⁵⁷ Comforts then, for an elderly man; and among them, her apple pies.

Emma's own assessment of herself and her marriage was even more positive. And there can be no doubt that she really was as anxious for him in his illnesses and really did nurse him as faithfully as she told Greville she did. On their wedding anniversaries she was sincerely glad when Hamilton told her he loved her more than ever. They became, in her view, exemplary in marriage. 'Everybody that sees us are edified by our example of conjugal and domestick felicity ... We are so happy, our situation is very flattering in the publick character, and in private we are models for all husbands and wives.'⁵⁸ Visitors, in varying degrees of amusement or disgust, conceded that they were indeed a loving couple. Lady Palmerston: 'She and Sir W. are rather too fond ... Sir William perfectly idolises her ...' Lady Holland: 'as tiresome as ever; he as amorous, she as vulgar'. As to Emma's vulgarity, naturally the English ladies and gentlemen made much of it. Sir Gilbert: 'Her manners are perfectly unpolished, of course very easy, though not with the ease of good breeding, but of a barmaid ... I was wonderfully struck with these inveterate remains of her origins.' Lady Holland made the usual fun of her accent. Emma, impersonating a water nymph, was resting her head on one of Hamilton's vases. He must have looked anxious. She said: 'Don't be afeard Sir Willum; I'll not break your joug.' Lady Holland thought it 'impossible to go beyond her in vulgarity'; but Sir Gilbert said he found Emma less vulgar once he had seen some Neapolitan ladies. And yet, on any objective assessment, there has perhaps never been a more vulgar spectacle than that of the English aristocracy season after season holidaying in Italy. Hamilton saw thirty-six years of them, more than enough. What they thought vulgar in Emma, he thought natural, and liked it. Lady Palmerston, shrewder than most, made this observation:

> Lady H. is to me very surprising, for considering the situation she was in she behaves wonderfully well. Now and then to be sure a little vulgarness pops out, but I think it's more Sir William's fault, who loves a good joke and leads her to enter into his stories, which are not of the best kind.[59]

Hamilton was twelve years in the army; in Naples he moved in every sort of company; he was wider in his taste and tolerance than the class and the circles he had left behind in England. And he was confident in Naples, for many years he had been the centre and the favourite there. His chief vulnerability was Emma herself, and until September 1798 she never did expose him to the kind of ridicule he had feared. Others thought her, and him with her, ridiculous, as he surely knew and just as surely did not care.

As a couple Hamilton and Emma *were* remarkable, but anyone thinking them merely risible and disgusting might look around at their near contemporaries: the poltroon King up to his ears in animal blood; the immoralist Beckford, fabulously rich on sugar from his plantations; the surpassingly futile Earl Bishop of Derry; and fraudsters, adventurers, serial fornicators without number. The late eighteenth century was rich in monsters, especially in the class that Emma, the blacksmith's daughter from the Wirral, and Mrs Cadogan, her mother, formerly Duggin or Doggins, had been translated into.

The Revolution meanwhile, begun as an onslaught against the parasitical classes and continuing abroad largely as a war for aggrandizement and plunder, was waiting in Upper Italy. Hamilton wrote to Bland Burges: 'I fear we shall beshit ourselves if the french shou'd ever penetrate as far as Naples ...'[60] That was in March 1795. He had three and a half years then watching them get closer. During his illness in April there was a deepening of the intimacy between Emma and the Queen. She wrote two or three times a day to ask after him, and sent some quinine. Her affection for Hamilton was real enough, but she also had an interest in him and in Emma as a means of influencing him, in her politics against the French. She was fearful, on good grounds, that since their allies on land were doing so badly, the British might pull their fleet out of the Mediterranean altogether, and she intrigued hard, making use of Emma, to prevent this. The two women, the one a veteran of seventeen pregnancies now turning all her energies to the politics of vengeance, the other becoming voracious for a massive public role, were so intimate and their surviving letters so thick with endearments, that in scurrilous writings, then and since, they appear as lovers. More likely power was the passion, each her own. It was at this time that Emma wrote to Greville:

Send me some news, political and private, for against my will, *owing to my situation here*, I am got into politicks, and I wish to have news for our dear much-loved Queen, whom I adore. Nor can I live without her, for she is to me a mother friend and everything. If you cou'd know her as I do, how you wou'd adore her! For she is the first woman in the world; her talents are superior to every woman's in the world, and her heart is most excellent and strictly good and upright. But you'l say it is because we are such friends, that I am partial; but ask everybody that knows her. She loves England and is attached to our Ministry, and wishes the continuation of the war as the only means to ruin that abominable French council.[61]

Hatred of the French worked like an aphrodisiac between the Queen and Emma, as it did later between Emma and Nelson.

Through Emma, behind Ferdinand's back, Maria Carolina passed on to Hamilton whatever she thought might help the British, and so her own, cause. Though himself very fond of Hamilton, Ferdinand, in so far as he had any policy, favoured neutrality; which was not good enough for Maria Carolina. She passed on information chiefly having to do with Spain, whose monarch, Ferdinand's elder brother, Charles IV, was seeking an accommodation with the French, first a separate peace then an alliance. Having already, it seems, put Hamilton in possession of Spain's cyphers, she gave him sight of letters too, for him to copy and send to London. Emma herself did some of the copying – for example, of Charles's letter to Ferdinand announcing that he had made peace with France. Hamilton kept that transcription, in the original Italian, endorsing it 11 August 1795. Emma's claim in the bitter last years of her life that England was in her debt rested largely on her part (which she greatly exaggerated) in this intrigue.

In June more revolutionary plotting was uncovered in Naples, this time largely among the aristocracy. The Queen's own assessment of her subjects was this:

[The nobility] is the most depraved and vicious class, which wants a King without strength or authority, without power or rights, a mere doll ... If they are slightly thwarted they become vipers. The worst are the lawyers, the corrupted young students and soldiers; the people are good; the class which comes in contact with the nobles (servants, etc.) bears their stamp.

She and the King feared assassination. Hamilton wrote to Lord Grenville about the latest plots: 'It is to be hoped that an example may be speedily made of some of the most guilty followed by a General pardon.'[62] But he knew the state of Naples and often wondered how long something so rotten could keep going and what use it was as an ally.

Peace with Spain allowed France to concentrate elsewhere. In April 1796 Napoleon's Italian campaign began. In his harangue he promised his ragged troops: 'I am about to lead you into the most fertile plains in the world; fruitful provinces and large cities will soon lie at your mercy; there you will find honour, profit and wealth.' As Northern Italy folded, Naples, on British advice – Naples was better neutral than occupied by the French – began to treat for peace. They got an armistice on 5 June and a treaty on 10 October, by which no more than four ships of any country still fighting France were allowed in her ports and all imprisoned French conspirators in the Kingdom were to be released. The British understanding of this treaty, as expressed by Hamilton in a letter to Acton, was that it was a necessary strategy for the moment. The Neapolitans, so Hamilton proposed and Acton agreed, would renege on their neutrality just as soon as they had any hope of moving effectively with Britain against the French. That was Maria Carolina's position too. She wrote to Emma: 'Nominally neutral but never in our feelings.'

On 5 October Spain, now allied with France, declared war on England. On 4 February 1797 French troops took Mantua. 'At Rome,' Hamilton wrote to Lord Grenville on 2 March, 'there is an appearance of general discontent and lately a very serious conspiracy of the people.' Napoleon was in the Papal States by then, and with the Peace of Tolentino (19 February) humiliated the Pope and began the systematic looting of Italy's art for France. Hamilton wrote to Banks (31 May): 'for want of union & firmness a Land full of Sans Culottes have robbed murdered plunder'd & now are giving the Law to Eleven million, which is the supposed population of Italy'. To Lord Grenville early in June he reported revolution in Venice and further discontent in Naples. He told Banks he feared that the kingdoms of Northern Italy 'must one day be drawn into the vortex of the great Republican System';[63] and by the end of the year that had happened. With the Peace of Campo Formio in October Austria took herself out of the wars for a while, leaving Britain more or less solitary.

Campo Formio was only a pause. The French wanted Rome, and worked with local Jacobins and like-minded exiles from Naples and elsewhere to destabilize the place for take-over. By the end of the year they had a pretext – the killing of a French general by papal troops – and on 10 February 1798 they occupied the city. Five days later Rome was a republic. So Naples' immediate neighbour had been 'drawn into the vortex', and it was natural, despite the declared neutrality, to suppose that Naples would be next. On 7 March Hamilton wrote to Lord Grenville that although there was no immediate danger from the French he expected them to invade just as soon as they could. He went on to say that in a month or so he proposed making use of the leave already granted him to come home. And he made a strange offer: to go via St Petersburg on a mission for the British Government to the Czar of Russia whom he had been in friendly correspondence with since his visit to Naples in 1782 and who had several times invited him to his court. Quite what Hamilton was up to here is hard to say. Presumably he thought he could be useful in trying to draw the Czar into an alliance with England (which was achieved, without Hamilton's aid, by December). But the spring of 1798 was an odd time for a conscientious ambassador to leave his post – having frequently said at times less desperate that he felt he ought not to. He had just heard from Grenville that they would not give him the retirement pension he had asked for. Did he think he might improve his chances by a strenuous and dangerous trip to Russia? His offer rather resembles one he made much earlier: to replace Stormont in Vienna, because the then Emperor of Austria was so fond of him. Now, no doubt thinking Grenville might wonder what he was after, Hamilton concluded: 'I throw this out to your Lordship not with any wish or view of serving myself but out of pure Zeal and earnest desire of serving my Good King and Country to the utmost of my ability.'[64] Needless to say, nothing came of his proposal.

One good thing the French did (in April) was to arrest Lord Bristol in Milan. Hamilton commented to Grenville: 'We all know that His Lordship's freedom in Conversation, particularly after dinner is such as to make him liable to accidents of this nature.' They kept him nine months. The French ambassador to Naples meanwhile, Citizen Garat, was appearing at Court in what Hamilton called 'their new exaggerated stile that is with rough cropt black hair the frock closely buttond up, boots and a huge Sabre hanging to a black leather belt over the Coat'. At a *fête champêtre* he and a secretary 'wore large Spectacles constantly ... Their terrific appearance actually frightened the Ladies.' These were little indicators of a larger intimidation. Hamilton wrote to Lord St Vincent: 'The last Message from the French Directory at Paris, is exactly the language of our High-waymen – Deliver your money or I will blow your brains out.' Naples, he said, wanted the protection of a British fleet.[65]

The city was crowded with artists, Grand Tourists, royalists, displaced from Rome, which French commissioners were sys-tematically plundering for the Louvre. Cornelia Knight and her aged mother had arrived. They were present at a dinner for George III's birthday, given by Hamilton on 4 June, at which he announced news just received from Lord St Vincent that a British squadron was on its way to their quarter of the Mediterranean, in pursuit of the French. Its commander was Rear-Admiral Nelson. Hamilton wrote to Grenville next day. He had arranged to get Prince Augustus out the only relatively safe way, through Manfredonia and Trieste to Vienna, and would now leave himself. Or, if the British fleet were indeed coming, he would stay on. The death of his consul Davenport meant there was more work than ever. But if the fleet got no co-operation from Naples (and Hamilton had been pressing Acton to supply them at least in Sicilian ports) he, Hamilton, would pull out with them. On 12 June the French occupied Malta, as a staging post on their way to Egypt (itself a stage on the way to British India) with forty thousand troops. Cornelia Knight set up a telescope, and on 17 June sighted British ships off Posillipo. Captain Troubridge, Nelson's second-in-command, came ashore to ask Hamilton if he had any idea where the French fleet might be. Hamilton knew nothing except that they had been heard of heading south. Troubridge and the whole squadron vanished. For six weeks then Nelson looked for the French, to and fro between Syracuse and Asia Minor.

On 14 July, through fifteen rooms, from the water closet to the library, Hamilton did an inventory of his pictures in the Palazzo Sessa.[66] He feared the French would loot them. There were 374 in all; he loved them and they were, besides, his capital for retirement. Among them were fourteen of Emma (three done by Tischbein for Goethe's *Iphigenia*), one of Mrs Cadogan, one of Catherine's dog Milk, views of Lake Celano in the Abruzzi, of Paestum, of the English Garden at Caserta, of Vesuvius and Stromboli. There were thirty or more by his painter Pietro Fabris, two bas-reliefs by Wedgwood and a fragment of an antique fresco from Baia. Listing his treasures looks like a preparation to leave if and when things got worse, and indeed long before he was forced out people thought his departure imminent. The Naples banker Alexander Macauley, for example, wrote on 24 July: 'Sir William Hamilton is on the eve of his departure from Naples if an opportunity offers of going home by sea.' To his Secretary of State, Hamilton himself was saying something rather different. He wrote on 8 August: 'In my humble opinion unless some unforeseen and fortunate Event should prevent it the french will pass their Christmas merrily at Naples.' And concerning his own intentions:

> Altho' I feel myself with all my personal property in danger of being involved in the general ruin of this Country ... I am still happy that I did not profit of the King's gracious leave of absence as my presence here at this moment has been & appears still to be essential to His Majesty's Service, nor will I quit Naples untill I can do so with a safe Conscience, let what may be the Consequence.

But to Spencer Smith in Constantinople (1 September):

> As I have had the King's leave to return home on my private concerns for more than a year past – I mean to profit of the first King's ship that is sent home to get a passage on her but realy my presence has of late been so necessary here that I cou'd not in conscience quit my Post altho' I am nearly worn out with the multiplicity of disagreable business.[67]

Two days later news reached Naples that, for an interlude at least, put a different face on everything. But had there been an opportunity to leave in July or August, had Hamilton and Emma taken it, the last years of his life would have been very different.

Cornelia Knight, still at her telescope, on the morning of 3 September saw a sloop flying a blue ensign in the Bay; next a boat putting out from the shore and going alongside; next the meeting of its passengers and two officers on deck. She writes: 'We fancied we could see them, with the commotion natural to sailors, and particularly on such an occasion, depict by their action the blowing up of some ships and the sinking of others.'[68] The sloop was the *Mutine*; her captain had brought dispatches for Hamilton: Nelson's fleet had destroyed the French in Aboukir Bay. Overtaking them south of Crete (without knowing it, they passed in the night), and so not finding them at Alexandria, he went off along the coast of Asia Minor, searching. Meanwhile the French arrived, landed their army and won the Battle of the Pyramids, but the fleet itself lay vulnerable in the bay when Nelson came back on them suddenly on the evening of 1 August. He attacked at once, half his squadron cutting through the French line to anchor between them and the shore, half keeping the seaward side. The French were destroyed by midnight, between two lines of fire.

This victory, which had little effect on the French armies in Egypt and none on the French armies in Italy, sent Royalist and pro-British Naples into a delirium of joy. The Queen, according to Emma, 'fainted cried kiss'd her Husband her children walked frantic with pleasure about the room cried kiss'd and embraced every person near her exclaiming *oh brave nelson oh God bless and protect our Brave deliverer oh nelson nelson what do we not owe to you oh victor saviour of itali* ...' Emma also fainted and hurt herself falling. 'But what of that,' she wrote to Nelson, 'I shou'd feil it a glory to die in such a cause.' She described her outfit to him: 'My dress from head to foot is alla nelson ... even my shawl is in Blue with gold anchors all over, my ear rings are nelson's anchors; in short, we are be-Nelson'd all over.' Hamilton too was delighted; thought – more cautious than most but still not cautious enough – that the victory had 'most probably put an end to the confusion and misery in which all Europe would soon have been involved';[69] and so far abandoned good sense as to ask Cornelia Knight to write some lines on the battle, which she did, entitling them, 'The Battle of the Nile, 1st of August, 1798 – A Pindarick Ode', a poem best described as long.

The British fleet arrived in dribs and drabs, Nelson's flagship, the *Vanguard*, being towed in damaged on 22 September. He had been further damaged himself in the battle, by a piece of shrapnel, above his blind eye. When it happened he thought it had killed him. He said to his captain: 'I am killed. Remember me to my wife.' He was ill on the voyage back, anxious about further strategies, and intending to spend as little time as possible in Naples. The *Mutine* met him with letters; Emma and Hamilton wanted him at the Palazzo Sessa; he would have preferred a hotel, but they prevailed. Five hundred boats went out to meet the *Vanguard* in the bay, the Hamiltons, with Cornelia as chronicler, in their barge, and the Royal Family in theirs. Boatloads of singers and musicians; endless renderings of 'God Save the King', 'Rule Britannia' and 'See the Conquering Hero Comes'; caged birds released in thousands. Hamilton's party came alongside first, fifteen guns saluted them. Nelson was on deck, dressed up, with the new scar very visible across his forehead. He described what happened next in a letter to his soon to be unhappy wife: 'Up flew her ladyship and exclaiming: "Oh God is it possible" fell into my arms more dead than alive. Tears however soon set the matter to rights.' 'Arms' is imprecise: his right had been amputated, very badly, just below the shoulder after the attack on Santa Cruz in July 1797. According to another account, Emma 'began to rehearse some of her theatrical airs, and to put on all the appearance of a tragic queen' even as they approached, and the boatman, fearful of capsizing, asked her to desist. Soon after, the King boarded, to a twenty-gun salute, and poked around the *Vanguard*, even down to the sick bay, like a schoolboy. He asked to touch the hat Nelson was wearing when the iron hit him. All then breakfasted sumptuously on board.

Their landing later in the city was one of those occasions that are instantly mythic; icon and tableau in the style of a city surpassingly good at spectacle. The Palazzo Sessa had Nelson's name appearing in three thousand lights. He was lodged upstairs, in the room lately vacated by Prince Augustus. There exhaustion, his wound, sickness, prostrated him, in Emma's enormous care, on a diet of asses' milk. He wrote to his wife Fanny that Emma, having 'made the turn' from her dubious beginnings, was one of the very best women in the world and an honour to her sex. He recovered for a vast fête on his fortieth birthday, 29 September, eighty to dinner, one thousand seven hundred to the ball, eight hundred staying on for supper. It cost Hamilton two thousand ducats and to accommodate so many he will have needed the space not just of the Palazzo Sessa but of much of the neighbourhood. Plates were emblazoned with Nelson's name, ribbons and buttons bearing his initials handed out, a victory column set up ... And Cornelia added a new verse to the National Anthem: 'Join we great Nelson's name/ First on the roll of fame/ Him let us sing ...' There was one unhappy incident. Nelson's stepson, Josiah, got drunk and 'in intemperate language' accused Emma of seducing Nelson's affections away from his mother. Captain Troubridge carried him out.[70]

Next morning Nelson wrote to Lord St Vincent: 'I trust my Lord in a week we shall be at Sea. I am very unwell and the miserable conduct of this Court is not likely to cool my irritable temper. It is a country of fiddlers and poets, whores and scoundrels.'[71] He didn't get away till 15 October, and before then the Austrian General Mack arrived, to lead a Neapolitan army against the French in Rome. Nelson's victory had encouraged them, falsely, and they were besides, by provisioning the British fleet in Syracuse and welcoming them in Naples, in breach of their alliance with the French and might expect retribution before long. The idea was to strike first, with, they hoped, Austrian support from the north. Nelson in the mean time went off to Malta, where the French were now besieged and blockaded.

Hamilton, though warned by Grenville to be sure of the Austrians first, was urging the Neapolitan Council into pre-emptive war; but at the same time, and very wisely, he was preparing for the worst and clearing the Palazzo Sessa of its treasures. From 26 October until the end of the year the painter and antiquary James Clark packed away Hamilton's paintings into thirteen large cases for shipment out of Naples, carefully noting the contents of each. A fourteenth case, of paintings from Caserta, was packed early in the new year by an assistant (Clark was ill). Five more cases took the marbles and bronzes. The vases of Hamilton's Second Collection were packed up separately and eight cases of them (not all and not the best, as it turned out) went out on a British warship, the *Colossus*, through Nelson's influence, about the middle of November.

Nelson was back in Naples on 31 October. In the way of rear-admirals then he seems to have pleased himself in his comings and goings; but it was already being said that desire rather than duty drew him to Naples. Emma had assailed him with letters during his fortnight away, the last but one concluding: 'Love Sir William and myself for we love you dearly. He is the best husband, friend, I wish I could say father allso, but I should be too happy if I had the blessing of having children, so must be content.' She was forgetting little Emma, and subconsciously looking forward to little Horatia. Nelson described his relationship with Hamilton as filial: 'I live as Sir William's son in the house'; and Hamilton said of him: 'So fine a Character I realy never met with in the course of my Life.'[72] They went with Emma to inspect the Neapolitan troops in training near Monte Cassino.

Nelson had a very low opinion of General Mack, and rightly. In manoeuvres organized by the General to show off the troops, the home side, commanded by him, was surrounded and defeated by the mock enemy, a truthful if not encouraging augury. The King and

Queen were there and the mood in the camp was, for no good reason, optimistic. Emma paraded Nelson as her captive charge. Rumours on that score getting back to England so alarmed Fanny that she spoke of coming out to join him.

Austria at the last minute refused to commit troops unless the French attacked Naples first, but by then what might be called the war party – the Queen, Emma, Nelson and Hamilton himself – had pushed the King beyond turning back. On 22 November, without any declaration of war, the Neapolitan army marched from San Germano, led by the unwarlike King Ferdinand and the incompetent General Mack; Nelson sailed with five thousands troops to Leghorn, there to disregard the neutrality of Tuscany and come at the French from that base. It is not clear whether Hamilton, in constantly urging war, was acting in accordance with British policy, or ahead of it. Grenville's view in January was that the only safety for Naples lay in submission, adding that 'no man can calculate the extent, or the effects of that submission'.[73] But by late November he and the London government press were commending the Neapolitans on their courage and urging them to seize the opportunity. What Grenville wanted, of course, was to force Austria back into the war. The Neapolitans might serve that purpose and if Hamilton and his strident party committed them, it was worth a try. Needless to say, being used like this did Naples no good; no more than it had Toulon.

King Ferdinand's crusade was an unhappy farce. In atrocious weather they floundered in the mud, forded the River Melfa up to their necks, and when they met the French, out of some residual scruple over the neutrality they had long since breached, they politely asked them to withdraw; which the French, outnumbered six to one, were glad to do. Ferdinand entered Rome on 29 November, tore down the liberty trees, moved into the Farnese Palace and invited the Pope to return. But the Neapolitan army, as was afterwards said, had been more exhausted by six days' marching than any of the armies in the Seven Years War had been by seven years' fighting. The French under Championnet regrouped, and when on 30 November Mack advanced from Rome his forces were at once humiliatingly dispersed. The King set them the example in running for his life. It was said he escaped disguised as a lackey; and whether literally true or not the story gets him right. On 6 December the Directory declared war on Naples, their armies reoccupied Rome and continued south.

Having abandoned his troops, Ferdinand, back in Naples, prepared to abandon his people. He and his family confidently expected to be butchered if they stayed, either by the incoming French, beheaders of Louis and Marie Antoinette, or by the disaffected finally rising at home. Even the loyal and francophobic mob were worrying. Their violence was often not very well directed. For example, they lynched the royal messenger Ferreri by mistake, and in a demonstration of their love and loyalty tied a rope around his foot and dragged him through the dirt, to show the King. In fact, their feelings for Ferdinand were rather like their feelings for Saint Januarius: they might turn in an instant from adoration to vilification and physical violence if he did not do the trick.

Nelson had warned in early October that evacuation might be necessary, and Hamilton at least, clearing the Palazzo Sessa of its works of art, had heeded his warning. On 16 December the blood of Saint Januarius failed to liquefy. On the 18th Mack wrote urging flight. The King and Queen and their numerous progeny began their secret preparations. It was like the Flight to Varennes, in Maria Carolina's view at least. The fact that the mob was loyal made no difference. Certainly they would not have let the King go had they been able to stop him; nor would the numerous Jacobins in the city. Hamilton had to organize the evacuation of the British residents, as well as of the French émigrés. Nelson stood by in the *Vanguard* to take off the Royal Family and all they could carry in the way of treasure. They shifted a good deal, £2,500,000 worth (in that day's reckoning) of gold, silver, diamonds, plate, coin of various realms, looting the country (as they always had) before the French or their own excitable citizens did. Nelson, the British Ambassador, the British fleet, assisted them. Britain's dealings with Naples in 1798–9 were no more salubrious than any Great Power's ever are with a client state. The *structures* of politics perhaps do not change very much.

In the débâcle Emma Hamilton really came into her own. Nightly at the Palazzo Sessa she received trunkloads of what the Royal Family could not possibly leave their capital without, and letter after letter from the hysterical Queen: 'I venture to send you this evening all our Spanish money, both the King's and my own, they are sixty thousand gold ducats. It is all we have, for we have never hoarded. The diamonds of the whole family, both men and women, will arive tomorrow ...' Emma, ecstatic in her self-importance and love of royalty, endorsed them: 'My adorable unfortunate Queen! God bless and protect her and her august family! *Dear, Dear, Dear Queen!*[74]

Nelson, mistrusting the people of Naples as much as their sovereigns did, had withdrawn his ships beyond the range of cannonshot from the forts. All the goods and money had to be rowed out there. On the evening of 21 December it was the turn of the refugees themselves. Hamilton, Emma and Mrs Cadogan, leaving their carriage waiting and the servants in the Palazzo Sessa expecting them home, slipped away from a fête at the Turkish Minister's and went on foot down to the waterfront, from where they were ferried to the *Vanguard* in a freezing wind. Nelson himself went for the royal party, and conducted them through a secret passage from the palace down to the quay. There his boats were waiting.

Nelson's ship took most of the English residents, but also, besides the royal family, General Acton, the Austrian Ambassador and sundry Neapolitan nobles and their servants. About two thousand others in flight, among them Cornelia Knight and her mother, were dispersed wherever they could be accommodated in the very heterogeneous armada assembled under Nelson's command. Next morning was too rough to sail. On 23 December boatloads came out to the ships to beg the King not to leave. Ferdinand would see only the Archbishop. He told him he had gone to sea because he had been betrayed on land; Acton added that he would return when the people had proved their loyalty with deeds. Meanwhile, the King said, the Archbishop should look after them as his, the Archbishop's, flock. The *Vanguard* waited a few hours more, until the King's favourite wolfhounds were fetched in safely from Caserta, and to receive the hapless General Mack, for whom, he was so abject, even Nelson felt some pity. Nobody had any useful advice to offer Mack; he was to do his best, and fall back towards Sicily when that failed. At seven the fleet set sail. The wind shifted to the north. Ferdinand at once perked up. He observed to Hamilton: 'We shall have plenty of woodcocks, *Cavaliere*, this wind will bring them – it is just the season, and we shall have rare sport ... You must get your *cannone* ready.' Then he summoned his gamekeeper and discussed woodcock with him.[75]

The wind increased to become the worst gale Nelson had experienced in all his years at sea. The *Vanguard* lost her fore-yard and three topsails, and was near to having to sacrifice her main-mast. The Austrian Ambassador, afraid he was about to meet his Maker, thought he had better not do so in possession of a snuffbox decorated with a naked portrait of his mistress, and threw it overboard. Hamilton composed himself with a loaded pistol in each hand. He told Emma he wasn't going to die with 'the guggle-guggle-guggle' of salt-water in his throat. Emma for her part was magnificent. Nelson mentioned her in dispatches to Lord St Vincent:

> It is my duty to tell your Lordship the obligations which the whole Royal Family as well as myself are under on this trying occasion to her Ladyship. They necessarily came on board without a bed, nor could the least preparation be made for their reception. Lady Hamilton provided her own beds, linen, etc, and became their *slave* ... nor did her Ladyship enter a bed the whole time they were on board.

He was beginning that pleading on her behalf that would end in the pathetic codicil to his will; but here at least her behaviour was fit for praise. While most were prostrate with fear and sickness and whilst Hamilton was preparing himself to die with a bullet through either temple, Emma heroically cheered and nursed and comforted the royal family. Her mother too, tough as they come, ministered to the King. Emma reported: 'The king says my mother is an angel.'[76] On Christmas morning Prince Carlo Alberto, the youngest of Maria Carolina's children, fell into convulsions. Emma nursed him all day, but he died that evening in her arms, aged six.

Early next morning the ships came into Palermo. The Queen went ashore at once, in her grief; the Hamiltons followed her, through driving snow, to accommodation in the damp and chilly Colli Palace, a residence only meant for summers. Ferdinand ate a hearty breakfast and waited till a reception of sufficient pomp had been organized. Then he landed in good spirits.

Chapter 12

WRECK AND DISGRACE, 1798–1800

The *Colossus*, Captain George Murray, though heavily armed, had been in service in the Mediterranean and at Aboukir as a storeship. After the battle she took on booty and the wounded and came back to Naples with Nelson's *Vanguard.* In Naples she was not refitted as she needed to be, priority being given to ships that would still have to fight. Indeed, Captain Murray reluctantly gave up his spare anchor for Nelson's use. When she sailed from Naples, still carrying spoils from Aboukir and French and English wounded and also now Hamilton's vases, she was not in good condition; but she reached Lisbon safely on 20 November. There she took on a further cargo: the body of Admiral Viscount Shuldham, the coffin being hidden in a large packing case so as not to alarm the superstitious sailors. In convoy with eight merchantmen she was piloted into St Mary's harbour, Isles of Scilly, in bad weather on 7 December, and the next day was driven by the gale (the spare anchor might have saved her) out of the roads and ran aground on a reef just south of Samson. Boats came out and all but one of the crew and all the passengers, including the wounded, were got off safely. Then the ship broke up.

Greville wrote to Hamilton on 9 January with the bad news of the wreck. He had it from their friend Lord Spencer that '4 large boxes' belonging to Hamilton had gone down with the ship. Exactly what vases were on the *Colossus* was and is still something of a puzzle. Hamilton, in letters of 22 March, 8 and 28 April and 14 July 1799 and 25 January 1800, speaks consistently of eight cases containing 'all of the best vases in my collection ... the cream of my collection'; but four is the only precise number given by anybody at the English end. Greville wrote again on 10 January, saying, incorrectly, that the ship had gone down 'in deep water near shore' (the wreck was half out of the water at low tide); and, correctly, that Hamilton's cases were 'deep in the hold'. There some at least seem to have escaped the terrible falling of shot, cannon and ballast into the hold as the ship broke up, and to have floated free. Greville sent this further report on 8 June 1799:

> I am sorry to inform you that only about ten vases and pateras, of which only one is of consequence, has been preserved from all the wreck. That a box was opened is most certain, but what I recover'd was obtain'd from the people by one of the many employed to watch the landing of any cases by the sea. I was assured by Major Bowen that these were thrown on the beach by the sea. The one I mention as of consequence is the drinking cup with the boar & sheep's head. I am still in hopes more may be thrown up.[1]

Bowen was the commander of Star Castle, the fortress on St Mary's. In a curious corroboration or repetition of what Greville already knew in June he responded thus to his enquiries, in a letter of 26 November:

> I fear there is no reasonable ground to hope that another article of Sir William Hamilton's interesting collection of antiquities will be recovered from the wreck of the Colossus. You will be sensible of this from the following statement of facts.
>
> The Colossus being, as is generally thought here, in a very weak state, broke up uncommonly soon after striking on the rocks. The people of St Martin's Island met several packages drifting out at Crow Sound, among the rest those described to them as Sir W. Hamilton's. They assert that, anxious to fulfil Captain Murray's and my earnest injunctions, they used the utmost efforts for recovery of the latter; but that the sea running very high and the wind blowing a storm, they found it impossible to lift the packages which were very large into their boats. They then tried to disengage the contents. Unfortunately, in this also they failed. Their solemn declaration to me is, in their own words, that 'they saw on opening the canvass cases, several large pieces of most beautifully painted clome' (the name for all earthen ware here); 'but that, on their trying to lift them, whether from the effect of seawater on them, or a cement

used in joining them, a single piece could not be taken into a boat, each giving way in their hands like wet dough'.

It will be evident to you Sir, that if articles of this, or even of a much more substantial nature, had remained in the hull when the guns shot, and ballast fell together in a mass, they must have been utterly demolished.

The few articles that were recovered were thrown on St Martin's Island by the sea. I had early intimation of it; and, though they were divided amongst the women of the island, to whom this part of the spoil was left, I succeeded after much toil and the distribution of four guineas in obtaining every piece saved.[2]

This extraordinary document, which came to light in a bookshop in Hampstead only a few years ago, confirms Hamilton's assertion in his letters of 14 July 1799 and 25 January 1800 that the cases were 'so very carefully packed ... They were excellently packed up, & the cases will not easily go to pieces'; but it is very odd that the vases being taken out gave way 'like wet dough'. Sea water itself would not harm glazed pottery. Hamilton said as much: 'the sea water will not hurt the vases'. Anyway, what few survived the wreck and were recovered reached Hamilton eventually via Major Bowen and William Augustus Pitt (of Camelford?). But they were very few, fifteen in all, according to Hamilton. From some other source he had already heard of the wreck before Greville's letters reached him in Palermo in the latter half of March 1799; and until March 1801 he continued in the belief that most and the very best of his Second Collection was at the bottom of the sea (off Plymouth, he would say: did he really have no idea where the Scillies are?)[3]

Hamilton was grieved by his loss. Sir Gilbert Elliot said: 'It will go far, I think, to break his heart.'[4] Hamilton's first response was to concede (as he had done years earlier at the death of Catherine) that this was something by which his philosophy had been 'put to the Trial'. He knew before Greville did that the corpse of Admiral Shuldham was safe and sound. 'Damn his body,' he wrote,

it can be of no use but to the Worms, but my Collection wou'd have given information to the most learned & have convinced every intelligent Being that there is but one Truth, & that God Almighty has never made himself known to the miserable Atoms that inhabit this globe otherwise than bidding them to increase & multiply & to leave the rest to Him – So thought the Wise Ancients when the Mysteries of Bacchus & Eleusis were established.

That is the highest claim Hamilton ever made for the art he had spent his life collecting: that it would, if properly considered, bring the beholder to a view of things far more stoically pagan than Christian. At that moment, as his life slipped further into distress and something approaching ignominy, he shows an interest in the vases far exceeding their function as improvers of contemporary taste, or as bearers of his name into posterity or as the means of paying off his debts. His one consolation was that he had had them engraved and published, and he adds: 'I have many living witnesses that the originals existed'; almost as though such *effective* beauty, like a Messiah, needed witnesses or succeeding generations would never believe in it. He could not let them go. Seven months after the wreck he was still urging Greville to spare no expense in his efforts at recovery; and a refrain in his letters is that those vases were unique: 'never in this world will such a collection be made again ... I do assure you never again will such a collection appear ... The like were never seen, or ever will be.' For a man not given to hyperbole this is high language. He had shipped them out to keep them from the French, but freely conceded that 'they had better be at Paris than at the bottom of the sea'. Hamilton concluded then (25 January 1800) by reverting to his old consolation: 'However, drawings were made of all, & the prints for the 4th volume were engraved and are with Tischbein, who I hear is in Germany.'⁵

In the general *sauve qui peut* in December 1798 Tischbein had asked Hamilton what he should do. Hamilton offered him a passage to Sicily; but by then it was too late to get his plates and engravings safely packed and on board. Tischbein was unwilling to leave them. Hamilton assured him that the French in their advance through Italy had never done artists any harm. He should be as friendly to them as possible, and hide his treasures before they arrived. Tischbein and his pupil Luigi spent two nights making a hole in the wall above a door and immuring in it all the work done on Hamilton's vases and on Tischbein's own *Homer*. Poor Luigi, Tischbein reports, almost broke his back lifting the heavy copper plates and crouching in the hole to lay them safely away.[6]

The French advanced steadily through a kingdom rapidly disintegrating under its own contradictions. Pignatelli, the unfortunate creature appointed regent by the departing King and Queen, so mistrusted the fanatical *lazzaroni* that he would not arm them for an effective resistance. While he dithered the Jacobins worked like a solvent in the body politic of the city. They wanted the French in because they wanted freedom, equality and fraternity, and believed Championnet and his troops would deliver it; others wanted them in because anything was better than the ferociously loyal mob. There was a stay in the advance when Pignatelli sued for an amnesty, which was granted, but on terms so ruinous and humiliating that the city revolted at them and collapsed into anarchy. The *lazzaroni* took on the defence of what their betters had abandoned, sacked the royal palace and slaughtered anyone they suspected of being at all pro-French. Pignatelli fled, dressed in his wife's clothes, and got to Sicily, where he was imprisoned. 'We regard him as a criminal,' the Queen said, 'for leaving and for making the armistice.'[7] Championnet, declaring the amnesty null and void (Naples having failed to comply), marched in, encouraged by local republicans now occupying the Castle of Sant' Elmo. Advancing from Capodimonte on 21 January, the French, and their supporters in Naples, fought the *lazzaroni* street by street. Tischbein's lodgings on the Piazza Alt Largo di Pinga were in the midst of the worst fighting. The French had a battery under his windows; by that and the incoming fire his house was so shaken he feared it would collapse. Towards evening on the third day the French got the upper hand and the firing decreased. But then a nunnery opposite and a palace nearby went up in flames, and he feared that his house, and *Homer* and the *Engravings from Ancient Vases* in it, would perish that way. Soon he was summoned below, the house was to be set alight and everyone in it shot. His own account deserves not to be paraphrased here:

> Thereupon I said: 'Addio Homero', ran downstairs and was met by an officer and some soldiers ready to perform the execution. I explained to the officer who I was and that I did not even know why they were waging war but only concerned myself with art. He

at once became very polite. The soldiers left and he and three others came upstairs with me, to eat a meal together, in friendship.

In the night the plunderers arrived, three lots of them, but departed in peace when he told them he was a German and an artist.[8]

The fighting ceased, on 23 January 1799 the Kingdom of Naples became the Parthenopean Republic, liberty trees were erected, a *Te Deum* was sung, there was a miraculous liquefaction of the blood of Saint Januarius, and the *lazzaroni*, for a while, went quiet as lambs. Tischbein now sought to leave Naples. He was offered a passage, with his copper plates, to Paris; accepted; got underway, but was intercepted by French privateers and carried into Leghorn, where he was quarantined and his belongings impounded. The Prussian consul intervened, but still all his cases had to be opened. The privateers were on the watch for anything English, and the first paper taken out was the title page of the *Engravings*, announcing them to be the property of his Britannic Majesty's Envoy Extraordinary and Plenipoteniary to the Court of Naples. But the sailor held the sheet upside down and could not read it as English. Tischbein was allowed to proceed, but leaving the plates in the customs house; from where, against all the odds, as picaresque in their adventures as the vases themselves, they were forwarded to him in Germany by a friend.

The Hamiltons, in Palermo, moved to the Villa Bastioni, which, like their first accommodation, was a place 'calculated only for summer'. There Sir William took to his bed for a week. On 7 January, sending a dispatch to Lord Grenville, he was, he said, still not well enough to write as fully as he could have wished; but the day before he had written Charles Greville a longish account of the Neapolitan defeat in which there is no glimmer of admission that he, Nelson, Emma and the Queen might have been at fault in urging the King into war. He blamed Mack and the army, for 'treachery and stinking cowardice', and the Austrians for failing to intervene. He sounds more and more like a man assailed too late in life by events too vast and complex for his energies and judgement. He told Greville that he was 'really ... in want of repose'; and, uniquely in the surviving documents of his life, he made mention of his father, to assert himself: 'I feel age creeping upon me, but I will bear up as long &

as well as I can, and not give up as my father did twenty years before he died, calling himself a dying man, and so we all are.'⁹

In Sicily, and really for the remaining years of his life, Hamilton had much to bear up against. Again in that letter to Greville he says he looks forward to coming home on leave, as soon as possible, perhaps in the spring. It had become the pathetic leitmotiv of somebody unhappy in his circumstances. The longer he waited, or the longer he was thwarted, the worse his life became. Even as late as the spring of 1799, had he left Italy then he would have been spared a good deal. Everything became crasser in Sicily. Characters shifted further into caricature. The Queen raged and lamented, but ever more uselessly. Ferdinand stirred himself enough to blame her for their situation and to allow somebody else to try his hand at improving it. On 25 January Cardinal Fabrizio Ruffo, who had crossed with the Court to Palermo, offered to lead a counter-revolutionary march through Calabria. Gladly the King agreed, authorizing him to act as his vicar-general with 'the unrestricted quality of *alter ego*' on the mainland of Italy. Ruffo landed at Punta del Pezzo on 7 February with only eight companions, but very soon assembled a fanatical horde and with them advanced in the name of God and the King with all possible savagery towards the capital. Austria entered the wars again on 1 March and the French on every front were put on the defensive.

Irrelevant in Palermo, the Hamiltons, the Bourbons, Nelson and numerous further displaced English tourists went on ever more grotesquely in their roles. The French émigrés, however, were obliged to go elsewhere. The Sicilians hated all the French, royalist or republican, with an equal passion and would not let them land. They headed for Trieste. They were luckier than their compatriots who did land on 20 January 1799. These were 120 men from the army in Egypt, all affected and forty or fifty of them almost blinded by the desert sun. They were quarantined in a house on the seafront, and having been there three weeks, ever more an object of hatred, on some slight provocation nearly all were massacred. The British Consul in Palermo, Charles Lock, reports: 'The rage of the populace went so far as to roast and eat their livers.'¹⁰ Since the Sicilians hated the Neapolitans, in fact all foreigners (in September they massacred 120 Turks), almost as much as they hated the French, Maria Carolina felt no safer in her alternative capital than she had in the care of the loyal mob in Naples.

Hamilton took up ambassadorial residence in the vast Palazzo Palagonia on the waterfront. Nelson and other English also had rooms there. Hamilton, on money he did not have, felt obliged to entertain as lavishly as before. Replying, on 22 March, to Greville's letters about the wreck of the *Colossus*, he spoke of 'the general Wreck that has attended my fortune of late'. His debts, he said, which had been £6000 when he first came abroad, now totalled more than £15,000; and he said again that he would leave on the first ship possible and hoped to be home in June or July, unless obliged to stay.[11]

Cardinal Ruffo's army, first increased by eighty 'persons of no good intention and stability', as he himself described them, before the end of February numbered seventeen thousand, not all like the first eighty but mostly. He called them the Christian Army of the Holy Faith, and promised them the best of both worlds: plunder in this, life everlasting in the next. By 1 March, requisitioning supplies, arms and funds on the way, he had reached Monteleone and was welcomed in. The King, diverting some of his bloodlust from animals to those humans in his kingdom who had been unfaithful to Almighty God and to himself, wrote to Ruffo urging him not to be lenient. He wanted, he said, 'summary, military, exemplary punishment'.[12] Corfu was taken by Russian and Turkish squadrons; the British, under Captain Troubridge, blockaded the port of Naples.

Nelson meanwhile was behaving in a way entirely customary and recognizable in the Kingdom of the Two Sicilies: as the *cicisbeo* of a woman with an elderly husband. Cornelia Knight, who moved in with the Hamiltons after the death of her mother in August 1799, said later that 'there was certainly at that time no impropriety in living under Lady Hamilton's roof. Her house was the resort of the best company of all nations, and the attentions paid to Lord Nelson appeared perfectly natural.'[13] But whatever the exact degree of intimacy already existing between Emma and Nelson, they were viewed as over-fond by many observing them, not least by Nelson's fellow officers.

Guests at the Palazzo Palagonia were treated to Emma's attitudes just as for years they had been at the Palazzo Sessa; but her performances had by now so run into the rest of her life that spectators often could not tell what was an act and what was (so to speak) real; and nor could she, and perhaps in her case such distinctions do not apply. Thus when Pryse Lockhart Gordon arrived in Palermo from Naples in April 1799 and presented himself at the Palazzo Palagonia she entered on Hamilton's arm, 'dying, she said, of chagrin for the loss of her beloved Naples'. One chief woe, so she told him in a '*mélange* of Lancashire and Italian', was the loss of all her possessions in the Palazzo Sessa 'which had fallen into the hands of the vile republicans'. He was able to assure her that everything from the house had been got safely away and should be in Palermo very soon; but he discovered afterwards that the transport ship had already arrived and that Emma knew perfectly well that her things were safe and sound. So she was acting. As she was on another occasion reported by the – it must be admitted – unfriendly Lockhart Gordon:

> On one occasion, being desirous to astonish a gentleman who had just arrived, and had not heard of her Ladyship's attitudinal celebrity, she dropped from her chair on the carpet, when sitting at table after dinner. The comb which fastened her superabundant locks had been removed (like Caesar she had fallen gracefully), and nothing could have been more classical or imposing than this prostrate position. Sir William started up to open a little of the curtain in order to admit the proper light, while the stranger flew to the sideboard for water, with which he plentifully sprinkled the fainting dame, before he discovered that it was a *scena* (and not a fit as he thought) which had been got up. – 'You have spoiled, my good friend,' said the Knight, 'one of the most perfect attitudes that Emma ever executed – how unlucky!'

There Hamilton appears disappointed by his guest, not embarrassed by his wife; and it has to be said that at this time, and even later when things got worse, there is more sense among observers that Hamilton *must surely* feel embarrassed, distressed, humiliated, than hard evidence that he did. Either he doted so much that he could not see or (more likely, in my view) he thought his audience at least as foolish.

Lockhart Gordon recounts another scene, one of the grossest ever witnessed in Emma's life. The Emperor of Russia had sent dispatches to Nelson and the courier, a Turk, 'a coarse savage monster', according to Lockhart Gordon, was given a dinner by Hamilton. The Turk got drunk on rum, a drink allowed him even as a Muslim. He had by him a Greek as interpreter:

> The monster, who had the post of honour at her Ladyship's side, entertained her through the interpretation of the Greek with an account of his exploits; among others, that of his having lately fallen in with a French transport, conveying invalids and wounded soldiers from Egypt, whom he had brought on board his frigate; but provisions and water having run short he found it necessary to get rid of his prisoners, and amused himself by putting them to death. 'With this weapon,' said he in his vile jargon, and drawing his shibbola, 'I cut off the heads of twenty French prisoners in one day! Look, there is their blood remaining on it!' The speech being translated, her Ladyship's eye beamed with delight, and she said, 'Oh, let me see the sword that did the glorious deed!' It was presented to her; she took it into her fair hand covered with rings, and looking at the encrusted Jacobin blood, kissed it and handed it to the hero of the Nile!

Gordon continues:

> Mrs. Charles Lock, the beautiful and amiable wife of our consul-general, was sitting *vis-à-vis* to the Turk, and was so horrified at the scene (being near her accouchement) that she fainted and was taken out of the room. Her Ladyship said it was a piece of affectation, and made no efforts to assist her guest...

So there Mrs Lock was acting, and Emma meant it.

> The toad-eaters applauded, but many groaned and cried 'shame' loud enough to reach the ears of the Admiral, who turned pale, hung his head, and semed ashamed. Lord Montgomery got up, and left the room, and I speedily followed.[14]

Gordon makes no mention of Hamilton's response.

With the Court now removed to Palermo, Sicily, and Palermo

especially, enjoyed a brief heyday. The idle classes, prevented from amusing themselves on the mainland, did so instead in Sicily. Some, like Cornelia Knight, were entranced by Art and Nature; others enjoyed Society, as it presented itself at the royal residence or the Palazzo Palagonia. The King hunted. There were riots in February over food prices; and there was the above-mentioned massacre of French soldiers on the waterfront; but by and large, with a deter- mination that must come with breeding, the classes who had always enjoyed themselves continued to do so in the last remotest bit of Italy where they still could.

In Calabria meanwhile Cardinal Ruffo and his merry men, afforced by local bandits, were speedily making it possible for King and Court and hangers-on to move back into the spaces rightly theirs. Catanzaro and Cotrone were sacked; after which those happy with their plunder dispersed and those unhappy mutinied. Through the agency of the local clergy however, the Cardinal soon raised another army, and his march on Naples continued. The Directory recalled the humane Championnet, replacing him with Field Marshal J. E. J. A. Macdonald, who acted strictly in the French interest and informed the Neapolitan Jacobins that they would have to fend for themselves. Troubridge oversaw the recapturing of the islands, 'the inhabitants,' Hamilton reports, 'very readyly assisted him in Cutting down the Trees of Liberty & giving into his hands the most notorious Jacobins employ'd by the french Government at Naples'. By early April Troubridge had sent to Palermo for a judge. He had republican prisoners to get rid of: 'the villains increase so fast on my hands eight or ten of them must be hung'. In the Abruzzi meanwhile King and Church had found another champion. He was, so Hamilton reported to Lord Grenville, 'an outlaw'd Priest that goes by the Name of the Grand Diavolo, a notorious Murderer who wishes to obtain his pardon by his Services'. He had raised an army at least as savage as Ruffo's, and was advancing against Naples from the north. The Parthenopean Republic waited to be erased. Neither Hamilton nor Lord Grenville had any illusions about the means being employed towards that end; nor about the quality of the government to be restored. Yet Hamilton writes with evident satisfaction that on the islands 'the abominable french Trees of Liberty have been cut down and the flags of His Sicilian Majesty are now flying'; he even thought it would be 'glorious indeed' if His Majesty could be enthroned again 'without any other foreign aid than that of Great Britain'.[15]

The Royalist armies, supported now by Russian and Turkish squadrons, closed in on Naples, to exterminate the Republic. In Palermo the King and Queen were kept informed, and exhorted their loyal forces to get on with it. Naturally, having already magnificently displayed his cowardice in the run from Rome, the King had no thought now of taking any part himself. First he insisted that his armies on land and the English at sea must make land and sea entirely safe for him. All the cleansing was to be done by them; his contribution consisted in demanding that it be bloody. The French withdrew; the violence done or connived in by Ferdinand's hench-men – among whom we have to number Hamilton, Emma, Nelson and his captains – was not against the French with whom at least Great Britain was at war, but against those Neapolitans foolish or idealistic or opportunistic enough to serve their brief republic. These were, Hamilton noted on 5 June, showing 'every mark of the greatest apprehension', as well they might with the Grand Diavolo advancing fast from Gaeta, Ruffo already under Vesuvius, the British in the Bay and executions proceeding on Procida, Ischia and Capri. Loyally, Hamilton, on the verge of involvement in worse and worse, again told his Secretary of State he would not come home, even though, he added, 'I am much worn and my private affairs in South Wales are suffering by my long absence.'[16]

There was one clear issue in all the complexity of that summer's politics: whether to treat the Neapolitan Jacobins leniently or harshly. Cardinal Ruffo, far wiser and far less murderous than either his army or his king, thought leniency the best way of re-establishing a viable social order. 'In winning back Naples,' he wrote, 'I foresee that our greatest obstacle will lie in the fear of deserved punishment.'[17] He had been given at the outset full powers by the King, and now in the last stages of the submission of Naples he was proceeding according to his humane lights. Having fought his way through Calabria and seen any amount of slaughter he might have been allowed to finish the business as moderately as he could. But the non-combatants, the watchers from a safe distance, the royal family, wanted vengeance, and were encouraged in this by Nelson who acted throughout and quite improperly as though he himself or his own

king were the offended party. Emma, the blacksmith's daughter, the
ex-prostitute, rabid in her love of royalty and hatred of republics,
urged him on; and Hamilton wrote the necessary letters. On 5 June
the *Foudroyant* arrived in Palermo; Nelson made her his flagship.

Ruffo and the Grand Diavolo overwhelmed Naples. Not surprisingly, their forces used that city much as they had all other human
habitation along the way. By 14 June only the castles still held out,
and in them some remaining French and many Neapolitan Jacobins
had taken refuge. Cardinal Ruffo, 'to prevent the Capital from
becoming a heap of Stones', negotiated their capitulation; Captain
Foote, representing the British, put his name to it, albeit rather
unwillingly. In essence the terms were that the French would be
allowed to leave unmolested and embark on ships for Toulon, and
that the Neapolitans might leave with them or return to their homes
in Naples, also unmolested. On 21 June the British fleet sailed from
Palermo, the Hamiltons and Nelson on board the *Foudroyant*. Emma
was there, in her own estimation, as Maria Carolina's 'Deputy'. At
Procida they learned the terms of the capitulation, as had also in the
meantime the King and Queen in Palermo. The Court and all their
loyal servants frothed with rage. The King accused Ruffo of playing
a treacherous game of his own, and wanted him removed from all
command; he offered Nelson supreme authority instead; the Queen,
through Emma, recommended him 'to treat Naples as if it were an
Irish town in a similar state of rebellion'.[18] Hamilton wrote to Ruffo
on 24 and 27 June, in French, on Nelson's behalf, to say that he
entirely disapproved of the capitulation and that, with the redoubtable
force at his command, he had no intention of remaining neutral in
the matter. He defined his role as the defeat of the common enemy
(the French) and the submission of the rebellious subjects to the
King's clemency. That conflation characterizes Nelson's subsequent
behaviour. He arrived with his ships to find all parties in a state of
truce. There were rumours of a French fleet heading towards Naples,
and Ruffo, understandably, for good tactical as well as humanitarian
reasons, wanted the evacuation concluded as swiftly as possible. But
Nelson was there in time to interfere. Twice he saw Ruffo on board
the *Foudroyant*, to browbeat him, with Hamilton as interpreter; they
reached no understanding. The gloss Hamilton put on it, in a long
apologia to Lord Grenville, was that Nelson merely acted to halt

proceedings that still wanted royal approval, which of course would never be forthcoming. On 28 June Acton got a message to Nelson from Palermo, in the King's name insisting on severity. Nelson acted accordingly. He halted the evacuation. Indeed, under his guns he had the Neapolitans taken off the Toulon ships. Those who had returned to their homes were ordered to surrender themselves forthwith. They were thrown into gaol, 'to lie at the King's mercy'. His vengeance more like.

Hamilton reads, in his dispatches at this time, like a man acting as mouthpiece for others more determined than he was on a brutal course. His long dispatch of 14 July 1799, for example, is remarkable in its draft form for the unusually high number of corrections and crossings-out. By then he had particularly unpleasant things to relate, and was struggling to put them in the best light possible. In fact now, politically as well as domestically, he was associating himself with Nelson in opprobrium.

The Court, and Nelson as their agent, especially wanted to get their hands on Admiral Caracciolo. He had crossed with the royal party to Sicily in December 1798 (and had felt insulted that they were on Nelson's and not on his ship), but had crossed back in March and served the Republic. He was captured by Ruffo's forces after three or four days in hiding. On 27 June, Hamilton, writing for Nelson, asked Ruffo, now thought untrustworthy, to hand Caracciolo over. Nelson, he wrote, would see to him ('il en disposera'). So it was that this admiral in the service of and then in rebellion against a foreign power was brought to a flagship of the British navy and there court-martialled and sentenced to death by hanging. He begged not for his life but to be spared the disgrace of hanging; but that clemency was refused him. Hamilton and Count Thurn (who had presided over the court martial) asked for a stay of twenty-four hours, 'for the care of the soul'; but Nelson refused that too. 'All is for the best,' Hamilton wrote to Acton. 'Lord Nelson's manner of acting must be as his conscience and honour dictate, and I believe his determination will be found best at last.' And he duly recounted the whole business to Lord Grenville:

Admiral Caracciolo the Chief of the Rebells of His Sicn Majest's Marine ... was by Lord Nelson's orders, tried on board the

Foudroyant by a Court Martial composed entirely of Neapolitan Marine officers, was condemn'd & hung up at the yard arm of the Neapolitan Frigate the Minerva ... at 5 o'clock in the Evening of the same day, where he hung untill Sun Set to the great Satisfaction of His Sicn Majesties Loyal Subjects thousands of which came off from Naples in boats with loud applause at so speedy an Act of Justice ... His body was afterwards thrown into the Sea.[19]

Doubtless as a rebel he could not have expected much better, and certainly the loyal subjects were pleased to see him hang; none the less Nelson and Hamilton with him were greatly demeaned by their involvement. Nelson's assiduity on behalf of a poltroon King and his hatred of rebels in a city he had always despised, having little or nothing to do with his war against the French, are perhaps best understood as a muddling of judgement and loyalties rather akin to the muddle he was in in his very public private life. If he was the agent of Ferdinand on board the *Foudroyant* he was also, on the same ship, more and more in thrall to Emma Hamilton.

In that same long dispatch of 14 July Hamilton included for Lord Grenville's perusal the letters sent to Emma from the Queen. The motive, ostensibly official (Grenville might benefit from the information they contained), was also and perhaps largely personal. Hamilton wanted Emma's importance acknowledged, for her own good and also for his, on his return. Rather pathetically, he seems to have thought these letters might help him in what he foresaw would be difficult dealings with his employers, the British Government. Indeed, he told Grenville he would want them back on his arrival home – and of that, he added, he now saw 'a real prospect'. He wrote: 'We mean to profit of the first Ship that Lord Nelson sends downwards after that their Sicilian Majesties shall have been happily reinstated on their throne of Naples, having had, as your Lp. knows, in my pocket for more than two years the King's gracious Permission to return home for a short time to look after my private concerns.'[20]

Ferdinand was now persuaded that he might do some good and run no risk by 'showing himself' in the Bay. He arrived with Acton on 10 July. To greet him, Caraccioli's corpse, sunk with shot at head and foot, bobbed to the surface and stood there like a cork. It was suggested that he had come to beg the King's pardon; or that he wanted a Christian burial. Some fishermen towed him ashore and shovelled him a hole in the sand. The King and Acton moved to Nelson's flagship. Nothing better symbolizes the indecent fusion of Neapolitan interests and British complicity than the weeks of the physical living together of Hamilton, Emma, Nelson and the Bourbon King on board the *Foudroyant*.

The French, still besieged in Sant Elmo, finally surrendered and were allowed to march out in good order and board their ships for Toulon. Neapolitan republicans, trying to slip out with them, were obligingly handed over by the French commandant General Méjean. The King stayed safely on Nelson's ship, but Emma and Hamilton went up into the fort and from there – presumably with a spyglass, it is a fair distance – they looked down on the Palazzo Sessa and on the Villa Emma at Posillipo – despoiled and plundered, Emma told Greville, and 'Sir William's new apartment – a bomb burst in it!'[21] That was their last sight of those places.

In Naples, still not fit for the King to land in, eight thousand republicans began to be tried and sentenced. Emma and Nelson were constantly petitioned to intercede, mostly on the grounds that the petitioner had surrendered in good faith, according to the terms negotiated with Cardinal Ruffo. All in all about a hundred were hanged; but to them need to be added those summarily dealt with on the islands and those torn limb from limb by the Army of the Holy Church when Ruffo let it loose. The trials themselves dragged on for a year, exciting great disgust in a Europe by then pretty well used to atrocity. Hamilton made a strange observation to his Secretary of State: 'My former despatches to Yr Lp have painted sufficiently the abominable & general Corruption of this Country and it has not been improved by the french government of Seven Months.'[22] He wrote this on 5 August, having overseen the restoration of precisely that corrupt old order. If the French had changed nothing for the better certainly the returning Bourbons would not.

On 1 August the people of Naples came out in boats to honour the Hero of the Nile and their reinstated sovereign who was wholly dependent on him. Four days later Ferdinand sailed away, leaving Ruffo (after all) as viceroy and a Supreme Junta to keep the gallows busy. He mistrusted Naples, he was happier in Palermo. Arriving there on 8 August, he and his party on the *Foudroyant* were welcomed with loyal joy and three nights of festivities. Then the Hamiltons and Nelson, back in the Palazzo Palagonia, were showered with presents by the King and Queen who were sincerely grateful and just as sincerely anxious that without British protection they would not last long, not in Sicily and certainly not in Naples. Hamilton was always pleased by presents from heads of state; he detailed them in letters home, to boost his standing with those who might advance him or depress him. This time, from the King and Queen, he got 'a thumping yellow diamond set round with Diamonds in a ring'. Emma got the Queen's picture set with diamonds in a bracelet, earrings of pearl and diamonds, an aigrette of the Queen's cypher in diamonds, a complete dress of the finest point lace, and more besides. Nelson, symbolically enough, got the King's own sword which had come down to him from Louis XIV through Philip and Charles of Spain. In addition he was made Duke of Brontë, with land under Etna worth a good deal more than Hamilton's in Pembroke.[23]

A week later there was another fête, in honour of Saint Rosalia and, again, of Nelson and the Hamiltons; and a fortnight after that, a third. On this last occasion – chiefly a replay of the Battle of the Nile in fireworks – the three suffered an apotheosis (by no means the last) of glory and risibility. They appeared in their proper persons but also in wax effigies, crowned with wreaths of laurel and bearing the motto of the Garter *Tria juncta in Uno*. Emma who had brought the statues to life and had herself been endlessly converted back into works of art now carried her husband and her lover into wax, into a sort of fairground equivalent of the bronzes of Herculaneum and the marbles of the galleries in Rome.

Hamilton reiterated his wish to come home. So what held him in Palermo? He believed himself – or rather the trio he was a part of – to be indispensable. He wrote to Spencer Smith on 25 July 1799 (from the *Foudroyant*):

When I wrote last to you I thought I was going to England having had the King's leave in my pocket these 2. years: but having been 35. years acquainted with this Country and it's inhabitants, language, & C, and Lady Hamilton being in as much favour with the Queen as I am with the K. of Naples, I cannot be spared yet; indeed what could Lord N. do without us? He would demand his recall from this station if I left him: this has decided my stay.[24]

The court wanted Nelson and his fleet; the Queen knew she could work on Nelson through Emma; they feared (rightly) that if Hamilton left they would get someone less amenable to their interests; Nelson spoke no Italian, had no patience with Italians and needed Hamilton as interpreter and go-between, if he was to act in the Neapolitan and (rather remotely) the British interest; but he was in love with Emma, she with him and Hamilton was complaisant; Palermo was a better location for such relations than, they feared, London would be; neither Emma nor Nelson wanted Hamilton to go home, not if by that they would be separated. Nelson meanwhile was telling Fanny that Hamilton insisted he must stay. And so on. He, the Hamiltons and the King and Queen were attached, almost fused, in a nexus of interdependence.

Having told Grenville he would leave on the next ship heading west, on 7 September Hamilton had to tell him that he had 'let the Goliath go down to Gibraltar' without him, though Captain Foley had offered him and Emma a passage home. The reason again: the King and Queen need Nelson, and Nelson will only stay if Hamilton does. He wrote that though the French had gone from Naples 'the pernicious Maxims thay have left behind them will require force & a watchful eye'.[25] Without a strong foreign garrison in Naples the King and Queen would not go back. A month later, by which time Hamilton thinks the King's presence in Naples really necessary, His Majesty still won't leave Palermo without Nelson's protection. Grenville must for a long time have been wondering why this state – about which his diplomats and naval officers to a man spoke with the utmost contempt – should ever have warranted so much propping up.

Hamilton wrote to Banks on 13 September: how they were fêted and rewarded in Palermo; of Emma: 'except being a little fatter she is as you saw her 8 years ago'; and of himself: 'I am nearly worn out.' And then about the possibility of returning, a passage worth quoting because, though a repetition, there is something peculiar and sad in it:

We were to have returned to England in the Colossus Captain

Foley & she came here to take us, but at the request of Ld. Nelson & this Court We have deferred our departure untill next Spring, when alive or dead I shall come home, for at my first wife's particular desire I am to lye by her in Slebech Church when I am dead and we shall roll soon together into Milford Haven for the sea is undermining that Church very fast.[26]

Foley's ship was the *Goliath*, of course. The mistake is a poignant one. The *Colossus* by then was a wreck off Samson with many of Hamilton's beloved vases. We shall come to Slebech in due course, but this sudden harking back to Catherine and looking forward to a sort of reunion with her is an admission, albeit wry and oblique, of how wearisome his life was in the toils of Emma, Nelson and the King and Queen.

Autumn, winter and the following spring it continued much the same. Hamilton was often unwell. Lock writes: 'Sir William's health is very much broken and his frame is so feeble that even a slight attack of bile, to several fits of which he has lately been subject, may carry him off.' All the more remarkable, given such bouts and any number of other trials and tribulations, is his resilience. Emma grew more and more into caricature, and there were the usual unfriendly witnesses *de passage* who sent word back to London society of what she and her husband and her *cavaliere servante* were like. Hamilton's 'a little fatter' seems to have been euphemistic. Lady Elgin, joining her husband (thief of the marbles) in Palermo en route to Constantinople in October 1799, said of her: 'She is indeed a Whapper! and I think her manner very vulgar.' And of Nelson: 'It is really humiliating to see Lord Nelson, he seems quite dying and yet as if he had no other thought than her.'[27] His own officers, notably Troubridge, were alarmed for him. Emma grew ever fonder of gambling, and his attendance on her into the small hours did his enfeebled constitution no good. It is unlikely he ever thought of himself as Antony and her as Cleopatra and Palermo as Egypt; but the parallel is near (the London *Times* used it on 14 November) and with or without the knowledge of it he did feel his humiliation at least as keenly as his officers did. He was best at sea. Hanging around in Palermo depressed him. Neither there nor in Naples did the Bourbon court whose servant he had become seem in any way estimable. He shared

Troubridge's view: 'So trifling a character as a Neapolitan I never before met with.'

Troubridge reported cheerfully on the executions continuing in Naples: 'Today *departed this Life Princes, Dukes, Commoners and Ladys*, to the amount of Eleven some by the *Axe* and others by the *halter.*' But Hamilton noted 'with regret' the execution, by hanging, 'of Doctor Domenico Cirillo – One of the first Phisicians, Botanists & Naturalists in Europe'.[28] Cirillo was a friend, and like Hamilton a Fellow of the Royal Society. He had appealed through Emma for mercy, but with no success. His death touched Hamilton closely, bringing the lingeringly murderous business home. Troubridge said death was 'a trifle' compared with conditions in the prisons. The King left his Junta and his hangmen to it, and enjoyed himself. By December 1799 Hamilton's dispatches to Grenville come close to frank disgust. He saw 'the general corruption at Naples & the infinity of defects in Government', and added: 'I am sorry to say I do not yet see any intention of endeavouring to mend it.' The King did have some sense that he

cou'd not with propriety lead the same dissipated life there, as formerly and He does not yet see such a Military force at Naples as He can rely on for His own personal Security & which I have observed always had a great influence upon His Majesty – At Palermo His Majesty diverts himself much the same as He did at Naples by going from one Country House to another & by shooting.

The truth was, he would not go back to Naples until he could *safely* divert himself there as he was diverting himself in Palermo. Hamilton and Acton were both of the opinion that he should return at once '& grant himself the General pardon & put an end to the numerous prosecutions on foot, and apply himself seriously to the formation of a better Government', forgetting the past. 'The utmost temper & humanity is requisite.'[29] Small hope of that. So Hamilton drew up a final balance on the court he had served at for thirty-five years.

As the century ended Napoleon, returning from defeat in Egypt, abolished the Directory and made himself First Consul in the *coup d'état* of 18 Brumaire. The émigrés were requested to return, France went under a military dictatorship and proceeded towards imperial autocracy. On 14 November it was announced in the London *Times* that Lord Keith was sailing to the Mediterranean to relieve Nelson of his command of the fleet. 'Upon his Lordship's arrival,' the paper said, 'Lord Nelson will return to England.' Then came the heavy allusion to Antony and Cleopatra. On 20 December Lord Grenville wrote to Hamilton: 'Your long and faithful service, and particularly your conduct at the difficult close of it have unquestionably well intitled you to His Majesty's favor on your retreat, and I have His Majesty's gracious permission to assure you of it.'³⁰ This being interpreted meant he was being removed. In fact, it was already settled who would replace him. In January Nelson sailed to meet Keith at Leghorn. They were back in Palermo together on 3 February, and Keith was accommodated at the Palazzo Palagonia. He hated his week there: 'The whole was a Scene of fulsome Vanity and Absurdity.'³¹ He left for Malta, taking Nelson with him.

Hamilton's debts were pressing. He owed his banker in Palermo, Abraham Gibbs, more than £3000, and Samuel Ragland, a merchant advancing him money in Naples, about the same. He tried to settle them, at least in part, with large drafts to be drawn on Ross and Ogilvie in London. Ross wouldn't honour them: Hamilton owed him £7000 already.³² Debts and attempts to settle them were a part of the long drawn-out business of leaving.

In England meanwhile Greville was doing his best with Lord Grenville. He was at his office several times in the first week of January 1800, and, having failed to get an audience, wrote a letter to his Lordship's secretary, setting out Hamilton's financial circumstances and his claims on Government. The former, in Greville's representation, did indeed look bad. Total debts: £19,000. Annual income from the estates: £2200, but from that had to be subtracted interest on the debts, mortgage repayments and income tax amounting to £1350. Greville concludes: 'Total income without any house to live in: £850.' Heartrending. He asked that his uncle should not get less than a minister retiring from Vienna would get, and made a bid also for a portion of the pension to be continued to Emma, after Hamilton's death. No response. Greville wrote again at the end of the month. He complained: 'it has never happened to me to experience a Similar mark of inattention & I may add under no Circumstance could I have been more sensible of neglect'. Hamilton would experience the same, and worse, in his own person when he returned.

In fact Hamilton's fate had largely been decided some time before these fruitless visits and letters, and Greville knew it. Really, he was pleading with Grenville to be as kind as possible after a fait accompli. He begged him to consider:

> What the pecuniary embarrassment of Sr William will be if dismissed without a liberal provision, & what the sentiment of his mind must be if the news of his disgrace & Supercession shall arrive as abruptly to him as it has been communicated to me.[33]

So that was how it was meant and seen in London: not just recalled, but disgraced. In Palermo, quite deludedly, Hamilton still thought he could leave on his own terms. He wrote to Greville on 25 January that he hoped to be home by the King's birthday (4 June), preferably by sea but otherwise he would cross to Naples and go through the Tyrol. In the event, he had no say in the choice of route, nor would the King have been pleased to see him on his birthday. More importantly, he said he had no intention of giving up his house or of resigning his post, unless he got from Government the deal (£2000 per annum clear) he had asked for in January 1798.

A week or so later he learned from the newspapers (abruptly, as Greville had hoped he would not) that his replacement was Sir Arthur Paget and that he was on his way, as Envoy Extraordinary and Plenipotentiary, a rank not accorded to Hamilton until he had been more than two years in the job. Hamilton wrote to Nelson that he didn't know whether he had been kicked up or down out of his post, but still managed to interpret it as meaning that he would after all be given what he had asked: 'I suppose it is a Cabinet job wishing to provide for Paget and they could do it no other way than by satisfying me.' In that illusion, on 22 March, he wrote to Lord Grenville, agreeing to come home, adding that he would do so 'with much satisfaction and with a thorough Confidence in His Majesty's goodness'; by which he meant that he trusted the (very vague) assurances given him on 20 December. Then he reminded his Lordship that it was not his 'retreat but a leave of absence for a short time to look after [his] private concerns' that he had applied for. Naturally Lord Grenville disregarded this. He promised Paget, who had written at length complaining about his reception in Palermo, that as soon as Hamilton got home he would explain to him 'without reserve the utter impossibility of his going back to Naples in any public situation'.[34]

Hamilton slid from favour on a number of grounds. Encouraging war against the French in November 1798 he was co-responsible for the catastrophes that ensued; and though Grenville had backed him once the invasion was underway, doubtless he blamed him after its failure. Then the client state itself presumed more and more and behaved worse and worse. Hamilton, at times (with Nelson and Emma) acting more like its agent than like His Britannic Majesty's Envoy, was tarred with their dirty brush. Besides that, he was willy-nilly part of a scandalous and ridiculous trio on a very public stage, and none the less continued to pester for a better deal than, in the view of the Foreign Office, he was due. All in all, ageing and ailing in a post now after thirty years at last of some importance, he needed replacing.

Arthur Paget arrived in Palermo on 9 April. Hamilton refused to present him at Court, made no effort to get on friendly terms with him, and Emma did her forthright best to discredit him. Paget lodged with Consul Lock, who detested Emma and she him; so the lines of hostility were very clearly drawn. To the bitter end Hamilton chose to view Paget as only his *temporary* replacement; he described him to Acton (20 April) as taking over in his, Hamilton's, absence. Emma told Greville they had sworn to be away not more than six months. Nelson meanwhile had written to Lord Keith for leave to return home and had offered the Hamilton ménage a lift on a warship, if Keith would spare him one. On 22 April Hamilton presented his 'recredentials' (effectively, his resignation, though he still insisted that he would be back again 'in a very few months')[35] and Paget his credentials to 'their Sicilian Majesties'. The Queen particularly was alarmed at Hamilton's going and, schooled by Emma, spoke of Paget in the most unfriendly way. With Hamilton, Nelson and Emma she would lose, she thought, her best allies and agents in the furtherance of her own interests.

The day after Paget took up his post, Nelson, the Hamiltons,

Cornelia Knight, an old Maltese nobleman by the name of Mushkin Pushkin, and one or two other hangers-on, left Palermo in the *Foudroyant*, for a month's holiday. Cornelia wrote some verses to raise their spirits. Their first recorded port of call is Syracuse, where they spent two days sightseeing; then they sailed on to Malta and in a detached and leisurely fashion joined the blockade of Valletta, where the French were still holed up. They had a couple of weeks ashore, in safe and pleasant places, first St Paul's Bay then Marse Scirocco Bay, Emma wearing her new cross of honour of the Order of Malta that Nelson had wangled for her from the Grand Master of the Order, Czar Paul I.

News reached them from England that on 3 February Charles Fox had denounced Nelson in parliament for reneging on the agreement given to the Neapolitan Jacobins. Altogether he and Emma with him, and Hamilton perforce as well, were in private correspondence but also now publicly at home and abroad being ridiculed and condemned. Lord Keith and the Admiralty grumbled and blustered but Nelson went his own sweet way. And it was now, on this holiday cruise in an idle war zone, that he and Emma chose to complicate things further. Before they left Malta she was pregnant with his child.

In Palermo Paget had been trying to persuade the King to move back to Naples. Still he would not. He was enjoying himself in Palermo and thought Naples unsafe. Paget wrote of him: 'the truth is that H.S.M. *has a very proper sense of Danger* – in other words he is a sad Poltroon'.[36] Nelson and party returned on 31 May. On 4 June Hamilton gave one last banquet in honour of George III, whose favour he had by now forfeited. Ferdinand agreed to a (selective) amnesty of his rebel subjects and the gallows were removed from the square where they had stood for nearly twelve months. But it was another year before he showed himself in his old capital; and Maria Carolina, more and more at odds with him, also decided to absent herself, and visit her daughter, the Empress, in Vienna. The long-suffering *Foudroyant* was refitted to accommodate her, one prince, three princesses and the necessary three dozen retainers. Another two dozen, as well as the baggage and Hamilton's pictures and more of his vases, went on board the *Alexander*. Hamilton closed his account with Abraham Gibbs, still owing him nearly £6000, and on

10 June, with many promises to return, he and Emma left the Kingdom of the Two Sicilies for ever.

It was 9 November before they reached London. In those five months Hamilton suffered cruelly. The way would have been hard in any case, but Emma and Nelson did nothing to make it easier. He was ill and distressed, but they travelled from place to place as though in triumph. They would do the same to him again the following year on the tour of Wales.

The *Foudroyant* arrived off Leghorn on 14 June, the day of the Battle of Marengo. The weather was so bad they had to wait two days to get ashore. In the city there was a service of thanksgiving, after false news of an Austrian victory. In fact, as the British and Neapolitan travellers soon learned, there were six thousand Austrian dead, the French had won, they took possession of the western provinces as far as Genoa. At Leghorn the parties had intended separating, Maria Carolina continuing overland to Vienna, Nelson and the Hamiltons by sea to England. The Queen distributed more gold and diamonds to her English friends; prematurely, as it turned out. They were still together, dithering, two weeks later. The French being so close, Maria Carolina thought she might return to Sicily, in the *Foudroyant*. She and the Hamiltons had come to regard this vessel as their private taxi; but not unreasonably, after Marengo, Keith wanted her back, and the *Alexander* too. Hamilton, certainly, was for going by sea in whatever ship. But Cornelia Knight wrote to Sir Edward Berry, Captain of the *Foudroyant*, from Leghorn, on 2 July: 'The Queen wishes, if possible, to prosecute her journey. Lady Hamilton cannot bear the thought of going by sea; and, therefore, nothing but impracticability will prevent our going to Vienna.' She added: 'Lord Nelson is well, and keeps up his spirits amazingly. Sir William appears broken, distressed, and harassed.'

There was a riot in Leghorn. The people wanted Nelson to lead them against the French. Maria Carolina, terrified of any populace whichever side it was on, took refuge in the *Alexander*, hoping for a passage to Messina. But then, on the 16th, Cornelia reported: 'It is, at length, decided that we go by land; and I feel all the dangers and difficulties to which we shall be exposed.' The decision was largely Emma's and the Queen's. Nelson agreed, against his better judgement. Emma, said Cornelia, 'hates the sea, and wishes to visit the different

Courts of Germany'. And her husband? 'Sir William says *he* shall die by the way, and he looks so ill, that I should not be surprised if he did.' Their goods, Hamilton's pictures and vases among them, were stowed on board the *Serapis*, bound for London, but they themselves left Leghorn on 17 July, on a very risky route across the breadth of Italy, for Ancona. They reached Florence in twenty-six hours, passing within a couple of miles of the French outposts. From there they headed south. At San Giovanni the coach carrying Nelson, Hamilton and Emma overturned, and the latter two were hurt; 'but not dangerously', Cornelia says. The wheel was mended, but broke again at Arezzo. The French were advancing. The Queen and her prince and princesses would have been a fine prize for them, but she had got two days ahead by now, leaving the English party to make out the best they could. At Arezzo there was another separation. Nelson, Emma and Hamilton took the good carriage, Cornelia and Mrs Cadogan stayed in Arezzo three days while the other was repaired. Cornelia spoke nobly for them both: 'It was of less consequence we should be left behind, or taken, than they.' They all met up in Ancona; sailed on Russian ships (the Austrian having been thought untrustworthy); narrowly avoided capture by privateers; and reached Trieste. They were eight days there, Hamilton too ill to move. 'The physicians had almost given him up.' Everyone was more or less ill, but Nelson at least had the satisfaction of being fêted by thousands whenever he showed his face.

On the eve of their departure Cornelia wrote: 'How we shall proceed on our long journey is to me a problem; but we shall certainly get on as fast as we can; for the very precarious state of Sir William's health has convinced everybody that it is necessary he should arrange his affairs ...'[37] Strange consideration. Were they hurrying him to a place where he could compose himself and die? Really, nobody seems to have considered his well-being at all. Their further route was Ljubljana, Klagenfurt, Graz, to Vienna on 18 August. All the towns were celebrating the second anniversary of the Battle of the Nile, Emma and Nelson walked the streets arm in arm, her black maid Fatima, Nelson's gift from Egypt, following behind.

They had six weeks in Vienna, during which time Hamilton seems to have recovered somewhat. He managed to go fishing, a pastime he looked to more and more, for solace. Nelson sat to Heinrich

Füger, in full regalia and also for the only portrait of him in civilian dress. He was the cynosure, Emma muscled in vigorously also to centre stage, and Hamilton continued in the role of attendant lord. They inspired the English they consorted with, notably Lord and Lady Minto (the Elliots) in their country villa at St Veit, to ever more hateful gossip.

Lady Minto wrote to Lady Malmesbury (her sister) of Emma and Nelson: 'she leads him about like a keeper with a bear'. Lady Malmesbury had already heard, from Consul Wyndham, of the behaviour of the party in Leghorn: 'They all sit and flatter each other all day long.' Nelson certainly could take any amount of adoration: 'She puffs the incense full in his face; but he receives it with pleasure, and snuffs it up very cordially.' And since he gave as good as he got – 'thinks her quite an *angel*, and talks of her as such to her face and behind her back' – perhaps those two at least had rendered themselves impervious. And doubtless also they meant it; whereas their hosts, receiving them, flattering them, were dipping their pens in bile ten minutes after carriages.[38]

Emma rounded apace, but was so fat by now nobody noticed. A Swedish diplomat, Suerstolpe, described her as the fattest woman he had ever laid eyes upon ('but with the most beautiful head'). In Dresden Mrs Melesina St George Trench thought her 'colossal', 'exceedingly *embonpoint*'. Nevertheless, she performed. She sang for Haydn, his setting of (some of) Cornelia's Pindarick Ode 'The Battle of the Nile', the effect of which Cornelia thought 'grand'. She did her attitudes all along the route, in every company; and everywhere she went there were people, mostly English, who thought her quite unspeakable. James Harris, the son of Lord and Lady Malmesbury, wrote home: 'Lady Hamilton is without exception the most coarse, ill-mannered, disagreeable woman I ever met with.' Mrs Trench thought her 'bold, forward, coarse, assuming, and vain'; her ruling passions seemed to Mrs Trench to be 'vanity, avarice, and love for the pleasures of the table'. Certainly she fed a good deal, and bawled and gambled. But there were some observers who thought that when she sang or posed she achieved or recovered something superior to her vulgar self. Suerstolpe, for example, had never heard anything so heavenly as her singing; and even Mrs Melesina St George Trench, having seen the attitudes, conceded: 'It is remarkable that, though coarse and ungraceful in common life, she becomes highly graceful, and even beautiful, during this performance.' But having conceded that much with one hand she at once took it back with the other: 'It is also singular that, in spite of the accuracy of her imitation of the finest ancient draperies, her usual dress is tasteless, vulgar, loaded and unbecoming.'

The Elliots, one lot in Vienna, another in Dresden, and Mrs Trench, friend of the latter branch, are not so very important in the end; whereas Emma (*'Moll* Cleopatra'), Nelson ('Antony') and Hamilton ('the grey-haired Lord'), three yolked in one, are heroically comical and poignant. Mrs Cadogan likewise is a figure no Trench or Elliot could hold a candle to. 'Mrs Cadogan ... is,' Mrs Trench reports, '– what one might expect.' But this enduring lady, when the party reached Hamburg, sat through an evening with the elderly poet Klopstock, as Cornelia reports:

> Mrs Cadogan and I supped one evening with Klopstock and his wife, a pleasing-featured, fat, fair woman, much younger than himself, and a good musician. He read to me some passages from his 'Messiah', and his room was hung with drawings by Füger, of subjects taken from that poem. At that time Klopstock was chiefly engaged in writing odes, very sublime, but too metaphysical to be easily understood.[39]

For that evening alone Mrs Cadogan deserves a place in the Golden Book of the Sublimely Comic. Where Hamilton was is not recorded; fishing, one hopes, or lying down.

In Vienna they left Queen Maria Carolina – tearfully – and on 26 September proceeded to Prague. There, with the Archduke Charles, they celebrated Nelson's birthday; Emma sang 'God Save the King', and more Cornelia. All the rest of their route was by water. They sailed from Lowositz on 1 October down the Elbe to Dresden and had a week there with Lord Minto's brother (and brother ambassador) Hugh Elliot. The Elliots certainly thought them guests from hell, and in letters soon put family and friends in the picture. Hamilton appears at a dinner on 3 October 'old, infirm, all admiration of his wife' and never speaking 'but to applaud her'. Emma, who had insisted on the land route because she wished to visit the courts of

Germany, was unlucky in Dresden. The Electress refused to receive her 'on account of her former dissolute life' ('former' is a nice touch). Nelson said: 'If there is any difficulty of that sort, Lady Hamilton will knock the Elector down.' She was finally put off by being told that the Elector never gave dinners or suppers, at which she cried: 'What? No guttling!' That evening, 9 October, she drank a (to Mrs Trench) astonishing amount of champagne and danced the tarantella. More importantly, 'Sir William also this evening performed feats of activity, hopping around the room on his backbone, his arms, legs, star and ribbon all flying about in the air.' For a man at death's door he could be very entertaining. Thin, burned to a cinder, a walking piece of verdigris, in his last few years he went again and again into the shadow of death and, true to his promise that he would bear up as long and as well as he could, came out again and again for another turn.

Emma knew very well that as Hamilton neared his end she was herself heading for uncertainty. On the journey back to England her mind was on her chances there. She confessed as much to Mrs Trench, who reported:

> I was so tired, I returned home soon after dinner, but not till 'Cleopatra' had talked to me a great deal of her doubts whether the Queen would receive her, adding, 'I care little about it. I had much rather she would settle half Sir William's pension on me.'

She would be disappointed on both counts.

On 10 October the Hamilton and Nelson party embarked for Hamburg. Mr Elliot saw them off. His report to Mrs Trench is worth quoting because it says more than he perhaps realized:

> The moment they were on board, there was an end of the fine arts, of the attitudes, of the acting, the dancing, and the singing. Lady Hamilton's maid began to scold in French about some provisions which had been forgot, in language quite impossible to repeat, using certain French words, which were never spoken but by *men* of the lowest class, and roaring them out from one boat to another. Lady Hamilton began bawling for an Irish stew, and her old mother set about washing the potatoes, which she did as cleverly as possible. They were exactly like Hogarth's actresses dressing in the barn.[40]

First, the 'fine arts' themselves had been thought by many to be quite as vulgar as the bawling for an Irish stew; secondly, the distinction between Emma acting and Emma not acting is, I think, impossible to make, and that may be true also of the others yoked with her; and thirdly, the Elliots and their circle in their peculiarly English snottiness doubtless incited the Hamilton and Nelson troupe to be ever more outrageous. Drifting downstream now slowly but surely towards a London scandal, they seem at times as wild as that naked picnic I mentioned a long time back: Winckelmann, d'Hancarville, and Baron Riedesel, toasting doves on the lava of Vesuvius and drinking lacrimae Christi. Cornelia Knight felt ever more uncomfortable; what Mrs Cadogan felt nobody knows.

They were eleven days reaching Hamburg, heading north, into the fogs and the cold, away from Italy (Dresden was known as the Florence of the Elbe) for ever. On board there was less and less 'guttling' and the inns were rough. In Hamburg Nelson bought his wife a 'magnificent lace trimming'[41] for a court dress. They sailed on the *King George* mail packet on 31 October and arrived in Great Yarmouth in the pouring rain a week later. There they were fêted, or Nelson was, and the Hamiltons perforce with him. Their carriage was dragged by the local men to lodgings at the Wrestlers' Arms. A message was waiting for Nelson from his wife. Would he like to bring his friends to visit at Roundwood, the Norfolk home? They obeyed. But Lady Nelson meanwhile had gone to London. The meeting would be there.

Chapter 13

'I WILL BEAR UP AS
LONG & AS WELL AS I CAN.'
NOVEMBER 1800–APRIL 1803

Hamilton and party arrived in London on the evening of Sunday 9 November 1800. The weather, atrocious all the way, broke over the capital in the worst storm for a century. Emma, Nelson and Hamilton put up at the usual hotel, Nerot's in Mayfair; Cornelia and Mrs Cadogan, on the long journey from Palermo often a pair, went to lodgings in Albemarle Street. Thus they were spared the meeting of Nelson with his wife in the hall of Nerot's Hotel, and the fraught dinner of the two married couples that followed. Even whilst this was in progress Cornelia was visited by one of Nelson's old captains, now Admiral Sir Thomas Troubridge. He came to warn her that for the sake of her good spinster name she would do well to distance herself from Nelson and the Hamiltons. Another caller, Mrs Nepean, whose husband was Secretary to the Admiralty, did the same; and offered her accommodation in her own house. Cornelia moved there next day, but staggered her severance, completing it on the 22nd when she refused an invitation to the theatre with the infamous trio. Cornelia was particularly at risk because she had been for so long in their company and her verses to two of them were in the London papers even as they arrived; and since London had known for months what was going on, it was hard for Cornelia to assert either their innocence or her ignorance. Breaking with them within two weeks of the homecoming, she might at least claim to have done the right thing as quickly as she could.

Emma inscribed her verdict on Cornelia in a Molière she had given her: 'Altho she is clever and learnd She is dirty illbred ungrateful bad mannered false and deceitful But my Heart takes a noble vengance I forgive her.' Nelson wrote: 'What a b—— that Miss Knight is!'[1]

On 10 November Nelson and the Hamiltons (his necessary adjuncts) were cheered and celebrated at the Lord Mayor's Parade; on the 11th husband and lover, resplendent in all their orders and decorations, were 'rumped' at St James's by His Majesty – that is, after the briefest of greetings, he turned his back on them and talked at great length to someone, so they thought, much less important. There could be no question of Emma's being presented to Queen Charlotte at the next or at any other of her Thursday receptions, which the London newspapers noted with satisfaction. The people fêted Nelson wherever they could find him, and cheerfully included the Hamiltons as part of the bargain; but the Court and certain parts of London society were fussier. Emma was the chief bugbear, much as she had been during her last visit, in the summer of 1791, in the weeks before Hamilton married her. Whether to receive her, be intimate with her, be in the same room as her – these were the questions exercising the nicer sensibilities in the winter of 1800. Those in Hamilton's own family, for example. Lady Frances Harpur (Greville's sister) wrote to Mary Dickenson:

> It was settled by my Brothers & Ld Cathcart, that it could not be avoided noticing *Ly H.*, without offence to *Sr Wm* or at least *affecting his feelings*; & as He has met with much *Vexation, & disappointment*, as to *His Recall*, & is in Weak Health, it was decided on *His Acct*, Ly H. was to be *Visited*.
>
> Sr Wm & Ly H. came to me one Morning, I explained that I could *not* be in their Society; but hoped He was assured of my affection; He was very kind, *laughed, & said* He knew *I was a Nun*; Would see me some times; said Every one must follow their own Plans ...
>
> Few Ladies visit Ly. H. except those have been at Naples, & some censure our Family for visiting *Ly Hamilton*; Ly Mansfield means to see them occasionally in *Gt Cumberland* St. but *not* to enter into their *Society* ... My Brother Warwick visits them; Ly Warwick & Family are at Warwick Castle. There is difficulty in inviting them to the Castle; My Brother wishes to see Sr Wm *there*; but altho' an *Occasional Visit*, or *Eveg* may be spent wth *Ly H.* it does not seem desirable or *proper* for my *Nieces* to be *intimate* wth *Ly H*...

Emma was more bothered than Hamilton by these delicate restrictions. Lady Harpur reports her as anxious to be worthy of the Hamilton clan, and begging permission to call occasionally. And yet they were by no means short of society. Less nice people were glad to be with them, some real friends, others curious to witness scandal in close proximity. Lady Harpur conceded: 'They have continual Company,' and added, 'but I don't know Their Set. Prince *Augustus* is one, & Foreigners.'² Augustus, in his nullified marriage, was a dubious seal of approval.

Hamilton had more serious worries than how often Lady Harpur and her kind would receive or visit him. Having seen Lord Grenville and been told by him that he had been recalled and replaced, not given leave, he began the struggle to get what he thought was his due: a pension of £2000 a year net, compensation for his losses in Naples (£10,000) and repayment of the large sums (£13,000) disbursed by him on official business during his last two years in Naples and Palermo. This petitioning would go on humiliatingly and to no great avail till he was dead. After so long on the periphery and having at the last, when events moved him to the centre, not come out of it blamelessly and being further harmed by the scandal of his wife and Nelson, Hamilton had no clout (having lost the King's favour) with a Foreign Office inveterately slow in settling its debts.

In his struggle he had an ally as much of a mixed blessing as Prince Augustus: William Beckford. Within a week of their arriving in London Beckford gave Hamilton and Emma the use of his house in Grosvenor Square and suggested that on the basis of thirty-seven years' loyal service, he, Hamilton, should seek not a financial settlement with Government, but a peerage; and he, Beckford, would not only campaign on his behalf but would also, if successful, top up his pension annually by £2000 and settle an annuity of £500 on Emma.³ This offer was by no means disinterested. Denied a peerage himself in 1784 (having been caught *in flagrante* with young William Courtenay), Beckford had the far-fetched idea that a deal might be done whereby Hamilton's title, if obtained, would pass to him and his heirs after Hamilton's death, which he might expect before too long. Needless to say, nothing came of this. The campaign was desultory, nobody in power gave it half a thought, Hamilton himself was rather embarrassed.

Considering all he had been through and the worries still plaguing him, Hamilton's appearance in London that winter was remarkably perky. Lord Palmerston visited on 25 November and reported to his wife: 'He is still thinner and yellower than he was when we saw him but in other respects seems much the same and seems occupied with the same pursuits as usual.' And two weeks later Lady Harpur reported: 'Sir Wm is very *thin*, much *aged*, & *stoops*; but is very Cheerful, & the same *pleasing Countenance*.' It should also be noted that in public he and Emma behaved as fondly as ever, and Nelson was certainly no issue between them. Palmerston again: 'Her attentions to Sir William do not seem to have relaxed in any degree and they both talk of Lord Nelson in every other sentence. His bust is in the room and Sir William says his friendship and connection with him is the pride and glory of his life'; and Lady Harpur: 'She appears much attached to Sr Wm He is in much admiration, & I believe She *constitutes* His *Happiness*; I cannot but *lament* this *Idolatory*.'

Hamilton wrote to Mary (then in Bath) on 5 December: 'I cannot leave London until my own confused affairs are settled, as yet I am ignorant of what is to be come of me ...'[4] But he was no nearer any settlement two weeks later when he, Emma and Nelson accepted Beckford's invitation to spend Christmas at Fonthill. Lady Nelson was not invited. Beckford had been spending money as though sugar and slaves would last for ever; his residence and outhouses (a tower, an abbey) were on their way to becoming the most ludicrously gothic pile in the universe; and he laid on a Christmas show that was worthy of his folly, the climax being Emma, eight months pregnant, in capacious white, carrying a golden urn and impersonating – some guessed, some didn't – the faithful Agrippina with the ashes of her noble spouse Germanicus. As an encore, and as further proof if any were needed that she operated on planes far removed from reality, Emma impersonated an abbess receiving two nuns into a convent, and was said, by some, to have acted the part 'with the greatest truth and propriety'.[5] The party ended; Nelson, recalled to duty, broke with Fanny, and prepared to sail. For £1000 Hamilton bought the lease on 23 Piccadilly, a small but elegant house, now vanished, opposite Green Park. Nelson took command of the Channel fleet; Gillray did a savage cartoon, 'Dido in Despair', showing an obese Emma, howling like a giant baby, a fleet of warships visible through the open window, and, to represent Sir William, a little clutch of priapic antiquities. On 28 January 1801, at no. 23, Horatia was born, and removed at once into discreet safe keeping. Within a week or so Emma was back in society, not noticeably slimmer.

Hamilton's financial problems were by now acute. He had left many loose ends behind him in Italy, one being whether his departure was final or not. He told Mary (having been told it clearly by Lord Grenville) that he would never return to Naples in any public capacity; but he left open the possibility that he might as a private citizen, and his agents in Naples and Palermo and his servants at the Palazzo Sessa continued to hope he would. Not until 1 November 1801 did he write to Sam Ragland, acting for him in Naples, to say that he would not be back and that the staff were to be dismissed. For twelve months before then letters had gone to and fro between the two men on the subject of Hamilton's intentions and his debts. Ragland wrote on 20 January 1801, begging for a speedy settlement. He had been advancing money to Hamilton from August 1799 and was owed 'little short of £2400'. At the end of 1800 Hamilton had instructed him, and also the banker Edmund Noble, to begin selling off furniture, pictures and other effects in the Palazzo Sessa, everything except 'the Harpsichord of two Rows of keys by Shudi', Catherine's instrument, and 'the 2 great Lava Tables & 2 other Marble & Lava Tables in the same dining Room'. These Hamilton wished to have sent home.[6] The house at Posillipo was to be given up, but rent on the Palazzo Sessa would be owing until May 1801, and Emma had made things difficult, especially for the sale of the furniture, by allowing a Marshal Rosenheim to live there until that date. Ragland continued to pay Vincenzo Sabatino and the other servants in Hamilton's name, and there were besides considerable and long overdue bills to various tradespeople, notably the tailor and Giovanni Plonqueur, the coachmaker. When Rosenheim moved out, in May 1801, sales went ahead but raised very little, no pictures were bought, and Ragland put the unsold things in storage, commenting: 'should the present unhappy Scene of Public affairs change, so that you should return hither, they are at your disposal'. Then it was more than six months before the servants learned they no longer had an English master. Receiving Hamilton's letter of 1 November 1801, Ragland replied on 22 December:

I observe Sir William that you do not intend to return hither again &
wish for to clear off all here Even to discharge Vincenzo & the two
livery servants – The communication of this to them has been
almost a Death Stroke after so many years in your Service, nor can
I extract from either, what Present would content them as they
submit it to your feelings particularly Vincenzo.

When Ragland next wrote, on 6 April 1802, the present submitted
to Hamilton's feelings had still not been paid and Vincenzo was,
Ragland reported, 'in very narrow Circumstances, with a large Family'.
The coachmaker and the tailor likewise were still waiting, and the
latter, himself owing money which he could not pay until Hamilton
paid him, had a writ out against him. Ragland advanced him a sum
to fend off arrest. Ragland meanwhile was in trouble with Cleasby
and Co, again on Hamilton's account. He was as pressing as he dared
be, having hoped, he said, 'that you would have arranged matters ere
this & answer'd my Letter'. He begged him in conclusion to 'pay the
Coachmaker & Taylor & relieve the distress of your poor Servants'.
By English standards the sums were small: £600 still owing the
coachmaker and the tailor together, Ragland's advance to the tailor
was 100 ducats (about £20); but the local hardship was none the less
real.[7]

There was a similar mess in Palermo, overseen (from Naples now)
by Abraham Gibbs. In Palermo they were still expecting Hamilton
back well into the summer of 1802. Gibbs wrote on 13 July that Mrs
Graefer (wife of the Caserta gardener now Nelson's agent on the
Brontë estate) 'assured me she had certain intelligence of your
returning shortly to Palermo'. Gibbs had acted 'under the constant
expectation of your returning to Sicily, which your silence confirmed
to me'. Hamilton's coach – the same no doubt for which he still
owed Giovanni Plonqueur – was left unsold in Palermo, 'being so
heavy, no tolerable offer was ever made for it'. Other bits and pieces
of Hamilton's effects were either sold (some silver and lace for 236
ducats), or shipped off to England (the four marble and lava tables
and two Raphael drawings). Gibbs seems to have been under
instruction from Mrs Cadogan to sell 'solely the old things'; and as
late as January 1803 he was writing to ask what he should do with
sixteen cases packed by Mrs Cadogan and sent to Malta and now

back in Naples. On 26 May 1802 Hamilton wrote to Ragland saying he was owed considerable sums by the Treasury, and sending for Vincenzo Sabatino, his servant for decades, 100 ducats. The interconnections in the cash nexus are legion.[8]

Hamilton does not come well out of all this, but at least it can be said in his favour that from the moment of his arrival in London he strove officiously to recoup his losses and to raise some cash. There was great material hardship in England that winter, riots in towns, rick-burning in the country, the people wanted bread and a living wage. To furnish the Piccadilly house Emma sold at least some of the diamonds given to her as a leaving present by Maria Carolina. That raised a certain amount, far less (Emma said) than they had hoped, but the times were bad. The banker Coutts told Henry Swinburne that the Pembroke estates were bringing in barely £1000 a year, half what Greville had confidently promised. (Hamilton had shifted his account to Coutts, being vexed with Ross and Ogilvie for not meeting the demands he had made on them from Palermo.)[9] Just before the birth of Horatia (23 January) Louis Dutens, acting for Hamilton, instructed his lawyer to draw up 'a deed of assignment ... to Mr Alexander Davison, in trust for Lady Hamilton, of the furniture and other contents of the house, No 23 Piccadilly'. On 4 February it was signed and sealed.[10] This was provision for her after his death (Davison, for his sins, had charge of her finances); it also made up in part for the diamonds she had been forced to sell; still, a week after the birth of her child by another man, it was honourable and generous.

Altogether, at this trying time, Hamilton seems to have been in tolerably good spirits. Writing on 11 February 1801 he gave the Naples banker Edmund Noble a cheerful enough account of his circumstances:

> I bear the Climate remarkably well am stronger sleep and digest better than I did at Naples – Emma does not like this Country so well as I do & threatens to return to Naples I am too old to move again. We have a very comfortable House in Piccadilly a good arm chair a Warm room a good dinner & a good bottle of Wine is all I can enjoy ...

A quiet last few years was what he wanted. Emma might be a trouble, but he did, that day, at last, confidently expect satisfaction from His Majesty's Government. The letter continues:

> I flatter myself Government will enable me to have such enjoyment for the short remains of my life – I have been just assured that my business is settled Net 2000£ per Annm Pension & a small sum of money to help me in my present difficulties ... My old Master the King is very kind to me & receives me at Windsor as one of His Family I beleive all will end well ...[11]

In that belief Hamilton called at Lord Grenville's office on 16 February. There he was shown a copy of the letter that Grenville had written to the Treasury in his affair. It stipulated only 'a nominal Pension of 2000£'. Hamilton wrote at once to Grenville, expressing his disappointment and going over old ground:

> Your Lordship must remember that altho' I had His Majesty's gracious assurance that I shou'd not be removed from my Post unless at my own desire I wrote some years ago that if your Lorp. wished to send any one to Naples in my room I shou'd be satisfied with a net income of 2000£ pa. but not with a nominal Pension to that amount – Having been removed from Naples without my consent or having had the smallest intimation of it from your Lordp. untill the moment Mr Paget arrived at Palermo, I took it for granted that Your Lp. had secured for me the net income I requested as my retreat after such long Service.

He went on to repeat to Lord Grenville what he had already submitted to his Lordship's secretary: that his disbursements in the last eighteen months in Palermo amounted to £13,222. In short, having sold his diamonds, he still needed £8000 from Government, or he would 'remain in distress' to the end of his life. 'Having passed my whole life in the service of my King & Country,' he concluded, 'I do not ask more than what is common Justice.'[12] The manner of his removal from Naples rankled. He must, so it seemed to him (and so he wrote to Richard Worsely), get the pension he was asking for or 'appear in the Eye of the World as a disgraced man'.[13] Lord Grenville was unmoved. He replied that what Hamilton was asking as pension 'considerably exceeds the usual proportion of salary retained by Foreign Ministers on their retreat'. He had, he said, left it to the King to authorize a larger sum if he saw fit,[14] and he overlooked the plea for the reimbursement of £8000.

That was on 19 February. Towards the end of the month Nelson came back on three days leave. From his flagship in the Channel he had conducted an agitated correspondence with Emma, ostensibly on behalf of a fictitious character, a Mr Thompson, who was supposed to be an uxorious sailor on board with him. Speaking for Mr Thompson he enquired passionately and jealously after his beloved wife and their child; that is, after Emma and Horatia. This ludicrous strategy, ever more convoluted and far-fetched, was resumed whenever he went to sea.[15] Hamilton appears in the letters as an elderly uncle whom Mr Thompson can't help wishing to be rid of. Unaware of this, if not of the liaison and its child, Hamilton continued until his death to revere Nelson and to think of him as his true friend.

In February 1801 Pitt's long administration ended; George III suffered another bout of porphyria so severe it seemed he might die. In that context, and with no capital of favour or goodwill to draw on, Hamilton's chances of getting a fair deal were slight. In the middle of March he learned that his actual pension would be £1200. The question of compensation for his disbursements and losses was left to the new Foreign Secretary, Lord Hawkesbury. Hamilton still owed Ragland £2000 and Ross and Ogilvie over £6000.

Then in March and April he did what was necessary and sold his collections. Hamilton was quite unsentimental about his treasures when he had to be. He owned them for as long as possible, valuing them both as works of art and as a capital he would liquidate when he had to. Christie's disposed of his pictures in two sales, the first on 27–8 March, the second on 17–18 April, in total bringing in £5700. Hamilton bought three or four of his own paintings back, when they failed to reach the reserve price, among them a Rembrandt (portrait of the artist's mother) and a Van Dyck Saint Sebastian. Vigée Le Brun's 'Lady Hamilton as a Recumbent Bacchante', which would have gone under the hammer, was bought by Nelson through a third party, for £300. He could not bear the thought of any other man possessing it. His jealousy over what company Hamilton was taking her into or allowing her to go into – the Prince of Wales's set worst of all – extended to include her likeness. He wrote: 'I see clearly, my dearest friend, you are on SALE. I am almost mad to think of the iniquity of wanting you to associate with a set of whores, bawds, & unprincipled lyars. Can this be the great Sir William Hamilton? I blush for him.' Had the picture cost him three hundred drops of blood, he said, he would have given it with pleasure.[16] He left it to her in his will.

On 7 March, Hamilton wrote Nelson a cheerful letter. Having finally opened the packing cases safely arrived from Naples and Palermo he discovered in them not, as he had persisted in believing, the worst of his vases, but most of the very best. Why it had taken him so long to find out is a mystery. The *Serapis*, to which the Hamilton and Nelson baggage was transferred (from the *Foudroyant*) at Leghorn in the summer of 1800, docked in London that October, and an agent collected the goods on Hamilton's behalf. They remained in storage then (in George Street, Westminster) until selling became a necessity in March the following year.[17] Perhaps the vases were among those things. Another possibility is that, intended for the *Colossus* (in November 1798), they were never in fact loaded, but were left by mistake on the quay, and were not among the tons of baggage taken on board the *Foudroyant* at that time either. They must then have come out to England through somebody else's good offices – James Clark, Ragland or Gibbs? – either just before or having survived, by being overlooked, all the violence of revolution and counter-revolution in Naples. One way or another they were now restored to Hamilton in March 1801, and at once, reunited with vases which, when he feared he had lost them, had seemed to him proof of the best in God and Man, he gave them to James Christie to sell. They would have been auctioned at the second sale in April but the collector Thomas Hope intervened and Hamilton, asking £5000, let him have them for £4000. How many they were is hard to say. It depends how many were lost with the *Colossus*.[18] Hope disposed of the worst of them but kept the rest, displaying them in his three Vase Rooms in the grand house in Duchess Street he had just bought from Hamilton's sister, the Dowager Countess of Warwick. They remained in his family till 1917. Then they were dispersed, a few going to the British Museum.

By the end of April Hamilton had raised £10,000, not enough, it seems, to settle his debts in Italy, but enough to pacify Ross and

Ogilvie and to live at 23 Piccadilly in the style to which Emma felt entitled. On 2 April Nelson disregarded orders and distinguished himself brilliantly against a nation the British were not, strictly speaking, at war with. News of his glorious victory at Copenhagen reached London two weeks later. Wraxall describes the celebrations in the Hamiltons' house. Emma danced a Tarantella:

> Sir William began it with her, and maintained the conflict, for such it might well be esteemed, for some minutes. When unable longer to continue it, the Duke de Noia succeeded to his place; but he, too, though near forty years younger than Sir William, soon gave in. Lady Hamilton then sent for her own maid servant; who being likewise exhausted, after a short time, another female attendant, a Copt, perfectly black, whom Lord Nelson had presented her, on his return from Egypt, relieved her companion.[19]

There was life in Hamilton yet, and again, as at the Elliots' in Dresden, he proved it dancing. And if Emma exhausted him, there was no disgrace; so she did everyone.

Hamilton, still surprising the world in bouts of mad vitality, had less than two years to live. On 25 May he saw Greville to discuss his will with him. This new will, signed on the 28th, replaced the one he had made in the summer of 1791 when he married Emma. He made a bequest to her of £300, and to her mother of £100; gave her an annuity of £800 (£100 of it for her mother so long as she lived); and the rest, as he had always intended, was to go to Charles.[20] In the event it would be no great fortune. Hamilton lived his last years as he always had, beyond his means; raising cash here to settle creditors, disbursing it there to please himself and Emma.

Palmerston had said of Hamilton that he seemed 'occupied with the same pursuits as usual'; and indeed he was. Selling pictures and vases may be numbered among them, but there were others, more positive, too. He continued in dealings with Tischbein, now in Hamburg and still busy on the illustrations of Homer, the work begun in Naples out of the study of Hamilton's Second Collection. After the auctions, and the sale of those vases to Thomas Hope, Hamilton sent him £100 in the assumption that, in order to get on with the Homeric work, he would have 'present need of money'.

Tischbein was to pay him back when sales of their joint publication of the vases (three volumes were out by now) should permit it. This was not in Hamilton's lifetime, needless to say. Tischbein, himself hard pressed for cash, wrote to Hamilton some time in the summer or autumn of 1801 with a proposal to sell the plates and his entire interest in the work. Hamilton, though much taken up with his own worries ('my own affairs require all my attention and it is impossible for me at my age and in my feeble state of health to engage myself much') did some canvassing on his behalf, but urged him to come to London in the following year 'towards the month of May when London is full – and when the rigours of our climate are over', and to prosecute the business in person with his, Hamilton's, immediate help.[21] But Tischbein could not absent himself from his duties in Hamburg and the proposal, like so many, came to nothing. In promoting the sale of the *Engravings from Ancient Vases* in Germany – there was a cheap German edition as well as the expensive original – Tischbein was a loyal advocate of Hamilton's achievement, against detractors who saw him as only a rich English aristocrat with no scholarship and moreover ridiculous because of his wife. To a correspondent in Weimar, for example, sending him drawings of vases in the Second Collection and urging him to make them known, Tischbein wrote:

> In the arts we owe Hamilton a great deal and as a person he is one in a million. Where would you find his equal for true understanding? We owe it to him that the vases were recognized as works of art ... He is the only one to have seen their true worth and spirit...
>
> Hamilton spent thirty thousand talers on the vases, and other people have the pleasure of them. Is that not deserving of praise and gratitude? Believe me, my dear friend, I know the art world pretty well by now and there are very few real connoisseurs in it. Hamilton is one of them, and when we lose him we shall lose a great deal, his loss will be a great one for the arts and I am afraid we may lose him soon, for he is ill.[22]

The letter was probably written in the autumn of 1800.

Hamilton attended his clubs, especially the Dilettanti and the Royal Society. They became a respite for him from his domestic circumstances. There he could continue to be in touch with the chief artistic and scientific passions of his life. On 14 June 1801 he made an important donation to the library of the Royal Society: Father Antonio Piaggi's diary of Vesuvius, eight volumes in all, kept scrupulously day by day, with drawings too, from 1779 till 1795, on Hamilton's behalf. They had come to him on Piaggi's death in 1796, and, through Banks, Hamilton had promised them to the Society, saying of them: '[They] are wonderfully curious & would I believe be the grounds of a very interesting publication.' The diary needed editing: the Padre had 'some strange ideas'. Hamilton said of him: 'My friend with much Philosphy & real knowledge had a good deal of the Rosicrucian in him, possessed the secret of making gold & many other articles & died as poor as a rat as these Gentlemen always do.' At first Hamilton intended to do this editing himself but then, finding himself 'too old & indolent', hoped someone in the Society would. Presenting the volumes he wrote:

> The Padre Antonio lived in a House at the Madonna Pugliano near Resina at the foot of Vesuvius & with a full view of the Vulcano from his Window – He always rose at day break & took his observations several times in the day, no man was ever more ready at his pencil as his masterly sketches testify – nor no man was ever more attached to truth.[23]

The diaries went into the Royal Society library on 7 February 1805, and are indeed a full and beautiful work.

Apart from the clubs, there was fishing. When Nelson came home on leave early in July he and the Hamiltons had a few days at the Fox and Hounds, Burford Bridge, by Box Hill, then another few days at the Bush, Shepperton, near Staines, where they went fishing. Naturally, whatever they did, the papers reported it, and Hamilton was always made to look the most foolish of the three: 'Lord Nelson is now at Staines with Sir William and Lady Hamilton on a fishing party. Sir William who is said to be one of the first *anglers* in the kingdom, devotes much of his time to that species of sport.[24] It is unlikely that all three sat along the bank together. Nelson and Emma had a good deal to discuss, doubtless they left Hamilton to his rod and line.

Back from that little holiday Hamilton went to Pembroke with Greville. He writes cheerfully enough from Burford on 27 July: 'Here we are my Dear Emma, after a pleasant day's journey! No extraordinary occurrence. Our chaise is good, and would have held the famous *tria juncta in uno* very well: but, we must submit to the circumstances of the times.'[25] If Hamilton was suffering from being one of the famous three, he did not show it. Indeed, his letter to Nelson from Milford on 12 August is positively jaunty. He describes a boat trip of 'some leagues' to view the light-houses erected at his expense on the dangerous Crow Rock, expresses perfect satisfaction with the improvements in the town, and even looks forward to being 'a gainer in the end' as housing, allotments and gardens spread all over the two thousand acres owned by him.[26]

The 'circumstances of the times' took Nelson back to sea, to defend the south coast against invasion, and to involve him in two débâcles at Boulogne. His mind was chiefly on Emma, their child, and on the possibility of setting up house. In his absence and Hamilton's Emma was looking for a place to buy with Nelson's money. Hamilton was back from Pembroke by 19 August, but before then she had found somewhere and written to tell Nelson of it. He wrote on 20 August: 'I approve of the house at Merton.' He had asked her to find him 'a little farm'; naturally, she came up with something grander, costing £9000. Nelson's lawyers had it surveyed, the surveyor was absolutely damning. He concluded: 'In short it is altogether the worst place under all its circumstances that I ever saw pretending to suit a Gentleman's family.'[27] But Nelson went ahead, because 'Paradise Merton', as they came to call it, was Emma's choice. The house, built around 1700, stood in about seventy acres, and they and it vanished under 'development' in the latter part of the nineteenth century. It stood in the square made by these modern streets: Quicks Road on the north, Merton Road and Morden Road on the west, Haydons Road and Abbey Road on the east, and (probably) High Path on the south. Nearest tube: South Wimbledon. Nelson, Hardy, Trafalgar, the *Victory* and the Hamiltons are commemorated in street names where the grounds of Paradise Merton lay.

The Hamiltons and Nelson's sister-in-law went to Deal in the last weeks of August and saw him there when, and for as long as, the

Admiralty allowed. Hamilton was a necessary presence, for tattered respectability's sake. Nelson bought Merton Place with his own money; he said he would rather be a beggar than borrow from Hamilton (who in fact had none to lend him). When the house was being furnished he was insistent that none of Hamilton's belongings, particularly not his books, should be moved in; but he needed him there as ostensible chaperon if he was to be with Emma. The world understood Hamilton's function, and thought it inglorious; mostly he seems to have minded less than the world did. At Deal he got in some more fishing, Emma some sea-bathing. When they returned to Piccadilly early in September, Nelson wrote to 'Mrs Thompson': 'My dearest wife, how can I bear our separation!'[28]

The purchase of Merton Place was concluded on 13 September. Emma could now give herself over to preparing it for Nelson's possession. Their daughter Horatia, farmed out with a Mrs Gibson in Little Titchfield Street, was fetched to 23 Piccadilly whenever Emma thought convenient. Perhaps she waited for times when Hamilton was not at home, perhaps between this odd husband and wife such tact or subterfuge had become unnecessary. At all events he took himself off for a few days to visit his elder nephew at Warwick Castle, leaving Emma to do as she pleased. One document of that visit, a letter to the younger nephew, Charles Greville, written on 9 October, shows Hamilton's extraordinary capacity for allowing himself to be put upon by insufferably tedious people, in this case the Earl of Warwick. He writes:

> I was bored to death by his Lordship's eternal talk & stories, chiefly of himself, as to strength, bravery, knowledge of improvement, so as to be actually now one of the richest men in England ... In short, I should be ungrateful if I did not feel the affection shown me, during this visit, from all the family, but it would drive me mad was I obliged to live a month with him; he does not give an echoe fair play.

In a 'rhapsody of incoherent boasting' the Earl praised himself for having paid off all his father's and his own debts, forgetting a sum he still owed Hamilton who was certainly not 'one of the richest men in England'.[29]

Whilst Hamilton was listening to the Earl, word came to London and Emma sent it on express to Warwick, that the preliminaries of a peace with France had been signed. For her the chief significance of this news was that Nelson would be allowed home. Hamilton joined her at Merton, where she was busy getting the place in order, and wrote enthusiastically to Nelson about the house and grounds he had bought through Emma's agency, sight unseen:

> You have nothing but to come and enjoy immediately; you have a good mile of pleasant dry walk around your own farm. It would make you laugh to see Emma & her mother fitting up pig-sties and hen-coops, & already the Canal is enlivened with ducks, & the cock is strutting with his hens about the walks. Your Lp's plan as to stocking the Canal with fish is exactly mine. I wil answer for it, that in a few months you may command a good dish of fish at a moment's warning...[30]

The canal, described by the surveyor as 'dirty black looking', and not so much a canal as 'a broad ditch, which keeps the whole place damp',[31] was, if anything, a tributary of the River Wandle (praised by the angler Izaak Walton) but Nelson and the Hamiltons soon rechristened it 'the Nile'. They, and Mrs Cadogan with them, generally managed to enjoy themselves where the world thought they could not (or should not). Nelson arrived in the early hours of 23 October, having driven through the night from Deal, and was delighted with 'all the territories and waters of Merton', as he put it, under the rule of Emma, or 'Lady Paramount', as he called her.[32]

So began their *ménage à trois* in Paradise Merton. They were punctilious in sharing the expenses, and had enough company – not the best, by society's standards, real ladies, such as Lady Harpur, stayed away. She wrote: 'I can *not* bring myself to Continue to visit *Ly Hamilton*; Her Conduct is so censurable.'[33] But the less fastidious came in good number. Several members of Nelson's family were induced to call, as well as representatives of the world of the arts, Signora Banti, the singer, for example, and Mrs Jane Powell, the actress, who had been with Emma many years before, both of them as maids, in the household of a Dr Budd of Blackfriars. Before seeing his home Nelson had written: 'Have we a nice church at

Merton? We will set an example of goodness to the under-parish-ioners';³⁴ and once in residence he and Emma did. Hamilton stayed home. In exuberant letters Emma told all and sundry how well Hamilton and Nelson got on together, and she was probably telling the truth. They appeared in public as good friends – at Court on 30 October, at the Lord Mayor's Parade (again) a week later in Hamilton's carriage, cheered (Nelson chiefly) by the crowds. For his more serious interests Hamilton's clubs and the British Museum were less than two hours' drive away; and at Merton, in the little domestic Nile, he could fish.

Necessary at Merton and yet redundant there, Hamilton kept on 23 Piccadilly, which he could not afford. Back from Warwick, for example, he had a bill of £400 for wine awaiting him. It was now, still in debt to Ragland and still keeping on (though not paying) his servants from the Palazzo Sessa, that he finally wrote to say he would not be back. Two establishments in England were enough. At the end of November, through Coutts, he sold £1000 of consols (government stock) for the poor price of £673.³⁵ Clearly, he needed the money and could not bide his time. Coutts dealt with him not at Piccadilly but at Merton. In January 1802 he sold more diamonds, to pay Ragland,³⁶ not the whole debt by any means. From Ragland and from Gibbs, in that spring and summer, came urgent letters asking to be paid, begging him to relieve the distress of tradespeople and servants who depended on him in Naples. He wrote to Ragland that the Treasury owed *him* money, and he would be well off when they finally honoured *their* debts;³⁷ but his efforts to persuade them to do so, early in June, were a humiliating failure, one rather typical of his dealings with those upon whom *he* depended.

He tried two or three times to get to see Lord Hawkesbury, the new Foreign Secretary and the son of an old friend of his, Lord Liverpool, whose assistance he had solicited in 1763, to get the Naples job. Now, on 12 June 1802, Lord Hawkesbury kept him waiting for two hours, then sent down word that he was too busy to see him. Would he come back next week? What Hamilton wanted was that Hawkesbury should make good the omission of his predecessor Grenville who had gone out of office in the previous December without forwarding to the Treasury Hamilton's claims for compensation of his losses and reimbursement of his extraordinary expenses during his last years in Naples and Palermo. When Hawkesbury would not see him Hamilton asked to see one of the private secretaries instead, and there he was luckier, and put in his request through him. But he found the whole business very demeaning, and in a long letter to Hawkesbury, written from 23 Piccadilly on the same day, he recounted his treatment and concluded:

> I must own, My Lord, feeling my Situation as having the honor of being His Majesty's Privy Council & having served his Majesty as His Minister at the Court of Naples to the best of my ability for 37 Years, that I felt myself humbled by waiting so many hours as I have done in Your Antichamber, and as I am not sensible of having been wanting in attention or civility to your Lordship (the Son of my very old and worthy friend Lord Liverpool) when you visited Naples, I hope Your Lordship will excuse the liberty I now take of expressing my feelings and that you will grant the just request I have made . . .[38]

Hawkesbury, then the Honourable Robert Banks Jenkinson, had visited Naples in the winter of 1791–2, just after Hamilton got back there after marrying Emma, but that connection didn't make him civil ten years later. The Treasury paid up very haltingly; even on the claims they recognized, they still owed £1700 when Hamilton died.[39]

Getting nowhere with them Hamilton allowed himself again to be taken up in Beckford's scheme to get him a peerage. It involved soliciting assistance from the Duke of Hamilton, head of the clan, and his son Lord Douglas. Again, it came to nothing. Douglas wrote to say that he feared the plan 'never could possibly succeed'; the part of it having to do with Beckford's own advantage was particularly unpromising, 'being of so peculiar a nature, & being so little consonant with the feelings and tempers of people'.[40] Hamilton admitted frankly to Douglas that he needed the extra money a peerage might have brought, but let the matter drop.

Hamilton's life by now was troublesome in many respects. Writing to Greville on 24 January 1802 (from Merton) he put a brave face on it:

> It is but reasonable, after having fagged all my life, that my last days should pass off comfortably & quietly. Nothing at present disturbs

me but my debt, and the nonsence I am obliged to submit to here, to avoid coming to an explosion, which wou'd be attended with many disagreeable effects, and would totally destroy the comfort of the best man and the best friend I have in the World. However, I am determined that my quiet shall not be disturbed, let the non-sensicall world go on as it will.[41]

But really he had a lot to bear and such efforts as he made to defend his peace and quiet were not very successful. He was included in 'the nonsensicall world' whether he liked it or not. In the house of 'the best man and the best friend', whose comfort he was not willing to destroy by a showdown, Hamilton cut rather a sad figure. Emma queened it at Merton Place as she had done at the Palazzo Sessa, as though she and Nelson were at home there and Hamilton only a guest. Lord Minto, back from Vienna, visited them in March, chiefly, it seems, in order to confirm his disgust. Emma's own account of at least one of the evenings he was at makes not only the vulgarity perfectly clear – 'Miss Furse eat so much that ... she vomited before us all ... Mrs Tyson was drunk ...' – but also that Minto joined in and that when it came to flattery he was as fulsome as any. But still he wrote:

> The whole establishment and way of life is such as to make me angry, as well as melancholy ... She looks ultimately to the chance of marriage, as Sir W will not be long in her way, and she probably indulges a hope that she will survive Lady Nelson ... She is in high looks, but more immense than ever. She goes on cramming Nelson with trowelfuls of flattery, which he goes on taking as quietly as a child does pap. The love she makes to him is not only ridiculous, but disgusting: not only the rooms but the whole house, staircase and all, are covered with nothing but pictures of her and him, of all sizes and sorts...[42]

In that last respect too, the narcissistic, Paradise Merton much resembled the Palazzo Sessa.

On 15 July Hamilton was in London to support a candidate of Lord Nelson's on the hustings. He arrived late. Had he arrived on time his life might have ended earlier and more violently than it did, since the platform collapsed – or was pulled down by the opponents, some said – and there were many injuries and two deaths. He reported this to Emma next day, in a long letter most of which was taken up with complaints, in ironic tone, about her extravagance. Knowing the terms of his will she had accused him of intending to leave her 'to poverty and distress'. He retorted now:

> I know your value and mean to do every thing in my power (when I know what I really possess) to prevent that distress, but it is not my fault if by living with a great *Queen* in *intimacy* for so many years that your *ideas* should so far outrun what my means can furnish.

On her relationship with Nelson he wrote: 'I know *the purity of your connection with him*,' and said to her what he had said to Greville: that he would do nothing to upset him, fearing 'that a sudden change from his present peace and tranquility might prove fatal to him'.[43] I doubt if he feared Lord Nelson, if upset, might fall down dead; and I'm certain he did not think Emma's connection with him pure.

A week later the *tria juncta in uno*, plus appendages in the form of Nelson's obnoxious brother and his wife and child, were on the road again, heading west this time, into Pembroke. They were six weeks away, and Hamilton suffered in a fashion that must have recalled to him the terrible journey home overland from Leghorn in the summer and autumn of 1800. Yet the trip, if not his idea, did have some bearing on his interests; or if not on his, since nobody expected him to live for long, then on those of his heir, Charles Greville. Emma too, dissatisfied with what she was promised in the will, might hope her lot would be increased if Hamilton and Greville could be surer of their fortune. The idea was to enhance the prestige and the prospects of the works at Milford by getting Nelson to view them and to talk them up in public. They left on Wednesday 21 July and their first stop, that night, was the Star Inn, Oxford, where dinner and rooms had been booked for them by two more of the family, Nelson's sister Kitty and husband, arrived ahead from Bath. On Thursday morning, in pouring rain, there was a procession through cheering crowds to the Town Hall, where Nelson was presented with the Freedom of the City in a gold box. Next day he and Hamilton were made honorary Doctors of Civil Law in the Sheldonian. Each in his way deserved some such honour; but wherever Nelson went his brother William, like a busy jackal, went too, for what he could pick up. On this occasion it was an honorary Doctorate of Divinity. But the *Morning Post* ridiculed Hamilton: 'When Lord Nelson had a degree conferred upon him at Oxford, it is said that his friend Sir William Hamilton had an *honorary* one also voted him at the same time, but whether that of L.L.D. or A.S.S. the Records of the University do not say.'[44]

That afternoon they jogged on to Woodstock and next morning arrived uninvited at Blenheim, the Duke of Marlborough's place. For whatever reason – shyness, scruples, disgust – the Duke would not see them, but sent out a servant instead, with an offer of some cold refreshments in the park. The trio refused. They were outraged. Hamilton and Emma heaped on the flattery, to console poor Nelson, who wiped away a tear, took Emma by the hand, and said he was content to have always done his duty. The snub is a marker of their dubious standing in the eyes of the higher classes; burghers and the common people welcomed Nelson throughout the tour, and generously included his companions. They proceeded to Gloucester; from there to Ross; by boat down the Wye to Monmouth; from there to Crickhowell and the great Cyfartha iron foundry at Merthyr Tydfil. The sight of Nelson – so diminutive, so maimed – moved the most unlikely people to tears. They loved and revered him as the saviour of their country. In Italy, Austria, Germany, Hamilton had witnessed such welcomes without number; these closer to home, along a route and in regions he was familiar with, were perhaps more affecting. He was a generous man, in a situation continually delivering him up to the kind of ridicule he had always feared; and if to the end of his days he insisted that friendship with Nelson was a privilege, it must be that he could see in him what the common people could, something amid all the folly and vanity that really was heroic.

They arrived at Milford on 31 July, in time, as planned, to celebrate the fourth anniversary of the Battle of the Nile next day. Greville was there to meet them. Over the next three or four days Nelson did what he could for the cause of Milford, Greville and Hamilton. At a great banquet in his honour he first paid tribute to a local man, Thomas Foley, who had been with him as a captain at the Nile and at Copenhagen; then moved on to praise Milford as one of the best harbours in the world, as good as Trincomalee in the East Indies, and to commend the shipbuilding going on there, and the development of the town 'under the judicious arrangements and unremitting perseverence of the Hon. Charles Greville',[45] whom he, as the last of the trio of Emma's lovers there present on that occasion, cordially disliked. Hamilton laid the foundation stone of a new church above the harbour, St Catherine's, which when completed housed for many years the truck of the mainmast of the French flagship *L'Orient*, sunk in Aboukir Bay. To the inn where they stayed, the New Inn, now the Lord Nelson, he presented Nelson's portrait done in full length by the Palermo artist Guzzardi. Then they went visiting the local gentry, by boat from Milford up the Eastern Cleddau as far as Picton, adjacent to Slebech where Catherine already lay and where Hamilton soon would. In Haverfordwest they met up with Foley, and stayed two days at Ridgeway, his brother's house; from there to Stackpole, Lord Cawdor's; and from there to Tenby.

Altogether Hamilton had nearly a fortnight in the one part of Britain outside London where he had any roots or extensive con-nections. Neither he nor Nelson nor Emma wrote up their tour. Nelson kept precise accounts day by day (and he and Hamilton were scrupulous in paying halves); besides that he wrote a swift memorandum to the Admiralty, urging them to make better use of the oaks in the Forest of Dean. But from Hamilton, nothing. Yet he must have reflected that he would return to those parts only in a coffin; doubtless he dwelled in his thoughts on his first marriage and his second; but of his thoughts and feelings, as usual, he left no record. The abundant other documentation of this last of his tours is not very helpful in that respect either. It is mostly adulatory, focusing on Nelson. After Blenheim there were one or two more little contretemps. The Vicar of Carmarthen, making the traditional distinction between the woman's and the man's blame in adultery, said he would be very glad to pay his respects to Lord Nelson but could not possibly receive Lady Hamilton; and John Foley's wife did not wish to have her in the house, but was persuaded. At Tenby then, where Hamilton had property, one observer left this jaundiced vignette:

I was yesterday witness to an exhibition which though greatly ridiculous, was not wholly so, for it was likewise pitiable; and this was in the persons of two individuals who have lately occupied much public attention. I mean the Duke of Bronte, Lord Nelson, and Emma, Lady Hamilton. The whole town was at their heels as they walked together. The lady is grown immensely fat and equally coarse, while her 'companion in arms' had taken the other extreme – thin, shrunken and to my impression in bad health. They were evidently vain of each other as though the one would have said 'This is Horatio of the Nile' and the other 'This is Emma of Sir William'. Poor Sir William, wretched but not abashed; he followed at a short distance bearing in his arms a cucciolo and other emblems of their combined folly.[46]

A cucciolo is a little dog, perhaps the replacement of Nilus, Nelson's gift to Emma in 1800, who had gone missing. What other emblems Hamilton was carrying, who knows. But there he is, the attendant lord, carrying milady's little dog and 'not abashed'.

The tour continued for another three weeks; the long way back took them through Swansea, Cardiff, Newport and Chepstow, then north into the midlands, to Worcester and Birmingham, and south finally towards London via Warwick and Althorp. Though it will have looked for the most part like the Triumph of Lord Nelson through a grateful nation it is striking how much of the whole thing either concerned Hamilton particularly, like the works on his estate at Milford, or lay through what might be called his territory and involved people who were his, rather than Nelson's or Emma's, friends and family. All the route to Pembroke he had travelled many times, with Catherine or with Greville. Then for two weeks or so he and his party, visiting in the county, actually passed among the scattered farms and manors of his estate. At Picton and Stackpole they were entertained by Hamilton's aristocratic country neighbours. At Merthyr and at Swansea they were met by industrialists, Richard Crawshay and John Morris, whom Hamilton had met and become friendly with on his trip with Greville the previous year. In Birmingham he took his party visiting two men, Henry Clay and Matthew Boulton, whom he had been in dealings with and materially assisted in their manufactures through the publication of his vases and through his good offices in Naples. At Rudhall, near Ross, they were the guests of Mr and Mrs Westfaling, whom Hamilton, as ambassador, had looked after during their visit to Naples in 1794. At Downton Castle they stayed a couple of nights with Richard Payne Knight, fellow Dilettanti, co-author of the *Remains of Priapus* and admirer of Emma since the summer of 1791. At Warwick their host was Hamilton's tedious nephew, the Earl, and at Althorp, the Earl of Spencer, with whose family, especially its females, Hamilton had long had dealings. Thus the tour, in accounts of which he mostly appears as playing, if anything, third fiddle, was in many ways a demonstration of the breadth of his interests, of his achievement, of the range of his social connections. It perhaps also demonstrates his generosity in this sense that everywhere he went, through localities that were his and among friends, family and acquaintances that were his, he introduced a national hero who at once eclipsed him and he presented himself publicly as the supernumerary member in a scandalous and risible *ménage à trois*.

They were back at Merton by 5 September. At once Emma organized another holiday, at Margate, and a meeting with her daughter at nearby Ramsgate. Letters from Hamilton in these last months are few and far between. It is a sad fact that two of the most substantial are complaints. The first probably belongs now, where he did not wish to be, at Margate early in September 1802. Emma must have told him she needed sea baths or she would die, a claim even less credible than that Nelson would if disturbed in his domestic felicity by any outburst of Hamilton's. She wrote:

> As I see it is a pain to you to remain here, let me beg of you to fix your time of going. Whether I dye in Piccadilly or any other spot in England, 'tis the same to me; but I remember the time when you wish'd for tranquility, but now all visiting and bustle is your liking. However, I will do what you please, being ever your affectionate and obedient EH.

Hamilton wrote on the back:

> I neither love bustle nor great company, but I like some employment and diversion. I have but a very short time to live, and every moment is precious to me. I am in no hurry, and am exceedingly glad to give every satisfaction to our best friend, our dear Lord Nelson. The question, then, is what can we best do that all may be

perfectly satisfied. Sea bathing is usefull to your health; I see it is, and wish you to continue it a little longer; but I must confess, that I regret, whilst the season is favourable, that I cannot enjoy my favourite amusement of quiet fishing. I care not a pin for the great world, and am attached to no one so much as to you.[47]

There is an almost formulaic repetition of certain things: his wish to go fishing, his attachment to her and to Nelson, his contempt for the world.

Nelson's birthday, 29 September, was celebrated at Merton with a dinner party hosted by Hamilton. Among the guests was the editor of the *Morning Chronicle*, who wrote up the event, especially Emma's rendition of an Italian cantata in praise of Nelson, with grateful enthusiasm. *The Times* and the *Morning Post* resumed the more usual satirical tone to report a fishing trip over the next two days at Kingston and Hampton: 'The HERO OF THE NILE sits, *die in diem* to witness the gudgeon fishing of Sir William and Lady H—. Sir William who is liberality itself, pays the boatman a Guinea a day for his exertions.[48] In that respect his last autumn was kindly. He got away from Merton a few times, it seems. On one day in October he came home from Teddington with an assorted catch of sixty pounds. But these excursions were respites. In November he wrote Emma what amounts to an ultimatum:

I have passed the last 40 years of my life in the hurry & bustle that must necessarily be attendant on a publick character. I am arrived at the age when some repose is realy necessary, & I promised myself a quiet home, & altho' I was sensible, & said so when I married, that I shou'd be superannuated when my wife wou'd be in her full beauty and vigour of youth. That time is arrived, and we must make the best of it for the comfort of both parties. Unfortunately our tastes as to the manner of living are very different. I by no means wish to live in solitary retreat, but to have seldom less than 12 or 14 at table, & those varying continually, is coming back to what was become so irksome to me in Italy during the latter years of my residence in that country. I have no connections out of my own family. I have no complaint to make, but I feel the whole attention of my wife is given to Ld N. and his interest at Merton. I well know the purity of Ld N's friendship for Emma and me, and I know how very uncomfortable it would make his Lp, our best friend, if a separation shou'd take place, and am therefore determined to do all in my power to prevent such an extremity, which wou'd be *essentially detrimental* to all parties, but wou'd be more sensibly felt by our dear friend than by us.

He concludes with one of his sayings from Shakespeare, this time from Hamlet: 'I think, considering the probability of my not troubling any party long in this world, the best for us all would be to bear those ills we have rather than flie to those we know not of.'[49]

On the 19th of that month the *Herald* noted: 'Sir William Hamilton sported an elegant new chariot on Wednesday last, for the first time.'[50] That gave him some freedom, to get away. He went fishing, or he went into London where he could choose his own company. He was at meetings of the Royal Society (chairing one when Banks was ill) and of the Dilettanti. His last surviving letter to Banks, on 30 January 1803, is a very characteristic document. In it he urges that all British ships be fitted with lightning conductors (perhaps remembering the relatively safe passage of lightning, down the gilding, in Lord Tylney's house in 1774), and he concludes: 'The greatest Satisfaction a man can feel is the reflection of his having been instrumental in removing Evil & promoting good to his fellow Creatures.'[51] Though never an active philanthropist – he was not an inventor, a reformer, an initiator of better practice – he could in a general way be said to have 'promoted good to his fellow creatures', and more particularly and chiefly through the publication of his vases, in the *efficacy* of whose beauty he did truly believe.

Having presented Piaggi's Diary of Vesuvius to the Royal Society, in whose library it can still be consulted, he presented something of equal or perhaps even greater importance to the Dilettanti: Piaggi's account of the excavations at Herculaneum, withheld by him during his lifetime because of his close connection with the Neapolitan Court; but what the Dilettanti did with it and where it has vanished to is a mystery. Their minutes for a meeting of 6 March 1803 read:

The Right Honble Sr William Hamilton KB. offered to this Society a collection of the original Notes and Drawings relative to the

Discoveries in the City of Herculaneum made during the course of the excavations in that City by the Padre Antonio Piazzi & by the Padre himself given to Sr Wm Hamilton: in order that the Society might publish the same in such manner as they may think Proper.

The Dilettanti resolved:

1 That the Society do accept from their worthy Member Sr Wm Hamilton this most valuable present & do return him their sincere thanks for the same. 2dly That the Papers presented by Sr William Hamilton be referred to the Committee of Publication who on inspection of them, shall report to the Society their sentiments with respect to the most eligible mode to be pursued in their publication.

There was a meeting of the Society on Sunday 27 March, to decide in principle whether to publish or not (practicalities could be left to the Publications Committee) but Hamilton had to send in his apologies. He wrote from 23 Piccadilly on 25 March:

Nothing cou'd have prevented my having had the honor of attending at the proposed meeting on Sunday of the Dilettante Society as the fate of a favorite child of mine that I have deposited in the hands of the Society will probably be decided – My present State of health & weakness is deplorable and makes it impossible for me to attend but my Friend Mr. Wyndham is thoroughly master of the business and will I am sure in my room give the most satisfactory acct to the Society of the probable benefit the arts will receive by the publication of these papers shou'd the Society think proper to adopt the Plan that will be proposed by the Committee appointed for Publications.

'Favourite child', it may be remembered, was the phrase Emma used to describe the childless Hamilton's feelings towards the English Garden at Caserta. At their meeting on 27 March the Dilettanti resolved that their Committee of Publications

should be authorised & empowered to proceed with the Inter-pretation & Arrangement of the Papers presented to the Society of Dilettanti by Sir William Hamilton KB and to draw from Time to

> Time on the Treasurer for such Sums as may be necessary to repay
> the Expence of completing such Interpretation & Arrangement

And further 'that when such Interpretation & Arrangement shall be completed, the Committee of Publications do lay the same before the Society together with their opinion thereof'. The papers never were published, nor is any further mention of them made in the Society's minutes. For a while at least they were with Charles Townley, a close friend of Hamilton's and one of the Dilettanti. But then they vanish.[52]

Having feared coming back to English winters, he survived three. He was ill in the early part of each year, as he had been often during his last years in Italy. When he wrote to Tischbein in June 1801 he told him his illness that spring had been severe. Taking ill again early in 1803 he never quite recovered his strength. He was at a levee on 16 February; that evening he and Emma hosted a grand concert at 23 Piccadilly; and, as we have seen, he attended the Dilettanti on 6 March; but after his letter to them on 25th he declined fast. On 31 March he made last amendments to his will, increasing Emma's legacy from £300 to £800 and leaving Vigée Le Brun's portrait of her, done in enamel by Henry Bone, to Nelson. On 1 April he sent away Mrs Cadogan who with Emma had been nursing him, in his phrase, 'with unremitted Tenderness', and had a long and last conversation with his nephew Charles Greville. Greville drew up a memorandum of this talk, to use in proving the will and particularly that part in the codicil by which he was left £7000 of stock. If we trust his account, Hamilton to the last was still grievously hurt by his treatment from the country whose servant he had been for nearly forty years. He would, he said, have had more to bequeath to Emma and would have left Charles an estate more intact and less encumbered with debt if the Treasury had only honoured its debt to him (he claims they only paid him half), forcing him to sell his valuables, which he had intended to use to 'exonerate' his estate, and his pictures, vases, and books, which were to have amused him in his old age and to have gone to Greville after his death. He bitterly resented being granted only the usual pension. He wondered if the King actually knew how badly his 'foster brother' was being treated. This is Greville's record of Hamilton's words to him:

I cannot think that the King has forgot that my Mother reared us & the same Nurse suckled us – that from his first Establishment as Prince of Wales untill Burks Bill I had been near his person. I have more than once told the king that my little Welch Estate would be my Sheet Anchor & I intended it to be yours entire – but one Farm is gone since my return & the King knows that another was on Sale. He wishes you & Robert [Greville's brother] well & I cannot think that he would have deserted me when he knew all – for when I go alone to Windsor nothing can be more Gracious & flattering –

So much for his grievances and distress. Beyond those, he seems to have maintained or achieved a good deal of equanimity before his death. He was at first, according to Greville, worried that his dying might be protracted. Greville assured him that it would not be.

He said, I hope so, I know the weakness of Humanity – In health I meditated without finding limits to the Sublimity of Power – or to the infinity of Goodness of the Almighty. In my weakness I dwell on it with increased humility & Resignation –

He was content with the philosophy he had reached, and wished to die undisturbed in it: 'I do not wish to see any Friend who is wiser or better than I am & may be desirous to prepare me for death. You will not, I know, let them intrude, to disturb my Tranquillity.' This means, I think, that he did not want any clergyman let in, and certainly none attended. Greville's account concludes: 'This was his Last Conversation with me alone. He lingered a few days & died without a groan.'[53] Nelson said: 'without a Sigh or a Struggle'. It was on the morning of 6 April 1803. He died in Emma's arms, with Nelson holding his hand. Emma endorsed the moment thus: 'Unhappy day for the forlorn Emma ten minutes past ten Dear Blessed Sir William left me.'[54]

Obituary notices, in *The Times* on 7 April and the *Sun* on the 9th, whilst acknowledging his royal connection and his long service at the Court of Naples, chiefly drew attention to his achievements in the Fine Arts. *The Times* dwelled also on his domestic happiness (with Emma) and made no mention of either his sharing it with Nelson nor of his substantial contribution to the new science of vulcanology.

Hamilton directed in his will that he should be buried beside his first wife Catherine, to fulfil the promise he had made her, and that the funeral was to be conducted 'in as private a manner as decency and propriety [would] permit'.[55] The long journey to that burial began on 12 April. Some years later Sir William Gell, who explored and described Pompeii more professionally than anyone in Hamilton's generation could have done, related the following anecdote, perhaps as the eyewitness in it:

> A gentleman passing along Piccadilly saw a crowd of people at Sir W. Hamilton's door, where they were putting the coffin into the hearse; but seeing everybody looking up at the window, he looked also, and there was to be seen Lady Hamilton in all the *wildness of her grief*. Some said her attitudes were fine; others that they were affected; others that they were natural. At last, as the gentleman was leaving this motley group, some of whom were crying and others laughing, he heard a child go up to its mamma, and say, 'Ma, mamma, don't cry, pray don't cry, for they say as how it's all *sham*.'[56]

I should say the performance was as false and true as that moment after the Battle of the Nile when she flung herself at Nelson, crying 'Oh God, is it possible?'

Hamilton was buried next to Catherine in the Barlow vault at Slebech on 19 April. By then the terms of his will were public knowledge. Emma's immediate legacy was £800; thereafter, from the Pembroke estates, she was to have £800 a year, £100 of it going to Mrs Cadogan for her share. Her outstanding debts, of about £450, were to be settled out of the money still owing from the Treasury. Annuities of 100 ducats were to be paid to four servants in Naples. Nelson got two guns and the aforementioned portrait of Emma. Hamilton's instruction read:

> The Copy of Madame Le Brunns Picture of Emma in Enamel, by Bone I give to my Dearest Friend Lord Nelson Duke of Bronte, a very small token of the great regard I have for his Lordship the most virtuous loyal and truly Brave character I ever met with God bless him and shame fall on those who do not say Amen.[57]

So Nelson was bequeathed a copy of a portrait of the woman who had long been his already in the flesh. If Hamilton's tone is mocking, then it is a mockery directed against a public and its press who duly made all the expected jokes. When Hamilton said, as he often did, that he cared not a fig for the great world, in this regard at least he meant it.

Nelson – that summer back on duty in Naples – wrote to Maria Carolina: 'You will be sorry to hear, that good Sir William did not leave [Lady Hamilton] in such comfortable circumstances as his fortune would have allowed. He has given it amongst his relations.'[58] Considering the debts he left and the burdens on the estate and bearing in mind what the Treasury owed him, there is more ungenerosity than justice in Nelson's comment; but there is *some* justice. At the last, as he had always made it clear that he would, Hamilton sided with his family, making Greville his heir and keeping his promise to Catherine. £800 a year, though not princely, would have been enough to keep Emma and her mother and one or both of her children in reasonable comfort, had she not been Emma. She knew very well that she would be straitened, and began at once, with the support of Greville and Nelson and a good deal of sympathy from society, to petition that at least some of Hamilton's pension should continue to be paid to her, though the rule was it would stop with his death. Her letter to Prime Minister Addington of 13 April nicely combined both her departed husband's and her own merits and services in a plea for recompense. Addington might have obliged – he was reported to be favourably inclined – but national politics supervened and put it out of his mind as the peace within which the *tria juncta in uno* had lived out the last scenes of their public role ended a month after the death of one of them, and took away another soon to sea, leaving the lady doubly widowed and desolate. She gave up 23 Piccadilly, now Greville's, and moved to a smaller house in Clarges Street, where Catherine had lived when Hamilton married her.

POSTSCRIPT

Just before leaving to command the British fleet Nelson found time to arrange the christening of his and Emma's daughter, Horatia. Mrs Gibson, the child's minder, saw to it on their behalf. They appear on the certificate as godparents, and the date of birth is false. The christening took place on 13 May in the convenient church of St Mary-le-Bone, where in September 1791 Emma and Sir William had had their sparse and hurried wedding ceremony. Then Nelson was away at sea chasing the French fleet hither and thither. He got no leave until August 1805, before Trafalgar, at which battle, parading in his plumes and medals so ostentatiously that some have thought it suicidal, he was shot through the spine and died. Emma got the news on 6 November, fainted and, coming round, seemed stricken through and through. 'What shall I do?' she asked repeatedly. 'How can I exist?' Even the uncharitable thought she meant more by that than money, means and practicalities. But those did increasingly concern her. In his testament Nelson had left her as a legacy to his King and Country; but the charge was not honoured and her efforts to get what she thought her due brought her into ever grosser attitudes and ridicule.

In November 1808 there was a meeting of her trustees, to consider how her debts might be paid. It was agreed that the furnishings of 23 Piccadilly, together with Hamilton's library, all assigned to her by him in February 1801 and since Nelson's death removed to Merton Place, should be auctioned; and the house too was to be sold. The trustees estimated that the books might be worth £1500. Christie's auctioned them, on 8 and 9 June 1809. Into the four winds went Hamilton's many books of travel and natural history; his collection of rarities on Vesuvius and vulcanology; his sumptuous folios of

285

antiquities; his Piranesi; the *philosophes* and the *belles lettres* of France; the poets, economists, novelists, historians of Britain and Italy; works by friends – by Saussure, Swinburn, Beckford, Dutens, Walpole, Burney; his copies of Winckelmann's letters, the *History of Ancient Art*, the *Monumenti Inediti*; things sent him by colleagues and admirers in the European world of learning; the vast and costly *Antichità d'Ercolano*; and his own *Vases*, the d'Hancarville and the Tischbein, the *Campi Phlegraei*, his *Philosophical Transactions*, and *The Worship of Priapus* ... on and on, over two days, two hundred and eighty lots, dozens of volumes sometimes in a single lot. Altogether, the books raised £1042 15s 6d. The first two Winckelmann went in one lot with a dictionary of antiquities for half a guinea.[1]

Next day, 10 June, in a sale of furnishings and works of art, many of them Nelson's, Emma herself, as St Cecilia, Cassandra, Thaïs, Niobe, the Comic Muse, a recumbent bacchante, likewise among other collectors was dispersed.

She outlived her old lover Greville and her doughty mother, Mrs Cadogan, the first dying in the autumn of 1809, the second early the following year. In gin and penury she ended her own days in Calais in January 1815, watched over by Horatia, old beyond her fourteen years. She had, by her own account, turned to Catholicism in her later years. The adult Horatia commented severely: 'That must be between her God and herself, but having lived so long with such a decided freethinker as Sir William Hamilton professed to be, it is not surprising that she should not have any very fixed principles.'[2]

Hamilton had prophesied that he and Catherine, buried in Slebech Church, would 'roll soon together into Milford Haven for the sea is undermining that church very fast'; and although that has not happened, still in a sense he and she have been obliterated. The church was built, probably in the twelfth century, by the Knights of St John of Jerusalem. It passed, with a great deal of land, to the Barlows at the Dissolution, and became their family church. They had their own heated pew in the south transept and a vault under the chancel for their dead. But in the years after Hamilton joined Catherine there the church fell more and more into ruin. Finally, in the early 1830s, a new lord of the manor, the first Baron de Rutzen, deliberately hastened its demise, in fact actively vandalized it, so that he could build a replacement higher up above the water, on what became the A40. That new church, St John's, inaugurated in 1838, is itself condemned now and dangerous to enter. The old church is roofless, the effigies of a knight and his lady that used to lie on a tomb in the south chancel have long since gone to a museum. But where the plaque has gone, once affixed to the northern wall in commemoration of Sir William Hamilton and his achievements, nobody knows. In the old place by the muddy Western Cleddau, under the rooks and the yew trees, no indication remains that Hamilton and Catherine are buried there. We know they are, because the church records attest their interment in the vault, the first on 22 February 1783, the second on 19 April 1803. The floor of the church, open to the sky, is thick grass, but if you stamp in the right spot the vault sounds, hollow. In 1945 a Field Ambulance unit, billeted at Slebech Hall, found the old church 'very much in need of a clean up', and together with a party of German prisoners-of-war, they set to work. The nave, full of earth and rubble, had trees and bushes growing in it. They cleared all this away and dug deeper to reach the original floor, hearing a hollow sound the nearer they got. 7349040 Sgt. Bernard Allcock wrote a report, which reads, at the critical point, as follows:

> We carried on digging. All this time the hollow sound had increased, and we were very much elated when a large slab was uncovered and then another; between the two there was a slight gap, through which we dropped small stones, and placing our ears to the gap, listened for the stone to either splash into water or hit a hard surface.
>
> It did neither; after talking a bit, we decided to try and lift up one of the slabs to see if it was an entrance; it was; there were about eight steps leading down to a crypt which looked very forbidding, but with so much success on our hands, we overcame that feeling and entered.
>
> With the aid of electric torches we saw seven coffins laying there and in the right hand corner an urn, about two feet high.
>
> We glanced at the coffins to see if names and dates could be found, but unfortunately there was nothing to give us any clues; we did notice that the coffins were hewn out of tree trunks and finished off by making the outsides very smooth, but whether they were

stained or not we could not tell; they were dark but this may have been through age and not stain.

I would like to point out that the coffins and ornaments were not interfered with or violated in any form by us, but it was noticed that at some time or other the crypt had been entered and interfered with, much to our sorrow.

After our visit, it was decided to close up the crypt entrance by replacing the slab, and putting down cement to seal it off from further violation; this seal was put down on V.E. Day, and the following inscription was carved in the cement:

177 Field Ambulance. R.A.M.C.

V.E. Day. May 8th 1945.

A penny was placed in the cement as a seal.[3]

Two among the coffins must be those of Catherine and Hamilton.

CONCLUSION

In January 1794 Emma wrote to Hamilton to tell him of the death of his old friend Lord Pembroke. Hamilton was at Venafro, hunting. He replied: 'The news ... gave me a little twist ... I have, for some time, perceived, that my friends, with whom I spent my younger days, have been dropping around me.' Then he added:

> My study of antiquities, has kept me in constant thought of the perpetual fluctuation of every thing. The whole art is, really, to live all the *days* of our life; and not, with anxious care, disturb the sweetest hour that life affords – which is, the present! Admire the Creator, all his works, to us incomprehensible: and do all the good you can upon earth; and take the chance of eternity, without dismay.[1]

He was harking back to the lines of verse he had written in his notebook a few years previously; but also summarizing things he had said (and would say again) about the transient human being's place and proper bearing in a world of such colossal phenomena as the volcano and such beautiful objects as the vases. Hamilton had a philosophy and through public and private vicissitudes tried to live by it. Though I regret not having found much documentation of the life of his heart and soul, my guess is that any such find – the journal which he kept after Catherine's death, for example, and promised to show Beckford – would not have revealed a very different man.

Hamilton's achievements in the Arts and the Natural Sciences are indisputable. Through the collecting and publication of the vases he made beautiful objects available to a wider and wider public (in the British Museum we can see them still); he advanced a better understanding of them – that they were Greek, not Etruscan – and

materially affected contemporary taste and manufacture. In Naples
and in London he was a great encourager and patron of the arts.
Many painters, British, Italian, French, German, owed some or most
of their livelihoods to him; musicians too, employed in his Academy
at the Palazzo Sessa. In vulcanology, much of his thinking seems
close to the modern; and he is besides, in his own writing, in the
pictures he commissioned from, especially, Pietro Fabris, and in the
journal he had (and donated) from Antonio Piaggi, a provider of
detailed and unslanted evidence for others even nowadays to evaluate
and interpret.

In the political and public world Hamilton's achievement was
much less. He would certainly and rightly be forgotten had he done
nothing else. His time in parliament seems to have been only nominal;
then as a diplomat his post was for most of his career of peripheral
importance, which his hundreds of letters to his Secretaries of State
do, it must be said, amply convey. He was on the margins, his
masters overlooked him, he never had much clout. In draft form
(among the Foreign Office papers) the recredentials he had to present
when he left his post refer to him simply as Envoy Extraordinary
and omit the 'additional character' (Plenipoteniary) given him in 1767.
Somebody noticed and inserted it before the copy went to him.[2]
That little accident is perhaps symbolic. For all his origins in and
loyalty to the establishment he put himself at some remove from
them, and could not rely on their goodwill when he needed it. And
having been peripheral for thirty years, when the consequences of
the French Revolution reached down the length of Italy, then he
was taken up into a politics and into complicities that became ever
more squalid. And during his last five years, in public and in private
life, in a triangle with Emma and Nelson, he seemed to many wholly
ridiculous.

Hamilton's feelings during that ridicule are hard to gauge. Though
severely tried and now and then protesting, he does seem, perhaps
to the bitter end, to have loved Emma and to have felt real friendship
and admiration for Nelson; and that despite knowing everything, as
I am sure he did. He upheld himself by his own keen interests – the
arts, the natural sciences, fishing, congenial company – and by an
ironic detachment, never expecting too much either of his nearest
and dearest or of himself, and certainly not of the world at large

whose opinions and behaviour he viewed on the whole with an amiable contempt.

That said, Hamilton must not be thought of as standing above the mêlée. He was a thorough participator in the life that mattered. His attachments to people – to his first wife Catherine, to his nephew Greville, his niece Mary, his distant cousin Beckford, his friend Banks – were real and lasting; and in his doting on Emma and admiration for the hero Nelson he is human and sympathetic and not, as the cartoonists and his disloyal guests thought, merely risible. He professed the usual doctrine of rational self-interest, but loved and was loyal often in contravention of it. He never dropped Beckford, for example, as many did.

Hamilton had passionate interests and he pursued them 'not wisely but too well'. Collecting and publishing the vases got him into serious debt. Among earthquakes and eruptions he risked life and limb; for the sake of science, he might say, but really because those violent energies in nature fascinated him. He was curious; the phenomena of the real world excited him. And he had a keen love of beauty – in people, especially young women, and in works of art, especially those of the Ancient World. He was a thorough and intelligent hedonist, and that will to live and to enjoy living sustained him, helped him 'bear up', as he said, in many circumstances – the journey home in 1800, for example, interminable dinner-parties, everlasting hunts, dirty politics, folly at Court – that would have been the death of a less determined man. He had stamina, and a sort of resolute patience, and an enviable ability actually to get enjoyment and interest among people and in situations one might think quite void of either.

Hamilton was well liked. In his appeal to Lord Grenville in January 1800, Charles Greville said of his uncle that he was loved by everyone from the King to the *lazzaroni*;[3] and though it did not move Lord Grenville it was certainly true. In a very un-English way Hamilton moved easily in every sort of company; he took a real interest in all manner of people; they felt attended to and responded warmly. On leave in England he must have seemed increasingly exotic. Wraxall said of him that in appearance – 'tall and meagre, with a dark complexion, a very aquiline nose' – he always reminded him of Rolando in Lesage's picaresque novel *Gil Blas*: an intriguing asso-ciation, since Rolando is a robber chief, whose physical appearance

Lesage never describes, only his violent deeds and rather cynical conversation, so that reading these, Wraxall must have thought of his friend and lent Rolando his looks and bearing. There is something predatory about Hamilton the collector, the hedonist, the tireless seeker after sights for his eyes and interest for his curious intelligence. But besides that (and no doubt more than the robber Rolando) his face, Wraxall says, 'powerfully attracted and conciliated every beholder'.[4]

Soon after Hamilton died the war against France resumed and dragged on bloodily for a further dozen years. Revolution and Romanticism sent a rift through the European social order and European consciousness that was vaster and more final than any observed by Hamilton in the Campi Phlegraei. He touched on the new sensibility in Goethe, lived with it tolerantly in Catherine and Beckford, but was himself of the world that was in the process of passing away. He was the servant of a social order that would before long have to accommodate itself to the demands first of the bourgeoisie then of the urban proletariat; and he was complicit with a regime – the Neapolitan – more backward and ripe for dissolution than any among the dubious allies ranged against the new ideals and the cynical self-interest of France. But that close association with things past does not make him *passé*. By the principle of common humanity no human life should pass quite out of our interest; and Hamilton's seventy-two years, so rich in dealings with remarkable men and women, so full of passionate curiosity about the phenomenal world, are worth knowing about. He is to an unusually high degree both individual and representative.

NOTES

Preface

1. Goethe, *Kampagne in Frankreich* and *Belagerung von Mainz*, in *Sämtliche Werke*, 18 volumes (Zürich 1977), XII, pp. 289, 430
2. Add. MS 41199, f. 53

1 Life Before Naples, 1730–64

1. Hervey, *Memoirs*, II, 475
2. Morrison, II, 34
3. Walpole, *Anecdotes of Painting in England*, V, 171, 173
4. Add. MS 42071, f. 39
5. Hervey, III, 757–59
6. Bodleian MS Eng. Hist. g.3, f. 32v
7. MS Eng. Hist. g.4, f. 707
8. Ibid, g.3, f. 17
9. Ibid, f. 23
10. Ibid, g.4, f. 210
11. Ibid, f. 164
12. Ibid, g.3, f. 18v
13. Wraxall, pp. 139–40
14. Walpole, XXI, 155
15. Beckles Willson, pp. 192–3
16. Add. MS 51315, f. 18
17. Pembroke Papers, I, 37
18. Casanova, IX, 179
19. Bodleian MS Eng. lett. d.36, f. 62
20. Tischbein (1956), p. 291
21. Bodleian MS Beckford, c.31, f. 119
22. And not of Hugh Barlow of Lawrenny Hall as Fothergill and others have asserted.
23. Morrison, I, 62
24. Add. MS 38201, f. 198
25. Anson, p.3.
26. Add. MS 41197, f. 1v
27. Add. MS 40715, ff. 227–9
28. Morrison, I, 3
29. Add. MS 38200, f. 299
30. Morrison, I, 3
31. Add. MS 38201, f. 191
32. Anson, p.3
33. Add. MS 42069, ff. 5–6
34. Bodleian MSS Eng. hist. g.5–g.13 (Hamilton's fifth notebook is missing.)
35. Acton, p. 116
36. Add. MS 40714, f. 1
37. Connell, p. 58
38. Walpole, XXII, 243
39. Ibid, 259

2 Naples

1. BL Add. MS 34048, f. 24v
2. BL Egerton MS 2634, f. 22

3. Eg. 2634, f. 8
4. Ibid, ff. 5–6
5. Ibid, f. 5
6. Connell, pp. 58–9
7. See Eg. 2634, ff. 101–3; Sharp, I, 138; and Elliot, I, 406
8. PRO SP 105/316, f. 137
9. Eg. 2634, f. 77
10. Eg. 2634, ff. 84–5
11. Bodleian, MS Eng. hist. g.5, f. 1
12. Eg. 2634, f. 10
13. Sharp, I, 76. Sharp's letters were published early in 1767. James Philipps, Hamilton's tenant at Colby, wrote to congratulate him on his 'honourable mention' in them. See Aberystwyth, 5.
14. PRO, SP 105/316, f. 36
15. SP 105/316, f. 92
16. Eg. 2636, f. 100
17. SP 105/316, f. 37
18. Anson, p. 4
19. Add. MS 41197, f. 30
20. For example after the death of Lady Hillsborough in January 1766, or of Lord Cavendish in September 1781. See Aberystwyth, 50 and Morrison, I, 77.
21. SP 105/316, ff. 342 and 280
22. Paris, Krafft Bequest
23. Krafft Bequest
24. Eg. 2634, ff. 93–4
25. Add. MS 40714, ff. 2–3

3 Vases and the Volcano
1. Ingamells, p. 453
2. Krafft Bequest
3. Winckelmann, *Geschichte der Kunst* (Dresden, 1764), p. 122

and *Sämtliche Werke* (Osnabrück 1965), III, 94, 382–3
4. Abstract in Krafft Bequest. Other figures, see my 'Winckelmann and Sir William Hamilton', p. 62; Tischbein's evidence, see Von Alten, p. 84.
5. Krafft Bequest
6. Ibid
7. PRO, SP 105/316, f. 342
8. Krafft Bequest
9. Fothergill, *Mitred Earl*, p. 23
10. To Palmerston, 18 March 1766, Krafft Bequest
11. This account first published in *Philosophical Transactions*, 57 (1767), pp. 192–200. Quotations here taken from the reprint in *Campi Phlegraei*, I, pp. 16, 18, 18, 14.
12. Add. MS 42069, ff. 46–7. See my 'Winckelmann and Sir William Hamilton' for a fuller account of the dealings between the two men.
13. First published in *Philosophical Transactions*, 58 (1768), pp. 1–14. Here quoted from the reprint in *Campi Phlegraei*, I, 25–6 and p. 28.
14. Winckelmann, *Geschichte der Kunst*, pp. 122–3 and *Sämtliche Werke*, III, 383
15. Mankowitz, appendix
16. Eg. 2634, f. 216
17. Ingamells, p. 454
18. Eg. 2641, f. 20
19. Winckelmann, *Briefe*, III, 289, 342, 354, 375
20. SP 105/318, f. 175

NOTES

21. Anson, pp. 251–2
22. *Briefe*, III, 375, 379
23. See *Vases and Volcanoes*, p. 92. See also a letter in the Krafft Bequest to Hamilton from James Byres in Rome, 22 January 1785: 'Your portrait by Mr. Maron and Mr. Hamiltons bust by Mr Hewitson have been cased up for some time and are waiting for a Bark for Naples …' Christopher Hewetson did [Gavin] Hamilton's bust in 1784. But can the portrait here referred to be the one begun by Anton Maron in 1768?
24. *Briefe*, III, 375
25. Add. MS 42069, f. 60v
26. SP 105/319, f. 99

4 The King
1. Add. MS 34048, f. 61
2. Acton, p. 138
3. Ibid, p. 137
4. Wraxall, p. 147
5. Eg. 2634, f. 44
6. Winckelmann, *Briefe*, III, 362, 330
7. Wraxall, p. 148
8. Acton, pp. 138–9
9. Morrison, I, 80
10. PRO, FO/70/4, f. 223a
11. Morrison, I, 48
12. Ibid, 65
13. Eg. 2636, f. 178
14. Acton, p. 141
15. Acton, p. 43. See Miller, II, 247–50. Sharp, I, 139, calls it 'a strange, wild, and barbarous entertainment given to the

populace here four *Sundays* successively in the Carnival', and describes it.
16. Acton, p. 44

5 Amusements and Successes, 1768–1773
1. PRO, SP 105/319, ff. 127, 99; Aberystwyth, 99
2. Eg. 2635, f. 64
3. Ibid, f. 83
4. Wraxall, p. 152
5. Morrison, I, 12
6. Aberystwyth, 54, 4
7. Add. MS 41197, f. 100
8. *Campi Phlegraei*, I, 38. The tour published first in *Philosophical Transactions*, 60 (1770), pp. 1–19.
9. *Campi Phlegraei*, I, 47, 48
10. SP 105/319, f. 596
11. Ibid, f. 597
12. Miller, II, 222
13. Mozart, *Briefe und Aufzeichnungen*, ed. by Wilhelm Bauer and Otto Deutsch, 7 vols (Kassel, 1962–75), I, 350, 347–8
14. See *Vases and Volcanoes*, p. 128
15. Burney, pp. 176, 177
16. Ibid, pp. 180–1
17. Ibid, p. 195
18. Ibid, p. 176; Eg. 2635, f. 124
19. SP 105/320, ff. 251–2
20. Eg. 2635, f. 27
21. Add. MS 40714, f. 70
22. Ibid, f. 79
23. Add. MSS 41197, f. 133 and 40714, f. 83
24. Eg. 2635, ff. 129–30
25. Add. MS 40714, ff. 104–5
26. Add. MS 41197, f. 163; Eg.

2635, ff. 163, 181, 230, 216, 224.
Add. MS 41197, f. 169; Add.
MS 40714, f. 108

27. SP 105/319, f. 730
28. Add. MS 41197, f. 175
29. Eg. 2635, f. 230
30. Ibid, ff. 230–1
31. Coke, III, 442
32. Walpole, XXII, 339
33. Walpole, XL, 460
34. Walpole, XXXII, 70–1
35. *Vases and Volcanoes*, pp. 60, 160, 183; Fothergill, p. 118
36. Morrison, I, 44
37. Add. MS 40714, f. 108
38. Coke, III, 445, 447
39. Add. MS 37077, f. 3; Add. MS 40714, f. 117
40. Add. MS 40714, f. 119v
41. Morrison, I, 16–17
42. Coke, IV, 151, 260
43. Morrison, I, 17
44. Walpole, XXIII, 448
45. Walpole, XXIII, 448–9
46. Eg. 2635, f. 233
47. Add. MS 41197, f. 253
48. Eg. 2635, f. 225
49. Add. MS 42069, f. 91v

6 'Going thru' Life Tollerably',
1773–1780

1. Add. MS 24159, f. 99
2. Eg. 2636, f. 100
3. Krafft Bequest
4. Morrison, I, 19
5. Ibid, 22
6. Ibid, 39
7. Krafft Bequest
8. Morrison, I, 41
9. Ibid, 44

10. Ibid, 25
11. *Philosophical Transactions*, 63 (1773), pp. 324–32
12. Add. MS 34710, ff. 9–10. And cf. a letter from Saussure to Hamilton, in a copy among Strange's papers, Add. MS 19309, f. 107v
13. Ingamells, p. 800
14. Add. MS 19309, ff. 107–25
15. *Campi Phlegraei*, I, 6, 5
16. Bodleian, Misc. Eng. Hist. g.16, f. 20
17. *Campi Phlegraei*, I, 3–4
18. Goethe, XI, 223
19. *Campi Phlegraei*, I, 53, 86
20. Morrison, I, 25; Add. MS 34710, f. 11v
21. *Philosophical Transactions* 68/I (1778), pp. 1–6
22. *Campi Phlegraei, Supplement*, p. 2
23. *Campi Phlegraei, Supplement*, p. 20. The account also in *Philosophical Transactions* 70/1 (1780), pp. 42–84
24. *Archaeologia*, IV (1777), pp. 161, 164, 172–3
25. *Philosophical Transactions*, 85 (1795), pp. 92–3
26. *Archaeologia* IV, Plates VI and IX
27. Miller, II, 295
28. *Archaeologia*, IV, p. 166
29. Eg. 2636, f. 116
30. *Campi Phlegraei, Supplement*, p. 12
31. Eg. 2635, f. 253
32. Eg. 2636, f. 161
33. Ibid, ff. 178, 181, 273
34. Ibid, ff. 129, 130, 185, 160, 206
35. Morrison, I, 36

36. Eg. 2636, f. 226
37. Ibid, f. 156
38. Ibid, f. 246
39. Ibid, f. 140
40. PRO, FO 70/1, 26v
41. Eg. 2634, ff. 371–2
42. Eg. 2635, f. 256
43. Morrison, I, 27
44. Eg. 2636, ff. 126, 138
45. Eg. 2636, ff. 6–7
46. Walpole, XXXV, p. 418. See also, Aberystwyth, 55
47. Eg. 2636, f. 100
48. Add. MS 40714, ff. 133–34; Eg. 2636, f. 114; Morrison, I, 37
49. Add. MS 40714, f. 136
50. Morrison, I, 38
51. Eg. 2636, f. 154
52. Add. MS 41198, f. 6
53. Ibid, f. 8
54. Morrison, I, 48
55. Eg. 2636, f. 184
56. Krafft Bequest
57. Morrison, I, 25, 26
58. Fothergill, p. 146
59. Morrison, I, 9
60. Add. MS 34710, f. 9
61. Morrison, I, 44, 45
62. Aberystwyth, 54
63. Morrison, I, 45, 48
64. Wraxall, p. 330
65. Anson, p. 37
66. Ibid, pp. 144–5
67. Morrison, I, 51
68. Eg. 2636, f. 192; Morrison, I, 51, 52
69. Anson, pp. 147–8
70. Morrison, I, 57
71. Anson, p. 145
72. Kelly, I, 29

73. Pembroke Papers, I, 225
74. Eg. 2641, f. 130v
75. Ibid, f. 132
76. Add. MS 34048, f. 5
77. Add. MS 34048, ff. 7–8
78. Morrison, I, 63; Pembroke Papers, I, 494
79. Pembroke Papers, I, 233, 494

7 Mixed Events, 1780–August 1783

1. Morrison, I, 60–1, 63
2. Morrison, I, 62, 64
3. Pembroke Papers, II, 76
4. Morrison, I, 65
5. Bodleian, MS Beckford c.31, f. 50v
6. MS Beckford e.1, f. 67
7. MS Beckford c.31, f.37
8. Ibid, f. 32
9. Ibid, ff. 39, 32, 48, 40v, 35, 59v
10. Ibid, ff. 31v–32
11. Ibid, f. 32
12. Ibid, ff. 35v, 35
13. Pembroke Papers, II, 76
14. MS Beckford, c.31, ff. 46v, 49v, 54
15. Add. MS 40714, f. 193
16. MS Beckford, c.31, ff. 60v, 72
17. Ibid, c.31, ff. 46–7, 39v, 72, 64
18. Morrison, I, 70
19. Worship of Priapus, pp. 8–9, 10, 11
20. Morrison, I, 70; Add. MS, 34048, f. 14
21. Anson, p. 146
22. MS Beckford, c.31, ff. 55–6
23. Ibid, ff. 59v–60
24. Ibid, ff. 75v–6
25. Morrison, I, 79

26. Wraxall, pp. 124–5
27. Morrison, I, 79–80
28. Ibid, 81
29. MS Beckford, c.31, f. 54
30. Morrison, I, 80–2
31. Add. MS 41198, f. 112
32. MS Beckford c.31, f. 47
33. Morrison, I, 81, 82
34. Ibid, 82
35. Walpole, XXV, 321
36. Add. MS 41198, f. 112v; Anson, pp. 151–2
37. Anson, pp. 151, 152; Add. MS 41198, f. 112
38. MS Beckford c.31, ff. 107v–109
39. Add. MS 41198, f. 113v
40. Anson, p. 153
41. MS Beckford, c.31, f. 110
42. Ibid, f. 111v
43. MS Beckford, c.31, ff. 108v, 116, 116v
44. Morrison, I, 84; MS Beckford c.31, f. 116v
45. The whole account in *Philosophical Transactions* 73 (1783), pp. 169–208. In the British Library (Add. MS 8967, ff. 34–48) there is a dossier of documents on the earthquake, collected by Banks.
46. Add. MS 8967, f. 45. And cf. Lalande, VII, 354
47. See Richard V. Fisher *Volcanoes* (Princeton 1997), p. 165
48. Bodleian, MS Eng. hist. g.16, ff. 4–5

8 The Widower on Leave, August 1783–November 1784

1. Walpole, XXV, 432; XXXIII, 375, 415; XXV, 391; XXX, 375
2. Anson, pp. 4, 251–2, 172
3. Add. MS 34048, f. 23
4. Anson, pp. 155–6
5. Walpole, XXXIII, 489
6. Anson, p. 163
7. Reilly, p. 315
8. Morrison, I, 100
9. Ibid
10. Add. MS 42071, f. 6
11. Anson, pp. 174–5
12. Anson, pp. 235, 252, 253
13. Anson, p. 244
14. Memoirs in private hands
15. Anson, p. 251

9 The Transaction of Emma, 1784–1786

1. Morrison, I, 95
2. Ibid, 176; Add. MS 34048, f. 24v
3. Bodleian MS. Eng. Hist. g.16, f. 33v
4. The whole tour edited with a commentary in *Oxford German Studies* 23 (1994), pp. 104–23
5. Morrison, I, 96
6. Add. MS 42071, f. 2
7. Anson, pp. 303–4
8. Morrison, I, 99–101
9. Add. MS 42071, f. 4v
10. Morrison, I, 103
11. Add. MS 34048, f. 27. The tour published in *Philosophical Transactions* 76 (1786), pp. 365–81
12. Anson, pp. 304–5
13. Morrison, I, 104
14. Ibid, 108–9
15. Ibid, 111
16. Ibid, 105
17. Ibid, 113

18. Krafft Bequest
19. Morrison, I, 114
20. Ibid, 114–15
21. Anson, pp. 305–6
22. Ingamells, p. 456
23. Morrison, I, 117
24. Ibid, 117–19
25. Add. MS 34048, ff. 30, 33; Fraser, pp. 96–7
26. Morrison, I, 119–20
27. Ibid, 119, 123

10 *Private Passions in Political Times, 1787–1791*

1. Add. MS 41198, f. 134
2. Tischbein (1956), pp. 289–90
3. Kelly, I, 54. See also Bodleian, Bland Burges 35, f. 154
4. Krafft Bequest
5. Tischbein (1956), pp. 288–9
6. Morrison, I, 123–28
7. Ibid, 129
8. Add. MS 34048, f. 35v
9. Ibid, ff. 36v–37
10. Morrison, I, 131
11. *Worship of Priapus*, p. 46
12. Add. MS 36495, f. 208v
13. Ibid, ff. 267–68
14. Tischbein (1956), pp. 352, 356–7
15. Add. MS 34048, ff. 31v, 32v, 35
16. *Archaeologia*, IV, 1777, pp. 165ff. See my 'Sir William Hamilton's "Account of a Journey into the Province of Abruzzo"' in *Oxford German Studies* 23, 1994, pp. 117ff. Also Fraser, pp. 121ff. And especially K. G. Holström, *Monodrama, Attitudes, Tableaux Vivants* (Stockholm 1967).

17. Walpole, XI, 337, 349
18. Morrison, I, 127, 133
19. Goethe, XI, 228–9
20. Morrison, I, 123
21. Smith, pp. 129–30. The dates don't quite tally: Smith was at Caserta, according to his account, on 17–18 March 1787, Goethe on 14–16, according to his; but they must in reality have coincided. It is odd that Smith does not mention Emma, and there is a view (which I don't share) that she has not yet begun her performances and that Goethe, editing his *Italienische Reise* thirty years later, inserted a fiction.
22. Goethe, XI, 228, 363
23. Tischbein (1956), p. 291
24. Casanova, XII, 50–1
25. Goethe, XI, 397. The sketch is shown in Tischbein, *Zeichnungen aus Goethes Kunstsammlung* (Weimar, 1991), p. 47.
26. Morrison, I, 130
27. Letters to Banks, Add. MS 34048, ff. 39, 42, 47v, 49, 52, 59
28. Morrison, I, 134–35
29. Morrison, I, 139
30. Add. MS 41199, f. 53
31. *Die Göchhausen. Briefe einer Hofdame aus dem klassischen Weimar*, edited by Werner Deetjen (Berlin 1923), p. 104
32. Add. MS 34048, f. 58
33. Ibid, f. 35v
34. Morrison, I, 136
35. Anson, pp. 307–8
36. See my 'Goethe and the Ham-

iltons', *Oxford German Studies* 26 (1997), p. 116

37. See Hugh Tours, *The Life and Letters of Emma Hamilton* (London, 1963), p. 88
38. Morrison, I, 140
39. Anson, p. 306
40. Morrison, I, 142
41. Add. MS, 34048, ff. 61–2; Anson, pp. 306–7
42. Morrison, I, 151
43. Ibid, 152
44. Add. MS 40715, ff. 3–4v
45. Morrison, I, 153
46. Ibid, 154
47. Anson, pp. 308–10
48. Minutes of the Society of Dilettanti
49. Anson, p. 310
50. Bodleian MS Beckford c.31, f. 120
51. See Fraser, p. 160
52. Anson, p. 311
53. See Fraser, p. 156
54. *The Letters of Lord Nelson to Lady Hamilton*, II, 144, 160, 150
55. Morrison, I, 140
56. Add. MS 46491, ff. 129–30
57. Anson, p. 313
58. Ibid, p. 312
59. See Tours, p. 93. Fothergill, p. 251, confuses Dutens with Edward Barry.
60. Morrison, I, 158
61. *Letters of Lord Nelson*, II, 148
62. Aberystwyth, 14
63. Morrison, I, 158, 160
64. Ibid, 159
65. Casanova, XII, 49
66. Connell, p. 218

67. Ibid, pp. 246–7
68. Ibid, p. 250
69. PRO, FO/70/5, f. 48
70. Anson, p. 315
71. See *Oxford German Studies* 26 (1997), p. 118

11 *Doing the State Some Service, 1792–1798*

1. *Prelude* (1805), IX, 93–5
2. Morrison, I, 157
3. Bodleian, Bland Burges 48, f. 32. Burges said of France: 'We live in the daily expectation of hearing strange things from that devoted Country, which must now, in a week or two, be the theatre of war, and the victim of an irresistible Prussian army.' 'Devoted', in that usage, means doomed. Like most commentators, he was quite wrong.
4. Morrison, I, 167, 171
5. Add. MS 34048, f. 70
6. Morrison, I, 173
7. Ibid, 174
8. Eg. 1615, f. 1
9. Acton, p. 254
10. Add. MS 41199, f. 111
11. Southey, pp. 79–80
12. Morrison, I, 183
13. Connell, p. 269
14. Morrison, I, 189
15. Add. MS 34048, f. 77v
16. The whole account, quoted from here, in *Philosophical Transactions* 85 (1795), pp. 73–116
17. *Philosophical Transactions* 85 (1795), p. 115
18. Krafft Bequest

19. Add. MS 34048, ff. 77–80
20. *Philosophical Transactions* 85 (1795), pp. 94, 73, 111
21. Eg. 2641, f. 151
22. Morrison, I, 187
23. Add. MS 34048, f. 75
24. MS Beckford c.31, ff. 118–19
25. Von Alten, pp. 49–52; letter to Cadell in the Krafft Bequest
26. MS Beckford, c.31, ff. 118v–119; Von Alten, p. 72; letter to Cadell: Bodleian, Montagu d.13, f. 191
27. Morrison, I, 148; Gordon, II, 384
28. Morrison, I, 148
29. The letter itself is Add. MS 41197, ff. 96–7. See also a letter from John Spencer Smith, Constantinople, 27–8 February 1800 (Add. MS 41200, f. 188), describing a find of vases in a tomb near Argos and supporting the view that the '*soi disant* Etruscan Vases' were Greek.
30. Morrison, I, 148
31. Morrison, I, 171–2
32. Bland Burges 48, f. 167
33. Morrison, I, 208, 217, 220
34. Add. MS 34710, f. 23
35. Add. MS 38361, ff. 52ff
36. Morrison, I, 144, 142
37. Morrison, I, 162, 165
38. Add. MS 42069, ff. 148ff
39. Add. MS 40715, ff. 42, 48, 49v, 145
40. Morrison, I, 192, 195, 211, 214
41. Add. MS 41200, f. 1; Morrison, I, 217, 221, 223; Add. MS 34048, ff. 90v–91

42. Walpole, XXXV, 440
43. Morrison, I, 204
44. Bland Burges 20, f. 12
45. Walpole, XXXV, 440–1
46. Morrison, I, 195–6
47. Add. MS 34048, f. 82v
48. Morrison, I, 204
49. Add. MS 59031, ff. 190–91
50. Add. MS 42071, ff. 11v–12
51. Add. MS 59031, f. 202
52. Von Alten, p. 62
53. Morrison, I, 176, 225
54. Connell, p. 276; Elliot, II, 364; Russell, p. 22
55. Von Alten, p. 69; Ingamells, p. 457; Elliot, II, 366
56. Walpole, XXXV, 441; Add. MS 34048, ff. 74, 82, 84v, 66v
57. *Letters of Lord Nelson*, II, 154, 168
58. Morrison, I, 194, 197, 209
59. Connell, pp. 276, 280–1; Fraser, pp. 193, 207; Elliot, II, 364–65; Fothergill, p. 300
60. Bland Burges 20, f. 12
61. Morrison, I, 208
62. Acton, p. 275; Add. MS 41199, ff. 231v–232
63. Acton, p. 280; Fothergill, p. 289; Add. MSS 41200, f. 73v, 87; 34048, f. 86
64. Add. MS 59031, ff. 204–6
65. Add. MS 41200, ff. 105–06; 34906, f. 384
66. Add. MS 41200, ff. 121–28, the last pages very faint. See also Fothergill, pp. 427–42, for Clark's inventory case by case.
67. Add. MS 40715, f. 83v; 37077, ff. 22, 19v; 42069, f. 180v

68. Luttrell, p. 102
69. Russell, pp. 38–40; Morrison, II, 18
70. Russell, pp. 36, 42, 43; Fraser, pp. 221, 224
71. Russell, p. 43
72. Ibid, pp. 49, 51; Fothergill, p. 320
73. Add. MS 59031, f. 202v
74. Fothergill, p. 326
75. Gordon, I, 205
76. Russell, p. 59; Fothergill, pp. 330–1; Morrison, II, 35

12 Wreck and Disgrace, 1798–1800

1. Morrison, II, 36, 37, 41, 49; Add. MS 42071, f. 14v. Roland Morris's team, diving on the wreck in the years 1974–8, took up altogether about 35000 sherds from an area on the seabed where they supposed the hold of the *Colossus* to have been. How many pots this might have amounted to is impossible to say.
2. *Vases and Volcanoes*, p. 58
3. Morrison, II, 54, 83
4. Elliot, III, 42
5. Add. MS 42071, ff. 14–15; Morrison, II, 41, 45, 54, 82
6. Oldenburg, PT 970
7. Acton, p. 327
8. Oldenburg, PT 970
9. Morrison, II, 34, 40; Add. MS 37077, f. 60
10. Gutteridge, p. 24; Acton, pp. 338–9
11. Add. MS 42071, ff. 14–16
12. Acton, pp. 342, 345
13. Luttrell, p. 116
14. Gordon, I, 201; II, 385, 210–11
15. Add. MS 37077, ff. 70v, 71v, 72v, 77v; Russell, p. 72
16. Add. MS 37077, ff. 85v–86
17. Fothergill, p. 348
18. Russell, p. 79; Morrison, II, 56; Gutteridge, p. 213
19. Add. MS 42780A, f. 31; Gutteridge, p. 279; Add. MS 37077, f. 111
20. Ibid 37077, f. 105v
21. Morrison, II, 57
22. Add. MS 37077, f. 116v
23. Ibid 34048, f. 95; 37077, f. 120
24. Ibid 34912, f. 74v
25. Ibid 37077, ff. 127v, 128v
26. Ibid 34048, ff. 94–5
27. Russell, pp. 95, 100
28. Ibid, p. 95; Add. MS 41200, f. 179
29. Add. MS 37077, ff. 134–5
30. Russell, p. 108
31. Paget, I, 200
32. Add. MSS 40715, ff. 98–99, 126; 41200, f. 195
33. PRO, FO/70/13, ff. 7–7v, 21.
34. Morrison, II, 82; Russell, p. 111; Add. MS 59031, f. 213; Paget, I, 237–8
35. Add. MS 41200, f. 198; Morrison, II, 62; Add MS, 37077, f. 149; Paget, I, 190, 198, 219
36. Paget, I, 202
37. Knight, I, 319–23
38. Elliot, III, 147; Fraser, p. 263; Trench, p. 106
39. Trench, pp. 105–6, 108–10; Lutterell, p. 125; Fraser, p. 268; Fothergill, p. 386; Knight, I, 157

40. Trench, pp. 105, 109–12
41. Knight, I, 163

13 'I will bear up as long & as well as I can.' November 1800–April 1803

1. Luttrell, pp. 128–9
2. Anson, pp. 325–7
3. Morrison, II, 192–3
4. Connell, p. 436; Anson, pp. 325–7
5. Russell, p. 155
6. Add. MS 41200, ff. 202–5; Westminster Archive, Broadley 2, 115
7. Add. MS 41200, ff. 208, 214, 217–18
8. Ibid, 41200, ff. 221–2, 225
9. Westminster Archive, Broadley 2, 115; Fothergill, p. 398
10. Add. MS 42071, f. 23; Morrison, II, 111, 116
11. Westminster Archive, Broadley 2, 115. Hamilton dated the letter '11 Feby 1800', but his account of the change of administration and much else besides proves it must be 1801. He made the same mistake, 1800 for 1801, in his letter to Grenville on 16 February, but corrected it.
12. Add. MS 59031, ff. 217–18
13. Fothergill, p. 400
14. Add. MS 59031, f. 219
15. Incomprehensibly, Greville did something rather similar, with reference to Emma's first child. See his letter to Hamilton, 7 June 1796, referring to 'the little protégé whose education you have paid for since your mar-riage ... I am still uncertain of her history, but I believe her to be a niece of Mrs. C., and that her parents are alive' (Morrison, I, 223)
16. Morrison, I, 128; and Nelson to Emma, 19 March 1801
17. Add. MS 40715, ff. 133–133v; Morrison, II, 132
18. In preparing the advertisement for the sale Hamilton said that one third of his collection had been lost with the *Colossus* (see Add. MS 42069, f. 199v). That would leave 1000 if Tischbein's figure of 1500 can be trusted. Watkin, p. 36, thinks Hope only bought 750; Tillyard, *The Hope Vases* (Cambridge 1923), pp. 1–2, 'rather fewer than seven hundred'.
19. Wraxall, p. 141
20. Add. MSS 42071, f. 19; 40715, f. 139v, 141v
21. Oldenburg, PT 75, 76, letters in Italian. And see PT 531, draft of a letter from Tischbein to Hamilton, in German.
22. Von Alten, pp. 77–8
23. Add. MS 34048, ff. 76, 89v–90; Royal Society, MS 2, Letter from Hamilton to RS, 14 June 1801
24. Russell, p. 215
25. *Letters of Lord Nelson*, II, 180
26. Ibid, II, 217–18
27. Russell, pp. 223, 228
28. Morrison, II, 165, 168; Fothergill, p. 406
29. Morrison, II, 174

30. Ibid, 176
31. Russell, p. 227
32. Fothergill, p. 408
33. Anson, p. 328
34. *Letters of Lord Nelson*, I, 62
35. Aberystwyth, 16. And cf. letter to Greville, 5 December 1801: 'I am living upon one of the 1000 l. stock sold out' (Morrison, II, 177).
36. Aberystwyth, 17
37. Add. MS 41200, f. 225
38. Ibid, ff. 219–20
39. Morrison, II, 203; Add. MS 40715, f. 144v
40. Morrison, II, 195
41. Ibid, 182
42. Russell, p. 254; Elliot, III, 242
43. Russell, p. 262
44. Ibid, p. 265
45. Gill, p. 37
46. Ibid, p. 40
47. Morrison, II, 195–6
48. Russell, p. 271
49. Morrison, II, 197
50. Russell, p. 275
51. Add. MS 34048, f. 97
52. Minutes and Hamilton's letter in the archives of the Dilettanti, held by the Royal Academy. And see *Vases & Volcanoes*, pp. 44–45.
53. Add. MS 42071, f. 40
54. Russell, p. 283; Fraser, p. 299
55. Add. MS 40715, f. 139
56. Fothergill, p. 419
57. Add. MS 34990, f. 14
58. *Letters of Lord Nelson*, I, 115

Postscript

1. See Morrison, II, 321–2 and, in the archives of Christie's, the annotated catalogues of the sales.
2. Russell, p. 363
3. Haverfordwest Public Library, Slebech file

Conclusion

1. *Letters of Lord Nelson*, II, 178. See also his letter to Edmund Noble, 11 February 1801 (Westminster Archive, Broadley 2, 115). Having lamented the current follies of the world, he concludes: 'One must do as well as one can in it & not repine at being forced out of it.'
2. PRO, FO/70/13, f. 3
3. FO/70/13, f. 8
4. Wraxall, p. 139

BIBLIOGRAPHY

I MANUSCRIPT SOURCES

British Library

Additional MSS, principally:

8967, earthquake of 1783

34048, Hamilton's letters to Banks, 1778–1803

34710, to Strange and to Greville, chiefly vulcanology, 1775, 1795

35609, to Earl of Hardwicke, 1769, chiefly vases

36495, to George Cumberland, 1787, vases, the arts

37076, Battle of the Nile

37077, French invasion of Naples and restoration, 1798–1800

38200–01, Hamilton to Jenkinson (Lord Liverpool), 1763

38361, works at Milford, 1790

40714–15, Hamilton and Greville Papers, 1764–1803

41197–41200, Hamilton's correspondence and papers, 1761–1803

42069–71, ditto, 1764–1803

46491, Hamilton to the Archbishop of Canterbury, 1791

59031, to and from Lord Grenville, 1796–1802

Egerton MSS, principally:

1614, Nelson's letters to Emma, 1798–1805

1615, letters to Emma from Queen Maria Carolina, 1793–99

2634–37, Hamilton's letters to Secretaries of State, 1764–81

2641, letters to Hamilton (several from Banks)

Bodleian Library:

Beckford MSS (especially correspondence with Catherine)

Bland Burges

Hamilton Notebooks (MSS Eng. hist. g.3–16, years in the army, notes from Sir James
   Gray's correspondence, tour in the Abruzzi, record of letters sent)

MS Eng. hist. c. 51 (army commission and resignation)

MS Autog. d. 11, Flaxman to Hamilton, 1792

MS Montagu, d. 7, d. 13, letters to Cadell (bookseller)

Goethe-Archiv, Weimar: letters from Tischbein and from Hamilton

Haverfordwest Public Library: Slebech File

Muséum national d'histoire naturelle, Paris: Krafft Bequest (the papers – letters to and from

Hamilton, many on the arts and natural sciences – are not numbered)

National Library of Wales: Hamilton and Greville Papers (especially on the Pembroke estates, letters from Catherine's mother)

Oldenburg, Landesmuseum: Tischbein Papers

Public Record Office:

State Papers 105/315–21, correspondence with Sir Horace Mann, 1764–71

Foreign Office 70/1–13, letters to Secretaries of State, 1780–1800

Westminster Archive: Broadley Collection (letter to Edmund Noble)

2 HAMILTON'S PUBLISHED WORKS

Note: Hamilton's works were translated – into French, German, Italian, Dutch, Danish – as they came out; they were also excerpted (usually in the *Annual Register*), and pirated. The following list is unlikely to be exhaustive. Most often I have abbreviated the titles. See also Uberto Limentani's *Bibliografia Hamiltoniana*, included in his re-issue of *Campi Phlegraei* and also published separately, Milan 1962.

1 'Two Letters ... containing an Account of the last Eruption of Mount Vesuvius', in *Philosophical Transactions* 57 (1767), pp. 192–200.

2 'An Account of the Eruption of Mount Vesuvius, in 1767', in *PT* 58 (1768), pp. 1–14. For 1 and 2 see also *Annual Register*, 1767 and 1769; and German translation, Bremen, 1770.

3 'A Letter ... containing some farther Particulars on Mount Vesuvius, and other Volcanos in the Neighbourbood', in *PT* 59 (1769), pp. 18–22. Also *AR*, 1770.

4 'An Account of a Journey to Mount Etna', in *PT* 60 (1770), pp. 1–19. Also *AR*, 1771; and a French translation printed with Riedesel's *Voyage en Sicile*, Lausanne, 1773.

5 'Remarks upon the Nature of the Soil of Naples, and its Neighbourhood', in *PT* 61 (1771), pp. 1–47. Also *AR*, 1772; and published by Bowyer & Nichols, London, 1771.

6 *Observations on Mount Vesuvius, Mount Etna and other Volcanos* (London, 1772). This collects all the *PT* letters to date. German translation Berlin, 1773.

7 'Account of the Effects of a Thunder-Storm ... upon the House of Lord Tylney at Naples', in *PT* 63 (1773), pp. 324–32.

8 'Account of the Discoveries at Pompeii', in *Archaeologia*, vol. IV (1777), pp. 160–75. Also Bowyer & Nichols, 1777; German translation Nuremberg, 1780.

9 *Campi Phlegraei*, 2 vols (Naples 1776). This collects all the *PT* letters on volcanoes and consists otherwise of 58 paintings by Pietro Fabris commented on by Hamilton. Text in English and French. A Supplement – a letter and more paintings and commentaries – was published in 1779, dealing with the violent eruption that year. There was a French edition in 1799, and an Italian in 1962.

10 'A Letter ... giving an Account of certain Traces of Volcanos on the Banks of the Rhine', in *PT* 68 (1779), pp. 1–6, 106. German translation Leipzig, 1784.

11 'An Account of an Eruption of Mount Vesuvius which happened in August, 1779', in *PT* 70 (1780), pp. 42–84. Also published as the *Supplement* to *Campi Phlegraei*.

12 *Oeuvres complettes de M. le chev. Hamilton*, (Paris, 1781). This handy volume, published with Hamilton's approval, collects together all the letters of *Campi Phlegraei* and its supplement plus 'Volcanos on the Rhine'. There are 200 pages of notes and commentary. Partial

German translation of this French publication, Frankfurt and Leipzig, 1784; Dutch same year.

13 'An Account of the Earthquake which happened in Italy, from February to May 1783', in *PT* 73 (1783), pp. 169–208. Italian and French (Florence and Paris) 1783; German (via the French) Strasburg 1784. Pirated English publication (Colchester and Edinburgh) 1783.

14 'The present State of Mount Vesuvius; with the Account of a Journey into the Province of Abruzzo, and a Voyage to the Island of Ponza', in *PT* 76 (1786), pp. 365–81. Also in *AR*, 1786; and published that year by Bowyer & Nichols. German, Dresden, 1786.

15 'An Account of the Remains of the Worship of Priapus', published in a volume with Richard Payne Knight's 'Discourse on the Worship of Priapus', London, 1786. New editions 1865 and 1883.

16 'An Account of the late Eruption of Mount Vesuvius', in *PT* 85 (1795), pp. 73–116. Danish, 1796.

17 *Collection of Etruscan, Greek, and Roman Antiquities from the Cabinet of the Honble. Wm. Hamilton His Britannick Majesty's Envoy Extraordinary at the Court of Naples*, 4 vols (Naples, 1766–67, actually 1767–76). Hamilton supplied the works of art and doubtless some opinions on them; but the text was written by d'Hancarville with some contribution from Winckelmann. Text in English and French.

18 *Collection of Engravings from Ancient Vases mostly of pure Greek Workmanship discovered in Sepulchres in the Kingdom of the Two Sicilies but chiefly in the Neighbourhood of Naples during the course of the years MDCCLXXXIX. and MXCCLXXXX. now in the possession of Sir Wm. Hamilton His Britannic Majesty's Envoy Extry. and Plenipotentiary at the Court of Naples with Remarks on each Vase by the Collector*, 5 volumes (Naples, 1791 [actually 1793] – after 1803). Text in English and French. The remarks seem mostly to have been composed by Count Italinsky, in French – Hamilton says he merely translated them; but he wrote at least the introductory letters to the Earl of Leicester and the 20-page address To the Reader. Partial German publication, Weimar, 1797–1800.

The Library of the Royal Society has the original letters (some with drawings) sent by Hamilton from Naples to be read at the Society's meetings. Not all of them were published. See, for example, a letter of 8 February 1770 'On the supposed change in the Italian climate', touching also on tarantulas and the volcano. The Library also holds Antonio Piaggi's diaries of Vesuvius, kept for Hamilton and donated by him.

3 OTHER PRINTED BOOKS AND ARTICLES

Acton, Harold, *The Bourbons of Naples* (London, 1957)
Anon., *Memoirs of Lady Hamilton* (London, 1815)
Anson, Elizabeth and Florence (eds.), *Mary Hamilton* (London, 1925)
Beckford, William, *Travel Diaries*, ed. Guy Chapman, 2 vols (London, 1928)
Black, Jeremy, *The Grand Tour in the Eighteenth Century* (London, 1999)
Burney, Dr Charles, *Music, Men and Manners in France and Italy*, ed. H. E. Poole (London, 1969)
Casanova di Seingalt, Giacomo, *Memoirs*, trans. A. Machen, 12 vols (London, 1922)
Christie, Ian, *Wars and Revolutions. Britain 1760–1815* (London, 1982)
Clarke, John, *The Life and Times of George III*, (London, 1972)
Colvin, Sir Sidney, and Cust, Lionel, *History of the Society of Dilettanti* (London, 1914)

Connell, Brian, *Portrait of a Whig Peer* (London, 1957)

Constantine, David, 'Winckelmann and Sir William Hamilton', in *Oxford German Studies*, 22 (1993), pp. 55–83)

'Sir William Hamilton's Account of a Journey into the Province of Abruzzo', in *OGS*, 23 (1994), pp. 104–23

'Goethe and the Hamiltons', in *OGS*, 26 (1997), pp. 101–31

Deetjen, Werner (ed.), *Die Göchhausen. Briefe einer Hofdame aus dem klassischen Weimar* (Berlin, 1923)

Fothergill, Brian, *Sir William Hamilton* (London, 1969), *The Mitred Earl* (London, 1974)

Fraser, Flora, *Beloved Emma* (London, 1986)

Garden, Francis Lord Gardenstone, *Travelling Memorandums made in a tour upon the Continent of Europe in the years 1786, 87 and 88*, 2nd edition, 3 vols (Edinburgh, 1802)

Gerning, Isaac, *Reise durch Oesterreich und Italien*, 2 vols (Frankfurt, 1802)

Gibbon, Edward, *Memoirs of my Life and Writings*, ed. A. O. J. Cockshut and Stephen Constantine (Keele, 1994)

Gill, Edward, *Nelson and the Hamiltons on Tour* (Gloucester and Monmouth, 1987)

Goethe, *Sämtliche Werke*, 18 vols (Zürich, 1977)

Goodden, Angelica, *The Sweetness of Life. A Biography of Elisabeth Louise Vigée Le Brun* (London, 1997)

Gordon, Major Pryse Lockhart, *Personal Memoirs*, 2 vols (London, 1830)

Gutteridge, H. C., *Nelson and the Neapolitan Jacobins*, Navy Records Society XXV (London, 1903)

Harnack, Otto (ed.), 'Zur Nachgeschichte der Italienischen Reise', *Schriften der Goethe-Gesellschaft* 5 (Weimar, 1890)

Herbert, Lord, *The Pembroke Papers*, 2 vols (London, 1939, 1950)

Herder, Johann Gottfried, *Italienische Reise, Briefe und Tagebuchaufzeichnungen 1788–89* (Munich, 1988)

Hervey, Baron John, *Some Materials towards Memoirs of the Reign of King George II*, ed. R. Sedgwick, 3 vols (London, 1931)

Hibbert, Christopher, *The Grand Tour* (London, 1974)

Holmström, K. G., *Monodrama, Attitudes, Tableaux Vivants* (Stockholm, 1967)

Home, J. E. (ed.), *The Letters and Journals of Lady Mary Coke*, 4 vols (Edinburgh, 1889–96)

Ingamells, John, *A Dictionary of British and Irish Travellers in Italy 1701–1800* (New Haven and London, 1997)

Jenkins, Ian and Sloan, Kim, *Vases and Volcanoes. Sir William Hamilton and his Collection* (British Museum Press, 1996)

Jones, Thomas, *Memoirs*, Walpole Society, vol. 32 (London, 1951)

Kelly, Michael, *Reminiscences*, 2 vols (London, 1826)

Knight, Cornelia, *Autobiography*, ed. Sir J. W. Kaye, 2 vols (London, 1861)

Lalande, Joseph Jérôme le François de, *Voyage en Italie*, 9 vols (Paris, 1786)

Leppmann, Wolfgang, *Winckelmann* (London, 1971)

The Letters of Lord Nelson to Lady Hamilton with a Supplement, 2 vols (London, 1814)

Limentani, Uberto, *Bibliografia Hamiltoniana* (Milan, 1962)

Llanover, Lady, *The Autobiography and Correspondence of Mary Granville, Mrs Delany*, 3 vols (London, 1862)

Lofts, Norah, *Emma Hamilton* (London, 1978)

Luttrell, Barbara, *The Prim Romantic. A Biography of Ellis Cornelia Knight* (London, 1965)

Mankowitz, Wolf, *Wedgwood* (London, 1953)

Mildenberger, Hermann, *J. H. W. Tischbein Goethes Maler und Freund* (Oldenburg, 1986)

Miller, Lady Anne, *Letters from Italy*, 3 vols (London, 1776)

Minto, Countess of (ed.), *Life and Letters of Sir Gilbert Elliot*, 3 vols (London, 1874)

Moore, Dr John, *A View of Society and Manners in Italy*, 5th edition, 2 vols (London, 1790)

Morris, Roland, *HMS Colossus: The Story of the Salvage of the Hamilton Treasures* (London, 1979)

Morrison Alfred, *The Hamilton and Nelson Papers*, 2 vols (privately printed, 1893–4)

Mowl, Timothy, *William Beckford* (London, 1998)

Paget, Sir Augustus (ed.), *The Paget Papers*, 2 vols (London, 1896)

Rathbone, Philip, *Paradise Merton. The Story of Nelson and the Hamiltons at Merton Place* (London, 1973)

Reilly, Robin, *Josiah Wedgwood* (London, 1992)

Russell, Jack, *Nelson and the Hamiltons* (London, 1969)

Sharp, Samuel, *Letters from Italy in the years 1765 and 1766* (London, 1767)

Smith, James Edward, *A Sketch of a Tour on the Continent in the years 1786 and 1787*, 3 vols (London, 1793)

Southey, Robert, *Life of Nelson* (re-issued London, 1999)

Swinburne, Henry, *Travels in the Two Sicilies*, 2 vols (London, 1783)

Tischbein, Johann Heinrich Wilhelm, *Aus meinem Leben*, ed. Kuno Mittelstädt (Berlin, 1956)

Tours, Hugh, *Life and Letters of Emma Hamilton* (London, 1963)

Trench, R. Chevenix, *Remains of the late Mrs Richard Trench* (London, 1862)

Von Alten (ed.), *Aus Tischbeins Leben und Briefwechsel* (Leipzig, 1872)

Walpole, Horace, *Correspondence*, Yale Edition, 48 vols (London, 1937–83)

Warner, Oliver, *Emma Hamilton and Sir William* (London, 1960)

Watkin, David, *Thomas Hope and the Neo-Classical Idea* (London, 1968)

Willson, Beckles, *The Life and Letters of James Wolfe* (London, 1909)

Winckelmann, Johann Joachim, *Briefe*, 4 vols (Berlin, 1952–7)

Wraxall, Sir Nathaniel, *Historical Memoirs of my own Time* (London, 1904)

INDEX

INDEX

Hamilton, Sir William: – *contd*
sense, 149, 168–9; sexuality, 9–10, 92, 131,
159; attitude to women, 46, 91, 134, 135,
139, 140, 174; attitude to royalty, 3, 4, 46;
love of presents from heads of state, 240;
his politics, 198; HIS RELATIONSHIPS
AND FRIENDSHIPS: relationship with
his parents, 1, 3, 229–30; 'foster-brother'
to King George III, 8, 66, 281–2; early
friendships, 9–10; affection for Charles
Greville, 2, 11, 53, 99, 128, 291; strained
relations with Greville, 144, 146;
association with Baron d'Hancarville, 33,
36–40, 43, 62–3, 68, 200; time spent
hunting with King Ferdinand, 48–9, 83,
86, 97, 101, 103, 108, 110, 134, 157, 171,
185, 289, 291; connection with Emperor
Leopold II, 52, 61, 67; his possible
adopted daughter, 92; correspondence
with Joseph Banks, 98–9, 109, 117, 125,
139–40, 151, 159–61, 163, 172, 174, 189,
194, 197–8, 204, 206, 209, 213, 241, 279;
affection for his monkey Jack, 99–100,
102–3, 105; confides in his niece Mary,
xxvi, 43, 115–16, 130, 136, 140, 146–7,
174, 178; his marriage with Catherine,
102, 109–12, 131; friendship and
admiration for Nelson, 219, 257, 262, 270,
272, 274, 278–9, 283, 290–91; love for
Emma, 290–91; loyalty to Beckford, 291;
HIS ENTHUSIASMS AND
ACHIEVEMENTS: as collector and
connoisseur, 10, 13–14, 17, 30, 33, 42,
64, 69, 74, 103, 199, 291–2; vases, xxvi,
10, 21, 31–4, 36–7, 39–41, 55, 59, 63–5,
72–3, 107, 134, 161–2, 198–203, 208, 227,
247, 263, 279, 281, 289, 291; First
Collection of vases in the British
Museum, 65, 71, 74, 95, 162, 199–200,
289; Second Collection of vases, 155, 172,
187, 198–9, 208, 219, 226, 265; classical
knowledge, 10; his influence on British
pottery design and manufacture, 72–4,
127, 161–2, 199, 290; pictures and works
of art, 8, 13–14, 17, 21, 30–32, 34–5, 42–
3, 55, 59, 140, 156, 215, 262, 281, 286,
291; volcanoes and vulcanology, xxvi, 21,
29, 34–9, 42, 49, 54–6, 59, 65, 68, 70, 75–
81, 91, 96, 98, 122–3, 139, 160–61, 169,
187, 194–7, 201, 282, 289, 290–1;
earthquakes, 117–23, 125, 291; natural

history, 73–6, 98; lightning, 75, 279; his
scholarship, 33, 35–6, 39, 65, 200, 265;
reports on Pompeii, 66, 81; cult of
Priapus, 98, 102–3, 108, 110, 126, 161,
179; music, 8, 11, 13, 26, 56–8, 64, 98,
103, 109, 116, 126, 136, 140; hunting, 48–
9, 115–17, 134; English Garden at
Caserta, 134, 140, 143, 162–3, 215, 280;
fishing, 135, 249, 266–8, 270, 278–9, 290;
home improvements, 147, 154, 202;
horse-riding, 201; dancing, 252, 264; as
writer, xxvii, 194, 290; WRITINGS AND
PUBLICATIONS: *Campi Phlegraei*, 76–9,
81, 286; *Etruscan Vases*, 39–41, 44, 55,
62–3, 65, 69, 94–5, 286; *Observations on
Mount Vesuvius, Mount Etna and other
volcanoes*, 65, 70; 'Account of the
Earthquake which happened in Italy,
from February to May 1783', 118–19; *The
Worship of Priapus*, 161, 179, 277, 286;
'The Mountain of Somma' (translation),
197; *Engravings from Ancient Vases*, 199,
228, 265; PORTRAITS: 8, 43, 65, 66, 95,
128–30; DOCUMENTS RELATING
TO HAMILTON: xxvii, 12, 116
Hamilton, third Duke of, 1
Hampden, Lady Catherine, 60, 132
Hampton Court, 3
Handel, Georg Friedrich, 58, 116, 126
Hardy, Captain, 267
Harpur, Lady Frances, 178–9, 255, 256, 257,
269
Harpur, Sir Harry, 136
Harris, James, 250
Hart, Banker, 158
Hart, Emma, *see* Hamilton, Emma
Hawarden, 111, 129
Hawkesbury, Robert Banks Jenkinson, Lord,
262, 270–71
Haydn, Franz Joseph, 250
Hayley, William, 179
Hekla, 78
Heraclitus, 155
Herald, 279
Herbert, George Augustus, Lord, 98, 99,
102, 105, 156
Herculaneum, 17–18, 21, 29, 37, 64, 80–81,
164, 196, 279–80
Herschel, William, 160
Hertford, Lady, 64
Hervey, Christopher, 92

318

Maria Carolina: Queen of Naples, 92, 97;
her marriage to Ferdinand, 45, 47, 50;
pregnancies, 82–3, 142; growth of her
political influence, 85–6, 154, 172, 176,
190–92, 211–13, 217, 228; visits Catherine,
102; sympathy after Catherine's death,
115; proposes the English Garden, 134,
163; her Bourbon relatives, 185, 188; her
attitude to Emma, 159–60, 185–6; Emma
becomes her confidante, 190, 211, 213;
her assessment of her subjects, 212; urges
King Ferdinand to fight, 220, 229; flees
Naples, 221–3; laments in Sicily, 230;
demands vengeance, 235; Emma
becomes her 'Deputy', 236, 238; her
dependence on Hamilton and Nelson,
240–41; detains Hamilton in Sicily, 241–
2; her anxiety at Hamilton's departure,
246; at odds with Ferdinand, 247; leaves
Naples for Vienna, 247–9, 251; her
parting gift to Emma, 248, 260; informed
of Hamilton's death, 284
Maria Josepha, 47
Maria Theresa, Empress, 44, 45
Marie Antoinette, 172, 177, 183–5, 188–9,
192, 221
Marlborough, Duke of, 274
Maron, Anton von, 43
Maximilian, Archduke, 83
Maynard, Lord and Lady, 96–7
Mecklenburg-Strelitz, Prince Georg August
von, 36
Medici Venus, 40
Méjean, General, 239
Melfa, River, 220
Mengs, Raphael, 43
Merthyr Tydfil, 274, 276
Merton Place, 267–9, 272, 277–9, 285
Messina, 25, 55, 117, 118, 120, 122, 123
Meyrick, John, 202, 203
Middleton, Lord, 139
Midhurst, 12, 16
Milford, 12, 129, 140, 189, 201–4, 242, 267,
273–6, 286
Milk, 215
Miller, Lady Anne, 50, 51, 56, 81
Minchin, Mr, 15
Minto, Lord and Lady (the Elliots), 250,
251, 253, 272
Mitchell, Sir Andrew, 66

Mollochi di Sotto, 121
Monte Cassino, 135, 219
Monte Dragone, 48
Monte Nuovo, 20
Monteleone, 119, 231
Moore, John, 84
Moore, Reverend, 134
Morning Chronicle, 278
Morning Post, 274, 278
Morris, John, 276
Morritt, John, 208
Mountstuart, John Stuart, 26
Mozart, Leopold, 13, 57, 58
Mozart, Wolfgang Amadeus, 13, 57, 96
Murray, Captain George, 224
Murrhine, 72, 127

Neapolitan Academy, 28
Nelson, Fanny, 218, 220, 241, 253, 257, 272
Nelson, Horatia, 219, 260, 262, 268, 285,
286
Nelson, Horatio, Viscount: Emma's passion
for, 159; meets Hamilton and Emma in
Naples, 192; his ambition, 192;
Hamilton's opinion of him, 192; at
Naples with Hamilton and Emma (1798),
215–21; helps Hamilton and Emma out
of Naples, 222; mentions Emma's
conduct in dispatches, 223; in Sicily, 230–
31, 233; growing intimacy with Emma,
163, 231; brutality towards Ferdinand's
enemies, 235–8; becomes object of
opprobrium, 237; in thrall to Emma, 238,
241; with Hamilton, Emma and
Ferdinand on the *Foudroyant*, 239; made
Duke of Brontë, 240; scandal and
humiliation, 66, 242, 247–53; seeks leave
to return home, 246; Emma pregnant by,
247; denounced in parliament, 247; return
home with Hamilton and Emma (1800),
248–53; reception in London (November
1800), 254–5; reunion with Fanny, 254;
break with Fanny, 257; recall to duty,
257; correspondence with Emma from
on board ship, 262; buys portrait of
Emma, 262–3; jealousy over Emma, 263;
fishing with Hamilton and Emma, 266–
7; returns to sea, 267; buys Merton Place
(1801), 267–8; attends church at Merton,
270; his friendship with Hamilton, 270;
travels to Wales with Hamiltons, 273–7;